STUART TRACTS

Scholarly Resources Inc.
Wilmington, Delaware

SCHOLARLY RESOURCES, INC.
Wilmington, Delaware

Reprint edition published in 1973
First published in 1903 by Archibald Constable
and Co., Ltd; Westminster

Library of Congress Catalog Card Number: 72-83161
ISBN: 0-8420-1419-5

Manufactured in the United States of America

AN ENGLISH GARNER

STUART TRACTS

1603-1693

WITH AN INTRODUCTION BY

C. H. FIRTH

FELLOW OF ALL SOULS COLLEGE, OXFORD

WESTMINSTER

ARCHIBALD CONSTABLE AND CO., LTD.

1903

PUBLISHERS' NOTE

THE texts contained in the present volume are reprinted with very slight alterations from the *English Garner* issued in eight volumes (1877-1890, London, 8vo) by Professor Arber, whose name is sufficient guarantee for the accurate collation of the texts with the rare originals, the old spelling being in most cases carefully modernised. The contents of the original *Garner* have been rearranged and now for the first time classified, under the general editorial supervision of Mr. Thomas Seccombe. Certain lacunae have been filled by the interpolation of fresh matter. The Introductions are wholly new and have been written specially for this issue. The references to volumes of the *Garner* (other than the present volume) are for the most part to the editio princeps, 8 vols. 1877-90.

Edinburgh: Printed by T. and A. CONSTABLE.

TABLE OF CONTENTS

INTRODUCTION

THE tracts which stand first in this volume describe the accession of James I. and the rejoicings which accompanied his progress from Scotland to London. To them is prefixed, in order to explain the narratives followed, Sir Robert Carey's account of the circumstances of Queen Elizabeth's death, and of the manner in which he brought the news to Edinburgh. Carey, whose *Memoirs* were first published by the Earl of Cork in 1759, was the youngest son of Henry Carey, first Lord Hunsdon, and the grandson of Mary, sister of Ann Boleyn. His kinship to the Queen and his gifts as a courtier secured him the favour of Elizabeth, and when that sovereign died he held the office of Warden of the Middle Marches. As soon as Carey perceived that her end was near, he resolved to use the opportunity to gain the favour of her successor, in the conviction, as he tells us, that it was neither 'unjust nor unhonest' for him to do so. The candid selfishness of his defence explains his character, but contemporaries as well as later historians censured his haste to profit by the death of his kinswoman and benefactress. 'It hath set so wide a mark of ingratitude on him,' writes Weldon, 'that it will remain to posterity a greater blot than the honour he obtained afterwards will ever wipe out.'[1] Carey would willingly have borne this general censure, but what he could not endure without lamenting was the failure of the

[1] *Secret History of the Court of James I.*, i. p. 314.

hopes which he had built upon the gratitude of the King. James had at once appointed the welcome messenger one of the gentlemen of his bedchamber, but after he reached England he dismissed Carey from this post, and forgot to fulfil his promises of further preferment. The cause which led to Carey's removal was no doubt a representation addressed by the Council to the King, in which they stigmatised Carey's conduct as 'contrary to such commandments as we had power to lay upon him, and to all decency, good manners, and respect.' However, later in the reign he succeeded in obtaining the offices and titles he desired, becoming successively master of the robes and chamberlain to Prince Charles, and being created Baron of Leppington (1622), and finally Earl of Monmouth (1626). He died in 1639.

While the account of the last days of Queen Elizabeth given in Carey's *Memoirs* is valuable as being the report of an eye-witness, it should not be forgotten that he was influenced by the desire to construe the acts and words of the Queen in the manner most favourable to the claim of James I. Elizabeth had always been reluctant to name a successor, and even when she was dying this reluctance was as strong as ever. A recent historian gives good reason for doubting whether she so explicitly nominated James as Carey asserts:—

'On her dying day her Council ventured a first and last despairing effort to obtain from her such assent to their negotiations as would place James's title beyond cavil; and although representations have been made that the effort was successful, there is little valid ground for crediting the Queen, even in her last hours, with any modification of her resolve to leave the subject of the succession severely alone.

The French ambassador is solely responsible for the statement that she at an earlier period admitted by word of mouth that "the King of Scotland would hereafter become King of Great Britain." More trustworthy witnesses merely depose that on two occasions in her latest weeks, when the comments of others in her presence compelled her to break silence, she took refuge in oracular utterances which owe all their significance to the interpretation that their hearers deemed it politic to place on them.

'Before leaving London she is said to have told the Earl of Nottingham that "her throne had always been the throne of kings, and none but her next heir of blood and descent should succeed her." "Her next heir of blood and descent" was, in the eyes of the law, Lord Beauchamp. The vague phrases attest her settled policy of evasion. According to Sir Robert Carey, on the Wednesday afternoon before her death, "she made for her Council to be called, and by putting her hand to her head when the King of Scotland was named to succeed her, they all knew he was the man she desired should reign after her." Throughout her illness her hand had passed restlessly to and from her head, and a definite meaning could only attach to the sign in the sight of those who, like the reporter, were already pledged to seat James VI. in her place. Lady Southwell gives a more disinterested account of this episode of the Wednesday afternoon. The Council were not invited to the royal presence, as Carey avers. They demanded admittance "to know whom" the dying Queen "would have for King." She could barely speak, but made what preparation her waning strength permitted for the interview. The Councillors desired her to lift her finger when they named whom she approved. They mentioned the King of France; she did not stir. They spoke of the King of Scotland; she made no sign. They named Lord Beauchamp, the rightful heir under Henry VIII.'s unrepealed settlement. Then only did Elizabeth rouse herself, and with something of her old vivacity she gasped, "I will have no rascal's son to sit in my seat, but one worthy to be a king." These are the only unquestioned words which afford any clue to the Queen's wishes respecting her successor. At the best they are negative, and cannot be tortured into a formal acceptance of James.'[1]

After Carey's account of how he brought the good news to Edinburgh follow three narratives describing the progress of James from Edinburgh to London, and his reception by his new subjects. All three are reprinted and copiously annotated by John Nichols in his *Progresses of King James I.* (vol. i. pp. 53, 135, 408). Very little is known of their authors. T. M., the author of the true narration, was probably an inhabitant of Berwick, from the particularity with which he describes incidents which happened there. John Savile, author of *King James his Entertainment at Theobald's*, is mentioned by Anthony Wood in his *Athenæ*, but merely as 'a pretender to poetry,' patronised by the young spark to whom the '*Entertainment* is dedicated.' Of Gilbert Dugdale, the author of *Time Triumphant*, nothing at all is known. Perhaps, as Nichols suggests, he was the 'old man of the age of three score and nineteen,' who had seen the changes of four Kings and Queens, and had prepared a political address to his new sovereign, which he printed in spite of the fact that it was never delivered.

The unfeigned rejoicing by which the accession of James was hailed was due to the relief of the nation at

[1] Mr. Sidney Lee. *Cornhill Magazine*, 1897, vol. lxxv. p. 302.

the peaceful settlement of a much disputed question, which might have caused a destructive civil war. The union of the two crowns of England and Scotland added to the public satisfaction. James himself by his affability and graciousness increased the popularity which he originally owed to circumstances. T. M., who was possibly a soldier, relates with great approbation, that the King, to show his respect to 'the art military,' fired a shot out of a cannon, and did it 'with such sign of experience that the most expert gunner there beheld it not without admiration.' He applauds with equal fervour the King's 'merry and well-seasoned jests,' adding that all his words were 'of full weight, and his jests filled with the salt of wit,' and that they were 'no less gracious' than 'facetious and pleasant.' One characteristic of the new sovereign he notes which other observers do not. 'This is one especial note in his Majesty. Any man that hath aught with him, let him be sure he have a just cause, for he beholds all men's faces with stedfastness.'

To cultivate popularity with his people, James overcame for a time the dislike to crowds, which was one of his characteristics. The Duke in Shakespeare's *Measure for Measure*, who expresses a similar distaste, has been supposed to represent the King in this—

> '"I love the people,"
> But do not like to stage me to their eyes;
> Though it do well, I do not relish well
> Their loud applause and Aves vehement;
> Nor do I think the man of safe discretion
> That does affect it.'
>
> (Act I. sc. i. l. 68.)

At first, however, James affected this applause. A coach was offered him when he entered York in order to convey him to the Minster. But he graciously answered, 'I will have no coach. For the people are desirous to see a king, and so they shall; for they shall as well see his body as his face.' Accordingly, 'to the great comfort of the people, he went on foot to the Cathedral.'

So far T. M., but Dugdale sounds a different note. By the time he reached London James was weary of crowds, and so the last of these three pamphleteers seizes the opportunity afforded by the King's visit to the Royal Exchange to rebuke the irreverent multitude for not respecting their monarch's desire to be private. 'You will say, perchance,' concludes Dugdale, '"It was your love." Will you, in love, press upon your sovereign thereby to offend him? Your sovereign may, perchance, mistake your love, and punish it as an offence.'

Once again we are reminded of *Measure for Measure.* 'Even so,' says Angelo,

> 'The general, subject to a well-wish'd king,
> Quit their own part, and in obsequious fondness
> Crowd to his presence, where their untaught love
> Must needs appear offence.'
>
> (Act II. sc. iv. l. 28.)

Twenty years later James was no longer inconvenienced by the love of his subjects, and for him popular applause had become a thing of the past.

Under his son the popularity of the House of Stuart revived for a moment, then sank lower than ever. In 1660 came a reaction, and the English nation, weary of civil strife and of new experiments in government, welcomed the restoration of monarchy with the same universal and extravagant joy with which it had hailed the union of the three kingdoms and the accession of James I.

The relation of the progress of Charles II. from Dover to London, entitled *England's Joy*, forms a kind of pendant to the narratives describing the reception of his grandfather in England. It is much less detailed and much less graphic. In some points, also, the anonymous pamphleteer is inferior to the contemporary diarists. His account has not the little personal touches which make the description of the King's landing given by Pepys of so much interest, nor has it the sincere emotion which breathes in the few lines Evelyn devotes to the King's entrance into London. On the other hand, it contains many picturesque details which are to be found nowhere else. We learn how the people of Rochester decorated their streets with garlands made up of costly scarves and ribbons 'decked with spoons and bodkins of silver'; how at Blackheath the King was met by 'a kind of rural triumph, expressed by the country swains in a morrice-dance, with the old music of taber and pipe'; and we are told for the first time of the 'hundred proper maids' of Deptford, with their 'flaskets full of flowers and sweet herbs.' There are also some new details about the King's journey through London; and though the tract is of no great historical value, it is sufficiently interesting to deserve reprinting.

To pass from these pictures of pageants and popular rejoicings to the serious records of Puritanism is a somewhat abrupt transition. Two of the tracts in this volume—and two only—illustrate the rise of the discontent which bore fruit in the Civil War, and both of them deal with the religious rather than the political history of the times. But though the cause of the breach between the Stuarts and their people was more religious than political, religion and politics were almost inseparably associated in the struggle from its origin to its close. In practice it was found that men who held a certain set of views about Church affairs held an equally definite set of views about State affairs, and that there was a definite connection between their political and their religious creeds. The verse tract called *The Interpreter*, printed in 1622, and probably in Holland, illustrates this connection. The object of its author is to explain the political significance of the three familiar names—'Puritan,' 'Protestant,' and 'Papist,' but his standpoint is throughout that of the members of the first party. Any honest man, he complains, if he opposes the Government for constitutional or religious reasons, is termed a Puritan. Sir Benjamin Rudyard, in one of his most famous speeches in the Long Parliament, echoes the complaint of the anonymous author of these verses in words that almost seem inspired by him. Speaking of the King's advisers, he says: 'They have so brought it to pass that under the name of Puritans all our religion is branded, and under a few hard words against Jesuits all Popery is countenanced. Whosoever squares his actions by any rule, either divine or human, he is a Puritan; whosoever would be governed by the King's laws, he is a Puritan. He that will not do whatsoever other men would have him do, he is a Puritan. Their great work, their masterpiece now is, to make all those of the religion to be the suspected party of the Kingdom.'[1]

This tract also suggests the famous pamphlet called *The Character of a Trimmer*, written by Halifax about December 1684, and first published in 1688. Just as Halifax sets forth the views of a moderate man on the questions of hereditary monarchy, foreign politics, ecclesiastical policy,

[1] May, *History of the Long Parliament*, p. 73, ed. 1854.

and other subjects of controversy, so the author of the earlier tract sets forth the opinions held by a moderate member of the opposition to James on the different points at issue between the popular party and the Government. But the difference between the halting verse of the first pamphleteer and the nervous prose of the second is more striking than the resemblance between their method of treatment.

The progress of the national opposition to the government of the Stuarts is further illustrated by Archbishop Abbot's narrative of his own sequestration from all his ecclesiastical offices. Born in 1562, made a bishop in 1609, and Archbishop of Canterbury since 1611, Abbot became popular with the Puritans, because he adhered firmly to Calvinistic doctrine and opposed the Spanish marriage. Clarendon describes him as 'a man of very morose manners and a very sour aspect, which in that time was called gravity,' who 'considered Christian religion no other than as it abhorred and reviled Popery and valued those men most who did that most furiously.' Puritan historians naturally took a more favourable view, and Whitelocke writes that Abbot left behind him 'the memory of a pious, learned, and moderate prelate.' As he was a man who had the courage of his convictions, the archbishop had not hesitated to defy King James when that monarch ordered him to marry the Earl of Somerset to the divorced Countess of Essex. He next defied King Charles in defence of the freedom of the subject. In 1626, after his rupture with his second Parliament, Charles levied a forced loan to provide for his military and naval expenditure. Chief-Justice Crew was ordered to sign a paper certifying the legality of the loan, and was dismissed from office upon his refusal. The King determined to procure for his exaction the sanction of the highest authority of the Church, so, like Crew, Abbot was summoned to declare himself. The demand took the shape of requisition to him to license the sermon which Dr. Robert Sibthorpe had preached before the judges at the Northampton Assizes. Its title was 'Apostolic Obedience, showing the Duty of Subjects to pay Tribute and Taxes to their Princes,' and its doctrine was that no Christian could refuse the loan the King demanded. Abbot relates the attempts made to cajole or threaten him into acquiescence with the King's desire, and the nature of the objections which led him to decline, and so caused his sequestration. Incidentally he sketches the characters of his two chief enemies, Laud and Buckingham, and defends his friendship with two of the leaders of the opposition, Sir Dudley Digges and Sir Thomas Wentworth.

Three of the tracts reprinted in this volume are narratives by military commanders of the campaigns and battles in which they took part. Of these the most valuable by far is that by Sir Francis Vere. He and his younger brother, Sir Horace, were the most famous of the school of English soldiers who fought in the wars of the Netherlands, and, having learned the art of war there, placed their skill at the disposal of their country when either Elizabeth or James had need of it. Excellent lives of both the brothers are contained in the *Dictionary of National Biography*, but the fullest account of their services is to be found in the volume entitled *The Fighting Veres*, published by Sir Clements Markham in 1888. Anything in Vere's *Commentaries* which needs explanation will be found explained there, though, like most biographers, the author is a little too much inclined to maintain that his hero was always in the right.

The *Commentaries*, which became at once a military classic, were first published in 1657. They had for many years before this passed from hand to hand in manuscript, and copies had been multiplied for the benefit of those who desired to learn from the famous soldier's recollections how battles should be fought or to study the history of the time in which he lived. Vere did not write his *Commentaries* for publication: at most, it is probable they were designed to be communicated to a few other soldiers. Hence the fragmentary condition in which they are, necessitating the additional narratives from the pen of his comrade, Sir John Ogle, and his page, Henry Hexham, which are here inserted. The object of the *Commentaries* was not autobiographical, and hence they do not give an account of all the actions in which he took part, but only of some of them. Vere wished to discuss simply those actions in which, as commander or adviser, he played a leading part; and though he naturally vindicated his own conduct whenever it had been called in question, his main purpose was to explain the military causes of failure or success for the benefit of soldiers. The number and the nature of the details which he gives show this. Look, for instance, at the account given of the capture of the fort at Wesel, and the minuteness with which Vere describes the preparations for the escalade, and calls attention to a new manner of assaulting which, 'well considered, is of wonderful advantage.' In the same way, when he relates the action at Turnhout, he dwells minutely upon the tactics by which, with a small force, he delayed the march of a numerous enemy, and gave time for the rest of the prisoners to come up. He notes also the mistake made by the enemy in drawing up their battalions of pike one behind the other instead of posting them chequerwise or in some other formation which would have enabled them to support each other. Notice also the detailed account of the manner in which the Dutch and English cavalry broke these squares of pikemen: 'We charged their pikes, not breaking through them at the first push, as it was anciently used by the men-of-arms with their barbed horses: but as the long pistols, delivered at hand, had made the ranks thin, so thereupon the rest of the horse got within them.' The picture of the battle in the original edition of the *Commentaries* shows this process admirably.

The most important battle in which Vere was engaged was that at Nieuport in 1600. Before this the Dutch armies had never beaten the Spaniards in the open country in a pitched battle. Their successes had been gained in the attack or defence of fortified places. The Spanish foot were still renowned as the best infantry in Europe, and those who fought at Nieuport were 'old trained soldiers and to that day unfoiled in the field.' Their discipline and their solidity were their chief characteristics, while the strength of the infantry who served under the Dutch colours lay chiefly in their superior mobility. 'Unluckily,' says Vere, 'by the situation of the country that skill and dexterity we presumed to excel our enemy in (which was the apt and agile motions of our battalions) was utterly taken from us.' Prince Maurice and his army had to fight a defensive battle with an inferior force and in a disadvantageous position. The 4000 infantry forming Maurice's van, under the command of Vere, bore the brunt of the fighting. The task which Vere set himself was to make the enemy expend their strength in the attack upon the van, so that when they were disordered and spent by the struggle they might be easily overthrown by the rest of the Dutch army. He describes the conformation of the ground, the dispositions by which he made the most of it, and the manner in which he used his small force to the best advantage. Through the tardiness of his reserves Vere's force was nearly overwhelmed, but an opportune charge of horse decided the fate of the day and justified his tactics.

Vere has been charged with taking all the credit of the victory to himself and the troops under his command, and with ignoring the services of others; but if his account is rightly read, it is evident that he does not profess to narrate the battle as a whole but only his particular part of it. His object is to state a military problem and show how it was solved, not to write a history. The controversy about the battle of Nieuport and the value of Vere's contribution to its history may be studied at length in Motley's *United Netherlands*, iv. 14-51; Markham's *Fighting Veres*, pp. 278-305; and Dalton's *Life of Sir Edward Cecil*, i. 47-59.

There are two parts of Vere's narrative which have a special interest for English readers: his account of the capture of Cadiz in 1596, and his account of what was called *The Islands Voyage*, that is the expedition to the Azores in 1597. Fortunately, both these subjects have recently been treated at length and very competently by Mr. Julian Corbett in his *Successors of Drake* (1900). Speaking of Vere's account in a critical appendix, Mr. Corbett says: 'It is especially valuable for technical details and the light it throws on the true intention of the tactics employed; but throughout it is a studied apology for the author, probably exaggerating the part he played and minimising that of officers he disliked, such as Raleigh.' In his narrative, however, Mr. Corbett is much more favourable to Vere, whom he praises as 'the greatest of the Elizabethan generals.' He confirms many of Vere's statements, and supplies the information which explains the carping, critical attitude adopted by Vere towards Raleigh and Essex. Towards Raleigh, Vere is extremely hostile, and, as Mr. Corbett says, his testimony against him must never be accepted without confirmation. Essex, whose relations with himself Vere narrates at some length, he justified when his conduct as commander of the expedition to the Azores was called in question by Elizabeth. But when Vere speaks of Essex it is always with something of the contempt with which the professional soldier is inclined to regard the amateur, however excellent the amateur's intentions may be. This feeling is shown in Vere's remarks on the disorderly manner in which the storming of Cadiz was managed, and again in his account of the landing at Terceira. Of the latter he says:—

'His Lordship, *as his fashion was*, would be of the first to land; and I, *that had learned me of his disposition*, took upon me the care of sending the boats after him. . . . His Lordship himself took great pains to put his men in order; and for that *I perceived he took delight to do all*, in good manners and respect I gave the looking on.' In each case the commander-in-chief was doing what a general who knew his business would have left to some capable subordinate. The scene described by Vere in the market-place at Villa Franca when Essex, instead of listening to Vere's report of the movements of the enemy and the preparations which he had made to meet them, 'called for tobacco' and began smoking, shows that some resentment for personal incivility may have been mingled with Vere's contempt. Vere also complains that he was excluded from the consultations in which the conduct of the expedition was decided.

In addition to all this the usual hostility between the naval and military commanders in joint expeditions manifested itself in both these two, and helps to colour Vere's narrative. While his opinions on military matters may be confidently accepted, many of the disputed questions connected with the management of both expeditions were matters on which the admirals were better judges than he was.

One more point requires notice. Vere describes himself as drawing up, at the outset of the expedition to Cadiz, a paper setting down in writing the duties which properly belonged to every rank of officer in the army. A manuscript of this document is in the British Museum.[1] It was published in 1672 under the title of 'Sir Francis Vere's Notes of Direction how far every man's office in a regiment doth extend and the duty of every officer,' in Thomas Venn's *Military and Maritime Discipline* (folio, 1672, pp. 186-193).

The *Commentaries* end suddenly with the repulse of the attack of the Spaniards on Ostend on July 25, 1601, though Vere's command there lasted until March 7, 1602. It was his last considerable exploit. In 1604, when James I. made peace with Spain, Vere retired from the Dutch service and returned to England, where he married, became Governor of Portsmouth, and died on August 28, 1609, at the early age of forty-nine. His brother, Sir Horace, who was five years younger, continued in the Dutch service till 1632, earning almost as much glory as Sir Francis. In English

[1] Harleian, MS. 168, *f.* 120; also Cotton MS. Galba D. xii.

history his name is remembered as the commander of the little expedition sent by James I. to the Palatinate in 1620 and for his valiant defence of Mannheim against the Spaniards in 1622. Sir Horace, who was created Baron Vere of Tilbury on 24th July 1625, died in 1635.

The history of the portion of Sir Francis Vere's command at Ostend, which he left untold, was supplied by two of his subordinates, Sir John Ogle and Henry Hexham. Ogle, who was Vere's lieutenant-colonel, related the last charge at the battle of Nieuport and the story of the parley at Ostend. He became subsequently Governor of Utrecht, left the service of the States-General in 1618, was one of the Council of War appointed by James I. in 1624, as a sort of Committee of National Defence, and died in March 1640. Henry Hexham, Vere's page, whom we see on p. 181 pulling up the stockings and tying the points of his master's habits, contributed accounts of several episodes in the siege, and in especial of the great assault made by the Spaniards on January 7, 1602. He became a voluminous military writer; and his *Principles of the Art Military*, first published in 1637, was one of the most popular textbooks for the soldiers of the early seventeenth century. Besides this he compiled an excellent dictionary of the Dutch and English languages. Some account of Hexham is given in the supplement to the *Dictionary of National Biography*, where it is said that he probably died about 1650.

The long struggle of the Dutch for their freedom ended in 1609 with a twelve years' truce, though Spain did not formally acknowledge their independence till 1648. A tract by Sir Thomas Overbury contains an account of the economic and political condition both of the United

Provinces and of the part of the Netherlands which still remained subject to Spain. Overbury's little work is not so valuable as the more elaborate and better-known account of Holland written by Sir William Temple sixty years later, but it is interesting as giving the impressions of a contemporary traveller at the moment when the War of Independence ended. It supplies also a description of the field in which the exploits of Vere and his comrades took place.

The two Veres were the heads of a school of soldiers who learnt the art of war under their command. A list of the most notable of these officers is given by the editor of the *Commentaries*, and the most famous name amongst them is that of Sir Thomas Fairfax, the Parliamentary General. Fairfax, who had served under Sir Horace, married in 1637 Anne Vere, the daughter of his old commander, and his memoirs appropriately accompany those of Vere. Neither of the two papers written by Fairfax was published till after his death. His nephew, Brian Fairfax, who printed them in 1699, explains his reasons for doing so in a letter prefixed to the original edition. Brian says that his uncle's manuscript 'was never intended by him to be published, but to remain for the satisfaction of himself and his relations.' Nevertheless imperfect copies of them had got abroad. 'And this being an age wherein every man presumes to print what he pleases of his own or other men's, we are plainly told, that my Lord Fairfax's memorials are ready to be published, and by the very same person who has lately set forth some memoirs, wherein his Lordship is scarce ever named but with reproach.' The publications alluded to are probably the Memoirs of Lord Holles and those of Edmund Ludlow, but especially the former, which contains the most direct personal attacks upon Fairfax. For this reason Brian thought that he was doing his uncle a service in publishing this vindication of his political conduct and the narrative of his military services which follow it. The history of the MS. is traced in Markham's *Life of the Great Lord Fairfax*, p. 393, and in the *Sixth Report of the Historical Manuscripts Commission*, p. 465. The best version in print is that in the *Antiquarian Repertory*, vol. iii. 1808, for Brian Fairfax made a number of small changes in the text which are reproduced in the reprints in the *Somers Tracts* and in the *Select Tracts* of Maseres.

The first memoir is simply a vindication. Fairfax describes himself as more anxious to clear his actions than declare them, and selects for the purpose 'those actions which seemed to the world most questionable.' On some points his defence may be accepted without hesitation. For instance, there is no reason for doubting that he did not seek for the command of the New Model army, and accepted it for public motives not for selfish ends. As little doubt is there that he had no hand in the seizure of King Charles I. at Holdenby, and was sincerely opposed to the execution of the King. Brian Fairfax tells us that he could never speak of the King's death without tears in his eyes, and a contemporary rumour describes Cromwell as necessitated to set guards over Fairfax to prevent him from endeavouring to release Charles. More doubtful is the success of Fairfax in vindicating his conduct with respect to the execution of Lucas and Lisle after the capture of Colchester. The question has been much controverted, and to give the arguments at length in this Introduction would require too much space. It may be briefly stated that by the capitulation Fairfax had a perfect right to execute the two knights if he thought fit to do so. On the other hand, the more merciful course of handing them over to the civil authority to be tried and sentenced would have been fairer and wiser. This was the course adopted with regard to the peers taken prisoners at the same time. So far as concerns Fairfax's performance of the articles on which these prisoners surrendered his defence is sound enough. The question is amply discussed in Mr. Gardiner's *History of the Great Civil War* (iv. p. 205).

Yet in spite of the fact that Fairfax successfully vindicates himself on some particular points, there is no doubt that he misrepresents his own attitude during the events which followed the attempt of Parliament to disband the army in the spring of 1647. All contemporary evidence goes to prove that he was not the passive and unwilling agent he represents himself as being. Cromwell was more energetic and more prominent in the quarrel; but Fairfax was by no means a mere puppet in Cromwell's hands. During 1647 he seems to have been in perfect agreement with the other leaders of the army in the policy adopted. His difference with them began in 1648, but did not come to a head until the King's trial. It is somewhat difficult to fix his exact part in events, and consequently the precise amount of his responsibility, but an attempt is made to do so in the life of Fairfax contributed to the *Dictionary of the National Biography* by the present writer.[1]

The feebleness of Fairfax as a politician was in striking contrast to his vigour and boldness as a soldier. It recalls Whitelocke's description of the difference between Fairfax

[1] See also Mr. Gardiner's *History of the Great Civil War*, iii. pp. 308, 350; iv. p. 304, and the *Clarke Papers*, ii. pp. 146, 147.

in council and Fairfax in battle. He describes the General as 'a person of as meek and humble carriage as ever I saw in great employment, and but of few words in discourse or council.' On the other hand, continues Whitelocke, 'in action in the field I have seen him so highly transported that scarce any one durst speak a word to him, and he would seem more like a man distracted and furious than of his ordinary mildness.'

There are signs of this Fairfax in the second of the two narratives printed here. He was not the man to boast of his own deeds, as he proved on many occasions, but he was obliged to give some account of them by the purpose which he set before himself in writing, 'My silence,' he says, 'seemed to accuse me of ingratitude to God for the many mercies and deliverances I have had. . . . Wherefore I shall set down, as they come into my mind, such things wherein I have found the wonderful assistance of God to me in the time of the war I was in in the north.' Just in the same way another soldier of the time, Sir William Waller, drew up a few pages of recollections, consisting almost entirely of a list of his remarkable escapes from the perils and accidents to which a military career had exposed him, attributing these escapes as Fairfax does to divine assistance. For this reason, therefore, Fairfax is led to say more about his personal share than he otherwise would have done. We see him always charging at the head of his men and exposing himself with reckless courage. At Sherburn, for instance, the royalists had barricaded the streets of the town, and Fairfax and his troops had to take one of these defences. 'At the end of the barricade, there was a straight passage for one single horse to go in. I entered there, and others followed one by one.' At the capture of Wakefield he gets so far ahead of his men that he has a narrow escape of being taken, and much the same thing happens to him in the fight at Selby and at Marston Moor. In the retreat from Bradford, Fairfax and a dozen others charge three hundred horse, and six of them cut their way through. He gives a pretty full account of Marston Moor, where, besides narrating his own escape, he had to explain the defeat of the troops under his command; but, on the other hand, he says little of Winceby, where an opportune flank charge made by the horse he led appears to have had a considerable share in obtaining the victory. Though he does not undertake to give an account of the campaigns themselves, but only of his personal share in them, Fairfax's narrative is one of the chief authorities for the history of the war in Yorkshire from 1642 to 1644. It was not meant for publication, and he apologises for not having set down things 'in that methodical and polished manner as might have been done; being but intended for my own satisfaction, and the help of my memory.' Only the salient incidents of the campaigns are therefore related, 'my intention being only to keep in mind what I had been present in.'

The third of the military authors whose narratives are here reprinted, is Major General Thomas Morgan. Having learnt war in Germany and the Low Countries, he returned to take part in the war in the north of England, under the command of Fairfax. 'One of Sir Thomas's colonels, a little man, short and peremptory,' is the manner in which a contemporary narrative describes him. During the first Civil War Morgan, being expert in sieges, was principally employed in the capture of Royalist castles. Later, as colonel of a regiment of dragoons, he helped Monck to complete the conquest of Scotland, and became finally second in command of the army in Scotland with the rank of Major-General. In 1657 Morgan was sent to Flanders as second in command of the six thousand English, whom Cromwell sent to help the French against the Spaniards, and it is his narrative of their exploits that now requires to be criticised.

The boasting tone of Morgan's narrative is a complete contrast to Fairfax's modest account of his adventures. It also contrasts very strangely with the style and tone of the letters written by Morgan himself during the campaign he relates, some of which are printed in Thurloe's *State Papers*. Some historians have doubted in consequence whether the narrative was really the work of Morgan, but evidence exists to show when and why it was written. Dr. Samuel Barrow, an old acquaintance of Morgan's in Scotland, thought of writing a history of the period, and desired Morgan to draw up an account of the services of the six thousand English who were sent by Cromwell to serve in the Netherlands. Morgan's answer, which is dated 1675, ran as follows:—

'SIR,—Since I see you, I have drawne a foule draught of all my proceedings in France and Flanders with the six thousand English, and if you have the conveniency to step hither, that you may see them before my man writes them faire over, it will doe well; the sooner you come the better it will be, seeing you are so desireous to have a viewe of them. I shall not need to ad further but that I am,—Your very loving friend and servant,

1675. THO. MORGAN.[1]

[1] See *The Academy*, February 17, 1892.

Morgan died about 1679, and the narrative was published in 1699. Its value is rather doubtful. Godwin in his *History of the Commonwealth*, speaking of the battle of the Dunes, says: 'There is an absurd narrative of this action, printed under the name of General Morgan, the second in command, and published in 1699, in which he represents the French as cowards, Lockhart a poltroon, and Turenne an idiot, and assumes all the honour of the battle and the campaign to himself.' Though this criticism is not entirely undeserved, it is overstated. Morgan certainly played a more important part, both in the battle and the campaign, than his nominal commander Lockhart. And it is also certain from other sources that the English soldiers he commanded did greatly distinguish themselves, both at the battle of the Dunes, the storming of Ypres, and elsewhere. But Morgan's narrative is so exaggerated and so highly coloured, that it cannot safely be followed where it is not confirmed by other authorities. Its value lies in the little picturesque touches which bring before us the incidents of the battle and the character of the English soldier. The shout of rejoicing which Morgan's men give when they see the enemy, their throwing up their caps in the air, their colloquy with the English soldiers serving on the Spanish sides, and many similar details, are brought before us with incomparable vividness.

Morgan amusingly describes Turenne's horror and wrath when he proposed to assault the outworks of Ypres before such an attempt seemed feasible to the French Marshal. 'He rose up and fell into a passion, stamping with his feet, and shaking his locks, and grinning with his teeth, he said, "Major-general Morgan had made him mad."' It is only fair to add a description of Morgan himself as he appeared to Turenne. After the taking of Dunkirk, we are told by Aubrey, Marshal Turenne and Cardinal Mazarin had a mind to see the famous English commander: 'They gave him a visit, and whereas they thought to have found an Achillean or gigantic person, they saw a little man, not many degrees above a dwarf, sitting in a hut of turfs with his fellow soldiers, smoking a pipe about three inches long, with a green hat-case on. He spake with a very exile (*i.e.* thin or shrill) tone, and did cry out to the soldiers when angry with them, "Sirrah, I 'll cleave your skull," as if the words had been prolated by an eunuch.'

From the narratives of the soldiers we pass to those written by the sailors. They are written by less important people, and deal with less important events; but while they contain little information of direct use to historians, they are indispensable to those who seek to understand the temper of seventeenth century Englishmen. Throughout the whole of the century, and indeed much later, the English merchant seaman had to face the constant risk of capture by the pirates of Algiers or Sallee, in the Atlantic as well as the Mediterranean, and even at times in the Channel. The story told by John Rawlins is a type of many others, save that such bold exploits as the recapture of the 'Exchange' were not frequent. The prominent part which English renegadoes play in his adventures is very notable, and his description of the cruise of the pirate ship on board which he embarked contains details which the stories of other captives do not supply. Some years ago the condition of the Christian captives at Algiers was admirably treated in a series of articles by M. H. De Grammont entitled 'La Course, l'esclavage et la rédemption à Alger,'[1]

[1] *Revue Historique*, vols. xxv. xxvi. xxvii.

but no English book exists in which the subject is adequately dealt with.

In the preface, Rawlins apologises for the defects of his story, on the ground that it is 'the unpolished work of a poor sailor.' Towards the close of the narrative he admits that he had the help of some one else in 'cementing the broken pieces of well-tempered mortar,' and providing by 'art and cunning' a seemly setting for his 'precious stones.' The substance was doubtless, as asserted, supplied by the 'poor sailor' himself, but the rhetorical exhortations addressed to the 'gentle reader' are clearly the handiwork of a professional writer.

It is also to the hand of some journalist of the time that the next narrative in the volume is due. The *True Relation of the Stratagem practised upon a sea-town in Galicia*, illustrates the history of the war between England and Spain which began in 1625, and ended in 1629. It is essentially a political pamphlet, written to incite Englishmen to courageous deeds against their ancient enemies the Spaniards, and the statements of fact which it contains are of little value. One of the stories it tells seems to be the earliest form of the narrative of the adventures of Richard Peeke, which is printed after it. Richard Peeke's account of his single combat has doubtless some basis of fact. A newsletter of the time records his return to England after his release by the Spaniards, and says that he brought with him a challenge from Gondomar to Buckingham.[1] His adventure became so famous, that besides being the subject of the poem here reprinted, he was also made the hero of a play called *Dick of Devonshire*.[2] Peeke's narrative is so

[1] *Court of Charles I.*, i. p. 104.
[2] Bullen's *Old Plays*, ii. pp. 1-99.

well written, that it is easy to understand its popularity. He has an appreciation of the dramatic and the picturesque; he brings each incident vividly before his readers, from the moment when he finds the three dead Englishmen lying on the seashore, to that when after his hard won victory the Spanish soldiers, murmuring and biting their thumbs, threaten him with death. There is something which reminds one of *Chevy Chase* and the heroic ballads of the Elizabethan age in the modest depreciation of his own prowess, with which Peeke protests that though of the fourteen thousand men in the English army, above twelve thousand were better and stouter men than he is, yet, nevertheless, he is willing to fight any one they choose to pit against him. Better still is the simplicity and the fortitude of his farewell to his fellow prisoner in the gaol at Cadiz.

Robert Lyde's account of the retaking of the ship 'Friend's Adventure' has some points of resemblance with Peeke's narrative. Each fights against desperate odds, and Peeke's quarter-staff may be paralleled by Lyde's iron oar. But there is a considerable difference in the characters of the two men, and Peeke has a chivalrous spirit which is wanting in Lyde. There is also the difference, that while Peeke was obliged to fight to save his life, Lyde's life was in no immediate danger, and his motive was simply to preserve his freedom. For the 'lusty young man about twenty-three years old,' as the latter terms himself, had seen the inside of one French prison, and preferred to die fighting rather than to set his foot in another. Lyde's account of the sufferings endured by English sailors, who happened to be prisoners in France, is fully confirmed by the detailed diary which another sailor, Richard Strutton, published in 1690. In Lyde the dread of a French prison is reinforced by the thirst for revenge. When he sets to work to recapture his ship, he determines in his own mind exactly how many of the seven Frenchmen on board are to die in the conflict. He will kill three and no more, because three of his old shipmates had perished in their prison at Dinan, and when he was back in England again, he would enter aboard a fireship, in order to avenge the other four hundred men who had died in the same prison. Lyde is singularly pious, and has no doubt that the bloody work he undertakes will be blessed by God. He reads the Bible to the boy who is his companion, in order to convince him of the justice of their enterprise. Special providences encourage him in his purpose: when he prays for a south wind, the south wind comes; when for a south-west, south-west it is. At the last, with one brief prayer, he springs upon his enemies: 'Lord, be with us and strengthen us in the action.'

Very remarkable too is Lyde's forethought. He throws away his cap, so that if he gets a blow upon the head in the struggle, he may be killed rather than stunned. He drinks a pint of wine and 'half-a-pint of oil' to make him 'more fit for action.'

Lyde's account of the death struggle in the little low cabin is extremely graphic; but the most horribly vivid thing in his story is the picture of the wounded man, with the blood streaming from his forehead, 'beating his hands upon the deck to make a noise, that the men at the pump might hear: for he would not cry nor speak.' Finally, to counterpoise this tragedy, we have just the one touch of comedy the drama requires, in the broken French Lyde puts into the mouths of the vanquished. 'Moy travalli pur Angleterre se vous plea,' cry his sometime masters, putting off their hats, and then like Pistol to the French prisoners after Agincourt, his fury abates, and he promises to show mercy. We leave Lyde at last after his return to England, robbed by the lawyers of the bulk of his well-earned salvage money, but wearing the golden chain Queen Mary has given him, and looking forward confidently to preferment in the navy.

The narrative of Henry Pitman, unlike those of Peeke and Lyde, is a narrative of sufferings, not of daring deeds. The adventures he met with were forced upon him by his attempt to escape from captivity; and apart from the boldness with which he faced the dangers of the sea, he was evidently not a man to thrust himself into perils which it was possible to avoid. The peaceable surgeon was drawn into his strange experiences by fortune, just as he was accidentally involved in the fate which befell the men who had fought for Monmouth. As an account of the servitude to which the western rebels were condemned Pitman's story should be compared with that of his fellow-sufferer, John Coad. Coad's narrative, probably written about 1692, was published first in 1849 under the title of '*A Memorandum of the Wonderful Providences of God to a poor unworthy creature during the time of the Duke of Monmouth's Rebellion and to the Revolution in* 1688.' But while Coad had actually fought for Monmouth and had received two wounds in his service, Pitman was a non-combatant, and the one passed his period of servitude in Jamaica, the other in Barbadoes. Pitman's narrative was freely employed by Sir Walter Besant, in the historical novel entitled *For Faith and Freedom*, which he published in 1889. Lord Macaulay, who read Coad's narrative in manuscript, refers to it as giving 'the best account of the sufferings of those rebels who were sentenced to transportation,' but it is evident that he never saw Pitman's *Relation.* Had he done so, it would have saved him from a serious error. As is well known to most of the readers of Macaulay's *History*, one of the most controverted questions connected with it is the justice of the author's treatment of the character of William Penn. Amongst other charges, Macaulay accuses Penn of being the agent employed to extract the ransom of the 'Maids of Taunton' from their relatives. The advocates of the Quaker hero showed that the mysterious 'Mr. Penne' employed in this transaction was probably a certain George Penne employed in another business of the same kind. Macaulay for a number of insufficient reasons refused to accept this correction, and insisted that 'Mr. Penne' necessarily meant Mr. William Penn. One of his arguments was that it was too big a business for an obscure scoundrel like George Penne to be employed in. Pitman's narrative, however, shows that George Penne was regularly engaged in the buying and selling of prisoners, and completes the case against Macaulay's view. Mr. John Paget in his *Paradoxes and Puzzles* (p. 13), published in 1874, undertook a refutation of Macaulay's charge against Penn, but Pitman's evidence on this point was unknown to him. Its bearing on the question was first pointed out by Mr. C. E. Doble in two letters to the *Academy* for April 15, 1893, and March 23, 1895. Entries in the *Calendar of Colonial State Papers for* 1685-1688 still further strengthen the case against George Penne (p. 651).

Apart from its value as a contribution to the history of the sufferers in Monmouth's rising, Pitman's tract also throws some light on the history of the West Indian pirates with whom the fugitives were thrown into contact during their stay at Tortuga. Captain Yanche, whom Pitman mentions, reappears in the *Colonial State Papers* as Captain Yankey, who surrendered in 1687 to the governor of Jamaica. New Providence, which Pitman visited, became subsequently the chief rendezvous of privateersmen in those seas.[1] It is curious to note that these pirates were all strongly in favour of Monmouth, no doubt because these constant hostilities with the Spaniards had sharpened their Protestant zeal. John Whickers's captivity at Santiago, and his enforced service on a Spanish privateer, supplies an instance of the fate which befell English sailors who fell into the hands of the Spaniards, whether the said sailors were pirates or traders.

The adventurous vôyage from Barbadoes, and the experiences of the castaways on the island of Tortuga, have an interest of a more romantic nature. Sometimes, as Mr. Arber is careful to point out, we are reminded of incidents in *Robinson Crusoe*; and it is by no means unlikely that Defoe was familiar with Pitman's narrative, for he claimed to have been out with Monmouth himself, and at all events was specially interested in the subject of the ill-fated rebellion. The picture of Pitman and his comrades living on turtles and whelks, with occasional sea birds 'which did eat extreme fishy,' suggests comparison with Crusoe; though Crusoe was never so destitute of tobacco as to be driven to smoke wild sage in a crab's claw.

C. H. FIRTH.

[1] Lucas, *Historical Geography of the British Colonies*, ii. p. 79.

SIR ROBERT CAREY.

Account of the Death of Queen ELIZABETH; *and of his ride to King* JAMES *at Edinburgh*

1603

Sir ROBERT CAREY,
Lord Warden of the Middle Marches; and afterwards Earl of MONMOUTH.

Account of the Death of Queen ELIZABETH; *and of his ride to King* JAMES *at Edinburgh, 25th-27th March* 1603.

IN this state was this Middle March when JAMES came in King of England: and in all the time I continued Officer there, GOD so blessed me and all the actions I took in hand, that I never failed of any one enterprise: but they were all effected to my own desire and the good of that Government. Thus passed I forty-two of my years; [? 1560-1602], GOD assisting with his blessing and mighty protection.

After that all things were quieted and the Border in safety, towards the end of five years [1598–1603] that I had been Warden there; having little to do, I resolved upon a journey to Court, to see my friends and renew my acquaintance there. I took my journey about the end of the year [*which, according to the old reckoning, ended on the 24th March: say then, March* 1603].

When I came to Court [*at Richmond*], I found the Queen ill disposed, and she kept her inner lodging.

Yet she, hearing of my arrival, sent for me.

I found her in one of her withdrawing chambers, sitting low upon her cushions. She called me to her.

I kissed her hand, and told her, It was my chiefest happiness to see her in safety and health, which I wished might long continue.

She took me by the hand, and wrung it hard; and said "No, ROBIN, I am not well!" and then discoursed with me of her indisposition, and that her heart had been sad and heavy for ten or twelve days: and, in her discourse, she fetched not so few as forty or fifty great sighs.

I was grieved, at the first, to see her in this plight: for, in all my lifetime before, I never knew her fetch a sigh, but when the Queen of Scots was beheaded. Then [in 1587], upon my knowledge, she shed many tears and sighs; manifesting her innocence that she never gave consent to the death of that Queen.

I used the best words I could to persuade her from this melancholy humour; but I found, by her, it was too deep rooted in her heart; and hardly to be removed.

This was upon a Saturday night [? 19*th March* 1603]: and she gave command that the Great Closet should be prepared for her to go to Chapel the next morning.

The next day, all things being in a readiness; we long expected her coming.

After eleven o'clock, one of the Grooms [of the Chambers] came out, and bade make ready for the Private Closet; for she would not go to the Great.

There we stayed long for her coming: but at last she had cushions laid for her in the Privy Chamber, hard by the Closet door; and there she heard service.

From that day forwards, she grew worse and worse. She remained upon her cushions four days and nights, [? *Saturday* 19*th to Tuesday* 22*nd March* 1603] at the least. All about her could not persuade her, either to take any sustenance, or [to] go to bed.

I, hearing that neither her Physicians, nor none about her, could persuade her to take any course for her safety, feared her death would soon after ensue. I could not but think in what a wretched estate I should be left: most of my livelihood depending on her life. And hereupon I bethought myself with what grace and favour I was ever received by the King of Scots, whensoever I was sent to him. I did assure myself it was neither unjust, nor unhonest, for me to do for myself; if GOD, at that time, should call her to his mercy. Hereupon I wrote to the King of Scots, knowing him to be the right heir to the Crown of England; and certified him in what state Her Majesty was. I desired him not to stir from Edinburgh: and if, of that sickness she should die, I would be the first man that should bring him news of it.

The Queen grew worse and worse, because she would be so: none about her being able to persuade her to go to bed. [The Earl of NOTTINGHAM] my Lord Admiral was sent for: who (by reason of my sister [CATHARINE]'s death, that was his wife) had absented himself some fortnight from [the] Court.

What by fair means, what by force, he gat her to bed. There was no hope of her recovery, because she refused all remedies.

On Wednesday, the 23rd of March [1603], she grew speechless. That afternoon, by signs, she called for her [Privy] Council: and by putting her hand to her head, when the King of Scots was named to succeed her, they all knew he was the man she desired should reign after her.

About six at night, she made signs for [JOHN WHITGIFT] the Archbishop, and her Chaplains to come to her. At which time, I went in with them; and sat upon my knees full of tears to see that heavy sight.

Her Majesty lay upon her back; with one hand in the bed, and the other without.

The [Arch]bishop kneeled down by her, and examined her first of her faith: and she so punctually answered all his several questions by lifting up her eyes, and holding up her hand, as it was a comfort to all beholders.

Then the good man told her plainly, What she was; and What she was to come to: and though she had been long a great Queen here upon earth; yet shortly she was to yield an account of her stewardship to the King of Kings.

After this, he began to pray: and all that were by did answer him. After he had continued long in prayer, till the old man's knees were weary, he blessed her, and meant to rise and leave her.

The Queen made a sign with her hand.

My sister [PHILADELPHIA, Lady] SCROOPE, knowing her meaning, told the Bishop, The Queen desired he would pray still.

He did so for a long half-hour after; and then thought to have left her.

The second time she made sign to have him continue in prayer.

He did so for half an hour more, with earnest cries to GOD for her soul's health; which he uttered with that fervency of spirit as the Queen, to all our sight, much rejoiced thereat: and gave testimony to us all, of her Christian and comfortable end.

By this time, it grew late; and every one departed: all but her Women that attended her.

This that I heard with my ears, and did see with my eyes, I thought it my duty to set down, and to affirm it for a truth upon the faith of a Christian; because I know there have been many false lies reported of the end and death of that good Lady.

I went to my lodging, and left word with one in the Cofferer's Chamber to call me, if that night it was thought she would die; and gave the Porter an angel [10*s.* = £2 *now*] to let me in at any time, when I called.

Between one and two of the clock on Thursday morning [25th March 1603], he that I left in the Cofferer's Chamber, brought me word, "The Queen was dead."

I rose, and made all haste to the Gate [of Richmond Palace], to get in.

There I was answered, I could not enter: the Lords of the [Privy] Council having been with him [*the Porter*] and commanded him that none should go in or out, but by Warrant from them.

At the very instant, one of the Council [Sir EDWARD WOTTON, *afterwards* Lord WOTTON; see page 526] the Comptroller [of the Household] asked, Whether I was at the Gate?

I said, "Yes."

He said, If I pleased, he would let me in.

I desired to know how the Queen was.

He answered, " Pretty well."

I bade him " Good Night ! "

He replied and said, " Sir, if you will come in ; I will give you my word and credit you shall go out again at your own pleasure."

Upon his word, I entered the Gate, and came up to the Cofferer's Chamber : where I found all the Ladies weeping bitterly.

He [*the Comptroller*] led me from thence to the Privy Chamber ; where all the [Privy] Council was assembled.

There I was caught hold of ; and assured I should not go for Scotland till their pleasures were further known.

I told them, " I came of purpose, to that end."

From thence, they all went to [Sir ROBERT CECIL] the Secretary's Chamber : and, as they went, they gave a special command to the Porters, that none should go out at the Gates but such servants as they should send to prepare their coaches and horses for London.

Thus was I left, in the midst of the Court, to think my own thoughts till they had done counsel. I went to [GEORGE, Lord HUNSDON] my brother's chamber : who was in bed, having been over-watched many nights before.

I got him up with all speed ; and when the [Privy] Council's men were going out of the Gate, my brother thrust to the Gate.

The Porter, knowing him to be a Great Officer, let him out. I pressed after him, and was stayed by the Porter.

My brother said angrily to the Porter, " Let him out, I will answer for him ! " Whereupon I was suffered to pass : which I was not a little glad of.

I got to horse, and rode to the Knight Marshal's Lodging by Charing Cross ; and there stayed till the Lords [of the Privy Council] came to Whitehall Garden.

I stayed there till it was nine a clock in the morning ; and hearing that all the Lords were in the Old Orchard at Whitehall, I sent the [Knight] Marshal to tell them, That I had stayed all that while, to know their pleasures ; and that I would attend them, if they would command me any service.

They were very glad when they heard I was not gone :

and desired the [Knight] Marshal to send for me; and I should, with all speed, be despatched for Scotland.

The [Knight] Marshal believed them; and sent Sir ARTHUR SAVAGE for me.

I made haste to them.

One of the [Privy] Council, [Sir WILLIAM KNOLLYS] my Lord of [BANBURY] that now is [see page 526], whispered the [Knight] Marshal in the ear, and told him, If I came; they would stay me, and send some other in my stead.

The [Knight] Marshal got from them; and met me coming to them, between the two Gates. He bade me, Be gone! for he had learned, for certain, that if I came to them, they would betray me.

I returned, and took horse between nine and ten a clock; and [by] that night rode to Doncaster [162 *miles from London; and* 235 *miles from Edinburgh*].

The Friday night [the 26th], I came to my own house at Widdrington [298 *miles from London; and* 99 *miles from Edinburgh*]; and presently took order with my Deputies [of the Middle Marches, HENRY WIDDRINGTON and WILLIAM FENWICK; see page 499] to see the Borders kept in quiet; which they had much to do: and gave order [that], the next morning, the King of Scotland should be proclaimed King of England [at Widdrington]; and at Morpeth [289 *miles from London*] and Alnwick [306 *miles from London*].

Very early, on Saturday [27th March 1603], I took horse [at Widdrington] for Edinburgh; and came to Norham [331 *miles from London*, 8 *miles South of Berwick, and* 66 *miles from Edinburgh*], about twelve at noon. So that I might well have been with the King at supper time: but I got a great fall by the way [*i.e. after leaving Norham*]; and my horse, with one of his heels, gave me a great blow on the head, that made me shed much blood. It made me so weak, that I was forced to ride a soft pace after: so that the King was newly gone to bed by the time I knocked at the gate [of Holyrood House, Edinburgh].

I was quickly let in; and carried up to the King's Chamber.

I kneeled by him, and saluted him by his title of "England, Scotland, France, and Ireland."

He gave me his hand to kiss; and bade me welcome.

After he had long discoursed of the manner of the Queen's sickness, and of her death; he asked, What letters I had from the [Privy] Council?

I told him, "None": and acquainted him how narrowly I [had] escaped from them. And yet I brought him a blue ring from a Lady,* that I hoped would give him assurance of the truth that I had reported.

He took it, and looked upon it, and said, "It is enough. I know by this, you are a true messenger."

Then he committed me to the charge of my Lord HOME; and gave straight command that I should want nothing.

He sent for his Chirurgions to attend me; and when I kissed his hand, at my departure, he said to me these gracious words:

"I know you have lost a near kinswoman and a loving Mistress: but take here my hand, I will be as good a Master to you; and will requite you this service with honour and reward."

So I left him that night, and went with my Lord HOME to my lodging: where I had all things fitting for so weary a man as I was. After my head was dressed, I took leave of my Lord and many others that attended me; and went to my rest.

* *The account of the blue ring which Lady ELIZABETH SPELMAN gave to Lord CORKE was this:—*

King JAMES kept a constant and private correspondence with several persons of the English Court, during many years before Queen ELIZABETH died. Among them was [PHILADELPHIA] Lady SCROOPE [see page 478], sister of Sir ROBERT CAREY: to whom His Majesty sent, by Sir JAMES FULLERTON, a sapphire ring; with positive orders to return it to him, by a special messenger, as soon as the Queen was actually expired.

Lady SCROOPE had no opportunity of delivering it to her brother Sir ROBERT, whilst he was in the Palace of Richmond; but waiting at the window till she saw him at the outside of the Gate [see page 480], she threw it out to him; and he well knew to what purpose he received it.

S.E.B. [Sir S. E. BRYDGES.] *Memoirs of the Peers af England during the reign of JAMES I.*, p. 413. Ed. 1802. 8vo.

The next morning [Sunday, 28th March 1603], by ten a clock, my Lord HOME was sent to me from the King, to know how I had rested: and withal said, That His Majesty commanded him to know of me, What it was that I desired most that he should do for me? [and] bade me, Ask, and it should be granted.

I desired my Lord to say to His Majesty from me, That I had no reason to importune him for any suit; for that I had not, as yet, done him any service: but my humble request to His Majesty was to admit me a Gentleman of his Bedchamber; and hereafter, I knew, if His Majesty saw me worthy, I should not want to taste of his bounty.

My Lord returned this answer, That he [*the King*] sent me word back, "with all his heart, I should have my request."

And the next time I came to Court, which was some four days after [Thursday, 1st April 1603], at night, I was called into his Bedchamber: and there, by my Lord [the Duke of LENOX, *afterwards* Duke] of RICHMOND, in his presence, I was sworn one of the Gentlemen of his Bedchamber; and presently I helped to take off his clothes, and stayed till he was in bed.

After this, there came, daily, Gentlemen and Noblemen from our Court; and the King set down a fixed day [Tuesday, 5th April 1603] for his departure towards London.

Upon the report of the Queen's death, the East Border broke forth into great unruliness; insomuch as many complaints came to the King thereof. I was desirous to go to appease them; but I was so weak and ill of my head, that I was not able to undertake such a journey [*expedition*]: but I offered that I would send my two Deputies, that should appease the trouble and make them quiet; which was by them, shortly after, effected.

Now was I to begin a new World: for by the King's coming to the crown, I was to lose the best part of my living. For [with the death of the Queen] my Office of Wardenry ceased; and I lost the pay of 40 Horse: which were not so little, both [of them] as £1,000 per annum.

Most of the Great Ones in Court envied my happiness, when they heard I was sworn of the King's Bedchamber: and in Scotland I had no acquaintance. I only relied on GOD and the King. The one never left me: the other, shortly after his coming to London, deceived my expectation; and adhered to those that sought my ruin.

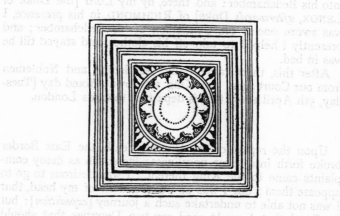

The

True Narration

of the

Entertainment of His Royal Majesty, from the time of his departure from Edinburgh till his receiving at London:

with all, or the most special, Occurrences.

TOGETHER WITH

The names of those Gentlemen whom His Majesty honoured with Knighthood.

AT LONDON.
Printed by THOMAS CREEDE
for THOMAS MILLINGTON.
1603.

To the Reader.

AFTER long travail to be informed of every particular, as much as diligence might prevail in; this small Work of His Majesty's Receiving and Royal Entertainment is brought forth: which, though it may seem to have been too long deferred [*This book was entered at Stationers' Hall on the 9th May* 1603, *ARBER, Transcript, etc. III., p.* 234. *It however contains information up to the* 18*th of that month, see page*]; yet seeing nothing thereof hath been public, no time can be too late to express so excellent a matter. Wherein the dutiful love of many noble subjects so manifestly appeared to our dread Lord and Sovereign, and his royal thankfulness in exchange for that which was indeed but duty; though so adorned with munificent bounty, that most Houses where His Highness rested were so furnished by the owners with plenty of delights and delicates, that there was discerned no negligence; but if there were any offence, the sin only appeared in excess—as more at large you shall hereafter perceive; where the truth of everything is rather pointed at, than stood upon.

All diligence was used to get the names of those Gentlemen that in sundry places received the honour of Knighthood; and what the Heralds have in register are duly set down, both for name, time, and place. If any be omitted; let it please them but to signify their names, and the House where they received that honour: and there shall be additions put to this impression; or, at least, which will be by order more fitly, placed in the next. Many, I am sure, there are not missing: and only in that point we are somewhat doubtful. The rest is, from His Highness's departure from Edinburgh [to] his coming to London, so exactly set down as nothing can be added to it but superfluous words; which we have strived to avoid.

Thine,

T. M.

A Narration of the Progress and Entertainment of the King's most excellent Majesty, with the Occurrents happening in the same Journey.

THE eternal Majesty, in whose hand are both the mean and mighty of the earth, pleased to deliver from weakness of body and grief of mind, ELIZABETH his Hand Maid, our late royal Mistress and gracious Sovereign: easing her age from the burthen of earthly Kingdoms, and placing her, as we steadfastly hope, in his heavenly empire; being the resting place, after death, for all them that believe faithfully in their life.

Thursday, the 24th of March, some two hours after midnight [*i.e. 25th March* 1603], departed the spirit of that great Princess from the prison of her weak body; which now sleeps in the Sepulchre of her grandfather [*i.e. in* HENRY *VII.'s Chapel in Westminster Abbey*].

The Council of State and the Nobility (on whom the care of all the country chiefly depended), immediately assembling together, no doubt assisted with the Spirit of Truth, considering the infallible right of our Sovereign Lord, King JAMES, took such order that the news of the Queen's death should no sooner be spread to deject the hearts of the people; but, at the instant, they should be comforted with the Proclaiming of the King.

Being hereon determined, Sir ROBERT CAREY took his journey in post towards Scotland, to signify to the King's Majesty the sad tidings of his Royal Sister's death; and the joyful hearts of his subjects that expected no comfort but in, and by, His Majesty's blessed Government.

This noble Gentleman's care was such that he intermitted no time: but, notwithstanding his sundry shift[s] of horses and some falls that bruised him very sore, he by the way, proclaimed the King at Morpeth.

And, on Saturday [26th March 1603], coming to Berwick, acquainting his worthy brother, Sir JOHN CAREY, how all things stood, posted on to Edinburgh; where he attained that night: having ridden near[ly] 400 miles in less than three days.

But before we come there, you shall understand what was instantly done at Berwick by Sir JOHN CAREY, upon the news brought by Sir ROBERT his brother. Who, like a worthy soldier and politic Statesman, considering it was a town of great import and a place of war [*Berwick was the Portsmouth of England at this time, and bridled Scotland*]; he caused all the garrison to be summoned together, as also the Mayor, Aldermen, and Burgesses: in whose presence he made a short and pithy Oration, including Her Majesty's death, and signifying the intent of the State for submitting to their lawful Lord.

And presently, with great contentment of all parties, His Majesty was proclaimed King of England, Scotland, France, etc. on Saturday, in the afternoon, being the 26th of March [1603], about three of the clock. Where all the people, though they grieved for their late Queen; yet was grief suddenly turned to pleasure, in expectation of their new King. But we will post from Berwick after Sir ROBERT CAREY, and overtake him in Edinburgh.

You understood before, that Sir ROBERT came to Edinburgh on Saturday night; where, being admitted to the King, be-blooded with great falls and bruises, [he] brought His Highness the first news of Queen ELIZABETH's death: which howsoever it presented him with kingdoms, glory, and immense wealth; yet, like his royal self, he showed apparent signs of princely sorrow. And dismissing Sir ROBERT CAREY, after so great toil, to his repose: His Majesty continued in his grief; and through that, expressed his true piety.

It was thought necessary in so high affairs to let slip no occasion, however sorrow particularly touched His Majesty for the loss of his private friend and royal Sister; yet the general care as well of those his people in Scotland as for us in England, caused him on Sunday, being the 27th of March [1603], to despatch [JOHN BOTHWELL] the Bishop of HOLYROODHOUSE to Berwick: that he might receive the town to his use, as the nearest place wherein, by right, he claimed possession.

Who accordingly, making all the speed he might, came to Berwick; where of the Governor he was honourably entertained: and, after signifying His Majesty's pleasure, reposed himself for that night.

On Monday, being the 28th of March, by sound of trumpet, the Governor, Mayor, Officers, and Council of the town were assembled at the Cross; where there the Governor [Sir JOHN CAREY] surrendered to the Bishop of HOLYROODHOUSE his staff and all his authority, unto the King's Majesty's use. So likewise did the Mayor deliver up the keys of the town.

And the said Bishop, being thus seised of all authority to His Majesty's use, ministered the Oath of Allegiance unto the Governor, Mayor, and the Superior Officers belonging to the garrison and to the town.

Which oath taken, the Bishop of HOLYROODHOUSE (expressing the gracious intention of His Majesty, as well to them as all others his subjects of England whom he found like them affected: which was rather to maintain, than to infringe, their Charters; to give, than to take from them anything) redelivered the keys and staff of authority to the Mayor and Governor. So likewise to every Commander, Captain, Lieutenant, and whatsoever Office they had before Her Majesty's death, there, in the King's name, he confirmed them: to their great joy and contentment. Thus spent the Lord of HOLYROODHOUSE the first part of Monday in Berwick; and dined with the Magistrates.

In the afternoon, the Lord Governor and his chief Officers of place called together all the soldiers that were under pay; so did the Mayor and Aldermen convene all the communalty of the town. To whom when the oath was read, and the Magistrates had certified them that they had been their example; the Lord of HOLYROODHOUSE wondered at, and much commended, their joy and readiness to be sworn servants to so regal a Master. Which he amply discoursed at his return to Edinburgh the next day; not hiding any of their forward applauses, but delivered their willingness to His Highness with express and lively words: assuring him, by his entrance into England at that little door, how welcome into the wide house His Excellence should be.

While this was a doing in Berwick, there drew to the King hourly most of the Nobility in Scotland, with sundry Knights and Gentlemen; gratulating the great blessings befallen His Highness, and attending his royal pleasure.

Besides, many numbers of Gentlemen came out of England to salute His Majesty; all [of] whom he graciously welcomed, and honoured one of them with the Order of Knighthood,*—being Master JOHN PEYTON [co. Norf.], son to Sir JOHN PEYTON, Lieutenant of the Tower of London. This being to that noble Gentleman no little glory that he was first Knight—yea, named by the King's Majesty "his first Knight"—that was made by our Sovereign after he was nominated and truly known to be the mightiest King in Europe.

During the continuance of His Majesty in Scotland, before his Progress towards England, his whole care was for the peaceable government of that Realm, from which he was a while to part. And to that end, he had sundry conferences with his Nobility, laying the safest projects that, in his wisdom and their experiences, seemed likely for effecting his royal desire: which, GOD willing, will come to pass to his great liking and [the] benefit of both the Realms.

But that it might more to his people appear; he in person came graciously to the city of Edinburgh, unto the Public Sermon. And after the Sermon was finished, in a most learned but more loving Oration, he expressed his occasion of leaving them, to the burgesses and a number of the people: exhorting them to continue in obedience, being the bond that binds Princes to affect their subjects, which broken

*As recorded in this Narrative, JAMES I. made 303 Knights during his Progress to London; and, in all, 2323 during his reign in England. The spelling of their names is given here according to J. P. [JOHN PHILIPOT], Somerset Herald, his *A perfect Collection of all Knight Bachelors made by King JAMES, &c.* London. 1660. 8vo. From which authority also, their Counties are here inserted between square brackets. Names in PHILIPOT, and not in this text, are also inserted in square brackets. E. A.

on their part he trusted should never be, and of his they were assured; persuading them also to agreement amongst themselves, being the bond of charity that tied all men, especially Christians, to love and bear with one another. In which obedience to him, and agreement amongst themselves if they continued: howsoever he was, in a manner, at that time, constrained to leave them; yet he would, in his own person, visit them, and that shortly, in times convenient and most necessary for his own advancement and their benefit.

Yet for all his kingly oratory, mild behaviour, and true intention; the people's hearts against his departure were even dead: and grief seized every private man's reins, saving only those that were made happy by attending his royal person into England.

For now they began duly to think upon his unmatched virtues, which never the most malicious enemy could impeach: being in the World's eye innocent of any capital and notorious crime, but such as may be incident to any just man; who daily falls, but never falls away. They now considered his affability, mercy, justice, and mägnanimity. They remembered how, in late years, Scotland, by his government, had increased in more riches than in the time of many [of] his predecessors: besides, his care for establishing true religion, his traffic almost with all nations, the royalty of his marriage, the blessings hoped for by his issue.

And such a universal sorrow was amongst them, that some of the meaner sort spake even distractedly; and [there were] none but, at his departing (which yet we are not come unto), expressed such sorrow as in that nation hath seldom been seen the like: albeit the King's Majesty was possessed of that which the common sort of the nation long wished for; I mean, the Kingdom [of England].

The 31st of March [1603], being Thursday, His Majesty, with great solemnity and pomp, was proclaimed King of England, Scotland, France and Ireland, at the Market Cross of Edinburgh, in presence of the whole Officers of Estate of the Realm, and many of the Nobility of Scotland, and sundry Knights and Gentlemen of England.

And in the evening of that day, there were many hundreds of bonfires made all about the city; with great feasting and merriment held till the appearing of the next day.

But as joyful as they were of His Majesty's great advancement, and enlarging of his Empire; so were they, as I before noted, for their private want of him no less filled with grief as, above all other times, was most apparently expressed at his departure from Edinburgh towards England: the cries of [the] poor people being so lamentable and confused that it moved His Majesty to much compassion; yet seeing their clamours were only of affection and not grounded on reason, with many gracious and loving words he left them, and proceeded on his Progress.

It was the 5th of April, being Tuesday, that His Majesty departed from Edinburgh, gallantly accompanied with multitudes of his Nobility, Lords, Barons, and Gentlemen of Scotland; and some French, as the French Ambassor, being Leger [*? resident*] in Scotland, whose wife was carried betwixt Edinburgh and London by eight pioneers or porters; one four to relieve the other four by turns, carrying her in a chair with slings.

As also His Majesty, being accompanied with his own attendants, as the Duke of LENOX, the Earl of ARGYLE, the Earl of MURRAY, the Earl of CASSILLIS, the Earl of MAR, the Lord HOME, the Lord OLIPHANT, and sundry others too tedious in this place to be repeated; for that several their names shall hereafter be more particularly expressed.

Besides, there were in His Highness's train, many numbers of gallant and well appointed English Knights and Gentlemen: who attended His Majesty that day from Edinburgh unto Dunglass, a House of the Lord HOME's; where His Excellence reposed himself that night.

Wednesday, the 6th of April, His Majesty progressed from Dunglass towards Berwick: having then attending on him many more Noblemen Knights and Gentlemen; besides the Lords Wardens of the Borders of England and Scotland, attended by the Borderers with several companies to receive him. The Lord Governor of Berwick also, being accompanied with all the Council of War, the Constables with their Cornets of Horse, and divers of the Captains; the

Band of Gentlemen Pensioners [of Berwick] with divers Gentlemen; advanced forward to entertain and conduct His Majesty into the town of Berwick.

Happy day, when peaceably so many warlike English Gentlemen went to bring in an English and Scottish King, both included in one person, into that town that, many a hundred years, hath been a town of the enemy; or at the least held, in all leagues, either for one nation or the other. But the King of Peace have glory, that so peaceably hath ordained a King, descended from the royal blood of either nation, to make that town, by his possessing it, a harbour for English and Scots, without thought of wrong or grudging envy.

Not to digress longer, these gallants met him and were graciously respected of His Highness; so falling in among the other Trophies, they set forward.

And when His Highness came within some half mile of the town, and began to take view thereof; it suddenly seemed like an enchanted Castle. For from the mouths of dreadful engines (not long before full fed, by moderate artsmen that knew how to stop and empty the brass and iron paunches, of those roaring noises) came such a tempest as dreadful, and sometimes more deathful, than thunder; that all the ground thereabout trembled as in an earthquake, the houses and towers staggering: wrapping the whole town in a mantle of smoke, wherein the same was a while hid from the sight of his royal owner.

But nothing violent can be permanent. It was too hot to last: and yet I have heard it credibly reported, that a better Peal of Ordnance was never, in any soldier's memory (and there are some [of] old King HARRY's lads in Berwick, I can tell you!) discharged in that place. Neither was it very strange, for no man can remember Berwick honoured with the approach of so powerful a Master.

Well, the King is now very near the gates: and as all darkness flies before the face of the sun, so did these clouds of smoke and gunpowder vanish at his gracious approach.

In the clearness of which fair time, issued out of the town Master WILLIAM SELBY [co. Northumb.] Gentleman, Porter of Berwick, with divers Gentlemen of good repute; and [he], humbling himself before the King's Majesty, presented unto him the keys of all the ports [*gates*]—who received them graciously: and when His Highness was entered betwixt the gates, he restored to the said Master SELBY the keys again, and graced him with the honour of Knighthood, for this his especial service; in that he was the first man that possessed His Excellence of those keys, Berwick indeed being the gate that opened into all his dominions.

This done, His Highness entered the second gate, and being within both the walls he was received by the Captain of the Ward: and so passed through a double Guard of soldiers, well armed in all points; but, with looks humble and words cheerful, they gave His Majesty to know their hearts witnessed that their arms were worn only to be used in his royal service.

Between this Guard, His Majesty passed on to the Market Cross, where the Mayor and his Brethren [*the Aldermen*] received him with no small signs of joy, and such signs of triumph as the brevity of time for preparation would admit. But the common people seemed so overwrapt with his presence, that they omitted nothing, their power and capacities could attain unto, to express loyal duty and hearty affection: kneeling, shouting, crying "Welcome!" and "GOD save King JAMES!" till they were, in a manner, entreated to be silent.

As soon as it pleased the people to give him leave that he might speak, Master PARKINSON, the Recorder of Berwick, being a man grave and reverend, made a brief speech to His Majesty, acknowledging him [as] their sole and Sovereign Lord. To whom, in the town's name, he surrendered their Charter: presenting His Highness also from them with a purse of gold; which, as an offering of their love, he graciously received. And for their Charter, he answered them most benignly and royally, That it should be continued: and that he would maintain their privileges, and uphold them and their town in all equity; by reason it was the principal and first place honoured with his mighty and most gracious person.

These ceremonies amongst the townsmen ended: as his usual manner is after any journey, His Majesty passed to the Church, there to humble himself before the Exalter of the humble: and [to] thank him for the benefits bestowed upon him and all his people. At which time preached before him, the Reverend Father in God, Doctor TOBY MATTHEW, Bishop of DURHAM: who made a most learned and worthy Sermon.

Which finished, the King departed to his Palace; and then they gave him a Peel of great Ordnance, more hot than before: Berwick having never had King to rest within her walls well nigh these hundred years.

The night was quickly overpassed especially with the townsmen that, never in a night, thought themselves securer: but the journey of the hours is always one, however they are made short or long by the apprehension of joy, or [the] sufferance of grief.

The morning's sun chased away the clouds of sleep from every eye; which the more willingly opened that they might be comforted with the sight of their beloved Sovereign: who, in his estate, attended upon by the Governor and the Noblemen, together with the Magistrates and Officers of the town, passed to the Church, where he stayed the Divine Prayers and Sermon; which when with his wonted humility he had heard finished, in the like estate he returned to his Palace.

This day, being Thursday the 7th of April, His Majesty ascended the walls; whereupon all the Cannoniers and other Officers belonging to the great Ordnance stood, every-one in his place: the Captains with their Bands [*Companies*] of soldiers likewise under their several Colours. Amongst which warlike train, as His Majesty was very pleasant and gracious; so to shew instance how he loved and respected the Art Military, he made a shot himself out of a cannon, so fair, and with such sign of experience, that the most expert Gunners there beheld it not without admiration: and there were none, of judgement, present but, without flattery, gave it just commendation.

Of no little estimation did the Gunners account themselves after this kingly shot: but His Majesty, above all virtues in temperance most excellent, left that part of the wall, and their extraordinary applause.

Being attended by his Nobility both of Scotland and England (the Lord HENRY HOWARD, brother to the late Duke of NORFOLK; and the Lord COBHAM, being then newly come to the town), and guarded by the Gentlemen Pensioners of Berwick; he bestowed this day in surveying of the plots [*plans*] and fortifications, commending the manner of the soldiers, and the military order of the town: being indeed one of the best places of strength in all the north of England. All which, when, with great liking, he had to his kingly pleasure beheld; he returned to his Palace, and there reposed till the next day.

The 8th of April, being Friday, the trumpets warned for the remove. And, all that morning, His Majesty, with royal liberality, bestowed amongst the garrison soldiers, and every Officer for war according to his place, so rich and bounteous rewards that all soldiers, by his bountiful beginning there, may be assured that they shall not, as they have been, be curtailed of their duties [*what is due to them*] by exacting Pollers; but used as the servants and servitors of a King: which very name, but more his largess, adds double spirit to a man of war.

After dinner, His Highness mounted on horseback and took leave of Berwick: where, near the bridge, he knighted Master RALPH GREY [co. Northumb.]; a Gentleman of great command and possession[s] near the Borders.

As his Excellence left Berwick, and entered the Realm of England, he was received by Master NICHOLAS FORSTER [of Bamburgh Abbey], High Sheriff of Northumberland, [*whom he knighted at Widdrington*]: who, besides his own servants and followers, was accompanied with a number of gallant Gentlemen of the Shire; who, riding before His Majesty, led the way towards Widdrington, where His Majesty intended to rest that night.

By the way, of his kingly goodness, and royal inclinations to the honour of arms and reverence of virtuous age, he vouchsafed to visit that worthy honourable soldier, Sir WILLIAM READ: who, being blind with age, was so comforted with the presence and gracious speeches of the King, that his spirits seemed so powerful within him, as he boasted himself to feel the warmth of youth stir in his frost-nipt blood. The way His Majesty had to ride, being long, enforced him to stay with this good Knight the less while: but that little time was so comfortable that his friends hope it will be a mean[s] to cherish the old Knight all his life long.

Not to be longer writing this than His Highness was riding the journey; he departed thence upon the spur, scarce any of his train being able to keep him company: for being near[ly] 37 miles, he rode it all in less than four hours. And, by the way, for a note, the miles, according to the Northern phrase, are a wey-bit longer than they be here in the South.

Well, as long as the miles were, His Majesty made short work, and attained [to] Widdrington [Castle]: where by the Master of the Place, Sir ROBERT CAREY [Lord Warden of the Middle Marches. He was afterwards made Earl of MONMOUTH. *See pages* 476-484], and his right virtuous Lady, he was received with all due affection; the House being plentifully furnished for his entertainment. Besides for situation and pleasure it stands very delightful.

His Majesty, having a little while reposed himself after his great journey, found new occasion to travel further. For, as he was delighting himself with the pleasure of the Park, he suddenly beheld a number of deer near the place. The game being so fair before him, he could not forbear; but, according to his wonted manner, forth he went, and slew two of them.

Which done, he returned with a good appetite to the House, where he was most royally feasted and banqueted that night.

On Saturday the 9th April [1603], His Majesty prepared towards Newcastle-[on-Tyne]. But before his departure from Widdrington; he knighted Master HENRY WIDDRINGTON, Master WILLIAM FENWICK, Master EDWARD GORGES [all co. Northum.].

After which, taking his leave with royal courtesy, he set forwards towards Newcastle; being 16 miles from Widdrington.

To pass the occurrents by the way, being not very material; when His Majesty drew near to Newcastle, the Mayor, the Aldermen, Council, and best Commoners of the same besides numbers of other people, in joyful manner met him.

The Mayor presented him with the Sword and Keys with humble duty and submission: which His Highness graciously accepting, he returned them again. He gave also to His Majesty, in token of their love and hearty loyalty, a purse full of gold. His Majesty gave them full power and authority under him as they lately held in Her Majesty's name: ratifying all customs and privileges that they were possessed of, and had a long time held.

And so, passing on, he was conducted to the Mayor's house, where he was richly entertained; and remained there three days.

Upon Sunday, being the 10th April [1603], His Majesty went to the Church, before whom [Dr TOBY MATTHEW] the Bishop of DURHAM preached. And that day, as it is his most Christianlike custom, being spent in devotion: he rested till Monday, which he bestowed in viewing the town, the manner and beauty of the bridge [over the Tyne] and key [*quay*]: being one of the fairest in all the north parts. Besides, he released all prisoners; except those that lay for treason, murder, and Papistry: giving great sums of money for the release of many that were imprisoned for debt; who heartily praised GOD, and blessed His Majesty, for their unexpected liberty.

So joyful were the townsmen of Newcastle of His Majesty there being, that they thankfully bare all the charge of his Household during the time of his abode with them, being from Saturday till Wednesday morning. All things were in such plenty and so delicate for variety that it gave great contentment to His Majesty: and on the townsmen's part, there was nothing but willingness appeared; save only at His Highness's departure, but [of that] there was no remedy. He hath yet many of his people by his presence to comfort: and forward no doubt he will; as he thence did, giving thanks to them for their loyal and hearty affection.

And on the bridge, before he came at Gateside; he made Master ROBERT DUDLEY [? DELAVALE, co. Northumb.], Mayor of Newcastle, Knight.

[JOHN PHILIPOT states that the following were also knighted at Newcastle on this 13th of April 1603:

Sir CHRISTOPHER LOWTHER,	co. Cumb.
Sir NICHOLAS CURWEN,	co. Cumb.
Sir JAMES BELLINGHAM,	co. Westm.
Sir NICHOLAS TUFTON,	co. Kent; *afterwards* Earl of THANET.
Sir JOHN CONYERS,	co. York.]

This Wednesday, being the 13th of April [1603], His Majesty set forward towards Durham. And at Gateside, near Newcastle; he was met by the Sheriff of the County and most of the Gentlemen in the same.

In his way, near Chester a Street, a little town betwixt Newcastle and Durham, he turned on the left hand of the road to view [Lumley Castle,] a pleasant castle of the Lord LUMLEY's: which being a goodly edifice of free stone, built in quadrant manner, stands on the shoring of a hill, in the middle of a green, with a river at the foot of it; and woods about it on every side but to the townward, which is, by the river [Wear], divided from it.

After His Highness had a while delighted himself with the pleasures of the place; he returned on his way towards Durham, being 6 miles from thence. Of which way he seldom makes [a] long journey.

And when he came near; the Magistrates of the city met him; and behaving themselves as others before them, it was by His Highness as thankfully accepted. And passing through the gates, whence His Excellence entered the Market Place, there was an excellent oration made unto him, containing in effect the universal joy conceived by his subjects at his approach; being of power to divert from them so great a sorrow as had lately possessed them all.

The oration ended, he passed towards the Bishop's House; where he was royally received: [Dr. TOBY MATTHEW] the Bishop attending His Majesty with a hundred Gentlemen in tawny liveries.

Of all his entertainment in particular at the Bishop's; [of] his [*the King's*] merry and well seasoned jests, as well there as in other parts of his journey; all his words being of full weight, and his jests filled with the salt of wit: yet so facetious and pleasant as they were no less gracious and worthy of regard than the words of so royal a Majesty—it is bootless to repeat them, they are so well known.

Thursday, being the 14th day [of April 1603], His Majesty took leave of the Bishop of DURHAM: whom he greatly graced and commended for his learning, humanity, and gravity: promising to restore divers things taken from the Bishopric; which he hath accordingly in part done, giving him already possession of Durham House in the Strand.

In brief, His Majesty left Durham, and removed towards [High] Walworth [*also called* Walworth Castle]; being 16 miles from Durham: where, by the Gentlewoman of the House, named Mistress GENISON [*or rather* the Widow of THOMAS JENISON], he was so bountifully entertained that it gave His Excellence very high contentment.

And after his quiet repose there that night, and some part of the next day; he took his leave of the Gentlewoman, with many thankful and princely congratulations for her extending costs in the entertainment of him and his train.

Friday, being the 15th of April [1603], His Majesty set forward from Mistress GENISON's of Walworth, towards York. His train [was] still increasing by the numbers of Noblemen and Gentlemen from the south parts, that came to offer him fealty and to rejoice at his sight. Whose love, although he greatly tendered; yet did their multitudes so oppress the country and make provision[s] so dear that he was fain to publish an Inhibition against the inordinate and daily access of people's coming, that many were stopped of their way; and only those that had affairs suffered to have access, some of great name and office being sent home, to attend their places.

All this notwithstanding; a number there were in His Highness's train; still increasing in every shire.

For now [Master HENRY BELLASSIS] the High Sheriff of Yorkshire, gallantly accompanied, attended His Majesty to Master [WILLIAM] INGLEBY's [*? at Baldersby Park*] besides Topcliffe, being about 16 miles from Walworth; who with great submission received His Majesty: and there he rested for that night.

On Saturday, being the 16th of April [1603], His Majesty removed from Master INGLEBY's towards York, being 16 miles from Topcliffe.

And when he came about some 3 miles from York, the Liberties of the City extending so far; Master BUCKE and Master ROBINSON Sheriffs of the City met him; and, with humble duty, presented him with their White Staffs: which His Majesty receiving, he delivered them instantly again [to them]. So they attended him towards the City.

Within a mile of which, when His Highness approached, there met him [WILLIAM CECIL] the Lord BURLEGH, Lord President of the North, with many worthy Knights and Gentlemen of the shire. These also attended on his person to York.

Where, when he came near unto the City, there met him three of the Sergeants at Arms, late servants to the deceased Queen: viz., Master WOOD, Master DAMFORT, and Master WESTROP: who delivered up their maces; which His Majesty, with royal courtesy, redelivered to them; commanding them to wait on him in their old places, which presently they did.

And, at the same time, the Sergeant Trumpeter, with some others of his fellows, did in like manner submit themselves, and render their service; which he benignly accepted, and commanded them in like manner to wait on him.

Then rode he on till he came to one of the gates of York; where [ROBERT WALTER] the Lord Mayor of the City, the Aldermen, and the wealthiest Commoners, with abundance of other people, met him.

There a long oration being made, the Lord Mayor delivered the Sword and Keys to His Majesty, together with a cup of gold, filled full of gold: which present His Majesty gratefully accepted; delivering the Keys again to the Lord Mayor.

But about the bearing of the Sword, there was some contention; the Lord President [of the North] taking it for his place, the Lord Mayor of the city esteeming it his.

But to decide the doubt, the King's Majesty merrily demanded, If the Sword being his, they would not be pleased that he should have the disposing thereof.

Whereunto when they humbly answered, It was all in his

pleasure; His Highness delivered the Sword to one that knew well how to use a sword, having been tried both at sea and on shore, [GEORGE CLIFFORD] the thrice honoured Earl of CUMBERLAND; who bare it before His Majesty, riding in great state from the gate to the Minster.

In which way, there was a conduit that, all the day long, ran white, and claret, wine[s]; every man to drink as much as he listed.

From the Minster His Majesty went on foot to his own House, being the Manor of St Mary's; having all the way a rich canopy over his head, supported by four Knights: and being brought hither, he was honourable received by the Lord BURLEGH; who gave cheerful entertainment to all the followers of His Majesty during the time of his continuance in York.

The 17th day [of April 1603], being Sunday, His Majesty passed towards York Minster; being one of the goodliest Minsters in all the land: England being as famous for churches as any one kingdom in Europe, if they were kept in reparations as that Minster is.

To this Minster, the King passed to hear the Sermon; and at the gate [*i.e., of the Manor House*] a coach was offered to His Highness. But he graciously answered, "I will have no coach. For the people are desirous to see a King, and so they shall: for they shall as well see his body as his face." So, to the great comfort of the people, he went on foot to the Church; and there heard the Sermon, which was preached by [Dr JOHN THORNBOROUGH, Dean of York and also] the Bishop of LIMERICK: whose doctrine and method of teaching was highly by His Majesty commended. And what his judgment is, is as extant to us all of any understanding as the light of the clear mid-day, or sun, to every perfect eye.

The Sermon ended, His Majesty returned afoot, in the same sort as he came, to his Manor; where he was royally feasted.

This Sunday was a Seminary Priest apprended, who before, under the title [*appearance*] of a Gentleman had delivered a Petition to His Majesty, in the name of all the English Catholics. When he was taken, His Highness had some conference with him: but, by reason of other great affairs, he referred him to be further examined by the Bishop of LIMERICK; who, presenting the effects of his Examination, the Priest was, the next day committed.

Dinner being ended, His Majesty walked into the garden of the Palace; being a most delightful place: where there awaited him a number of Gentlemen of great name and worth; whose commendations he received from honourable persons, and beheld honour charactered in their faces. For this is one especial note in His Majesty. Any man that hath aught with him, let him be sure he have a just cause! for he beholds all men's faces with steadfastness, and commonly the look is the window for the heart.

Well, to that I should handle. Amongst these Gentlemen it pleased His Majesty to make choice of these following; whom he graced with the honour of Knighthood:

Sir WILLIAM CECIL	[Lord BURLEGH].
Sir EDMOND TRAFFORD	[co. Lanc.]
Sir THOMAS HOLCROFT	[co. Lanc.]
Sir JOHN MALLORY	[co. York]
Sir WILLIAM INGLEBY	[co. York]
Sir PHILIP CONSTABLE	[co. Durh.]
Sir CHRISTOPHER HAWARD	[co. York]
Sir ROBERT SWIFT	[co. York]
Sir RICHARD WORTLEY	[co. York]
Sir HENRY BELLASSIS	[co. York]
Sir THOMAS FAIRFAX	[co. York]
Sir HENRY GRIFFITH	[co. York]
Sir FRANCIS BOYNTON	[co. York]
Sir HENRY CHOLMLEY	[co. York]
Sir RICHARD GARGRAVE	[co. York]
Sir MARMADUKE GRIMSTONE	[co. York]
Sir LANCELOT ALFORD	[co York]
Sir RALPH ILLERKER [or ELIKER]	[co. York]
Sir GEORGE FREVILE	[co. Durh.]
Sir MAUGER VAVASOR	[co. York]
Sir RALPH BABTHORPE	[co. York]
Sir RICHARD LONDER	[not in J. PHILIPOT's List.]
Sir WALTER CRAPE	

The same day, His Majesty caused five Gentlemen to be sworn his servants, which served Queen Elizabeth before time: whose names were Master RICHARD CONNIGSBY, Master GEORGE POLLARD, Ushers, Daily Waiters; Master THOMAS ROLLES and Master HARIFFE, Gentlemen, Quarter Waiters; and Master RICHARD READ-HEAD, Gentleman Sewer in Ordinary of His Majesty's Chamber.

This day likewise, the Mayor of Kingston upon Hull delivered to His Majesty a petition, which was also subscribed and justified by divers Aldermen of the said town, to be done in the behalf of all the poor inhabitants: who, with one voice, besought His Majesty that they might be relieved and succoured against the daily spoils done to them by those of Dunkirk, that had long molested them and others the English coastmen.

His Highness, as he is naturally inclined to much pity, so at that time he seemed to have great compassion of their wrongs and afflictions; which were not hidden from him, though they had been silent: but he comforted them with his princely and heroic reply, That he would defend them; and no Dunkirker should after dare to do any of his subjects wrong.

In which assurance they departed: and, no doubt, shall find the effect of his kingly promise.

I told you before, what bounty the Lord BURLEGH used during the continuauce of the King's Majesty in the Manor [of St Mary's at York]: but it was indeed exceeding all the rest in any place of England before. Butteries, Pantries, and Cellars [being] always held open in great abundance, for all comers.

Monday, being the 18th day [of April 1603], His Majesty was feasted by the Lord Mayor of York, whom he knighted by the name of Sir ROBERT WALTER [co. York]: at whose house there was such plenty of all delicates [*delicacies*] as could be possibly devised.

After dinner, His Majesty, following the rule of mercy he had begun with, commanded all the prisoners to be set at liberty, except Papists and wilful murderers.

Which deed of charity effected, he left York, and rode to Grimstone [Hall], being a house of Sir EDWARD STANHOPE'S;

where he lay that night, and dined the next day: His Majesty and all his train having their most bountiful entertainment; all the Offices in the house standing open for all comers, every man without check eating and drinking at pleasure.

Before His Majesty's departure from Grimstone, he knighted these Gentlemen:

Sir ROGER ASTON	[co. Chest.]
Sir THOMAS ASTON	[co. Chest.]
Sir THOMAS HOLT	[co. Chest.]
Sir JAMES HARINGTON	[co. Rutl.]
Sir CHARLES MONTAGUE	[co. Northt.]
Sir THOMAS DAWNEY	[co. York]
Sir WILLIAM BAMBROUGH	[co. York]
Sir FRANCIS LOVELL	[co. Norf.]
Sir THOMAS GERRARD	[co. Lanc.]
Sir ROBERT WALTER [Lord] Mayor of York	[co. York]
Sir RALPH CON[N]I[G]SBY	[co. Hertf.]
Sir RICHARD MUSGRAVE	[co. York]

The 19th day [of April 1603] being Tuesday, His Majesty took his journey towards Doncaster. Where, by the way, he went to Pomfret [*Pontefract*], to see the Castle: which when he had at pleasure viewed; he took horse and rode to Doncaster where he lodged all night at the sign of the *Bear* in an Inn; giving the host of the house, for his good entertainment, a lease of a Manor House in a reversion, of good value.

The 20th day [of April 1603], being Wednesday, His Majesty rode towards Worsop [Manor], the noble [GILBERT TALBOT] Earl of SHREWSBURY's House: and at Batine [*? Bawtry*] the High Sheriff of Yorkshire took his leave of the King, and there Master [ROGER] ASKOTH [*or* ASCOUGH, *or* AYSCUE] the High Sheriff of Nottinghamshire received him; being gallantly apppointed both with horse and man.

And so he conducted His Majesty on, till he came within a mile of Blyth: where His Highness lighted, and sat down on a bankside to eat and drink.

After His Majesty's short repast, to Worsop His Majesty

rides forward. But, by the way, in the Park he was somewhat stayed. For there appeared a number of Huntsmen, all in green; the chief of which, with a woodman's speech, did welcome him, offering His Majesty to shew him some game: which he gladly condescended [*agreed*] to see; and, with a train set, he hunted a good space, very much delighted.

At last he went into the House, where he was so nobly received, with superfluity of things, that still every entertainment seemed to exceed others. In this place, besides the abundance of all provision[s] and delicacie[s], there was most excellent soul-ravishing music; wherewith His Highness was not a little delighted.

At Worsop, he rested on Wednesday night, and in the morning stayed breakfast. Which ended, there was such store of provision left, of fowl, of fish, and almost everything, besides bread beer and wine, that it was left open for any man that would, to come and take.

After breakfast, His Majesty prepared to remove: but before his departure he made these Gentlemen, Knights; whose names are following:

Sir JOHN MANNERS	[co. Derb.]
Sir HENRY GREY	[co. Bedf.]
Sir FRANCIS NEWPORT	[co. Salop.]
Sir HENRY BEAUMONT	[co. Leic.]
Sir EDWARD LORAINE	[co. Derb.]
Sir HUGH SMITH	[co. Som.]
Sir EDMOND LUCY	[co. Warw.]
Sir EDMOND COKAYN	[co. Derb.]
Sir JOHN HARPER	[co. Derb.]
Sir WILLIAM DAMCOURT	[not in J. PHILIPOT's List]
Sir HENRY PERPOINT	[not in J. PHILIPOT's List]
Sir THOMAS GRESLAY	[co. Notts]
Sir JOHN BIRON	[co. Notts]
Sir PERCIVAL WILLOUGHBY	[co. Linc.]
Sir PETER FRESCHVILE	[co. Derb.]
Sir WILLIAM SKIPWITH	[co. Leic.]
Sir RICHARD THEKESTON	[co. York]
Sir THOMAS STANLEY	[co. Derb.]
[Sir WALTER COPE	co. Oxon.]

The 21st [day of April 1603], being Thursday, His Highness took his way towards Newark upon Trent; where, that night, he lodged in the Castle, being his own house: where the Aldermen of Newark presented His Majesty with a fair gilt cup, manifesting their duties and loving hearts to him: which was very kindly accepted.

In this town, and in the Court, was taken a cutpurse, doing the deed; and, being a base pilfering thief, yet was all Gentleman-like on the outside. This fellow had [a] good store of coin found about him: and, upon his examination, confessed that he had, from Berwick to that place, played the cutpurse in the Court. His fellow was ill missed, for no doubt he had a walking mate. They drew together like coach horses, and it is pity they did not go hang together. For His Majesty, hearing of this nimming gallant, directed a Warrant presently to the Recorder of Newark, to have him hanged: which was accordingly executed.

This bearing small comfort to all the rest of his pilfering faculty, that the first subject that suffered death in England, in the reign of King James, was a cutpurse: which fault, if they amend not, heaven suddenly send the rest [the same fate]!

The King, ere he went from Newark, as he had commanded this silken base thief, in justice, to be put to death; so, in his benign and gracious mercy, he gives life to all the other poor and wretched prisoners: clearing the Castle of them all.

This deed of charity done; before he left Newark [on the 22nd April], he made these Knights:

Sir John Parker	[co. Suss.]
Sir Robert Brett	[co. Devon.]
Sir Lewis Lewkenor	[co. Suss.]
Sir Francis Ducket	[co. Salop.]
Sir Richard Mompesson	[co. Bucks.]
Sir Richard Warburton	[co. Chest.]
Sir Richard Wigmore	[co. Heref.]
Sir Edward Foxe	[co. Salop.]
[Sir William Davenport	co. Chest.]

The 22nd day [of April 1603], being Friday, His Majesty departed from Newark, towards Belvoir Castle; hunting all the way as he rode: saving that, in the way, he made four Knights, [the first] one being the Sheriff of Nottinghamshire.

Sir ROGER ASKOTH [*or* ASCOUGH, *or* AYSCUE]	[co. Chest.]
Sir WILLIAM SUTTON	[co. Notts.]
Sir JOHN STANHOPE	[co. Derb.]
Sir BRIAN LASSELS	[co. York]

Sir ROGER ASKOTH [or ASCOUGH, or AYSCUE], High Sheriff of Nottinghamshire, being knighted, took leave of His Majesty; and Master WILLIAM PELHAM, High Sheriff of Lincolnshire, received His Highness, being gallantly appointed both with horse and men; divers worshipful men of the same country [*County*] accompanying him: who convoyed and guarded His Majesty to Belvoir Castle, being the Right Noble [ROGER MANNERS, the] Earl of RUTLAND's. Where His Highness was not only royally and most plentifully received: but with such exceeding joy of the good Earl and his honourable Lady, that he took therein exceeding pleasure.

And he approved his contentment in the morning [of the 23rd April 1603]; for, before he went to break his fast, he made these Knights whose names follow:

Sir OLIVER MANNERS	[co. Linc.]
Sir WILLIAM WILLOUGHBY	[co. Linc.]
Sir THOMAS WILLOUGHBY	[co. Linc.]
Sir GREGORY CROMWELL	[co. Hunts.]
Sir GEORGE MANNERS	[co. Linc.]
Sir HENRY HASTINGS	[co. Leic.]
Sir WILLIAM PELHAM	[co. Linc.]
Sir PHILIP TIRWHIT	[co. Linc.]
Sir VALENTINE BROWNE	[co. Linc.]
Sir ROGER DALLISON	[co. Linc.]
Sir THOMAS GRANTHAM	[co. Linc.]
Sir JOHN ZOUCHE	[co. Derb.]
Sir WILLIAM JEPSON	[co. Southt.]
Sir EDWARD ASKOTH [or ASCOUGH, or AYSCUE]	[co. Linc.]
Sir EVERARD DIGBY	[co. Rutl.]
Sir ANTHONY MARKHAM	[co. Oxon.]
Sir THOMAS CAVE	[co. Leic.]
Sir WILLIAM TURPIN	[co. Leic.]

Sir JOHN FERRERS	[co. Warw.]
Sir HENRY PAGENHAM	[co. Linc.]
Sir RICHARD MUSGRAVE	[not in J. PHILIPOT's List]
Sir WALTER CHUTE	[co. Kent]
Sir WILLIAM LAMBERT	[not in J. PHILIPOT's List]
Sir EDWARD ROSSETER	[co. Linc.]
Sir EDWARD COMINES	[not in J. PHILIPOT's List]
Sir PHILIP STIRLEY	[co. Leic.]
Sir EDWARD SWIFT	[co. York]
Sir BASIL BROOKE	[co. Salop.]
Sir WILLIAM FAIRFAX	[not in J. PHILIPOT's List]
Sir EDWARD BUSSY	[co. Linc.]
Sir EDWARD TIRWHIT	[co. Linc.]
Sir JOHN THORNE[HAUGH]	[co. Notts.]
Sir NICHOLAS SANDERSON	[co. Linc.]
Sir EDWARD LITTLETON	[co. Salop.]
Sir WILLIAM FOMPT [or FAWNT]	[co. Leic.]
Sir THOMAS BEAUMONT	[co. Leic.]
Sir WILLIAM SKEFFINGTON	[co. Leic.]
Sir PHILIP SHERRARD	[co. Leic.]
Sir JOHN TIRRIL [or THOROLD]	[co. Linc.]
Sir EDWARD CARRE	[co. Linc.]
Sir RICHARD OGLE	[co. Linc.]
Sir HAMAN SWITHCOATE [*or rather* HUGH WHICHCOT]	[co. Linc.]
Sir WILLIAM HICKMAN	[co. Linc.]
Sir WILLIAM FIELDING	[co. Warw.]
Sir HUMPHREY CONI[G]SBY	[not in J. PHILIPOT's List]
[Sir WILLIAM CARRE	co. Linc.]
[Sir WILLIAM ERMINE	co. Linc.]
[Sir JOHN WENTWORTH	co. Essex]

The 23rd day [of April], being Saturday, after the making of these Knights, and having refreshed himself at breakfast; His Majesty took kind leave of the Earl of RUTLAND, his Countess, and the rest: and set forward towards Burlegh.

And, by the way, he dined at Sir JOHN HARINGTON's [House ? *at Harington-Burley*]; where that worthy Knight made him most royal entertainment.

After dinner, His Highness removed towards Burlegh, being near Stamford in Northamptonshire. His Majesty on the way was attended by many Lords and Knights. And, before his coming, there were provided train-cents and live hares in baskets [that] being carried to the Heath [*? Empington Heath*], made excellent sport for His Majesty. All the way between Sir JOHN HARINGTON's and Stamford, Sir JOHN's best hounds with good mouths followed the game; the King taking great leisure and pleasure in the same.

Upon this Heath, not far from Stamford, there appeared to the number of a hundred high men, that seemed like the Patagones [*Patagonians*], huge long fellows of twelve or fourteen feet high, that are reported to live on the Main [*mainland*] of Brazil, near to the Straits of Magellan. The King, at the first sight, wondered what they were; for that they overlooked horse and man. But, when all came to all, they proved a company of poor honest suitors, all going upon high stilts, preferring a Petition against the Lady HATTON. What their request was, I know not: but His Majesty referred them till his coming to London; and so passed on from those giants of the Fens towards Stamford.

Within half a mile whereof, the Bailiffs and the rest of the chief townsmen of Stamford presented a gift unto His Majesty; which was graciously accepted. So rode he forward through the town, in great state, having the Sword borne before him; the people joyful on all parts to see him.

When His Highness came to Stamford Bridge; the Sheriff of Lincolnshire humbly took his leave, and departed greatly in the King's grace.

On the other part, the town standing in two Shires, stood ready [Master WILLIAM TATE] the High Sheriff of Northamptonshire, bravely accompanied, and gallantly appointed with men and horse; who received his Majesty, and attended him to Burlegh: where His Highness with all his train were received with great magnificence; the House seeming so rich as if it had been furnished at the charges of an Emperor. Well, it was all too little, His Majesty being worthy [of] much more; being now the greatest Christian monarch, of himself as absolute.

The next day [24th April 1603], being Easter Day, there

preached before His Highness, [Dr WILLIAM CHADERTON] the Bishop of LINCOLN; and the Sermon was no sooner done, but all [the] Offices in the house were set open, that every man might have free access to Butteries, Pantries; [and] Kitchens; to eat and drink in at their pleasures.

The next day, being Monday the 25th of April [1603], His Highness rode back again to Sir JOHN HARINGTON's [House at Harington-Burley]; and by the way his horse fell with him, and [he] very dangerously bruised his arm; to the great amazement and grief of all them that were about His Majesty at that time. But he, being of an invincible courage, and his blood yet hot, made light of it at the first: and being mounted again, rode to Sir JOHN HARINGTON's; where he continued that night.

And, on Tuesday morning, the pain received by his fall was so great that he was not able to ride on horseback; but he turned from Sir JOHN HARINGTON's, to take a coach: wherein His Highness returned to Burlegh, where he was royally entertained as before; but not with half that joy, the report of His Majesty's hurt had disturbed all the Court so much.

The next day, being Wednesday the 27th day of April [1603], His Majesty removed from Burlegh towards Master OLIVER CROMWELL's.

And, in the way, he dined at that worthy and worshipful Knight's, Sir ANTHONY MILDMAY's [at Apethorpe]; where nothing wanted in a subject's duty to his Sovereign, nor anything in so potent a Sovereign to grace so loyal a subject. Dinner being most sumptuously furnished, the tables were newly covered with costly Banquets [*Dessert*]; wherein everything that was most delicious for taste proved [the] more delicate by the art that made it seem beauteous to the eye: the Lady of the House being one of the most excellent Confectioners in England; though I confess many honourable women [to be] very expert.

Dinner and Banquet [*Dessert*] being past, and His Majesty at point to depart; Sir ANTHONY, considering how His Majesty vouchsafed to honour him with his royal presence, presented His Highness with a gallant Barbary horse, and a very rich saddle with furniture suitable thereto: which His Majesty most lovingly and thankfully accepted: and so, taking his princely leave, set forward on the way.

In this remove towards Master OLIVER CROMWELL's did the people flock in greater numbers than in any place northward. Though many before pressed to see their Sovereign, yet here the numbers multiplied.

This day, as His Majesty passed through a great common (which, as the people thereabout complain, Sir I. SPENSER [JOHN SPENCER] of London hath very uncharitably molested [*enclosed*]), most of the country [*district*] joined together, beseeching His Majesty that the common might be laid open again for the comfort of the poor inhabiters thereabouts: which His Highness most graciously promised should be performed, according to their hearts' desire.

And so, with many benedictions of the comforted people, he passed on till he came within half a mile of Master OLIVER CROMWELL's [at Hinchinbrook Priory]; where met him the Bailiff of Huntingdon, who made a long oration to His Majesty, and there delivered him the Sword, which His Highness gave to the new[ly] released [HENRY WRIOTHSLEY] Earl of SOUTHAMPTON [*the Patron of* SHAKESPEARE] to bear before him.

O admirable work of mercy! confirming the hearts of all true subjects in the good opinion of His Majesty's royal compassion: not alone to deliver from the captivity such high Nobility, but to use vulgarly with great favours not only him, but also the children of his late honourable fellow in distress [*i.e.* of ROBERT DEVEREUX Earl of ESSEX]. Well, GOD have glory, that can send friends, in the hour he best pleaseth, to help them that trust in him.

But to the matter. His Majesty passed, in state, the Earl of SOUTHAMPTON bearing the Sword before him, as I before said he was appointed, to Master OLIVER CROMWELL'S house: where His Majesty and all his followers, with all comers whatsoever, had such entertainment, as the like had not been seen in any place before, since his first setting forward out of Scotland.

There was such plenty and variety of meats: such diversity of wines, and those not riffe ruffe but ever the best of the kind; and the cellars open at any man's pleasure. And if it were so common with wine, there is little question but the Butteries for beer and ale were more common; yet in neither was there difference. For whoever entered the house, which to no man was denied, tasted what they had a mind to: and after a taste, found fullness: no man, like a man, being denied what he would call for.

As this bounty was held back to none within the house; so for such poor people as would not press in, there were many open beer-houses erected: where there was no want of beef and bread for the comfort of the poorest creatures. Neither was this provision for the little time of His Majesty's stay; but it was made ready [for] fourteen days: and, after His Highness's departure, distributed to as many as had [a] mind to it.

There attended also at Master OLIVER CROMWELL's, the Heads of the University of Cambridge, all clad in scarlet gowns and corner-caps; who, having presence of His Majesty, there was made a most learned and eloquent Oration in Latin, welcoming His Majesty, as also intreating the confirmation of their Charter and privileges: which His Majesty most willingly and free granted. They also presented His Majesty with divers books published in commendation of our late gracious Queen: all which was most graciously accepted of His Highness.

Also Master CROMWELL presented His Majesty with many rich and acceptable gifts: as a very great and a very fair wrought Standing Cup of gold, goodly horses, float [?*fleet*] and deep-mouthed hounds, divers hawks of excellent wing. And at the remove, [he] gave £50 [=£200 *now*] amongst His Majesty's Officers.

Upon the 29th day [of April 1603], being Friday, after His Highness had broke his fast; he took kind and gracious leave of Master OLIVER CROMWELL* and his virtuous Lady, late widow to that noble and opulent Knight, Signor HORATIO PAULO VICINO.

Thence, with many regal thanks for his entertainment, he departed to Royston.

* Sir OLIVER CROMWELL was uncle of his great namesake. E. A.

And as he passed through Godmanchester, a town close by Huntingdon, the Bailiffs of the town with their Brethren met him; and acknowledged their allegiance. There, convoying him through their town, they presented him with threescore and ten team[s] of horse all traced to fair new ploughs; in shew of their husbandry.

Which, while His Majesty, being very well delighted with the sight, demanded, Why they offered him so many horses and ploughs? he was resolved [*answered*], That it was their ancient custom whensoever any King of England passed through their town, so to present His Excellence. Besides, they added, that they held their lands by that tenure; being the King's tenants.

His Majesty not only took well in worth their good minds; but bade them use well their ploughs: being glad he was landlord of so many good husbandmen in one town.

I trust His Highness, when he knows well the wrong, will take order for those, as Her Majesty began, that turn ploughland into pasturage: and where many good husbandmen dwelt there is now nothing left but a great house without [a] fire: the Lord commonly at sojourn near London; and for the husbandmen and ploughs, he only maintains a shepherd and his dog. But what do I talking of sheep! when I am to follow the gests of a King. I will leave them and their wolfish Lords, that have eaten up poor husbandmen like sheep: and proceed where I left [off].

His Majesty, being past Godmanchester, held on his way to Royston; and drawing near the town, the Sheriff of Huntingdonshire humbly took his leave. And there he was received by that worthy Knight, Sir EDWARD DENNY, High Sheriff of Hertfordshire, attended upon by a goodly company of proper men, being in number seven score, suitably apparelled. Their liveries [were] blue coats, with sleeves parted in the midst, buttoned behind in jerkin fashion; and white doublets: and hats and feathers: and all of them mounted on horses with red saddles.

Sir EDWARD, after his humble duty done, presented His Majesty with a gallant horse, a rich saddle, and furniture correspondent to the same; being of great value: which His Majesty accepted very graciously, and caused him to ride on the same before him. This worthy Knight, being of a deliver spirit and agile body, quickly mounted, managing the gallant beast with neat and eiduing workmanship [*? eye-doing horsemanship*]: being in a rich suit of a yellow dun colour; somewhat near the colour of the horse, and the furniture.

And thus, in brave manner, he conducted His Majesty to one Master CHESTER's house [at Cockenhatch]: where His Highness lay that night, at his own kingly charge.

The 30th day [of April 1603], being Saturday, His Majesty took his journey towards Standon, to Sir THOMAS SADLER's: and, by the way, [Dr RICHARD BANCROFT] the Bishop of LONDON met him; attended on by a seemly company of Gentlemen in tawny coats and chains of gold.

At SIR THOMAS SADLER's, His Majesty was royally entertained, for himself and his kingly train: nothing being wanting the best desired, nor the meanest could demand.

There His Majesty stayed [on] Sunday: before whom the Bishop of LONDON preached.

His Majesty, now drawing near to London, the numbers of people more and more increased, as well of Nobility, Gentry, Citizens, country people, and all; as well of degree as of no degree. So great a desire had the Noble that they pressed with the ignoble to see their Sovereign: this being the difference of their desires, that the better sort, either in blood or of conceit, came to observe and serve; the other to see and wonder.

The 1st of May [1603], being Monday, His Majesty removed to Sir HENRY COCK's [at Broxburn Bury], being 9 miles from Sir THOMAS SADLER's: where provision for His Majesty and his royal train was so abundant that there was no man of what condition soever, but had what his appetite desired. For His Majesty's private and most to be respected entertainment: it was such as ministered His Highness great contentment.

Continuing there but one night, and departing the

next day; [he] honoured the good Knight for his greater expenses.

The 3rd of May [1603], being Tuesday, His Majesty took his journey towards Theobalds, a house belonging to Sir ROBERT CECIL, and about 4 miles distant from Sir HENRY COCK's: where met him [Sir THOMAS EGERTON, *afterwards* Lord ELLESMERE,] the Lord Keeper [of the Great Seal], [THOMAS SACKVILLE, Earl of DORSET,] the Lord Treasurer, [CHARLES HOWARD, Earl of NOTTINGHAM,] the Lord Admiral, with most of the Nobility of the land and [the] Council of Estate; who were graciously received.

At which time, the Lord Keeper made a most grave, learned, brief, and pithy oration to His Majesty: to which His Highness answered with great grace and princely wisdom.

At this house there met His Majesty all, or the most part, of the old servants and Officers in [the] Household of our late royal Mistress, Queen ELIZABETH; and with them, the Guard of His Majesty's Body: all of them being courteously received to their own content.

Also in this house of Theobalds, His Majesty made divers Noblemen of Scotland, of his Honourable Privy Council [of England], viz:

[LODOWICK STUART,] the Duke of LENOX.
[JOHN ERSKINE,] the Earl of MAR.
[ALEXANDER HOME,] the Lord HOME.
Sir GEORGE HOME [, *afterwards* Earl of DUNBAR], Treasurer of Scotland.
Sir JAMES ELPHINSTON [, *afterwards* Lord BALMERINOCH], Secretary to the King.
[EDWARD BRUCE,] the Lord of KINLOSS, now Master of His Majesty's Rolls. [He received that appointment on 18th May 1603.]

Also of the English Nobility, he made these of his secret and Honourable [Privy] Council;

The Lord HENRY HOWARD [, *afterwards* Earl of NORTHAMPTON].
The Lord THOMAS HOWARD [, *afterwards* Earl of

SUFFOLK]: who was also made there, Lord Chamberlain.

[CHARLES BLOUNT,] the Lord MOUNTJOY [, *afterwards* Earl of DEVONSHIRE].

His Majesty stayed at Theobalds four days [*3rd–6th May* 1603]; where to speak of Sir ROBERT's cost to entertain him were but to imitate geographers that set a little o for a mighty Province: words being hardly able to express what was done there indeed, considering the multitude that thither resorted, besides the train; none going hence unsatisfied. [*See Vol. V., pp.* 623–656].

At Theobalds, His Majesty made these Knights [on 7th May]:

Sir WILLIAM KILLIGREW	[co. Cornw.]
Sir FRANCIS BARRINGTON	[co. Essex]
Sir ROWLAND LITTON	[co. Hertf.]
Sir WILLIAM PETERS [? PETRE]	[co. Essex]
Sir JOHN BROGRAVE	[co. Hertf.]
Sir WILLIAM COOKE	[co. Essex]
Sir ARTHUR CAPEL	[co Hertf.]
Sir HERBERT CROFT	[co. Heref.]
Sir EDWARD GREVILL	[co. Warw.]
Sir HENRY BOTELER	[co. Hertf.]
Sir HENRY MAYNARD	[co. Essex]
Sir RICHARD SPENCER	[co. Hertf.]
Sir JOHN LEVENTHORP	[co. Hertf.]
Sir MICHAEL STANHOPE	[co. Suff.]
Sir THOMAS POPE BLOUNT	[co. Hertf.]
Sir RICHARD GIFFORD.	
Sir THOMAS MEDCALFE	[co. York.]
Sir GAMALIEL CAPEL	[co. Essex]
Sir WILLIAM SMITH	[co. Essex]
Sir JOHN FERRERS	[co. Hertf.]
Sir ROBERT BITTON	[not in J. PHILIPOT's List]
Sir VINCENT SKINNER	[co. Middl.]
Sir HUGH BEESTON	[co. Chest.]
Sir JOHN LEIGH	[not in J. PHILIPOT's List]
Sir THOMAS BISHOP	[co. Suss.]
Sir EDWARD LEWIS	[co. Glam.]

Sir GERVASE ELWES [or ELLYS]
Sir RICHARD BAKER [the Chronicler, co. Kent]
[Sir HENRY FANSHAW co. Hertf.]

The 7th of May [1603], being Saturday, His Majesty removed from Theobalds, towards London, riding through the meadows: where, within two miles on this side of Waltham, Sir HENRY DENNY discharged his followers.

And there, Master SWINNERTON, one of the Sheriffs of London, accompanied with the Sheriff of Middlesex, met his Majesty, with sixty men in livery cloaks; where an eloquent and learned oration was made to His Highness.

Besides these men in livery cloaks that attended the Sheriff, all well mounted on gallant horses; most of the Sheriff's Officers attended him: who conducted His Majesty [to] within two miles of London.

And at Stamford Hill [Master ROBERT LEE] the Lord Mayor of London presented him with the Sword and Keys of the City: with whom were the Knights and Aldermen in scarlet gowns and great chains of gold about their necks, with the Chief Officers and Council of the City. Besides 500 citizens, all very well mounted, clad in velvet coats and chains of gold; with the chief Gentlemen of the Hundreds: who made a gallant shew to entertain their Sovereign.

There also met his Majesty, all his Officers of Estate, as Serjeants at Arms with their rich maces; the Heralds with their Coats of Arms, and Trumpeters: every one in their order and due place.

The Duke of LENOX bore the Sword of Honour before His Majesty: and so His Highness passed on in royal and imperial manner.

At this time, that honourable old Knight Sir HENRY LEIGH met with His Majesty, being attended by sixty gallant men well mounted on fair horses, thirty of them being great horses: many of his men having chains of gold; the rest wearing yellow scarfs embroidered with these words, *Constantia et fide.* To this old Knight, His Majesty spake very lovingly: and so paced through his troops very well pleased.

The multitudes of people in high ways, fields, meadows, closes, and on trees, were such that they covered the beauty of the fields; and so greedy were they to behold the countenance of the King that, with much unruliness, they injured and hurt one another. Some even hazarded to the danger of death. But as uncivil as they were among themselves; all the way, as His Majesty past [they welcomed him] with shouts, and cries, and casting up of hats (of which many never returned into the owners' hands).

He passed by them, over the fields; and came in at the back side of the Charterhouse.

Thither being come, he was most royal received and entertained by the Lord THOMAS HOWARD. Where was such abundance of provision of all manner of things that greater could not be; both of rare wild fowls, and many rare and extraordinary banquets; to the great liking of His Majesty, and contentment of the whole train.

He lay there four nights [*7th to 10th May* 1603]: in which time the Lords of the Council often resorted thither, and sat upon their serious affairs.

At his departure [*11th May* 1603], he made divers Knights, whose names are these:

Sir CHARLES HOWARD	[co. Suss.]
Sir AMBROSE WILLOUGHBY	[co. Linc.]
Sir EDWARD HOWARD	[co. Surr.]
Sir HENRY HASTINGS	[co. Leic.]
Sir GILES ALLINGTON	[co. Camb.]
Sir RICHARD VERNEY	[co. Warw.]
Sir JOHN THINNE	[co. Wilts.]
Sir WILLIAM FITZWILLIAMS	[co. Linc.]
Sir WILLIAM CARREL	[co. Suss.]
Sir EDWARD BACON	[co. Suff.]
Sir FRANCIS ANDERSON	[co. Bedf.]
Sir JOHN POULTNEY	[co. Notts.]
Sir EDWARD DARCY	[co. York]
Sir JOHN SYDENHAM	[co. Som.]
Sir JOHN TUFTON	[co. Kent]
Sir THOMAS GRIFFIN	[co. Northt.]
Sir VALENTINE KNIGHTLEY	[co. Northt.]
Sir RALPH WISEMAN	[co. Essex]
Sir WILLIAM AYLOFFE	[co. Essex]
Sir JAMES CROMER	[co. Kent]

Sir THOMAS ROUSE	[co. Suff.]
Sir RODNEY	[not in J. PHILIPOT's List]
Sir HENRY VAUGHAN	[not in J. PHILIPOT's List]
Sir JOHN SMITH	[co. Kent]
Sir JOHN HUNNAM	[co. Chest.]
Sir THOMAS MEDE	[co. Kent]
Sir EUSEBIUS ISHAM	[co. Northt.]
Sir ARTHUR COOPER	[co. Surr.]
Sir ROBERT WINGFIELD	[co. Northt.]
Sir THOMAS JOSLING	[co. Herts.]
Sir HENRY GOODERICK	[co. York.]
Sir MAXIMILIAN DALLISON	[co. Kent]
Sir WILLIAM COPE	[co. Northt.]
Sir GEORGE FLEETWOOD	[co. Bucks.]
Sir PETER EVERS	[co. Linc.]
Sir HENRY CLEERE	[co. Norf.]
Sir FRANCIS WOLLEY	[co. Linc.]
Sir ARTHUR MAINWARING	[co. Chest.]
Sir EDWARD WATERHOUSE	[co. York]
Sir WILLIAM TWYSDEN	[co. Kent]
Sir HATTON CHEEKE	[? co. Essex]
Sir HENRY GORING	[co. Suss.]
Sir ROBERT TOWNSEND	[co. Salop.]
Sir WILLIAM HYNDE	[co. Camb.]
Sir RICHARD SANDYS	[co. Kent]
Sir ROBERT BRUCE COTTON	[co. Hunts.]
Sir OLIVER LUKE	[co. Bedf.]
Sir THOMAS KNEVET	[co. Norf.]
Sir HENRY SECKFORD	[co. Suff.]
Sir EDWIN SANDYS	[co. Kent]
Sir JOHN ASHLEY	[co. Kent]
Sir WILLIAM FLEETWOOD	[co. Bedf.]
Sir WALTER MILDMAY	[co. Essex]
Sir EDWARD LEWKENOR	[co. Suff.]
Sir MILES SANDYS	[co. Camb.]
Sir WILLIAM KINGSMILL	[co. Southt.]
Sir THOMAS KEMPE	[co. Kent]
Sir EDWARD TYRREL	[co. Bucks.]
Sir THOMAS RUSSELL	[co. Worc.]
Sir RICHARD TICHBORNE	[co. Southt.]
Sir THOMAS CORNWALL	[co. Salop.]

Sir RICHARD FERMOR	[co. Northt.]
Sir WILLIAM STAFFORD	[co. Hunts.]
Sir THOMAS CARRELL	[co. Suss.]
Sir EDWARD CARRELL	[not in J. PHILIPOT's List.]
Sir THOMAS PALMER	[co. Kent]
Sir ROBERT NEWDIGATE	[co. Bedf.]
Sir GEORGE RAWLEIGH	[co. Essex]
Sir THOMAS BEAUFOE	[co. Warw.]
Sir WILLIAM LOWER	[co. Cornw.]
Sir THOMAS FAIRFAX	[co. York]
Sir HENRY SIDNEY	[co. Norf.]
Sir GEORGE HARVEY	[co. Essex]
Sir HENRY CRIPPES [*or* CRISPE	co. Kent]
Sir JOHN HEVENINGHAM	[co. Norf.]
Sir WILLIAM BOWYER	[co. Bucks.]
Sir JEROME WESTON	[co. Essex]
Sir EDMUND BOWYER	[co. Surr.]
Sir NICHOLAS HASLEWOOD	[co. Northt.]
Sir JOHN JENNINGS	[co. Worc.]
Sir AMBROSE TURVILLE	[co. Linc.]
Sir JOHN LUKE	[co. Bedf.]
Sir JOHN DORMER	[co. Bucks.]
Sir RICHARD SAUNDERS	[co. Linc.]
Sir JOHN SHERLEY	[co. Suss.]
Sir THOMAS WAYNEMAN	[co. Oxon.]
Sir GODDARD PEMPTON	
Sir THOMAS METHAM	[co. York]
Sir EDMUND BELLINGHAM	[co. Camb.]
Sir JOHN HARINGTON	[co. York]
Sir EDWARD HARINGTON	[co. York]
Sir WILLIAM DYER	[co. Som.]
Sir WILLIAM DYER	[co. Som.]
Sir WALTER MONTAGUE	[co. Som.]
Sir GUY PALMES	[co. Rutl.]
Sir HENRY ASHLEY	[co. Surr.]
Sir THOMAS VACKATHELL [*or* VACHILL.]	
Sir THOMAS STUKELEY	[co. Suss.]
Sir EDWARD WATSON	[co. Northt.]
Sir THOMAS PRESTON	[co. Dors.]

Sir WILLIAM LEEKE	
Sir CHARLES CORNWALLIS	[co. Suff.]
Sir EDWARD FRANCIS	[not in J. PHILIPOT's List.]
Sir HUGH LOSSE	[co. Middl.]
Sir WILLIAM LYGON	[co. Worc.]
Sir THOMAS [LE] GROSSE	[co. Norf.]
Sir JOHN TASKEROW [or TASBURGH	co. Suff.]
Sir THOMAS FOWLER	[co. Middl.]
Sir EUSEBIUS ANDREW	[co. Northt.]
Sir EDWARD ANDREW	[not in J. PHILIPOT's List.]
Sir WILLIAM KINGSMILL	[co. Southt.]
Sir ROBERT LUCY	[co. Warw.]
Sir WILLIAM WALTER	
Sir JOHN CUTTS	[co. Camb.]
Sir RICHARD BLOUNT	[co. Oxon.]
Sir ANTHONY DERING	[co. Kent]
Sir H. VAUGHAN	[not in J. PHILIPOT's List.]
Sir JOHN CAREW	[co. Som.]
Sir EDWARD APSLEY	[co. Suss.]
Sir BERTRAM BOOMER	
Sir WILLIAM ALFORD	[co. York]
Sir ROBERT LEE	[co. Linc.]
Sir THOMAS BEAUMONT	[co. Leic.]
Sir ROBERT MARKHAM	[co. Oxon.]
Sir FRANCIS CASTILION	[co. Berks.]
Sir GEORGE SAVILE	[co. York]
Sir GEORGE MARTHAM	[not in J. PHILIPOT's List.]
Sir ARTHUR ATTIE [or ATEY	co. Middl.]
Sir PECKSALL BROCAS	[co. Southt.]
Sir JOHN WASHALL [or ? Sir ROBERT MARSHALL]	
Sir ROBERT CLEVELAND	
Sir RICHARD FERMOR	[co. Northt.]
[Sir THOMAS CHEKE	co. Essex]
[Sir THOMAS AYLOFFE	co. Essex]
[Sir WALTER TICHBORNE	]
[Sir THOMAS BAKER	]

Upon Wednesday, the 11th of May 1603, His Majesty set forward from the Charterhouse, to the Tower of London; in going quietly on horseback to Whitehall, where he took [his] barge.

Having shot the Bridge [*London Bridge*], his present landing was expected at [the] Tower Stairs. But it pleased His Highness to pass the Tower Stairs, towards St Katharine's: and there stayed on the water to see the ordnance on the White Tower, commonly called JULIUS CÆSAR's Tower, being in number 20 pieces; [together] with the great ordnance on Tower Wharf, being in number 100; and chambers to the number of 130, discharged off. Of which all services were so sufficiently performed by the Gunners, that a peal of so good order was never heard before: which was most commendable to all sorts, and very acceptable to the King.

Then his royal person arrived at his own Stairs, so called the King's Stairs; and with him these Nobles, besides other gallant Gentlemen of worthy note, viz:

[CHARLES HOWARD, the Earl of NOTTINGHAM,] the Lord Admiral,
[HENRY PERCY,] the Earl of NORTHUMBERLAND,
[EDWARD SOMERSET,] the Earl of WORCESTER,
Lord THOMAS HOWARD, &c.

At his coming up the Stairs, the Sword was presented to His Majesty by Sir THOMAS CONI[G]SBY, Gentleman Usher of his Privy Chamber; and by the King delivered to the Duke of LENOX: who bare it before him into the Tower.

Upon the Stairs, the Gentleman Porter delivered the Keys of the Tower to [Sir JOHN PEYTON] the Lieutenant of the Tower; and the Lieutenant presented them accordingly to the King's Majesty: who most graciously acknowledged the most faithful discharge of the loyal and most great trust put in him; so, taking him about the neck, [he] redelivered them again.

After his repose in the Tower some [*i.e. about an*] hour; it was His Majesty's pleasure to see some [of the] Offices: as the Armory, the Wardrobe, the rich Artillery, and the Church. And after, for recreation, he walked in the garden: and so rested for that night.

The next day, being Thursday and the 12th of May [1603] he saw the Ordnance House; and after that, the Mint Houses; and, last of all, the lions.

The next day, being Friday the 13th of May [1603], he made these Lords and Knights following, viz:

In his Presence Chamber, before dinner.

[Sir ROBERT CECIL,] Lord ESSENDON [, co. Rutl.: *afterwards* Earl of SALISBURY].

[Sir ROBERT SYDNEY,] Lord SYDNEY of Penshurst [, co. Kent: *afterwards* Earl of LEICESTER].

[Sir WILLIAM KNOLLYS,] Lord KNOLLYS of Grays [, co. Oxon.: *afterwards* Earl of BANBURY].

[Sir EDWARD WOTTON,] Lord WOTTON of Mar[her]ley [, co. Kent].

Sir JOHN DEANE [co. Essex]
Sir JOHN TREAVOR [co. Flint]
Sir THOMAS SMITH [co. Kent]
Sir THOMAS HUBERT [co. Norf.]

And [in the] afternoon, in the Gallery.

Sir WILLIAM DETHICK, Garter [King at Arms co. Surr.]
Sir ROBERT MACKLARAND [co. Oxon.]
Sir GEORGE MORTON [co. Dors.]
Sir EDMUND BELL [co. Norf.]
Sir THOMAS PEYTON [co. Kent]
Sir DAVID FOWLES
Sir WILLIAM GARDNER [co. Surr.]

KING JAMES
his entertainment
at Theobalds.

With his welcome to London,
together with a salutatory
Poem.

By JOHN SAVILE.

Dicito Iö pæan: et Iö his dicito pæan.

LONDON:
Printed by THOMAS SNODHAM, and are to be sold
at the house of T. ESTE.
1603.

To the right worshipful Master GEORGE SAVILE, son and heir to Sir GEORGE SAVILE knight, his most approved kind patron; health, honour, and happiness.

OFFSPRING of Gentry, sprig for Honour drest,
'Tis half your loss (O hell!) but all my blame,
In proper words your worth should not b'exprest.
Let it suffice that I adore your name!
Then pardon what is wanting! I will owe it;
And as I'm able, I will pay, I vow it!

Meanwhile, accept this Poem to our King!
Peruse it at your leisure, half or all!
Your Worship's worth, our Muse shall shortly sing;
Though in true Poesy, her skill 's but small:
Howe'er it be, accept her pure goodwill!
She rests at your command, in all save Ill.

Your Worship's
Ever ready at command in all duty.

JOHN SAVILE.

King JAMES his entertainment at Theobalds; with his welcome to London.

COURTEOUS Reader! for the better understanding of this description following, especially [those] to whom the situation of the place is either less known or not at all: they are therefore to note that Theobalds (whither the King's Majesty came on Tuesday, being the 3rd of May, accompanied with his whole train) is a princely manor belonging to the Right Honourable Sir ROBERT CECIL, Principal Secretary to His Majesty, and one of His Highness's Privy Council, seated in the county of Essex [*or rather Hertfordshire, near Cheshunt*], twelve miles distant from London, directly by north, near to an ancient town called Walton [*Waltham*] Cross.

This house is not placed adjoining to the highwayside, as many sumptuous buildings are in that country and thereabouts (and especially between that place and London), the most part whereof belong to the city merchants: but it hath a most stately Walk from the common streetway, whereby passengers travel up to the palace, by the space of one furlong in length, beset about, either side, with young elm and ash trees confusedly mixed one for another, from the highway to the first court belonging to the house; containing in breadth three rods (which amount to some fifteen yards), in fashion made like a high ridgeland, or the middle street-way without Bishopsgate.

His Majesty having dined upon that same day, with Sir HENRY COCKS at Broxbourne, four miles distant from Theobalds, about half an hour after one a clock in the afternoon, His Highness proceeded forward towards Theobalds. He was accompanied by Sir EDWARD DENNY, then Sheriff of Essex [? *Hertfordshire*], who had 150 followers in parti-coloured hats, red and yellow bands, round rolled, with a feather in every one of them of the same colour; besides two trumpeters: all which were in blue coats, and gallantly mounted. There did accompany His Majesty from Broxbourne, many of the nobility of England and Scotland.

As His Highness was espied coming towards Theobalds, for very joy many ran from their carts, leaving their team of horse[s] to their own unreasonable direction.

After his nigh approach unto Theobalds, the concourse of people was so frequent, every one desiring a sight of him, that it were incredible to tell of. And it was wonderful to see the infinite number of horsemen and footmen that went from the city of London that day, thitherwards; and likewise from the counties of Kent, Surrey, Essex, and Middlesex, besides many other countries.

There were in my company two others. After I had put it into their minds, what infinite numbers of horse and foot passed by us, after our breakfast at Edmonton, at the sign of the *Bell*, we took occasion to note how many would come down in the next hour. So coming up into a chamber next the street, where we might best both see and likewise take notice of all passengers; we called for an hourglass, and after we had disposed of ourselves as to who should take the number of the horse [*riders*], and who the foot [*walkers*], we turned the hourglass; but before it was half run out, we could not possibly truly number them, they came so exceedingly fast. There we broke off, and made our account of 309 horse, and 137 footmen; which course continued that day, from four a clock in the morning till three a clock [in the] afternoon; and the day before also, as the host of the house told us, without intermission. Now whether every equal space [of time] did equal the number of this I cannot justly say; therefore I forbear to set it down.

When we were come to Theobalds, we understood His Majesty to be within the compass of three quarters of a mile from the house. At which tidings, we divided ourselves into three parts, each one taking a place of special note, to see what memorable accidents might happen within his compass; one standing at the upper end of the Walk, the second at the upper end of the first court, the third [*i.e., J. SAVILE himself*] at the second court's door; and we made choice of a gentleman of good sort to stand in the court that leads into the hall, to take notice what was said or done by His Highness to the nobility of our land, or said or done by them to His Majesty, and to let us understand of it. All which accidents, as they happened in their several places, you shall hear in as few words as may be.

Thus then for His Majesty's coming up the Walk. There came before His Majesty some of the nobility, some Barons, Knights, Esquires, Gentlemen, and others; amongst whom was the Sheriff of Essex [*? Hertfordshire*] and most of his men, the trumpets sounding next before His Highness, sometimes one, sometimes another; His Majesty not riding continually betwixt the same two [noblemen], but sometimes [with] one, sometimes [with] another, as seemed best to His Highness; the whole nobility of our land and Scotland round about him, observing no place of superiority, but all bare-headed; all of whom alighted from their horses at their entrance to the first court, save only His Majesty, who alone rode along still, with four noblemen laying their hands upon his steed, two before and two behind. In this manner he came till he was come to the court's door where I, myself, stood, where he alighted from his horse; from which he had not gone ten princely paces but there was delivered to him a petition by a young gentleman; His Majesty returning his gracious answer, that "He should be heard, and have justice."

At the entrance to that court stood many noblemen; among whom was Sir ROBERT CECIL, who there meeting His Majesty, conducted him into his house; all which was practised with as great applause of the people as could be, hearty prayer and throwing up of hats.

His Majesty had not stayed above an hour in his chamber, but hearing of the multitude thronging so fast into the uppermost court to see His Highness, as His Grace was informed; he shewed himself openly, out of his chamber window, by the space of half an hour together. After which time, he went into the labyrinth-like garden to walk; where he recreated himself in the meanders, compact of bays, rosemary, and the like overshadowing his walk, to defend him from the heat of the sun, till supper time. At which, there was such plenty of provision for all sorts of men in their due place, as struck me with admiration [*astonishment*].

And first, to begin with the ragged regiment, and such as were debarred the privilege of any Court, these were so sufficiently rewarded with beef, veal, mutton, bread, and beer, that they sang "holiday!" every day, and kept a continual feast. As for poor, maimed, and distressed soldiers, which repaired thither for maintenance; the wine, money, and meat, which they had in very bounteous sort, hath been a sufficient spur to cause them to blaze it abroad since their coming to London: whose thankfulness is not altogether unknown to myself, some of whom hearing that I was about to publish this small Remembrance, made means to me to give me true information of such princely exhibition, as they daily received during the time of His Majesty's abode at Theobalds.

But let us a little look back into the Mirror of Majesty, to our Sovereign's own self! who in his princely wisdom, considering the multitude of people assembled together, had that provident care over us his loving subjects, that (foreseeing that victuals would be dear, both for horse and man, had they been permitted to have been disposed of, according to the unsatiable desire of the town inhabitants) he ratified a deposition to that effect before the Clerk of the Market, for such and such victuals, meal, bread, butter, eggs, cheese, beef, mutton, veal, and the like, with lodgings and many more such necessary matters, that they should not be out of measure dear, beyond ordinary course and custom, within the verge of His Majesty's Court, so long as it continued at Theobalds. What his princely intention was in this, towards the public good of all his faithful subjects then and there assembled together, drawn merely with the bonds of love and bounden duty, may easily be gathered by the publication of the same by His Majesty's privilege: but how effectually this was observed by all estates of people within the verge of His Majesty's Court at the said time, I refer it to the censure of them that are assured of the certainty of it.

Upon Wednesday morn, being the 4th of May [1603], His Majesty rode, very early in the morning, into Enfield Chase, accompanied with many of the nobility. His return was shorter than was expected by a great deal, by reason that the morning seemed to promise a shower, but did not perform it. I could have wished that either it had never lowered at all, so should we have enjoyed the presence of His Majesty the longer at that present, or that the middle region would have given us just cause to have railed against it, by urging His Highness's return into the house before his full recreation.

He rode the most part of the way from the Chase, between two honourable personages of our land, the Earl of NORTHUMBERLAND upon His Majesty's right hand, and the Earl of NOTTINGHAM upon his left hand.

Now one word concerning His Majesty's proceeding towards London, upon Saturday, the 7th of May; and so I will end.

For the number of people that went forth of the city of London to see His Majesty that day; doubtless they were contained in a number, but, without all doubt, were not to be numbered. I heard many grey heads speak it, that in all the meetings they had seen or heard of, they had never heard or seen the tenth man of those that were to be seen that day, betwixt Enfield and London. Every place in this space was so clogged with company, that His Highness could not pass without pausing, ofttimes willingly enforced, though more willing to have proceeded, if conveniently he could without great peril to his beloved people.

After our return to our houses, in our recreating prattle, a gentleman then sojourning in my house, one Master TH[OMAS] PA: a man upon my own knowledge of sufficient wealth; yet he would have been content to have exchanged his state so he might but have had actually, for every reasonable creature there was there that day, a bee; and a hive to put them in. Another, more reasonable than he, would ask for no more living, than for every one, a pin; which (according to an arithmetical proportion and by the judgement of two or three martial men (who had seen great companies together), as near as they could guess by their seeming show, would have amounted to 150 lbs., receiving but of every one a pin.

His Majesty coming to Stamford Hill, there was an oration made unto His Highness; the effect of which I could not truly learn: and hear it, I could not, by reason of the crowd. For even there, being three miles from London, the people were so throng, that a carman let his cart for eight groats [2*s.* 8*d.*] to eight persons, whose abode in it was not above one quarter of an hour.

From Stamford Hill to London, was a train [*hunt*] made with a tame deer, with such turnings and doubles that the hounds could not take it faster than His Majesty proceeded; yet still by the industry of the huntsman and the subtilty of him that made the train in a full mouthed cry all the way, it was never further distant than one close [*field*] from the highway whereby His Highness rode, and for the most part directly against His Majesty; who, together with the whole company, had the lee wind from the hounds; to the end they might the better perceive and judge of the uniformity of the cry.

After His Majesty had come from Kingsland, there was a division amongst the people, which way His Highness would take when he came at Islington; but, in fine, he came the higher way, by the west end of the church; which street hath ever since, and I guess ever will be called King's Street by the inhabitants of the same.

When His Highness had passed Islington, and another place called New Rents, and entered into a close called Wood's Close by a way, cut of purpose, through a bank, for His Majesty's more convenient passage into the Charterhouse garden; the people that were there assembled, I can compare to nothing more conveniently than to imagine every grass to have been metamorphosed into a man in a moment, the multitude was so marvellous. Amongst whom were the children of the Hospital [*the Bluecoat School, see Vol.* IV. *p.* 240] singing, orderly placed for His Majesty's coming along through them; but all displaced by reason of the rudeness of such a multitude.

After His Majesty was come among the press of the people, the shouts and clamours were so great that one could scarce hear another speak; and, though there was hope to find what was lost especially by the loser, notwithstanding, in token of excessive joy inwardly conceived in the heart, many threw up their caps.

Now, at last, he is entered into the garden; from which time, till his going to the Tower, mine eyes were never blessed with his encounter.

Now he is amongst us, GOD long preserve him over us! whose presence makes old men say, *Satis se vixisse se viso.*

FINIS.

A salutatory Poem to the Majesty of King JAMES.

HAIL, mortal god! England's true joy! great King
All hail! Thy coming forceth my Muse to sing!
Too forward, so untutored in these lays,
Unfit to blazon Kings' befitting praise,
Yet ne'ertheless I'm forced perforce to write:
Some Fury doth my head, my hand incite.
Antiquity hath taught, next that day
That English hearts first for your state did pray,
The angel GABRIEL, from JEHOVAH sent,
Told to the creature, what her Maker meant.
How She, a maiden-wife, should bear a son,
Mankind's sole Saviour when we were undone.
This blessed Eve of th'blest Annunciation
Was first day of your Highness's proclamation.
What hopes, what haps this proclamation brings
Is cause efficient why our Muses sing.
Hail, full of grace! this 'gins the Salutation,
Striking the Blessed with deepest admiration;
Half daunted first, then straight no whit dismayed,
Mildly made answer, *Be't as my Lord hath said!*
Look what surpassing solace, joy without measure,
Possessed her soul for this celestial treasure,
Entombing in her womb our Saviour dear,

Deigned only worthy, man's Saving Health to bear.
The like, and more, if more or like could be,
Possessed our souls, longing so long for thee,
She blessed the author of her good, the incarnate Word,
Singing, *My soul doth magnify the Lord!*
At tidings of your proclamation we,
In hands, in hats, in hearts did all agree.
The world hath our applause, heav'ns have our hearty praying,
Yourself, hands, hats, and hearts from you ne'er straying.
The fruit which came by the angel's *Ave!* t'all
Is easily gathered by old ADAM's fall;
The world, the flesh, the Devil, each one our foe,
By *Ave!* had their final overthrow.
The fruit we hope to reap by "GOD save the King!"
Which England's Council, unto the world did ring
'Pon that same day, 's, doubtless, beyond compare
Yourself in virtue, learning, valour rare.
GABRIEL! why stay'st? Angel! why art thou slack?
Tell me, Eternal Messenger! what holds thee back?
To take thy wings, leave demi-deity,
And bid "GOD save King JAMES his Majesty!"
Since thou 'rt create to tell thy Maker's mind,
And for no other end wert first assigned.
Old HOMER writes a silly dog would say
"Welcome" to's master κρᾶς αινόμενη;
PERSIUS hath told us, for great CÆSAR's sake,
A speechless parrot, χαῖρε to's welcome spake:
What shall our hearts devise? or hands set down?
Worthy thy great (O worthy King!) renown!
But thousands of "Welcomes!" millions of χαῖρες send;
Plaudites numberless, shouts wanting end.
Should we not this do, thankless were we then,
But oft it's seen, beasts are more kind than men.
Witness old BARDUS's ape, freed from the pit

That held a Senator and snake within it!
ADRIAN promised BARDUS half of all
His goods, to rid him from his hunting fall.
Poor man, untied his truss, let down his rope;
To pull out ADRIAN first was all his hope.
The ape espying it, out of the prison burst,
Clipping the line in 's arms, was hauled up first.
BARDUS lets down his cord the second time,
Intending ADRIAN up thereby should climb;
When 'twas come down, near to th'imprisoning ground,
The serpent close himself about it wound.
He was released the next: whom BARDUS seeing,
Ran, all aghast, hoping t'escape by fleeing.
Lastly, the Senator, fast by it caught:
Released, ne'er thanked him for the deed he had wrought.
Th' aforesaid two, wanting Words, Reason, Art,
Did several duties to him in their heart.
In thankfulness, poor ape did give him wood;
A precious stone, for his received good
The serpent gave him. Thus we plainly see;
For good received, thankful, dumb creatures be.
Why do I instant in ungrateful man,
Sith all are pressed to do, say, show the best they can,
To entertain England's undoubted King;
JAMES, First of that name, to his own to bring?
Do not our parrots, PERSIUS! equal thine?
When one, 'mongst many, so truly could divine
Could augurize aright, foresee, foresay
A full month since, bidding "King JAMES, good day!"
Unseen of most, hearing his only name,
Tell'st in the streets, recks not her teacher's blame,
Naming him twenty times at least together,
Ceasing no longer than oiling of a feather,
'Twixt each "King JAMES," or "King," or "good," or "day;"

And oft, poor fool, she totally did pray
Withouten ceasing, utter the whole throughout
To th'admiration of the gazing rout.
I cannot deem it now gulling toy
Which VENNARD (inspired!) entitled *England's Joy*;
I rather guess he did our good divine,
Nor daring to disclose 't before full time.
Be bold! go on! Now's thy presaging plain!
King JAMES is *England's Joy*, long hoped for gain.
That it is he, who cannot easily prove!
Sith it is only he, we only love.
'Tis he that *England's Joy* did first awake,
After sad sorrowing for ELIZA's sake.
Then reck no clownish frumps! regard them nought!
Banish such fooleries from thy purer thought!
We know the fruit sprung from foreknowing pen,
"King JAMES is *England's Joy*!" Say all "Amen!"
Tokens of *England's Joy*, who list to seek
That night might find strawed in London street,
Making the night, a day; Phœbe, a sun,
This was the first sign when our *Joy* began:
Continued still t'England's eternal good,
In the happy issue of your royal blood.
Make haste to make us happy, worthy King!
Our Muse desires to write th'enthronizing
At famous Westminster, in thy Elders' Chair;
Where England's peers will yield our Crown to th'heir,
To th'heir legitimate, yourself, dread Sovereign!
Wishing your happy and victorious reign.
Besides a Trine of Kingdoms are your own
Possess them all! possessing England's crown,
France, and froward Ireland, with our English land,
Are feal subjects to your royal hand.
Besides, your sacred Self doth bring with you,

A kingdom never knit to these till now,
As CAMDEN's *Britain* tells, since BRUTUS' days;
Then let us thank our GOD! sing roundelays!
England, rejoice! "St. George for England!" shout!
For joy, 'St. Denis!" cry all France throughout!
Double our joys, O Albion! Hark, Cambrian banks!
GOD hath enriched thee with a Prince, give hearty thanks!
You that, of long, had Lords in judgement sit
Deciding causes, for your country fit.
Clap hands! sing *Iῶ*! changed is your government:
Our King's dearest son's your Prince, your President!
St. DAVID, ring! for joy, set up your leek!
Your prayer's heard, you have got you long did seek!
Brave HENRY FREDERICK, that imperial name
I guess from his nativity foretold the same.
Thrice happy in his threefold name, are you!
HENRY, bold FREDERICK, is a STEWARD true,
How well these titles, with your names agree?
You, almost all, at least possessing three;
Welcome them heartily! welcome brave Prince HENRY!
Sing carols for his sake! keep wakes! be merry!
Ireful cold Ireland, cease from thy rage at last!
To yield subjection to thy King, make haste!
Sound out "St. Patrick!" Scotland, "St. Andrew!" sing!
King JAMES is England's, Scotland's, France's, Ireland's
King,
What can I add to eke our joys withal.
Sith JAMES is King of all, contained in all.
But thou hast, dear King! t'ease our expecting mind
Unstayed while your Highness stays behind,
Indeed ne'er truly stayed, till we, you greet
With *χαῖρε βασιλεὺς* in London street;
Nor then indeed, till we do all resort
To see your face shining in England's Court,

And then (O but till then make haste !) your Grace shall see
Your stranger subject's faithful loyalty.
Now to return where first I did begin,
'Mongst all estates, Poets have cause to sing
King JAMES his welcome; for he doth excel
(As his *Lepantho* and his *Furies* tell)
In Poesy. All kings in Christendom,
Then welcome him (quick spirits !), blush to be dumb!
And pardon him that boldly makes this suit
Forced by some Fury, scorns to be longer mute,
Rejoice ! Your patron is your country's King.
Judge ! of all states, have not you cause to sing ?
For shame, then, rouse your spirits ! Awake, for shame !
Give CÆSAR's due ! Acquit yourselves from blame !
All wish his welcome, 'mongst all sorts of men,
Save only such as are past sixty-ten :
These wayward old ones grudge to leave behind
What our succeeding Age is sure to find.
The peace, the plenty, pleasure, and such like gain
Which we are sure t'enjoy in JAMES his reign ;
Wishing, Would he had lived in their youth's prime;
Or Old Age would return to ten and nine !
Were they but nineteen who have ninety seen,
They would then wish to see King JAMES and 's Queen.
And so indeed they do, the whitest heads
That lived in antique time, and prayed on beads
These holiest fathers crave no longer life
Than once to see King JAMES his Queen and wife
With hands upreared, giving JEHOVAH praise,
That length'ed their lives to see his happy days.
That these his happy days full grace may bring,
Let English hearts cry all, "GOD save our King!"

FINIS.

THE

Time Triumphant,

Declaring in brief the arrival of our Sovereign liege Lord, King JAMES, into England, His Coronation at Westminster; together with his late Royal Progress from the Tower of London through the City to His Highness's Manor of Whitehall.

Shewing also the varieties and rareties of all the sundry Trophies or Pageants, erected as well by the worthy citizens of the honourable City of London, as also by certain of other nations, namely, Italians, Dutch, and French.

With a Rehearsal of the King and Queen's late coming to the Exchange in London.

By GILBERT DUGDALE.

¶ *At LONDON. Printed by R. B.* 1604.

TIME

Triumphant,

in King JAMES his happy coming to the Crown of England, &c.

WHAT time it pleased GOD omnipotent, to seize upon the soul of our late Sovereign Queen of famous memory, that worthy gentleman, Sir ROBERT CARY, night and day omitting no industry, brought, as I have heard it credibly reported, the first fame of the happened honour to our thrice famous and heroic King JAMES: whose haste though it unhappily threw him from his horse near his journey's end, yet it foretold the ensuing Majesty to come, and worthily entertained of one so gracious as our blessed and dread Sovereign, gave him to understand the power of the Almighty in his behalf; seating him as lawful and immediate in the English Throne, to rule Israel with a happy hand.

I shall not need to relate the good orders of the Most Honourable, grave, and wise Council of this land; the great love of the whole nobility; the affective humours of all the Court to shew their duties in that behalf; the worthy usage of the citizens of London in general, and in what excellent manner he was proclaimed, with what quiet love and government. For mine own part, I have known the city of London many years, but I never did see the retainers, inhabitants, both young and old, of that excellent order and government; nothing of that giddy rashness, as in times before they were accustomed to be: but all in one, and one in all, most worthily received the Imperial name of King JAMES, and freely consented to his titles as *By the Grace of God, of England, Scotland, France, and Ireland, King; Defender of, &c.*

The day then generally known of his coming forward to the possession of the Regal Seat; let me tell you, by the way, the joy was not so great in England by the English to fetch him, as the sorrow was in Scotland of the Scots to leave him. And that which was more confounding to their joys than the rest, the parting betwixt his Queen and him in the open street, in the full eye of all his subjects, who spent tears in abundance to behold it. Here English and Scottish in one sympathy, joined first in hearty affected love; in sign whereof the floods of their eyes drawn from their kind hearts, conjoined their amity: and no doubt, they that in kindness, being possessed with one joy, can weep together: they will now, and at all times, live and die together.

But to make haste to the principal, whereof this is part. Towards England he comes.

His royal entertainment in Berwick, both of the train of England and the soldiers there I need not set down. Yet I will tell you of a wise answer of the King to a question propounded.

When he entered in the town, it rained small drops, whereby some things had hindrance which should have royalised the time: but His Grace graciously, being attended in his chamber, on the sudden, looking from his window, might see the sunshine.

One by, of no small account, began to question thus. "I muse, why the temperate season was so quickly overcast by a shower of rain; and now that rain so overthrown by this sunshine: it presages somewhat sure[ly]!"

The King smiling, "No great matter!" quoth he, "only this imagine! the first fair shew of weather, my prosperous setting forwards, by GOD's sufferance; the latter shower, the universal tears of my country to leave their King; and this sudden sunshine, the joy of England for my approach." Which undoubtedly it was so, as it appeared; for the cost, and love pains, of his subjects (all the way from Berwick to York, from thence to Stamford, from thence to Theobalds, and so to the Charter House in London, where he remained for certain days, and then went to the Tower of London, and so seating his most royal person there), as the like hath seldom been, or I think ever will be again to the world's end, to any man's imagination.

Well here he is, happily planted and heartily welcome! What wants then but his blessed coronation! At which was no small triumph. For had you seen him in progress to it, as many did, when he took barge at Whitehall, on Saint James's day [*25th July*]; such was his salutation to the people, and theirs to him. But anon comes forth England's Triumph, the worth of women, ANNE, Queen of England, and happy wife to our most gracious King (whose father was King, brother no less a King, and whose husband four Kings in one), accompained with lovely ladies (the only wedstars of the world for beauty and good graces), following her dear husband to Coronation, with her seemly hair down trailing on her princely bearing shoulders, on which hair was a coronet of gold. She so mildly saluted her subjects, that the women weeping ripe, cried all in one voice "GOD bless the Royal Queen! Welcome to England! long to live and continue so!"

To Westminster they went, and took on them the royalty of the time, the complete order of Coronation; and, by a general and free consent, enjoyed the rights of Royalty and were invest in Honour, possessed of Majesty, owners of Royalty, and made the only Commander of all Principality.

The Triumph of that time, I omit; but let me turn to the Londoners whose hearts were wild fire, and burned unquenchable in love to this royal couple, and expressing her desires and their heads together to solemnize in triumph that happy day: which hour of glory was dashed by the omnipotency of GOD's power; who, mortally visiting the City and land with a general Visitation, hath, since that time, taken thousands to His mercy, and laid their heads low that else, in these actions, would have held them high.

Yet see again a new love of His Majesty! He nobly regarding the cost together with their loves, and that their expectations should go current, appoints when the full possession of their joys should be; that was when the angry hand of GOD had worked the will of His all-commanding power when the infection ceased, then should the Triumph of the day be solemnized. To this consent, cost prepared, and the City with the strangers, merchants, and others, erected Trophies of Glory, Pageants of that magnificence that never were the like.

Well, the time appointed, when His Highness would set forward, should be in the holy time in Lent, the joyful Spring time when the ground in triumph of the time should likewise flourish in ample equipage; and she (no niggard of her pomp) attires hers in a green livery embroidered with flowers of a thousand divers and sundry colours. Thus heaven and earth applaud the Triumph of King JAMES, and mortals all agree to make that hour famous.

In the meantime, His Grace, with his Queen and children, progressed in the country, and dealt honours as freely to our nation as their hearts would wish, as creating Knights, of Gentlemen; Lords, of Knights; and Earls, of Lords; and, no doubt, hereafter Dukes, of Earls: I [*ay*], and raised up an Honour in England that, to this day, has been long in oblivion, which as now it is honourably living, so it will never die: I mean our noble Knights of the Bath, young and gallant, worthy and valiant.

Nay, see the bounty of our all kind Sovereign! Not only to the indifferent of worth, and the worthy of honour, did he freely deal about these causes; but to the mean, gave grace: as taking to him, the late Lord Chamberlain's servants, now the King's Actors: the Queen taking to her the Earl of WORCESTER's servants, that are now her Actors; the Prince, their son HENRY, Prince of Wales, full of hope, taking to him the Earl of NOTTINGHAM his servants, who are now his Actors. So that of Lord's servants, they are now the servants of the King, Queen, and Prince.

But to return again to our Time Triumphant. Now the hour is come, and the day appointed. The preparation of which is mighty, I [*ay*] and so great as neither can my tongue tell, nor my pen set down. Yet to make a flourish of a flourish, thus it was.

Our heroic King hearing the preparation to be great, as

well to note other things, as that he was desirous privately, at his own pleasure, to visit them; accompanied with his Queen in his coach, he came to the Exchange, there to see for his recreation, thinking to pass unknown. The wily multitude perceiving something, began with such hurly burly to run up and down, with such unreverent rashness as the people of the Exchange were glad to shut the stair doors to keep them out. Here they lost the pleasing sight they might have enjoyed but for their rashness.

When His Highness had beheld the merchants from a window, all below in the walks, not thinking of his coming, whose presence else would have been more: they, like so many pictures, civilly seeming, all bare [headed], stood silent, modesty commanding them so to do. Which sight so delighted the King, that he greatly commended them saying, "He was never more delighted that seeing so many, of divers and sundry nations, so well ordered and so civil one with the other:" but withal discommended the rudeness of the multitude, who, regardless of time, place, or person, will be so troublesome.

And, countrymen, let me tell you this! If you heard what I hear, as concerning that; you would stake your feet to the earth, at such a time, ere you would run regardless up and down! Say, it is His Highness's pleasure to be private, as you may note by the order of his coming; will you then be public, and proclaim that which Love and Duty cries silence to? This shews his love to you: but your open ignorance to him! You will say, perchance, "It was your love!" Will you, in love, press upon your Sovereign thereby to offend him? Your Sovereign may, perchance, mistake your love, and punish it as an offence!

But, hear me! When hereafter he comes by you, do as they do in Scotland! Stand still! see all! and use silence! So shall you cherish his Visitation, and see him thrice for once amongst you! But I fear my counsel is but water turned into the Thames. It helps not!

But to our Solemnity. The Court, the City, and Country, all make preparation to the day: the Court, the order for the King's person; they in the City, his welcome to it, and his quiet pass through the streets; the Country, they post up to attend: so that all are busied to this Solemnity; and the reason, I trow, being the Day of Triumph so long expected.

The Tower was empty of his prisoners; and I beheld the late [!] Sir WALTER RALEIGH, the late [!] Lord COBHAM, the late [!] Lord GREY, MARKHAM, with others, conveyed some to the Marshalsea, others to the Gatehouse, and others to appointed prisons [*in* November, 1603].

The Tower itself was prepared with that pomp as eye never saw, such glory in the hangings! such majesty in the ornaments of the chambers! and such a necessary provision, as when I beheld it, I could no less than say

GOD gives King JAMES the grace
And glory of the day,
As never a King possessed like place
That came the Northern way,
And since the heavens will have it so,
What living soul dares say "No!"

Upon the Thames, the water works for his entertainment were miraculous, and the fireworks on the water passed pleasing. As of a castle or fortress built on two barges, seeming as a settled fort in an island, planted with much munition of defence: and two pinnaces ready rigged, armed likewise to assault the castle: that had you beheld the managing of that fight, with the onset on the castle, repulse from the castle, and then the taking of it, it was a show worthy the sight of many Princes. Being there placed at the cost of the Cinque Ports: whereat the King, all pleased, made answer that "their love was, like the wild fire, unquenchable!" And, I pray GOD, it may ever be so!

Well, from the Tower, he came. Here, Cost was careless; Desire was fearless, and Content flourished in abundance. But so royally attended, as if the gods had summoned a Parliament, and were all in their steps of triumph to JOVE's High Court. This worthy train attending so majestic a presence, the Companies of London in their liveries, placed in the street which was double railed [*i.e., a rail on each side of the street*] for them and the passengers, the Whifflers in their costly suits and chains of gold walking up and down, not a conduit betwixt the Tower and Westminster but runs with wine, drink who will! coming thus, with his royal assembly, all so gallantly mounted, as the eye of man was amazed at the pomp.

In Fenchurch street was erected a stately Trophy or Pageant, at the City's charge; on which stood such a shew of workmanship and glory as I never saw the like! Top and topgallant, whereon were shews so embroidered and set out, as the cost was incomparable! who spake speeches to the King of that incomparable eloquence, as, while I live, I shall commend.

The city of London was very rarely and artificially made; where no church, house, nor place of note, but your eye might easily find it out: as the Exchange, Cole Harbour, Paul's, Bow Church, &c.

There, also Saint GEORGE and Saint ANDREW, in complete armour, met in one combat, and fought for the victory; but an old Hermit passing by, in an oration, joined them hand in hand, and so, for ever, hath made them as one heart: to the joy of the King, the delight of the Lords, and the unspeakable comfort of the comminalty.

Our gracious Queen ANNE, mild and courteous, placed in a chariot of exceeding beauty, did all the way so humbly and with mildness, salute her subjects, never leaving to bend her body this way and that, that women and men in my sight wept with joy.

The young hopeful HENRY FREDERICK, or FREDERICK HENRY, Prince of Wales, smiling as overjoyed, to the people's eternal comfort, saluted them with many a bend.

Before whom, the Lord Mayor of the City in a crimson velvet gown, bearing his enamelled golden mace on his shoulder, ushered the King, Queen, and Prince; bringing them to Temple Bar, took his leave, and received many thanks of the King and Queen: who were after met by the Aldermen and Sheriffs, that came to guard him home.

Well, the glory of that Show passed, the King and his train passed on through Gratious [*Gracechurch*] street. But there let me tell you I was not very near: but, in my eye, it was super excellent Justice, as I take it, attired in beaten gold, holding a crown in her hand; guarded with shalmes and cornets, whose noise was such as if the Triumph had been endless.

There, likewise, were, on both sides, speeches spoken; Shows appointed with several harmonies of drums, trumpets, and music of all sorts.

The Italians spared no spending in that behalf, at whose charge this glorious prospect was so pompous and full of shew, to the wonder of every beholder for the height, strength, and quality. Through it our King and his train passed.

At the corner of the street stood one, an old man with a white beard, at the age of seventy-nine, who had seen the change of four Kings and Queens, and now beheld the triumphs of the fifth; which, by his report, exceeded all the rest. Wherefore, as hopeful never to behold the like, yet he would, of his own accord, do that which should show his duty and old love, that was to speak a five lines that his son had made him: which lines were to this purpose, he himself being attired in green—

Peerless of Honour, hear me speak a word!
Thy welcomed glory and enthroned renown
Being in peace, of earthly pomp and State,
To furnish forth the beauties of thy Crown.
Age thus salutes thee, with a downy pate.
Threescore and nineteen is thy servant's years,
That hath beheld thy predecessors four
All flourishing green; who deaths, the subjects' tears
Mingled with mine, did many times deplore,
But now again, since that our joys are five,
Five hundred welcomes, I do give my King!
And may thy change, to us that be alive,
Never be known, a fifth extreme to bring!
My honest heart be pattern of the rest!
Whoever prayed for them before now thee,
Both them and thine, of all joy be possest!
Whose lively presence, we all bless to see.
And so pass on! GOD guide thee on thy way!
Old Hind concludes, having no more to say.

But the narrow way, and the pressing multitudes so overshadowed him, with the noise of the Show, that opportunity was not favourable to him; so that the King passed by: yet noting his zeal, I have publicly imprinted it, that all his fellow subjects may see this old man's forwardness; who missed of his purpose by the concourse of the people. Besides the King appointed no such thing, but at several stays and appointed places.

Along Cornhill, they trooped with great majesty. But His Highness, being right over against the Exchange, smiled, looking toward it; belike, remembering his last being there, the grace of the merchants, and the rudeness of the multitude: and casting his eye up to the third Trophy or Pageant, admired it greatly; it was so goodly, top and top many stories, and so high as it seemed to fall forward.

On the top, you might behold the sea dolphins as dropping from the clouds on the earth, or looking to behold the King; pictures of great art, cost, and glory, as a double ship that, being two, was so cunningly made as it seemed but one, which figured Scotland and England in one, with the arms of both in one escutcheon, sailing on two seas at once.

Here, was a speech of wonder delivered too. But the glory of this Show was in my eye as a dream, pleasing to the affection, gorgeous and full of joy: and so full of joy and variety, that when I held down my head, as wearied with looking so high, methought it was a grief to me to awaken so soon. But thus the Dutch and French spared for no cost to gratify our King.

Still the streets stood railed, and the Liveries of all the Companies on both sides guarding the way; and the strong stream of people violently running in the midst towards Cheapside. There, our Triumphant rides, garnished with troops of royalty and gallant personages.

And passing by the Great Conduit, on the top thereof, stood a prentice, in a black coat, flat cap, servant-like, as walking before his master's shop. Now whether he spake this or not, I heard it not: but the manner of this speech was this; it coming to me at third, or second hand.

"What lacks you, gentlemen? What will you buy? Silks! Satins! Taffetas! &c.

But stay, bold tongue! Stand at a giddy gaze!
Be dim, mine eyes! What gallant train are here,
That strike minds mute, and put good wits in maze?
O 'tis our King! Royal King JAMES is near!
Pass on in peace, and happy be thy way!
Live long on earth, England's great crown to sway!

Thy City, gracious King, admires thy fame,
And on their knees, prays for thy happy state!
Our women, for thy Queen ANNE, whose rich name
Is their created bliss, and sprung of late.
If women's wishes may prevail thus being,
They wish you both long lives, and good agreeing!

Children for children pray, before they eat,
At their uprising, and their lying down:
Thy sons and daughters, Princely all complete,
Royal in blood, children of high renown.
But generally together they incline,
Praying in one, great King, for thee and thine."

Whether he were appointed, or of his own accord, I know not; but howsoever forward, love is acceptable; and I would the King had heard him, but the sight of the Trophy at Soper Lane end, made him more forward.

There was cost both curious and comely, but the devices of that, afar off, I could not conjecture. But by report, it was exceeding. It made no hugh high shew like the other; but was pompous, both for glory and matter; a stage standing by, on which were enacted strange things; after which, an oration was delivered of great wisdom. Both sides of this Pageant were decked gallantly; and furnished so as all the broad street, as the King passed, showed like a Paradise.

But here, His Grace might see the love of his subjects, who, at that time, were exceedingly in the Shows. Passing by the Cross [*in Cheapside*] beautifully gilt and adorned; there the Recorder and the Aldermen on the scaffold, delivered him a gallant oration; and withal a cup of beaten gold.

So he passed on to the Pageant at the Little Conduit, very artificial indeed, of no exceeding height, but pretty and pleasing, in the manner of an arbour; wherein were placed all manner of wood inhabitants, divers shews of admiration as pompions, pomegranates, and all kinds of fruits: which the Lords highly commended: where, after strange musics had given plenty of harmony; he passed toward Fleet Street, through Ludgate, where the Conduits dealt so plenteously both before and after he was passed, as many were shipped to the Isle of Sleep, that had no leisure, for snorting, to behold the day's Triumph.

When he came to the Trophy in Fleet Street, the Lords considered that the same, for royalty, was so richly beautified, and so plenteous of shew, that with the breath of the street, it seemed to them to have gone back again, and that they were but then at the Cross in Cheap, but otherwise saluted, as with variety of speeches.

All sundry sorts of music appointed by the City too, as that at the Little Conduit, and all else but the Exchange and Gratious Street. On the top of this Pageant was placed a globe of goodly preparation.

Thus, while wondering at the glory of it, setting on unawares, were they at the Pageant at Temple Bar: neither great nor small, but finely furnished; some compared it to an Exchange shop, it shined so in that dark place and was so pleasing to the eye. Where one, a young man, an Actor of the City, so delivered his mind, and the manner of all, in an oration, that a thousand gave him his due deserving commendations.

In the Strand, also, was another, of small proportion, a Pyramid fit beseeming time and place. But the day was far spent, and the King and the States, I am sure, wearied with the Shows, as the stomach may glutton: the daintiest Court stayed not long, but passed forward to the place appointed; where I leave them to GOD's protection and their own pleasures.

Thus have you heard a short description of this day's Progress, in which all the Peers and Lords of England, and a part of those of Scotland were assembled, to beautify the triumphs of their most gracious King. The multitude of people present at this, was innumerable; but to conclude, GOD be thanked for it! such was the care of the worshipful citizens of London, and all things so providentially foreseen by them, that little or no hurt ensued to any: which was greatly feared of many to have happened, by reason of the great multitudes that were in the City, being come both far- and near this, to see this most glorious and happy Show.

And I beseech Almighty GOD, of His infinite mercy and goodness, so to keep our King, Queen, and Prince, and all their princely progeny, that no harm may ever come near them, nor touch them; but that may ever live to His great glory, and to maintain His glorious Gospel, for evermore. Amen.

THE COMMENTARIES OF Sir FRANCIS VERE,

Being
divers Pieces of Service, wherein he had command; written by himself, in way of *Commentary*.

Published by
WILLIAM DILLINGHAM, D.D.

Ut V*ERUS in suis* Commentariis *prodidit.* CAMDEN, *Annal.*
Mihi sufficit hæc summatim è V*ERI* Commentario *annotasse.* Idem. *Ibid.*

CAMBRIDGE:
Printed by JOHN FIELD, Printer to the famous University. *Anno Dom.* MDCLVII.

[*Brave* VERE*! who hast by deeds of arms made good*
What thou hadst promisèd by birth and blood,
Whose Courage ne'er turned edge, being backed with wise
And sober Reason, sharpened with Advice.
Look, Reader, how from Nieuport hills, he throws
Himself a thunderbolt amongst his foes!
And what his Sword indited, that his Pen
With like success doth here fight o'er again!
What MARS *performed,* MERCURY *doth tell!*
None e'er but CÆSAR *fought and wrote so well!*
Why may not then his book this title carry,
The Second Part of CÆSAR's Commentary?

VERI SCIPIADÆ
duo fulmina belli.]

To the Right Worshipful *HORACE TOWNSHEND,* *Baronet.*

RIGHT WORSHIPFUL,

I HERE present you with the Works, that is, with the Actions and Writings of your great uncle, Sir FRANCIS VERE; unto which, as you have a right by blood, common to some others with you, so have you also right by purchase, proper and peculiar to yourself alone: having freely contributed to adorn the impression [*contributed towards the engravings of the original edition*]; wherein you have consulted, as the reader's delight and satisfaction, so the honour and reputation of your family.

I have read of one that used to wear his father's picture always about him; that, by often looking thereon, he might be reminded to imitate his virtues, and to admit of nothing unworthy of the memory of such an ancestor. Now, Sir, I think you shall not need any monitor than your own name! if, but as often as you write it or hear it spoken, you recall into your thoughts, those of your progenitors, who contributed to it: your honoured father, Sir ROGER TOWNSHEND, and your grandfather, the truly honourable and valiant the Lord VERE of Tilbury; men famous in their generations, for owning religion, not only by profession, but also by the practice and patronage of it. Whose virtues, while you shall make the pattern of your imitation, you will increase in favour with GOD and man, and answer the just expectations of your country. And that you may so do, it is the earnest desire, and hearty prayer of,

Sir,

Your very respectful friend and humble servant,

WILLIAM DILLINGHAM.

To the ingenuous Reader.

ALTHOUGH this book can neither need, nor admit of any Letters Recommendatory from so mean a hand: yet I thought it not incongruous to give thee some account of it; especially coming forth so many years after the author's death [Sir FRANCIS VERE died 28th August, 1608, æt. 54].

Know then, that some years since, it was my good hap to meet with a copy [i.e., in manuscript] *of it, in the library of a friend, which had been either transcribed from, or at least compared with another in the owning and possession of Major General SKIPPON: which I had no sooner looked into, but I found myself led on with exceeding delight, to the perusal of it. The gallantry of the action, the modesty of the author, and the becomingness of the style, did much affect me: and I soon resolved that such a treasure could not, without ingratitude to the author and his noble family, nor without a manifest injury to the repute our English Nation, yea, and unto truth itself, be any longer concealed in obscurity.*

Whereupon, I engaged my best endeavours to bring it into the public view: but finding some imperfections and doubtful places in that copy, I gave myself to further inquiry after some other copies; supposing it very improbable that they should all stumble at the same stone.

And so, I was favoured with another copy out of the increasing library of the Right Honourable the Earl of WESTMORELAND, which had been transcribed immediately from the author's own;

another, the Honourable the Lord FAIRFAX *was pleased to afford me the perusal of: but that which was* instar omnium, *was the Original itself, written by the author's own hand, being the goods and treasure of the Right Honourable the Earl of* CLARE, *but at present, through his favour, in my possession.*

These, Reader! are the Personages whose favour herein, I am, even upon thy account, obliged here to remember and acknowledge.

I have subjoined Sir JOHN OGLE*'s account of the Last Charge at Nieuport battle: whom, I suppose, our author himself would have allowed (being his Lieutenant-Colonel) to bring up the rear. I have also inserted his account of the Parley at the siege of Ostend. Both were communicated to me, by the same friendly hand* [the Earl of CLARE] *that first lent me the copy* [manuscript] *of Sir* FRANCIS VERE.

And, for thy further satisfaction, I have adventured to continue the story of that Siege, from the time that our Author put up his pen, to the time that he put up his sword there: having first, by his example, taught others the way how to defend the town. . . .

I will not here mention anything concerning our author's life and extraction. The one whereof is sufficiently known: and for the other, I shall content myself with what Sir ROBERT NAUNTON *hath briefly written of him, which I have printed here before the book; which is all but a larger Commentary upon that which he hath there delivered.*

Only give me leave to bemoan a little our own loss, and the author's unhappiness in this, that his noble brother [Sir HORACE VERE], *having been in courage equal, and in hazards undivided, should leave him here to go alone. For as he must be allowed a great share in these actions recorded by his brother: so were his own services afterwards, when* General of the English, *so eminent and considerable, that they might easily have furnished another Commentary; had not his own exceeding modesty proved a step-mother to his deserved praises.*

He was a religious, wise, and valiant Commander: and, that which quartered him in the bosom of the Prince of ORANGE, *he was always successful in his enterprises; sometimes, to the admiration both of friends and enemies. Take an instance or two.*

When he took Sluis, there was one stronghold first to be taken, which he found some difficulty to overcome; and that was, the opinion of his friends of the impossibility of the enterprise. And for his enemies, SPINOLA *himself, were he now alive, would, I question not, do him the right which he did him in his lifetime: and bear witness of his gallant retreat with* 4,000 *from between his very fingers; when, with three times that number, he had grasped up the Prince and his men against the seashore.*

And because the proficiency of the Scholars was ever accounted a good argument of their Master's ability; I shall make bold, with their leaves, to give you a list of some of his [Sir HORACE, afterwards Lord VERE of Tilbury, who died in 1635].

HENRY, Earl of OXFORD.
THOMAS, Lord FAIRFAX.
Sir EDWARD VERE, Lieut.-Colonel.
Sir SIMON HARCOURT, Sergeant Major.
Sir THOMAS DUTTON, Captain.
Sir HENRY PAITON, Captain.
Sir JOHN BURROUGHS, Captain.
Sir JOHN CONYERS, Captain.
Sir THOMAS GALE, Captain.
Sir WILLIAM LOVELACE, Captain.
Sir ROBERT CAREY, Captain.
Sir JACOB ASHLEY, Captain.
Sir THOMAS CONWAY, Captain.
Sir JOHN BURLACY, Captain.
Sir THOMAS WINNE, Captain.
Sir GER[*VASE*] *HERBERT, Captain.*
Sir EDWARD HARWOOD, Captain.
Sir MICHAEL EVERID, Captain.
Sir THOMAS GATES, Captain.

Besides divers others, whose effigies [portraits] *do at once, both guard and adorn Kirby Hall in Essex; where the truly religious and honourable the Lady* VERE *doth still survive* [in 1657], *kept alive thus long by special Providence, that the present Age might more than read and remember, what was true godliness in* [at] *eighty-eight.*

As for her Lord and husband, who died long since [in 1635], *though he left no heir male behind him, to bear his name; yet hath he distributed his blood, to run in the veins of many honourable and worshipful families in England. For his daughters were, The Right Honourable, Honourable and virtuous, the Countess of* CLARE, *the Lady* TOWNSHEND *now Countess of* WESTMORELAND, *the Lady* PAULET, *the Lady* FAIRFAX, *and Mistress* WORSTENHOLME: *whose pardon I crave, for making so bold with their names; but my hope is, they will be willing to become witnesses unto their Uncle's book (though a warlike birth), and to let their names midwife it into the world.*

Thus, Reader, I have given thee a brief account of this piece, and so recommend me to Sir FRANCIS VERE!

Sir ROBERT NAUNTON, in his *Fragmenta Regalia*, p. 41.

VERE.

SIR FRANCIS VERE was of that ancient, and of the most noble, extract of the Earls of OXFORD; and it may be a question whether the Nobility of his House or the Honour of his Achievements might most commend him; but that we have our authentic rule,

Nam genus, et proavos, et quæ non fecimus ipsi
Vix ea nostra voco, &c.

For though he was an honourable Slip of that ancient Tree of Nobility, which was no disadvantage to his virtue: yet he brought more glory to the Name of VERE, than he took blood from the Family.

He was, amongst all the Queen's Swordsmen [*military and naval officers*], inferior to none; but superior to many. Of whom, it may be said, "To speak much of him, were the way to leave out somewhat that might add to his praise, and to forget more that would make to his honour."

I find not, that he came much to the Court, for he lived almost perpetually in the Camp: but when he did, none had more of the Queen's favour, and none less envied. For he seldom troubled it, with the noise and *alarms* of supplications: his way was another sort of *undermining*!

They report, that the Queen, as she loved martial men, would Court this Gentleman, as soon as he appeared in her presence: and, surely, he was a soldier of great worth and Command! 30 years in the service of the States [*United Netherlands*], and 20 years over the English in Chief, as the Queen's General. And he that had seen the battle at Nieuport, might there best have taken him, and his noble brother, the Lord of Tilbury, to the life.

THE COMMENTARIES OF Sir FRANCIS VERE.

Boemeler Waert.

IN THE year of our Lord 1589, the Count CHARLES MANSFELDT having passed part of his army into the Boemeler Waert (the rest lying in Brabant over against the island of Voorn), prepared both troops to pass into the said island, with great store of flat-bottomed boats; his artillery being placed to the best advantage to favour the enterprise.

The Count MAURICE had to impeach him, not above 800 men: the whole force that he was then able to gather together, not being above 1,500 men; whereof the most were dispersed along the river of Waal, fronting the Boemeler Waert, to impeach the enemy's passage into the Betuwe. Of these 800 men; 600 were English, of which myself had the command.

These seemed small forces to resist the enemy, who was then reckoned about 12,000 men; and therefore Count MAURICE and Count HOLLOCK [*the popular name of Count PHILIP WILLIAM HOHENLO*], one day, doing me the honour to come to my quarters, put in deliberation, Whether it were not best to abandon the place?

Whereunto, when others inclined; my opinion was, That in regard of the importance of the place, and for the reputation of Count MAURICE, this being the first enterprise wherein he commanded in person as chief; it could not be abandoned but with much reproach, without the knowledge and orders of the States General: and that therefore they were first to be informed in what state things stood; I undertaking in the meantime, the defence of the place.

Which counsel was followed; and I used such industry both in the intrenching of the island and planting artillery, that the enemy, in the end, desisted from the enterprise.

The relief of Rheinberg.

IN THE year of our Lord 1589, the town of Berg upon the Rhine, being besieged by the Marquis of WARRENBON, and distressed for want of victuals: I was sent to the Count MEURS, Governor of Gelderland, by the States, with nine companies of English.

At my coming to Arnheim, where he lay, in a Storehouse of munitions; in giving order for things necessary for his expedition, the powder was set on fire, and he so sorely burnt, that he died within few days after.

The States of that Province called me before them, told me in what extremity the town was, the importance of the place, and facility in succouring it; desiring me to proceed in the enterprise: which I did willingly assent unto; and they appointed seven companies of their own nation to join with me, which were to be left in Berg in lieu of so many other companies to be drawn out hence.

To the Count OVERSTEIN, a young Gentleman and then without any charge [*command*], as a kinsman and follower of the Count of MEURS, they gave the command of twelve companies of horse.

With these troops, we passed to the Fort Caleti, made by SKINK, over against Rees. Where, finding the carriages appointed for that purpose, ready laden with provisions; we marched towards Berg, taking our way through a heathy and open country: and so, with diligence surprising the enemy (who lay dispersed in their forts about the town), in full view of them, we put our provisions into the town; and so returned to the said Fort by Rees, the same way we had gone.

The second relieving of Rheinberg.

AFTER some days' refreshing, new provision of victuals being made, it was thought good by the States, who, in the meantime had advice how things had passed, that we should with all speed, put in more provisions.

Being advertised that the enemy gathered great forces at Brabant, under the conduct of the Count MANSFELDT, for the strait besieging of the town; this made us hasten, and withal take the ordinary and ready way near the Rhine side. But because it was shorter, and not so open as the other; and so more dangerous, if perchance the enemy with his full power should encounter us: and because there were upon it certain small redoubts held by the enemy; we took along with us two small field pieces.

When we came within two English miles of Berg, at a Castle called Loo [*afterwards the favourite residence of* WILLIAM *III.*], which stands on the side of a thick wood within musket shot of the way we were [*intended*] to take through the said wood: [it] being very narrow and hemmed in, on both sides, with exceeding thick underwood (such, as I guess, as those dangerous places of Ireland). The enemy from the Castle first shewed themselves: and then came out towards the place, along the skirt of the wood, to gall our men and horses in their passage, with such bravery, as I might well perceive they were not of the ordinary garrison.

I first sent out some few Shot [*infantry with muskets*] to beat them back; giving order to our Vanguard in the meantime, to enter the passage, the Dutch footmen to follow them, and the horsemen, and the carriages [*waggons*]: with orders to pass with all diligence to the other side of the place, and then to make a stand, until the rest of the troops were come up to them; keeping with myself, who stayed in the Rearward, 50 horse, 6 trumpeters, and all the English foot.

In the meantime, the enemy seconded [*reinforced*] their troops of Shot, to the number 400 or 500; insomuch as I was forced to turn upon greater numbers with resolution to beat them home to their castle: which was so thoroughly performed, that, afterwards, they gave us leave to pass more quietly.

When the rest of the troops were passed, I made the English enter the strait [*ravine*]: who were divided into two troops; of which I took 100 men with 6 drums, placing them in the rearward of all; myself with the 50 horse, marching betwixt them and the rest of the English footmen.

This strait is about a quarter of an English mile long: and hath, about the middle of it, another way which cometh into it from Alpen, a small town not far off.

When we were past this cross way, we might hear a great shout of men's voices redoubled twice or thrice, as the Spanish manner is, when they go to charge: but, by reason of the narrowness and crookedness of the place, had no sight of them.

I presently caused the troops to march faster; and withal gave order to the trumpeters and drums that were with me, to stand, and sound a *Charge*: whereupon there grew a great stillness amongst the enemy; who, as I afterwards understood by themselves, made a stand expecting to be charged.

In the meantime, we went as fast from them as we could, till we had gotten the plain. Then having rid[den] to the head of the troops, who were then in their long and single orders, and giving directions for the embattling of them, and the turning their faces towards the strait, and the mouth of pieces also; and so riding along the troops of English towards the place, I might see from the plain, which was somewhat high raised over the woods which were not tall, the enemy coming in great haste, over a bridge some eightscore [yards] within the strait, with ensigns [*colours*] displayed, very thickly thronged together; and, in a trice, they shewed themselves in the mouth of the strait.

My hindermost troops, which were then near the strait, were yet in their long order: and with the suddenness of the sight somewhat amazed. Insomuch that a Captain, well reputed and that had, the very same day, behaved himself very valiantly, though he saw me directing as became me, often asked What he should do? till, shortly and roughly, as his importunity and the time required I told him, that "I was never less to seek [*i.e., never had less trouble to know what to do*]!" that "he therefore should go to his place, and do as I had commanded, till further orders."

And so doubting [*fearing*] the enemy would get the plain before my troops would be thoroughly ordered to go against them; I took some of the hinder ranks of the Pikes, and some Shot, with which I made out to the strait's mouth, [at] a great pace, willing the rest to follow: whereupon the enemy made a stand, as it were doubtful to come on; and so I came presently to the push of pike with them.

Where, at the first encounter, my horse being slain under me with a blow of a pike, and falling on me so as I could not suddenly rise, I lay as betwixt both troops till our men had made the enemy give back; receiving a hurt in my leg, and divers thrusts with pikes through my garments.

It was very hard fought on both sides, till our Shot spreading themselves along the skirt of the wood, as I had before directed, flanked and sore galled the enemy: so that they could no longer endure, but were forced to give back: which they did without any great disorder, in troop. And, as they were hard followed by our men, they turned and made head manfully; which they did four several times before they broke: and, at last, they flang away their arms, and scattered asunder, thrusting themselves into the thickets; for backwards, they could not flee, the way being stopped by their own men.

I commanded the men not to disband [*scatter*], but to pursue them; and passing forward, easily discomfited the 500 horsemen, who presently left their horses, and fled into the bushes: amongst whom, it was said the Marquis of WARRENBON was in person; for the horse he was mounted on, was then taken amongst the rest.

The horsemen who fled into the thick[et]s, we followed not: but went on the straight way, till we encountered with the 24 companies of Neapolitans; who discouraged with our success, made no great resistance. We took 18 of their ensigns [*colours*], and made a great slaughter of their men, till we had recovered the bridge before mentioned of them.

My troop being small of itself, made less by this fight, and less by the covetousness of the soldiers (whereof a good part could no longer be kept from rifling the enemy and taking horses); I thought good, not to pursue the enemy further than the said bridge: where, having made a stand till our men had taken full spoil of all behind us, the enemy not once so much as shewing himself; night growing on, I made my retreat, and two hours after sunset, came with the troops into the town of Berg.

This fight was begun and ended with one of the two English troops [*battalions of infantry*], which could not exceed 400 men: the other, which Sir Oliver Lambert led, only following, and shewing itself in good order, and ready if occasion required; the Netherlanders remaining in the plain, with the horsemen and the Count Overstein.

The enemy lost about 800 men [killed]; and by an Italian Lieutenant of Horsemen, who was the only man taken alive, I understood, that Count Mansfeldt was newly, before this encounter, arrived; and had joined his forces with those of the Marquis of Warrenbon, in which were all the Spanish regiments making 220 ensigns, besides other forces: so that the whole strength was supposed to be 13,000 or 14,000 foot, and 1,200 horse, of their oldest and best soldiers.

They had intelligence of our coming, but expected us the way we had taken before; and made all speed to impeach us by cutting off this passage, sending those harquebussiers we first met with by the Castle, to entertain us in skirmish.

Presently, upon my coming to Berg, though in great pain with my wound, we fell to deliberation what was to be done. We knew the enemy's strength, and the danger we were to abide in returning: and to stay in the town were to hasten the loss of it, by eating the provisions we had brought.

Of the two, we chose rather to return. And so giving order for the change of garrison and refreshing our men, and bestowing those who were hurt, on the empty carriages; by the break of day, the morning being very foggy and misty, we set forward, in as secret manner as we could, taking the open and broader way: without sight of any enemy till about noon, when some troops of horse discovered themselves afar off, upon a very spacious heath, and gave us only the looking on. So that, without any impeachment, we arrived, that night, at the fort before Rees.

The relieving of the Castle of Litkenhooven.

IN THE year of our Lord 1590, in the Castle of Litkenhooven in the Fort of Recklinghausen, there was a garrison of the States' soldiers besieged by the people of that country, aided with some good number of the Duke of CLEVE's, the Bishops of Cologne and Paderborn's soldiers, whom they call Hanniveers.

The States gave me order, with some companies of English foot, to the number of 700 or 800, and 500 Horse, to go to the relief of the said Castle: which I accepted, marching with all possible speed, in good hope to have surprised them at unawares. Arriving there one morning by break of day; I found the chief troop was dislodged, and that they [*the garrison*] wrought hard upon a fort before the entry of the Castle in which they had left good store of men.

I did expect to have found them without any entrenchment, and therefore had brought no provision of artillery or scaling ladders: without the which, it seemed very dangerous and difficult to carry it by assault. [The entrenchment] was reared of a good height with earth, and then with gabions thereupon, of six feet high, which made it almost unmountable: and to besiege them, I had no provision of victuals. So that I was to return without making of any attempt; or to attempt in a manner against reason: which notwithstanding, I resolved to adventure.

And therefore, dividing the English troops into eight parts, I conveyed them as secretly as I could, so as two of these troops might readily assault every corner of the said Fort, being a square of four small bulwarks [*bastions or batteries*], but with a distance betwixt the troops: to give on each corner with a signal of drums, at which, the first four troops should go to the assault; and another signal to the other four troops to second [*support*], if need required.

While this was in doing, I sent a drum, to summon them of the Fort to yield: who sent me word, "They would first see my artillery."

I saw by their fashion, there was no good to be done by entreaty: yet to amuse them, I sent them word, "The artillery was not yet arrived. If they made me stay the coming of it, I would give them no conditions!"

They answered, "That I should do my worst!"

At the very instant of my drum's return, I gave the signal, and the troops speedily gave upon the Fort, as I had appointed them. Though they did their utmost endeavours, they did find more resistance than they were able to overcome; nevertheless, I gave them no second [*reinforcement*] till I might perceive those within had spent their ready powder in their furnitures. At which time, I gave the second signal; which was well and willingly obeyed, and gave such courage to the first troops, that the assault was more eager on all hands; insomuch that one soldier helping another, some got to the top of the rampires [*ramparts*]: at which, the enemy gave back, so that the way became more easy for others to climb to the top; and so finally, the place was forced, and all the men put to the sword, being in number 350, all chosen men, with the loss and hurting of about 80 of my men.

The place thus succoured, and my men refreshed for some few days, I returned homewards: and found in my way, that Burick a small town of Cleve, and a little fort on that side the Rhine, were in the meantime surprised.

The enemy then held a Royal Fort not far from Wesel, which served to favour the passage of his forces over the Rhine. This place, I understood by those of Wesel, to be slenderly provided of victuals, so as they had but to serve them from hand to mouth, out of the town; and that their store of powder was small.

I knew the service would be acceptable to the States, if I could take that Piece from the enemy; and therefore resolved to do what lay in me.

I first appointed a guard of horse and foot to hinder their recourse to the town, for their provisions.

Then passing into the town of Burick; with such stuff as I could get on a sudden, and such workmen, I began to make ladders, so as, the night following, I had forty ladders in readiness, upon which two men [at a time] might go in front. For I being so weak, and the enemy having the alarm of my being abroad, I was to expect their coming: so as it was not for me to linger upon the starving of those of the Fort.

With this provision, I resolved to give a *scalado* to the Fort: which as it was high of rampire; so had it had neither water in the ditch, nor pallisado to hinder us.

The Fort was spacious, capable of [holding] 1,500 men, and had had four very royal Bulwarks [*bastions*]; upon one of which, I purposed to give an attempt, and only false alarms on the other quarters of the Fort. And to this end, for avoiding confusion in the carriage, rearing, planting, and scaling; as also for the more speedy and round execution: I appointed eight men to every ladder, to bear, plant, and mount the same; whereof four were Shot, and four Pikes, one of either sort to mount a-front.

And being come near the Fort, in a place convenient to range the men; they were divided into two parts, and ranged a-front [*in line*]; with commandment, upon a signal given, the one half to give upon one face of the bulwark, the other upon the other: which they did accordingly, and gave a furious attempt, mounting the ladders and fighting at the top of them; the enemy being ready to receive us. But by reason many of the ladders (which were made, as I said, in haste and of such stuff as could be gotten on a sudden) were not of sufficient strength: they broke with the weight and stirring of the men.

Seeing no likelihood to prevail, and the day now growing on; I caused our men to retire, and to bring away with them their ladders that were whole: with no great harm done to our men, by reason the enemy, being diverted by the false alarms, did not flank us; neither if they had played from the Flanks [*bastions*] with small shot, could they have done any great hurt, by reason of the distance. The most hurt we had, was with blows on the head from the place we attempted, both with weapons and stones: for the journey being long, to ease the soldiers, they had brought forth no morions [*helmets*].

I therefore, purposing not to give over the enterprise, provided headpieces for them in the town of Wesel, and used such diligence that, before the next morning, I was again furnished with ladders, and in greater number. For I had persuaded the horsemen, that were well armed for the purpose with their pistols, to take some ladders also, and be ready to give the *scalado* in the same manner: but somewhat later, for even then day began to break; which not giving us time to persevere in the attempt, was the only hindrance of our victory.

For our Shot having orders, when they came to the top of the ladders, not to enter, but taking the top of the wall for a breast [work] and safeguard, to shoot at the enemy fighting at the work side and standing in the hollow of the bulwark, till the same were cleared of defendants, for to enter more assuredly: which manner of assaulting, though it be not ordinary, yet well considered, is of wonderful advantage. For having the outside of both the faces of the Bulwark not flanked as I said before, on their backs, which in the darkness of the night, and for the alarms given on the other parts, they could not see or intend.

And in this manner having galled and driven many of the enemy from the wall; and being in a manner ready to enter: day came upon us, and the enemy having discovered us from the other flanks, turned both small and great shot against us; so as we were forced to retire, carrying our ladders with us, with less loss than the day before in the fight, though more in the retreat by reason of the daylight.

The same day, I provided more ladders, purposing, the next morning, to try fortune again: when, in the evening, the Governor of the Fort, by a drum [*drummer*] wrote me a letter complaining that, against the ordinary proceedings of men of war, I assaulted before I summoned: and the drum in mine ear told me, that "if I would but do them the honour to shew them any piece of ordnance, I should quickly have the Fort!"

By which drawing of theirs, I perceived they were in fear, and in discretion thought it meeter to make my advantage thereof, by drawing them to yield, than to despair them, to my greater loss, by further attempting to carry them by force.

And so, taking a piece out of the town of Burick, I planted the same before morning; and, by break of day, sent a trumpet to summon them to yield.

Which they assented to, so they might pass away with their arms: which I granted.

And so they came forth, the same morning; two companies of Almains [*Germans*] and two half companies of Italians: being nearly as strong in number as those that attempted them; for besides the English, I used none, but some few horsemen.

Most of their officers were hurt and slain, and of the soldiers, more than of mine.

This is true, and therefore let it be thought, that howsoever this attempt may seem rash with the ordinary proceedings of other Captains; yet, notwithstanding, I was confident upon a certain and infallible discourse of reason.

In the place, I found four double-cannon, with a pretty store of ammunition and victuals.

The same night, I and the troops were countermanded by the States: but I left the place with some guard and a better store of necessaries, before my departure.

The surprise of Zutphen Sconce.

IN THE year of our Lord 1591, I lying then at Doesburg, with the English forces; the Count MAURICE wrote unto me, that, by a certain day, he would be, with his forces, before Zutphen, to besiege the same, willing me, the night before, with my troops of horse and foot of that country [*Dutch troops*], to beset the town on the same side of the river on which it standeth.

On the same side, those of the town held a Fort, which made my Lord of LEICESTER lose many men and much time before he could get it.

The Fort I thought necessary to take from the enemy, before he had knowledge of our purpose to besiege him: and because I wanted force to work it by open means, I put this sleight following in practice.

I chose a good number of lusty and hardy young soldiers, the most of which, I apparelled like the country women of those parts; the rest, like the men: and gave to some, baskets; to others packs, and such burdens as the people usually carry to the market; with pistols, short swords, and daggers under their garments. Willing them, by two or three in a company, by break of day, to be at the ferry at Zutphen, which is just against the Fort, as if they stayed for them; for besides the English, I used none, but some few horsemen.

Most of their officers were hurt and slain, and of the soldiers, more than of mine.

This is true, and therefore let it be thought, that howsoever this attempt may seem rash with the ordinary proceedings of other Captains; yet, notwithstanding, I was confident upon a certain and infallible discourse of reason.

In the place, I found four double-cannon, with a pretty store of ammunition and victuals.

The same night, I and the troops were countermanded by the States: but I left the place with some guard and a better store of necessaries, before my departure.

The surprise of Zutphen Sconce.

IN THE year of our Lord 1591, I lying then at Doesburg, with the English forces; the Count MAURICE wrote unto me, that, by a certain day, he would be, with his forces, before Zutphen, to besiege the same, willing me, the night before, with my troops of horse and foot of that country [*Dutch troops*], to beset the town on the same side of the river on which it standeth.

On the same side, those of the town held a Fort, which made my Lord of LEICESTER lose many men and much time before he could get it.

The Fort I thought necessary to take from the enemy, before he had knowledge of our purpose to besiege him: and because I wanted force to work it by open means, I put this sleight following in practice.

I chose a good number of lusty and hardy young soldiers, the most of which, I apparelled like the country women of those parts; the rest, like the men: and gave to some, baskets; to others packs, and such burdens as the people usually carry to the market; with pistols, short swords, and daggers under their garments. Willing them, by two or three in a company, by break of day, to be at the ferry at Zutphen, which is just against the Fort, as if they stayed for escape. He was excepted in the Composition, taken from them, and executed as he well deserved, not for his first, but his second offence.

The defeat given to the Duke of PARMA at Knodsenburg Fort.

IN THE year of our Lord 1591, whilst the Count MAURICE was busied in Friesland, and with good success took many forts, as Delfziel, and others about Groeningen, the Duke of PARMA passed with his army into the Betuwe, and besieged the Fort on that side the river, upon the ferry to Nimeguen.

Whereupon the States countermanded the Count MAURICE, with their forces; who, being come to Arnheim, encamped in the Betuwe, right over against that town.

The Duke still continuing his siege, the States, who were then present at Arnheim (desirous us to hinder his purpose, if it were possible) in their Assembly, to which I was called with the Count MAURICE, propounded the matter, and insisted to have something exploited [*achieved*]: though we had laid before them the advantage the enemy had of us, in the number of his men, the strength of his encamping, as well by the site of the country as entrenchments. So as much time was spent, and the Council dissolved without resolution upon any special enterprise: albeit, in general, the Count MAURICE and the men of war agreed to do their utmost endeavour, for the annoying and hindering of the enemy.

I had observed by the enemy's daily coming with good troops of horse, and forcing of our scouts [*videttes*], that they were likely to bite at any bait that was cunningly laid for them; and therefore, having informed myself of the ways and passages to their army, and projected with myself a probable plot to do some good on them, I brake the same to the Count MAURICE: who liked my device well, and recommended to me the execution thereof; giving me the troops I demanded, which were 1,200 foot and 500 horse.

The distance betwixt the two armies was about four or five English miles; to the which there lay two ready ways serving for the intercourse betwixt Arnheim and Nimeguen: the one a dike or causeway which was narrower, and most used in winter, by reason of the lowness and miriness of the country; the other larger [*broader*]: both hemmed in with overgrown ditches and deep ditches.

Nearly half a mile from the quarters, this causeway was to be passed to come to the other way, which led to the main quarters of the enemy, where most of his horse lay. About two-thirds of the way from our camp, there was a bridge.

To this bridge I marched early in the morning, sending forthwith towards the enemy's camp 200 light and well-mounted horse, with orders to beat [*drive in*] the guards of the enemy's horse, even to their very quarters, and guards of foot; to take such spoil and prisoners as lay ready in their way: and so to make their retreat, if they were followed, more speedily; otherwise at an ordinary marching pace.

In the meantime I divided my footmen into two parts, whereof, one I laid near the hither side of the bridge, in a place very covert; the other, a quarter of a mile behind: and in the rearward of them, the rest of my horse.

If the enemy came in the tail of our horse (whom for that purpose I had appointed, as beforesaid, to come more leisurely, that the enemy might have time to get to horse), I knew they could bring no footmen: and therefore was resolved to receive betwixt my troops of foot, all the horsemen they could send. But if they pursued not our men in the heat, I judged they would either come with good numbers of both kinds of men ordered [*in order*], or not at all. And if they came with good advice, that they would rather seek to cut off my passage near home, by the causeway and higher way, than to follow me directly. For the better preventing whereof, the Count MAURICE himself, with a choice part of the horse and foot of the army, was to attend at the crossway to favour my retreat.

My horsemen, about noon, gave the enemy the alarm; and according to their directions, made their retreat, no enemy appearing. Whereupon I also retired with the rest of the troops till I came to the crossway, where I found the Count MAURICE with his troops.

In the head of which, towards the way of the causeway, with some distance betwixt his troops and mine, I made a stand in a little field by the side of the way, where they were at covert.

We had not been here half-an-hour, but our scouts brought word the enemy were at hand: which Count MAURICE's horsemen hearing, without any orders, as every one could get foremost, to the number of 700 or 800, they made with all speed towards the enemy.

I presumed, and said, "They would return faster, and in more disorder!" as it fell out. For the enemy coming as fast towards them, but in better order, put them presently in rout: and the greater the number was, the more was the amazement and confusion. Thus they passed by us, with the enemy at their heels, laying on them.

I knew not what other troops they had at hand, nor what discouragements this sight might put into the minds of our men; and therefore (whereas I purposed to have let the enemy pass, if this unlooked disorder had not happened amongst our horsemen) I shewed my troops on their flanks, and galled them both with Shot and Pikes; so that they not only left pursuing their chase, but turned their backs. Which our horsemen perceiving, followed, and thus revenged themselves to the full; for they never gave over until they had wholly defeated the troop, which was of 800 horse: of which, they brought betwixt 200 and 300 prisoners, whereof divers were Captains, as Don ALPHONSO D'AVALOS, FRADILLA, and others; with divers Cornets, and about 500 horses.

This defeat so troubled the Duke of PARMA, that, though so forward in his siege, and having filled part of the ditch of the Fort, he retired his army thence, and passed the river of Waal a little above Nimeguen, with more dishonour than in any action that he had undertaken in these wars.

The Calis [Cadiz] *Journey.*

IN THE year of our Lord 1596, I was sent for into England, at that time when the journey to the Coast of Spain was resolved on: which because of the taking of Calis, was, after, commonly called the Calis [*Cadiz*] Journey.

I returned speedily into the Low Countries, with Letters of Credence from Her Majesty, to acquaint them with Her Majesty's purpose, and to hasten the preparation of the shipping they had already promised to attend Her Majesty's Fleet in those seas: withal to let them know Her Majesty's desire to have 2,000 of her own subjects, as well of those in their pay as her own, to be employed in that action, and to be conducted by me, to the Earl of ESSEX and the Lord Admiral of England [*Lord* HOWARD *of Effingham*], Generals of that action, by joint Commission.

Whereunto the States assented: and I (according to my instructions given me in that behalf), by the time appointed, shipped and transported to the *rendezvous* which was assigned me before Boulogne on the coast of France, by reason that Calais in France was then besieged by the Cardinal ALBERT.

Upon that occasion, it was resolved to have employed this army for the succour and relief thereof; but coming into that road [*Boulogne*], I found no shipping of ours: and understanding that Calais was yielded the day before, I crossed the sea to Dover, where I found the whole Fleet, and the Generals; who received me with much joy and favour, being then, though far unworthy of so weighty a charge, chosen to supply the place of Lieutenant General [*second in command*] of the Army, by the name and title of Lord Marshal.

The Fleet set sail shortly after, and my Lord of ESSEX, leaving his own ship, embarked himself in the *Rainbow* with myself and some few of his ordinary attendant servants; of purpose, as I suppose, to confer with me at the full and at ease, of his Journey.

After two days' sailing, his Lordship landed at Beachim, near Rye, with divers other noblemen that he had, attending him so far on his Journey.

He took me along with him to the Court; and thence despatched me to Plymouth, whither most of the [other] land forces were to march, to see them lodged, provided with necessaries, trained, and ordered [*marshalled into companies, &c.*]; which I did accordingly: to the great contentment of the Generals, when, at their coming, they saw the readiness of the men, which were then exercised before them.

During the stay of this Army near Plymouth, which (by reason of the contrariety of wind) was nearly a month, it pleased my Lord of ESSEX to give me much countenance, and to have me always near him; which drew upon me no small envy, insomuch as some open jars fell out betwixt Sir WALTER RALEIGH, then Rear-Admiral of the Navy, Sir CONNIERS CLIFFORD, Serjeant-Major General of the Army, and myself: which the General qualified for the time, and ordered that in all meetings at land, I should have the precedence of Sir WALTER RALEIGH; and he, of me at sea.

[As to] Sir CONNIERS CLIFFORD, though there were grudging, there could be no competition. Yet being a man of haughty stomach, and not of the greatest government or experience in martial discipline, lest ignorance or will might mislead him in the execution of his Office, and to give a rule to the rest of the High Officers, who were chosen rather for favour, than for long continuance in service; to the better directing of them in their duties, as also for the more readiness in the General himself, to judge and distinguish upon all occasions of controversy: I propounded to my Lord of ESSEX, as a thing most necessary, the setting down in writing what belonged properly to every Office in the field. Which notion his Lordship liked well, and at several times in the morning, his Lordship and myself being together, he, with his own hand, wrote what my industry and experience had made me able to deliver: which was afterwards copied, and delivered severally to the Officers; and took so good effect that no question arose in that behalf, during the Journey. [*It is quite clear that VERE was used to teach this army the Art of War, as he had learnt it by actual experience in the Netherlands.*]

The wind serving, and the troops shipped, I embarked in the foresaid *Rainbow*, as Vice-Admiral of my Lord of ESSEX's Squadron.

The one and twentieth day after, being as I take it, the 1st of July [*O.S.*], the Fleet arrived early in the morning before Calis-Malis [*the city of Cadiz*], and shortly after, came to an anchor as near the Caletta as the depth would suffer us.

In the mouth of the bay, thwart of the rocks called *Los puercos*, there lay, to our judgement, 40 or 50 tall ships; whereof four were of the King's greatest and warlikest galleons, eighteen merchant ships of the West Indian Fleet outward bound and richly laden; and the rest were private merchant ships.

Because it was thought these could not escape us in putting to sea, the first project of landing our men in the Caletta went on: and so the troops appointed for that purpose, were embarked in our barges and long-boats. But the wind blowing hard, the landing was thought too dangerous; the rather for that the enemy shewed themselves on the shore, with good troops of horse and foot.

Notwithstanding, in hope the weather would calm, the men were still kept in the boats, at the ships' sterns.

This day, the Generals met not together: but the Lord Admiral had most of the sea officers aboard with him, as the Lord of ESSEX had those for land service; and Sir WALTER RALEIGH was sent to and fro betwixt them with messages. So that, in the end, it was resolved and agreed upon, to put, the next tide, into the Bay: and after the defeating of the enemy's fleet, to land our men between the town [*Cadiz*] and Punthal; without setting down any more particular directions for the execution thereof.

I then told my Lord of ESSEX that mine was a floaty [*light of draught*] ship, and well appointed for that service, that, "therefore, if his Lordship pleased! I was desirous to put in before his Lordship, and the other ships of greater burden." To which his Lordship answered suddenly, that "In any case, I should not go in before him!"

With this, I and the rest of the officers went to our ships, to prepare ourselves.

I took my company of soldiers out of the boats into my ship: for their more safety, and better strengthening of my ship.

And because we had anchored more to the north of the Fleet, more astern, and to the leeward of the Fleet as the wind then blew, than any other ship; I thought to recover these disadvantages by a speedier losing of my anchor than the rest. And, therefore, not attending to the General's signal and warning, so soon as the tide began to favour my purpose, I fell to weighing my anchor.

But the wind was so great, and the billows so high, that the capstan, being too strong for my men, cast them against the ship's side, and spoiled [*hurt*] many of them; so that after many attempts to wind up the anchor, I was forced to cut cable in the hawse. When I was under sail, I plied only to windward, lying off and on from the mouth of the Bay to the sea, which lieth near at hand, east and west: by that means gathering nearer to the Fleet.

The Lord THOMAS HOWARD, Vice-Admiral of the Fleet, with some few other ships, set sail also, beating off and on before the mouth of the Bay; but the General, and most of the Fleet kept their anchors still.

The tide being far spent, loth to be driven again to the leeward of the Fleet, and to endanger another cable, and perchance the ship itself on that shore, which was flat and near; and the benefit of entering the Bay with the first, which was not the least consideration: I resolved to put into the mouth of the Bay as near to the enemy's fleet as I could without engaging fight, and there to cast anchor by them; which I did accordingly. So that they made a shot or two at me; but since I made no answer, they left off shooting.

I was no sooner come to anchor, but the Generals set sail, and the rest of the Fleet; and bare directly towards me, where they also anchored.

It was now late ere the Flag of "Council!" was shewn in my Lord Admiral's ship; whither my Lord of ESSEX and the rest of the Officers repaired; and there it was resolved, the next morning, with the tide to enter the Bay, and board the Spanish ships, if they abode it. And ships of ours were appointed to begin this service, some to keep the channel and midst of the Bay; and others more floaty, to bear nearer the town to intercept the shipping that should retire that way, and hinder the galleys from beating on the flanks of our great ships.

I was not allotted with my ship to any special service or attendance. My desire was great, having till that time been a stranger to actions at sea, to appear willing to embrace the occasions that offered themselves; and therefore wound my ship up to her anchor, to be the more ready to set sail in the morning with the beginning of the flood.

The Spanish ships set sail, and made to the bottom of the Bay, rather driving than sailing; our ships following as fast as they could.

As the Spanish ships loosed from their anchors and made from us; their galleys, seventeen in number, under the favour [*cover*] of the town, made towards us ranged in good order. My ship (as before said) was floaty, stored with ordnance, and proper for that service; which made me hasten towards them, without staying for any company. Indeed, my readiness was such, by reason of my riding with my anchor a-pike [*taut*], that no other ship could come near me by a great distance. So I entered fight with them alone, and so galled them with my ordnance, which was cannon and demi-cannon, that they gave back, keeping still in order and in fight with me, drawing as near the town as they could: and with purpose, as I thought, as our ships thrust further into the Bay, to have fallen upon our smaller ships in the tail of the whole Fleet; and having made a hand with them, so to have put to the seaward of us the better to annoy us, and save themselves from being locked up.

Wherein to prevent them, I made toward the shore, still sounding with our leads till the ordnance of the town might reach me, and I the shore, with mine. Insomuch as I put them from under the town, and took certain ships which rode there at anchor forsaken of their men; and followed them, continuing fight till they came under the Fort of the Punthal: where, thwart the bottom of the Bay, which was not broad, lay their four great ships, with a pretty distance betwixt them, spreading the breadth of the channel, and at an anchor; and were now in hot fight of ordnance with our Fleet.

I was nearer Punthal and the shore of Calis by much, than any ship of the Fleet, and further advanced into the Bay. So that now growing within shot of the fort which lay on my right hand; and in like distance to the galleons on the left hand, and having the galleys ahead of me, betwixt them all, I was plied with shot on all sides very roundly: yet I resolved to go on, knowing I had good seconds [*support*] and that "many hands would make light work." But my company, either wiser or more afraid than myself, on a sudden, unlooked by me, let fall the anchor; and by no means, would be commanded or intreated to weigh it again.

In the meantime, Sir WALTER RALEIGH came upon my left side, with his ship, and a very little ahead of me, cast his anchor; as did also the Generals, and as many of the Fleet as the channel would bear: so that the shooting of ordnance was great; and they held us good talk, by reason their ships lay thwart with their broadsides toward us, and most of us, right ahead, so that we could use but our chasing pieces.

I sent my boat aboard Sir WALTER RALEIGH, to fasten a hawse to wind my ship, which was loosed soon after my boat was put off.

About me, the galleons let slip cable at the hawse, and with the topsails wended and drew towards the shore on the left hand of the Bay; and the Indian Fleet with the rest of the shipping did the like, more within the Bay.

It was no following of them with our great ships [*which were too deep in the water*]; and therefore I went aboard my Lord of ESSEX, whose ship lay towards that side of the channel, to see what further orders would be given.

At my coming aboard, the galleons were run on ground near the shore; and their men, some in their boats, began to forsake their ships.

I was then bold to say to my Lord of ESSEX, that "it was high time to send his small shipping to board them: for otherwise they would be fired by their own men." Which his Lordship found reasonable, and presently sent his directions accordingly. And in the meantime, sent Sir WILLIAM CONSTABLE with some long-boats full of soldiers;

which his Lordship had towed at his stern, since the first embarking, to have landed at the Caletta.

But notwithstanding he made all haste possible, before he could get to the galleons, two of them were set on fire; and the other two, by this means saved and taken, were utterly forsaken of their men, who retired through the fens, to Puerto de Santa Maria.

The Spanish Fleet thus set on ground, the prosecution of that victory was committed to, and willingly undertaken by, the sea forces by a principal Officer of the Fleet.

And because longer delay would increase the difficulty of landing our forces, by the resort of more people to Calis, it was resolved forthwith to attempt the putting of our men on shore; and to that end, commandment was given that all men appointed for that purpose should be embarked in the long-boats: and that my Lord of ESSEX should first land with those men which could be disembarked; and then my Lord Admiral to second [*support*], and repair to the General, who, the better to be known, would put out his flag in his boat.

The troops that were first to land, were the regiments of the General, my own, and those of Sir CHRISTOPHER BLUNT, Sir THOMAS GERRARD, and Sir CONNIERS CLIFFORD.

On the right hand, in a even front, with a competent distance betwixt the boats, were ranged the two regiments first named; the other three on the left: so that every regiment and company of men were sorted, together with their Colonels and chief officers in nimble pinnaces, some in the head of the boats, some at the stern, to keep good order. The General himself with his boat, in which it pleased him to have me attend him, and some other boats full of Gentlemen Adventurers and choice men to attend his person, rowed a pretty distance before the rest: whom, at the signal given with a drum from his boat, the rest were to follow according to the measure and time of the sound of the said drum, which they were to observing in the dipping of the oars; and to that end, there was a general silence as well of warlike instruments as otherwise.

Which order being duly followed, the troops came, all together, to the shore betwixt Punthal and Calis; and were landed, and several regiments embattled in an instant, without any encounter at all: the Spaniards, who, all the day before, shewed themselves with troops of horse and foot on that part, as resolved to impeach our landing, being clean retired towards the town.

The number of the first disembarking was not fully 2,000 men; for divers companies of those regiments, that had put themselves into their ships again, could not be suddenly ready, by reason the boats to land them, belonged to other great ships.

Calis on that side was walled, as it were, in a right line thwart the land, so as the sea, on both sides [*ends*] did beat on the foot of the wall: which strength, together with the populousness of the town (in which, besides the great concourse of Gentlemen and others, upon the discovery of our Fleet, and alarm of our ordnance; there was an ordinary garrison of soldiers) had taken from us all thought of forcing it without battery. And therefore, being landed, we advanced with the troops to find a convenient place to encamp, till my Lord Admiral, with the rest of the forces, and the ordnance were landed.

Being advanced with the troops half the breadth of the neck of the land, which in that place is about half a mile over, we might perceive that, all along the seashore on the other side of this neck of land, men on horseback and foot repaired to the town: which intercourse it was thought necessary to cut off. And, therefore, because the greatest forces of the enemy were to come from the land; it was resolved on to lodge the better part of the army in the narrowest of the neck, which, near Punthal, is not broader than an ordinary harquebus shot.

To which strait, Sir CONNIERS CLIFFORD was sent with three regiments, viz., his own, Sir CHRISTOPHER BLUNT's, and Sir THOMAS GERRARD's, there to make a stand, to impeach the Spaniards from coming to the town, till he received further orders for the quartering and lodging of his men.

Which done, the Lord General, with the other two regiments and his Company of Adventurers, which was of about 250 worthy Gentlemen; in all, not fully a 1,000 men, advanced nearer the town, the better to discover the whole ground before it.

And as we approached afar off, we might perceive the enemy

standing in battle under the favour of the town, with cornets [*standards of the cavalry*] and ensigns [*colours of the infantry*] displayed; thrusting out some loose horse and foot towards us, as it were to procure a skirmish.

I, marking their fashion, conceived hope of a speedier gaining the town than we intended, and where then about; and said to his Lordship, at whose elbow I attended, that "those men he saw standing in battle before the town would shew and make way for us into the town that night, if they were well handled." And at the instant, I propounded the means: which was, to carry our troops as near and covertly as might be, towards the town; and to see, by some attempt, if we could draw them to fight further from the town, that we might send them back with confusion and disorder, and so have the cutting of them in pieces in the town ditch, or enter it by the same way they did.

His Lordship liked the project, and left the handling thereof to me.

I presently caused the troops to march towards the other side of the neck of land, because the ordinary and ready way to the town lay on that side, low and embayed to the foot of the hilly downs, so as troops might march very closely from the view of the town.

Then I chose out 200 men, which were committed to the conduct of Sir JOHN WINGFIELD, a right valiant Knight, with orders that he should march on roundly to the enemy where they stood in battle, and to charge and drive to their Battles the skirmishers: but if the enemy in gross proffered a charge, he should make a hasty and fearful retreat, to their judgement, the way he had gone, till he met with his seconds that followed him; and then to turn short, and with the greatest speed and fury he could, to charge the enemy.

The seconds were of 300 men, led, as I remember, by Sir MATTHEW MORGAN, who were to follow the first troops at a good distance and so as both of them, till the enemy were engaged, might not at once appear to them; and to advance with all diligence when the troops before them did retire, to meet them, charge the enemy, and enter the town with them pesle mesle [*pell mell*].

With the rest of the forces, his Lordship and I followed.

The place served well for our purpose, being covert [*hid*

with trees] and of no advantage for their horsemen ; and the directions were so well observed, that the enemy were engaged in following our first troop before they discovered the rest. And so in hope and assurance of victory, being, beyond expectation, lively encountered ; they fled in disorder towards the town, so nearly followed of our men, that most of the horsemen forsook their horses, and saved themselves, some by the gates, others clambering over the walls, as did also their footmen ; our men following them at the heels to the very gate, which they found shut against them, and men standing over it and upon the walls to resist us.

The ditch was very hollow but dry. Out of which was raised a massy rampire, with two round Half-Bulwarks, the one towards the one sea, the other towards the other ; for height and thickness, in their perfection, but not steeped and scarped : so as it was very mountable, and lay close to the old wall of the town, which somewhat overtopped it no higher than, in many places, a man might reach with his hand.

To the top of the rampire, our men climbed ; who being, for the most part, old and experienced soldiers, of the Bands [*regiments*] I brought out of the Low Countries, boldly attempted to climb the wall, from which they beat with their shot, the defendants ; wanting no encouragements that good example of the chiefs could give them, the General himself being as forward as any.

Whilst it was hard stroven and fought on that side, I sent a Captain and countryman [*of the same county, Essex*] of mine, called UPSHER, with some few men alongst the ditch, to see what guard was held along the wall towards the Bay-ward ; and whether any easier entrance might be made that way or not, willing him to bring or send me word : which he did accordingly, though the messenger came not unto me.

He found so slender a guard, that he entered the town with those few men he had ; which the enemy perceiving, fled from the walls, and our men entered as fast on the other side.

My Lord of ESSEX was one of the first that got over the walls, followed by the soldiers as the place would give them leave ; and such was their fury, being once entered, that as they got in scatteringly, so they hasted towards the town, without gathering [into] any strong and orderly body of men as in such case is requisite, or once endeavouring to open the gate for more convenient entry for the rest of the troops.

I, therefore, foreseeing what might ensue of this confusion, held the third body of the men together; and with much ado, brake open the gate, by which I entered the town: and so keeping the way that leads from the gate towards the town, joined to my foot those men I met withal, scattered here and there.

Not far from the Market Place, I found my Lord of ESSEX at a stand with 40 or 50 men; whence I might see some few of the enemy in the Market Place, which made me advance towards them, without attending any commandment: who, upon my approaching, retired themselves into the Town House; whither I pursued them, broke open the gates, and, after good resistance made by the Spaniards in the upper rooms of the House, became master of it.

In which, I left a guard, and went down into the Market Place, and found my Lord of ESSEX at the Town House door. I humbly entreated his Lordship, to make that place secure, and give me leave to scour and assure the rest of the town: which I did accordingly.

And though I was but slackly and slenderly followed, by reason of our men's greediness for spoil: yet such Spaniards as I found making head, and coming towards the Market Place, I drove back into the Fort St. Philip and the Abbey of St. Francis.

Those of the Abbey yielded, to the number of 200 Gentlemen and others; and being disarmed were put into a chapel; and there left guarded. Those of St. Philip, it being now in the evening, cried to us that "in the morning, they would render the place." Before which also having put a guard: and understanding by some prisoners that there was no other place of strength but the Old Town near the Market Place; I repaired to my Lord of ESSEX, whom I found in the Market Place, and the Lord Admiral with him.

And after I had made report upon what terms things stood, and where I had been: I went to the said Old Town to visit the guards which were commanded by Sir EDWARD CONWAY, with part of the forces landed with my Lord Admiral; and from thence, to that part of the town where we entered.

And thus all things in good assurance, I returned to the Market Place; where the rest of the forces were, being held together to be readily employed upon all occasions.

Their Lordships went up to the Town House, and there gave GOD thanks for the victory: and, afterwards, all wounded and bloody as he was, yet undressed [*i.e.*, *his wounds*], gave the honour of knighthood to Sir SAMUEL BAGNALL, for his especial merit and valour in that day's service.

The loss was not very great on either side: for as the Spanish troops that stood ordered without the walls, got into the town confusedly and disorderly before we could mingle with them; so everyone, as he was counselled by fear or courage, provided for his own safety, the most flying to the Old Town and Castle.

Those that made head after the first entrance, being scattered here and there; our men as they followed with more courage than order, so encountered them in the like scattering manner, falling straight to handstrokes: so that it seemed rather an inward tumult and town fray than a fight of so mighty nations.

The next day, the Old Town and the Fort of St. Philip were delivered unto us: and the people that were in them, except some principal prisoners, were suffered to depart; with great courtesy shewed, especially to the women of the better sort. There went out of the town, Gentlemen and others, likely men to bear arms, betwixt 4,000 and 5,000. The brunt of this exploit was borne with less than 1,000 men.

We could have no help of Sir CONNIERS CLIFFORD; who mistaking his directions, went, with his troops to the bridge called Punto Zuarro, about three leagues distant: and my Lord Admiral, notwithstanding his Lordship used all possible diligence in the landing of his men, arrived not till we were, in a manner, full masters of the town.

It was long disputed whether the town should be held or not. I offered with 4,000 men, to defend it till Her Majesty's pleasure might be known. The Lord of ESSEX seemed to affect to remain there in person: which the rest of the Council would not assent to, but [determined] rather to abandon the town and set it on fire.

Which we did, about fourteen days after the taking of it.

I got there, three prisoners worth 10,000 ducats [£3,000 =

£15,000 *now*]. One of which was a Churchman [*ecclesiastic*], and President of the Contractation of the Indies: the other two, were ancient Knights, called Don PEDRO DE HERERA and Don GERONIMO DE AVALLOS.

In the meantime, whether of design and set purpose or negligence, the Indian Fleet, being unseized on by those who had undertaken it; some of the prisoners of the town dealt [*negotiated*] with the Generals to have those ships and their lading set at ransom. Whereupon, they had conference with the Generals, divers times, till the said ships were set on fire by the Spaniards themselves: in which was lost, by their own confession, to the worth of 12,000,000 [*i.e., ducats* = £3,600,000 = *about* £18,000,000 *now*] of merchandise.

The troops being embarked, the Generals met and consulted upon their next exploit. It was long insisted on, to put to sea, and lie to intercept the West Indian Fleet, which commonly, at that time of the year, arriveth on the coast of Spain. But the scarceness of our victuals overthrew that purpose: and resolution was taken to sail towards England; and on our way to visit the ports of that coast, and so to spoil and destroy the shipping.

And so, first, we made towards Ferrol, a good town and Bishop's see of Portugal [*which country at this time belonged to Spain see Vol. III. p.* 13]: to which, by water, there was no safe entrance for our shipping; the town lying better than a league from the sea, served with a narrow creek, though a low and marshy bottom.

For the destroying of such shipping as might be in this creek, as also for the wasting of the country adjoining, and the town itself, which though it were great and populous, was unfenced with walls; it was thought meet to land the forces in a bay, some three leagues distant from the town, and so to march thither.

Which was done; the town forsaken by the inhabitants, was taken by us. Our men being sent into the country, brought good store of provisions for the refreshing of the army. The artillery we found, was conveyed into our ships. And we, after five or six days' stay, returned to our ships, the way we came.

The regiments embattled marched at large, in a triple front, in right good order; which was so much the more strange and commendable, the men, for the most part, being new: and once ranged, having little further help of directions from the high Officers; who were all unmounted, and for the great heat, not able to perform on foot the ordinary service in such cases belonging to their charges.

The troops embarked, we made towards the Groine [*Corunna*], and looked into the Bay, but the wind blowing from the sea, it was thought dangerous to put in, and therefore, victuals daily growing more scant so that in some ships there was already extreme want, it was resolved to hasten to our coast: and so, about the midst of August, we arrived in the Downs, near Sandwich.

My Lord of ESSEX having taken land in the West parts [of England], to be with more speed at the Court, left orders with me, for the dissolving of the land forces and shipping; and sending back of the English forces into the Low Countries.

At this parting, there arose much strife betwixt the mariners and the soldiers, about the dividing of the spoil. For the mariners, envying and repining at the soldiers, who, as it fell out, had gotten most, purloined and detained their chests and packs of baggage, perforce! insomuch that, to satisfy the soldiers, I went aboard my Lord Admiral to desire of his Lordship redress; who promised to take order therein.

But some other principal Officers of the Fleet shewing themselves more partial, asked me, "Whether the poor mariners should have nothing?"

To which, I answered, "There was no reason they should pill the poor soldiers, who had fought and ventured for what little they had: and that the mariner's hope (having so rich a booty as the Indian Fleet at their mercy) was more to be desired than the trash the landsmen had got; so as they had none to blame for their poverty, but their Officers and their bad fortune."

This answer was taken to the heart, and is not forgotten to this hour [? 1606]; of which I feel the smart.

The troops dissolved [*disbanded*]; I went to Court, and there attended the most part of the winter.

The Islands Voyage.

IN THE year of our Lord 1597, being the next year after the journey of Calis, another journey was made by the Earl of ESSEX to the coast of Spain and the Islands [*the Azores*], with a royal navy, as well of Her Majesty's own shipping as of her best merchants; to which also was joined a good number of the States' ships, in all about 140; with an army of 7,000 or 8,000 landsmen, as well voluntary as pressed: and commonly called the Islands Voyage.

To which I was called, by Her Majesty's commandment, to attend his Lordship: as also to deal with the States, that besides the shipping which they were to send with Her Majesty's Fleet by virtue of the contract, they would suffer 1,000 of her subjects in their pay, to be transported by me, to her said General and Fleet, for that service.

Which having obtained, I hastened into England, and found my Lord of ESSEX at Sandwich, and his Fleet in readiness, anchored in the Downs.

It was early in the morning, and his Lordship was in bed, when I was brought to him. He welcomed me, with much demonstration of favour, and with many circumstances of words.

First he told me, "My Lord MOUNTJOY was to go as his Lieutenant-General (not of his own choice, but thrust upon him by the Queen), before me in place; yet that I should retain my former office of Lord Marshal: which as it had been ever in English armies, next the General in authority; so he would lay wholly the execution of that office upon me. And as for the Lieutenant-General; as he had a title without an office, so the honour must fall in effect upon them that did the service." With much more speech to this purpose, all tending to persuade me, that it was not by his working; and to take away the discouragement I might conceive of it.

I answered that "I had partly understood, before my coming out of the Low Countries, of my Lord MOUNTJOY's going as Lieutenant-General; so that I had forethought and resolved what to do. For though I was sensible, as became me, who saw no cause in myself of this reculement [*putting back*] and disgrace; yet my affections having been always subject to the rules of obedience, since it was my Prince's action and that it could not be but that my Lord MOUNTJOY was placed there by Her Majesty's consent, my sincerity would not give me leave to absent myself, and colour my stay from this action with any feigned excuse: but counselled me to come over, both to obey my Lord MOUNTJOY, and respect him as his place [*rank*], which I had always much honoured, required; much more his Lordship, who was General to us both. Though I was not so ignorant of his Lordship's power as to doubt that my Lord MOUNTJOY or any subject of England could be thrust upon him, without his desire and procurement.

"That therefore, as I had good cause to judge that his Lordship had withdrawn much of his favour from me, so I humbly desired his Lordship that, as by a retrenchment of the condition I was to hold in this Journey, I held it rather a resignment to his Lordship again, of the honour he had given me the last year (so far as concerned my particular respect to his Lordship, unsought for by me, than a service to him); so, hereafter, he would be pleased not to use me at all in any action, wherein he was to go Chief."

He would seem to take these speeches of mine as proceeding rather of a passionate discontentment, than of a resolution framed in cold blood; and that it would in time be digested. And so, without any sharpness on his part, the matter rested.

The purpose and design of this Journey was to destroy the Fleet that lay in Ferrol by the Groine [*Corunna*] and upon the rest of the Spanish coasts; and to that end to land our forces, if we saw cause: as also to intercept the [Spanish West] Indian Fleet.

Part of our land forces were shipped at the Downs; and we did put into Weymouth, to receive those which were to meet us there.

In that place, the Generalcalled myself and Sir WALTER RALEIGH before him; and for that he thought there remained some grudge of the last year's falling out, would needs have us shake hands: which we both did, the willinger because there had nothing passed betwixt us that might blemish reputation.

From thence, we went to Plymouth; and so towards Spain,

where, in the height [*latitude*] of 46° or 47°, we were encountered with a storm; against which the whole navy strove obstinately, till the greater part of the ships were distressed: amongst which, were the General's, mine, Sir WALTER RALEIGH's, and Sir GEORGE CARY's. My mainmast was rent in the partners [*sockets*] to the very spindle, which was eleven inches deep; insomuch as, to avoid the endangering of the ship, the Captain and Master were earnest with me, to have cast it overboard: which I would not assent unto, but setting men to work, brought it standing to Plymouth; and there strengthened it, so that it served the rest of the voyage.

The Lord THOMAS HOWARD, Vice-Admiral, with some few ships, got within sight of the North Cape [? *Finnistere*]: where, having plied off and on three or four days, doubting [*fearing*] that the rest of the Fleet was put back, because it appeared not; he returned also to our coast.

Our stay at Plymouth was about a month: more through want of wind than unwillingness or unreadiness of our ships, which, with all diligence were repaired.

In the meantime, our victuals consuming: it was debated in council, Whether the Journey could be performed or not, without a further supply of victuals? It was judged extremely dangerous; and, on the other side, as difficult to supply the army with victuals: which having to come from London and the east parts of the realm, and to be brought up at adventure, there being no sufficient store in readiness, would hardly be ministered unto us so fast as we should consume them. And therefore, it was first resolved to discharge all the land forces; saving the 1,000 I brought out of the Low Countries, with the shipping they were embarked in.

Then it was further debated in council, How to employ the Fleet? the purpose of landing the army at the Groine being dissolved.

A West Indian Voyage was propounded; whereupon every one in particular being to give his advice, it was assented to by them all. Only myself was of opinion, it could not stand with the honour, profit, and safety of Her Majesty and the State: the Fleet being so slenderly provided of forces and provisions, that nothing could be exploited [*achieved*] there answerable to the expectation that would be generally conceived. And yet, in the meantime, through the want of Her Majesty's Royal Navy and other principal shipping, with the choice Commanders both for sea and land, the State might be endangered by an attempt made by the Spaniards upon our own coast: whom we certainly knew to have then, in readiness, a great power of sea and land forces in the north parts of Spain.

Things thus handled, the Lord General posted to the Court.

After his return, no more speech was had of the Indian Voyage; but a resolution taken to attempt the firing of the Fleet at Ferrol and on the rest of the coast of Spain, and to intercept the [Spanish West] Indian Fleet, as in our discretions we should think fittest, either when we came to the coast of Spain or by going to the Islands.

With this resolution, we set forwards, directing our course to the North Cape, with reasonable wind and weather; yet the Fleet scattered: as, in a manner, all the squadron of Sir WALTER RALEIGH, and some ships of the other squadrons that followed him; who, for a misfortune in his mainyard, kept more to seaward.

The Lord General, whilst he and the rest of the Fleet lay off and on before the Cape (attending Sir WALTER RALEIGH's coming, who with some special ships had undertaken this exploit of firing the Fleet), suddenly laid his ship by the lee: which, because it was his order when he would speak with other ships, I made to him, to know his Lordship's pleasure.

He spake to me from the poop, saying I should attend and have an eye to his ship: in which at that instant, there was an extreme and dangerous leak, though he would not have me nor any other of the Fleet know it.

Which, leak being stopped, he directed his course along the coast southward; and, about ten leagues from the Groine, called a council, in which it was resolved to give over the enterprise of Ferrol (which as it was difficult to have been executed on a sudden, so now that we had been seen by the country, it was held impossible): and not to linger upon the coast of Spain, but to go directly to the Islands, the time of the year now growing on, that the Indian Fleet usually returned.

And to advertise Sir WALTER RALEIGH, divers pinnaces were sent out, that, till such a day, the wind and weather serving, the General would stay for him, in a certain height [*latitude*], and thence would make directly for the Azores. At this council, his Lordship made [*wrote*] a despatch for England.

I do not well remember where Sir WALTER RALEIGH and the rest of the Fleet met us; but, as I take it, about Flores and Corvo, the westerliest islands of the Azores: where we arrived in seven or eight days after we had put from the coast of Spain.

We stayed there some few days; and took in some refreshing of water and victuals, such as they could yield: which being not so well able to supply us, as the other islands, it was resolved in council to put back to them; and the squadrons, for the more commodity of the Fleet, were appointed unto several islands.

The General with his squadron were to go to Fayal; the Lord THOMAS with his squadron, and I with my ship, were to go to Graciosa; and Sir WALTER RALEIGH with his, either to Pico or St. George.

But Sir WALTER RALEIGH (whether of set purpose or by mistake, I leave others to judge), making with his squadron, more haste than the rest of the Fleet, came to Fayal afore us, landed his men, and received some loss by the Spaniards that kept the top of the hill, which commanded both the haven and the town.

The General with the rest of the Fleet, came to an anchor before the island; and hearing of Sir WALTER RALEIGH's landing and loss, was highly displeased, as he had cause: it being directly and expressly forbidden, upon pain of death, to land forces without orders from the General; and there wanted not [those] about my Lord, that the more to incense him, aggravated the matter.

Seeing the Spanish ensign upon the hill, his Lordship prepared to land with all haste; and so, about an hour before sunset, came into the town.

A competent number of men were given to Sir OLIVER LAMBERT to guard the passages; and then it was consulted how to go on with the enterprise of forcing them.

They were entrenched on the top of the hill, to the number

of 200; which hill was so steep, that it seemed artillery could not be drawn towards the said trench.

The night growing on, I desired his Lordship to give me leave to go up to discover the place: which his Lordship assented to. So taking 200 soldiers, I sent forwards; the young Earl of RUTLAND, Sir THOMAS GERMAN, and divers other Gentlemen Adventurers accompanying me.

At our coming to the top of the hill, finding no watch in their trenches, we entered them, and possessed the hill: where we found some of our men slain by the Spaniards. The hill was abandoned as we supposed in the beginning of the night, unseen or undiscovered by us or those that were placed at the foot of the hill.

We were all very sorry they so escaped, as was also the Lord General: for there was no following or pursuing them in that mountainous island.

The Captain and Officers that landed with Sir WALTER RALEIGH were presently committed: and before our departure thence, Sir WALTER RALEIGH was called to answer for himself, in a full assembly of the Chief Officers both by sea and land, in the General's presence. Where, every one being to deliver his opinion of the crime, it was grievously aggravated by the most. For my part, no man shewed less spleen against him than myself.

The General's goodness would not suffer him to take any extreme course: but with a wise and noble admonition, forgave the offence; and set also at liberty the Captains that had been committed.

After the Fleet had taken the refreshing that island could afford, which was in some good measure, we put from thence: and for three days, were plying off and on betwixt Graciosa and the island of Terceira, the ordinary way of the Indian Fleet.

In the meantime, certain were sent ashore by the General, at Graciosa, to draw from the inhabitants some portion of money and provisions, to redeem them from spoiling.

They brought word to the General, in the afternoon, that from the island, a great ship was discovered on the road-way [*track*] from the Indies: but they being sent again, with some others, to make a full discovery; at their return, which was sudden, it was found to be but a pinnace.

I must confess, in this point I may be ignorant of some

particulars; because things were not done as they were wont, by council: or if they were, it was but of some few, to which I was not called. But, in all likelihood, there was wilful mistaking in some, to hinder us of that rich prey which GOD had sent, as it were, into our mouths.

Howsoever it was, that same night, when it was dark, the General with the Fleet altered their course, and bare directly with the island of St. Michael; as it was given out, to water [*i.e., the bulk of the English Fleet deliberately went out of the track of the Indian Fleet, twelve hours before its arrival*].

A pinnace coming to me, in the Lord General's name, told me "it was his pleasure my ship and the *Dreadnought*, in which Sir NICHOLAS PARKER was, should beat off and on betwixt the island of St. George and Graciosa: for that the Indian Fleet was expected." The *Rainbow* in which was Sir WILLIAM MONSON, and the *Garland*, my Lord of SOUTHAMPTON's ship, were to lie, by the like order, on the north part of Graciosa. Willing us, if we discovered any Fleet to follow them, and to shoot off, now and then, a piece of ordnance; which should serve for a signal to the rest of the Fleet.

This order, as I take it, was delivered us about ten of the clock at night.

About midnight, or one of the clock, those of our ships might hear shooting, acording to this direction, rather in the manner of signal than of a fight, toward that part of the island [*Graciosa*] where the other two ships were to guard. This, as we afterwards understood, was from the *Rainbow*; which fell in the midst of the Indian Fleet; whom in their [*Rainbow's*] long-boat, they hailed, and by the Spaniards' own mouths, knew whence they were: who held them in scorn, and in a great bravery, told them what they were ladened withal.

The wind was very small [*light*], so as it scarce stirred our ships; but we directed our course as directly as we could, and so continued all night. The morning was very foggy and misty, so that we could not discover far: but still we might hear the shooting of ordnance, when we listened for it.

About eight or nine of the clock before noon, it began to clear: and then we might see a Fleet of twenty sails, as we judged some five or six leagues off; which was much about halfway betwixt us and Terceira.

The wind began a little to strengthen, and we to wet our

sails to improve the force of it; and somewhat we got nearer the Spanish Fleet: more through their stay, to gather themselves together; than our good footmanship.

All this while, the *Rainbow* and *Garland* followed the Fleet so near, that they might to our judgements, at pleasure have engaged them to fight. But their Fleet being of eight good galleons, the rest merchants' [ships] of good force: though the booty were of great inticement, it might justly seem hard to them to come by it; and so they only waited on them, attending greater strength, or to gather up such as straggled from the rest.

The *Garland* overtook a little frigate of the King's, laden only with cochineal; which she spoiled, and I found abandoned and ready to sink: yet those of my ship took out of her, certain small brazen pieces.

The Indian Fleet keeping together in good order, sailed still before us about two leagues; and so was got into the haven of Terceira [*Angra, see Vol. III. p.* 444], into the which, they towed their ships, with the help of those of the island, before we could come up to them.

It was evening when we came thither, and the wind so from the land, as with our ships there was no entering.

It pleased my Lord of SOUTHAMPTON and the rest of the Captains to come aboard me; where it was resolved to get as near the mouth of the haven as we could with our ships, and to man our boats well, with direction in as secret manner as they could, to attempt the cutting of the cables of the next [*nighest*] ships: by which means, the wind, as is foresaid, blowing from the land, might drive them upon us. This, though it were a dangerous and desperate enterprise, was undertaken: but being discovered, the boats returned without giving any further attempt.

The same night, we despatched a small pinnace of an Adventurer, to St. Michael, to give the Lord General advice where he should find the Indian Fleet: and us to guard them from coming out.

For we had determined to attend his Lordship's coming, before the said haven: which I accordingly performed with my ship, though forsaken of the rest [the *Dreadnought*, *Rainbow*, and *Garland*], the very same night; I know not whether for want of fresh water, or what other occasion.

Three or four days after, his Lordship came with the Fleet. Who sending into the haven, two nimble pinnaces to view how the Fleet lay; upon report that they were drawn so far into the haven, and were so well defended from the land with artillery, that no attempt could be made on them, without extreme hazard, and the wind blowing still from the land that no device of fire could work any good effect, and all provisions growing scant in the Fleet, especially fresh water: his Lordship gave over that enterprise, and put with the whole Fleet from thence to St. Michael.

The General had resolved to land in this island; and therefore called a Council to advise on the manner. In which, it was concluded that the greatest part of the Fleet should remain before St. Michael [? *the town of Ribeira Grande*] to amuse the enemy; and that the soldiers, in the beginning of the evening, should be embarked in the least vessels, taking with us the barges and long-boats, and so in the night, make towards Villa Franca, which was some four or five leagues off. His Lordship, and the rest of the chief Officers of the land forces, embarking with him in a small ship, left the sea Officers before St. Michael.

The next day, about evening, we were come near Villa Franca. I moved his Lordship, to give me leave, in a boat, to discover the shore and best landing-place; whilst his Lordship gave orders for the embarking the men into the other boats: which his Lordship granted, and I performed accordingly. So as, in due time, his Lordship was advertised of it, to his contentment; and proceeded to the landing of his forces upon the sandy shore before the town: where I could discover none to give impeachment, but a few straggling fellows which now and then gave a shot.

His Lordship, as his fashion was, would be of the first to land; and I, that had learned me of his disposition, took upon me the care of sending the boats after him. The seege [? *surf*] was such that few of the men landed with their furniture [*arms, &c.*] dry. His Lordship himself took great pains to put his men in order: and, for that I perceived he took delight to do all, in good manners and respect I gave the looking on.

In the meantime, some that were sent towards the town

to discover, gave the alarm that the enemy were at hand: and I told his Lordship it were good to send presently some good troops to possess the town of Villa Franca, before the enemy got thither.

His Lordship willed me to take with me 200 men, and to do with them what I thought good myself. I took so many of those men that were readiest, and bade them follow me: amongst which, were some Gentlemen of good account, as Sir JOHN SCOT and Sir WILLIAM EVERS, which accompanied me.

I went directly to the town, which I found abandoned: and leaving some guard in the Church which stood upon the Market Place, I passed somewhat further towards St. Michael: but neither seeing nor hearing news of any enemy thereabouts, I returned to the town. To which his Lordship was come, with the rest of his army, making in all, about 2,000 soldiers, Adventurers, Officers and their trains: all which were orderly quartered in the town, where we found good store of wheat.

His Lordship having thus gotten landing, advised with Council, Whether it were better to march to St. Michael, spoil that town, and water the Fleet there; or to send for the rest of the Fleet?

The difficulties in going to St. Michael were the roughness and unevenness of the way, being, for the most part, stony hills, in which a few men, well placed, might resist and impeach the passage to many; that the people and goods of the town would be withdrawn into the Castle, which was held by a garrison of Spaniards, and not to be forced without battery and much loss of men and time; that till it were gotten, there was no watering in that part, and our general necessity could endure no delay. It was therefore resolved to send for the Fleet to Villa Franca.

In the meantime, news came from the Fleet, that a West Indian [? *East Indian*] carrack, and a ship were come into St. Michael, and rode near the Castle.

His Lordship presently determined to go thither himself, for the better ordering of things. He took my Lord of MOUNTJOY with him; and by an especial Commission under his hand, committed to my command the land and sea forces at Villa Franca.

Before his Lordship could arrive at St. Michael, the carrack had run herself on ground under the Castle: and the other ship (which was not great), laden with sugar and Brazil commodities, had been taken by Sir WALTER RALEIGH.

The third day, his Lordship returned, with the Fleet, to Villa Franca, and gave orders presently to fall a watering. There was plenty of water; but the shipping of it into boats was tedious and troublesome: for, by reason of the greatness of the seege [? *surf*], we were fain, by wading and swimming, to thrust the barrels into the sea where the boats floated. This made the work the longer.

In the meantime our victuals consumed, and grew low; though we got some little refreshing from the land: which made us content ourselves with the less water.

After some four or five days watering, his Lordship gave order to embark the army; which he began early in the morning, and continued all the day: for the seege going high, the boats took in their men at a place where but one boat could lie on at once; which, together with the distance to the shipping, made the less riddance and despatch.

His Lordship, for the better expedition, was most of the time at the water's side: sending still to me for men from the town, as he was ready to embark them.

About five of the clock, in the afternoon, the sentinels that stood on the top of the steeple, discerned troops of men on their way to St. Michael. I sent up to the steeple, Sir WILLIAM CONSTABLE, and some other Gentlemen then about me, to see what they could discern: who all agreed that they saw troops, and as they guessed some ensigns [*colours*]. I willed Sir WILLIAM CONSTABLE to hasten to his Lordship, and tell him what he had seen.

I had yet remaining with me about 500 soldiers. Of these I sent out 60, whereof 30 Shot were to go as covertly as they could to a chapel, a great musket shot from the town, on the way the enemy was discovered; with orders, upon the enemy's approach, to give their volley; and suddenly and in haste to retire to the other 30 that were placed betwixt them and the town; and then all together, in as much haste and shew of fear as they could, to come to the town; where I stood ready with the rest of the men in three troops, to receive them, and to repulse and chase those that should follow them.

This order given, my Lord of ESSEX, with the Earl of SOUTHAMPTON and some other Lords and Gentlemen, came to the Market Place: where he found me with the troops.

His Lordship inquired of me, "What I had seen?"

I said, "I had seen no enemy; but what others had seen, his Lordship had heard by their own report: and might, if it pleased his Lordship, send to see if the sentinel continued to affirm the same."

His Lordship made no answer, but called for tobacco, seeming to give but small credence to this alarm; and so on horseback, with those Noblemen and Gentlemen on foot beside him, took tobacco, whilst I was telling his Lordship of the men I had sent forth, and orders I had given.

Within some quarter of an hour, we might hear a good round volley of shot betwixt the 30 men I had sent to the chapel, and the enemy; which made his Lordship cast his pipe from him, and listen to the shooting, which continued.

I told his Lordship, it were good to advance with the troops to that side of the town where the skirmish was, to receive our men, which his Lordship liked well; and so we went at a good round pace, expecting to encounter our men: who unadvisedly in lieu of retiring in disorder, maintained the place; which the enemy perceiving, and supposing some greater troops to be at hand to second, held aloof with his main force (for the highway to the town lay by the chapel, and there was no other passage for a troop by reason of the strong fence and inclosure of the fields), but sent out light men to skirmish.

Thus perceiving that our men held our ground, we stayed our troops in covert in the end of two lanes leading directly to the highway.

Those of the island, as we were certainly informed, could make [out] 3,000 fighting men, well armed and appointed; besides the ordinary garrison of the Spaniards. Of that number, we supposed them; because they had sufficient time to gather their strength together, and for that they came to seek us. And therefore as, on the one side, we were loth to discover our small number to them, unless they provoked us by some notable disorder, or necessity in the defence of ourselves: so we thought it not good to lessen our men by embarking of men, till the night was come, that silence and darkness might cover our retreat. And for these reasons, I opposed their heat that propounded to charge the enemy, and their haste that would needs have the men shipped without delay.

In the beginning of the evening, which ended the skirmish, keeping our sentinels in view of the enemy, his Lordship began to embark some troops, and so continued, till about the last troop was put into the boat: his Lordship seeing all embarked before he went aboard, but those forlorn men which made the last retreat, which were committed to Sir CHARLES PERCY; with whom, I embarked, without any impeachment of the enemy, or shew to have discovered our departure.

His Lordship made the young Noblemen and some other principal Gentlemen, Knights; as Sir WILLIAM EVERS, Sir HENRY DOCKWRAY, Sir WILLIAM BROWN, and a Dutch Gentleman that accompanied that Voyage in my ship.

We were no sooner aboard, but that the wind blew a stiff gale, so as some were fain to forsake their anchors.

And with this wind, we put for England; which continuing vehement, drave us to the leeward of our course, towards the coast of Ireland. I got an extreme leak in my ship, which kept both my pumps going without intermission many days before I got to harbour; wherewith my company were much wearied, and discouraged even to despair: which made me keep aloof from other ships, lest the hope of their own safety might make them neglect that of the ship.

The Fleet kept no order at all, but every ship made the best haste home they could: which as it might have proved dangerous if the Spanish Fleet, which was then bound for our coast, had not been scattered by the same weather; so it was in some sort profitable to us. For some of our smaller shipping, which were driven most leeward towards the coast of Ireland, met with two or three Spanish ships, full of soldiers, which they took: by which, we not only understood, at our coming to Plymouth, their purpose to have landed at Falmouth, with 10,000 men; but saw the instructions and orders of the sea fights, if they had met with us, which were so full of perfection, that I have ever since redoubted [*anxiously estimated*] their sufficiency in sea cases.

The Fleet arriving thus weather-beaten at Plymouth, his Lordship posted to the Court; leaving my Lord THOMAS, now Earl of SUFFOLK [*created July* 21, 1603], my Lord MOUNTJOY, and the rest of the Officers there. And, shortly, came provision of money, with Commission to the said Lords, Sir WALTER RALEIGH, and myself, to see the same issued and distributed by common advice, for the repairing, victualling, and sending about the Fleet to Chatham; and the entertaining of the 1,000 men I had brought out of the Low Countries, which were then disposed along the coast of Cornwall, and, after, sent to Ireland.

Which business despatched, I passed by post to London; and near Mary-bone [*Marylebone*] park, I met with Sir WILLIAM RUSSELL in his coach: who being my honourable friend (then newly returned from Ireland, where he had been Deputy), I [a]lighted to salute him, with much duty and affection; who stepping out of his coach, received me with the like favour. With whom, whilst I stood bareheaded, being in a sweat, I got cold: which held me so extremely, that for three weeks after, I could not stir out of my lodging.

I understood my Lord of ESSEX was at his house at Wanstead, in great discontentment; to whose Lordship I gave presently knowledge of my arrival, as also that I would forbear to attend his Lordship till I had been at Court: which then I hoped would have been sooner than it fell out my sickness would permit.

For I supposed, at my coming to Court, Her Majesty, after her most gracious manner, would talk and question with me concerning the late Journey: and though it pleased her always to give credit to the reports I made (which I never blemished with falsehood, for any respect whatsoever!) yet I thought this forbearance to see my Lord, would make my speech work more effectually.

So soon then, as I was able to go abroad, I went to the Court, which was then at Whitehall; and (because I would use nobody's help to give me access to Her Majesty, as also that I desired to be heard more publicly) I resolved to shew myself to Her Majesty, when she came into the garden: where so soon as she set her gracious eye upon me, she called me to her, and questioned with me concerning the Journey; seeming greatly incensed against my Lord of ESSEX, laying the whole blame of the evil success of the journey on his Lordship, both for the not burning of the Fleet at Ferrol, and missing the [West] Indian Fleet. Wherein with the truth, I boldly justified his Lordship, with such earnestness, that my voice growing shrill, the standers by, which were many, might hear; for Her Majesty then walked: laying the blame freely on them that deserved it.

And some, there present [*probably Sir W. Raleigh*], being called to confront me, were forced to confess the contrary of that they had delivered to Her Majesty; insomuch that I answered all objections against the Earl: wherewith Her Majesty, well quieted and satisfied, sat her down in the end of the walk, and calling me to her, fell into more particular discourse of his Lordship's humours and ambition; all which she pleased then to construe so graciously, that before she left me, she fell into much commendation of him. Who, very shortly after, came to the Court.

This office I performed to his Lordship, to the grieving and bitter incensing of the contrary party against me; when notwithstanding I had discovered, as is aforesaid, in my reculement, his Lordship's coldness of affection for me; and had plainly told my Lord himself, my own resolution (in which I still persisted) not to follow his Lordship any more in the wars: yet, to make as full return as I could, for the good favour the world supposed his Lordship bare me; fearing more to incur the opinion of ingratitude, than the malice of any enemies, how great soever, which the delivery of truth could procure me.

The Government of Brielle.

I STAYED the winter following in England.

In which time, my Lord SHEFFIELD making resignation of his Government of the Brielle into Her Majesty's hands; I was advised and encouraged by my good friends, to make means to Her Majesty for that charge: which it was long before I could hearken unto, having no friends to rely on.

For as I had good cause to doubt [*fear*] my Lord of ESSEX would not further me in that suit, so I was loth to have anything by his means, in the terms I then stood in with his Lordship; much less by any other person's, that were known to be his opposers.

Being still urged to undertake the suit, I began at length to take some better liking of it, and to guess there was some further meaning in it. And therefore, I answered that "if I were assured that Master Secretary [*Sir* ROBERT CECIL] would not cross me, I would undertake the matter."

Whereof, having some hope given me, I took occasion, one day, in the Chamber of Presence, to tell his Lordship as much: who answered me that "as he would be no mover or recommender of suit for me or any other; so he would not cross me."

I desired his Lordship of no further favour than might be looked for from a man in his place, for public respects.

And hereupon, I resolved to have Her Majesty moved; which Sir FULKE GREVILLE performed effectually.

Her Majesty, as her manner was, fell to objecting, that "I served the States, and that those two charges could not well stand together."

My Lord of ESSEX was, before this, gone from Court, discontented because of the difficulty he found in obtaining the Earl Marshalship of England. I went therefore to Wanstead to his Lordship, in good manners to acquaint him with what I had done: who rather discouraged me than otherwise in the pursuit.

Notwithstanding, I waited and followed my business hard, and one evening, in the garden, moved Her Majesty myself; who alleging, as before she had done to Sir FULKE GREVILLE, that "it could not stand with her service, that both those places should go together;" I told her Majesty that, "I was willing, if there were no remedy, rather to forsake the States' service, than to miss the place I was a suitor to Her Majesty for, in hers." And so, for that time, Her Majesty left me without any discouragement.

The Earl of SUSSEX was my only competitor; and for him my Lord NORTH professed to stand earnestly; who as soon as I was risen from my knees, told me, that "such places as I was now a suitor for, were wonted to be granted only to Noblemen."

I answered, "There were none ennobled but by the favour of the Prince; and the same way I took."

About this time, Her Majesty being in hand with the States, to make a transaction from the Old Treaty to the New, in which the States were to take upon them the payment to Her Majesty yearly, of so much money as would pay the ordinary garrison of the Cautionary Towns, it fell into deliberation, What numbers were competent for the guard of the said towns?

Wherein, before my Lords would resolve, they were pleased to call before them my Lord SIDNEY and myself, to hear our opinions, addressing their speech concerning the Brielle to me: whereunto I made such answers as I thought fit; not partially, as one that pretended to interest in that Government [*Governorship*]; but as I thought meet for Her Majesty's service.

And hereupon, Master Secretary took occasion merrily to say to my Lords, that they might see what a difference there was, betwixt the care of Sir FRANCIS VERE, a neutral man, and that of my Lord SIDNEY, who spake for his own Government; "but," saith his Lordship, "he will repent it, when he is Governor!"

And then he told their Lordships I was a suitor for the place; and that I should have for it his best furtherance. My Lords gave a very favourable applause to Master Secretary's resolution; and severally blamed me, that I had not acquainted them with my suit, and taken the furtherance they willingly would have given me.

It is true, I never made anybody acquainted with my suit, but Sir FULKE GREVILLE and Master Secretary. From thenceforward, I addressed myself more freely to Master Secretary; and conceived by his fashion [*manner*], an assurance of good issue: though I had not a final despatch in two months after.

In the meantime, my Lord SIDNEY and my Lord GREY were labouring to succeed me in the States' service. My Lord of ESSEX had promised his assistance to my Lord SIDNEY: insomuch as when I told him, at his coming to the Court, in what forwardness I was for the Brielle, and danger to lose my other charge, and who were competitors to succeed me; he plainly said that "he had given my Lord SIDNEY his promise, to procure him a regiment in the States' service."

I answered that "the command of the nation [*all English troops in the Dutch service*] belonged to me by commission"; that "there was as little reason for my Lord [SIDNEY] to be under my authority, as for me to yield my authority to him"; that "in respect of his Government [*Governorship*], he was uncapable of that charge as myself."

By this again, I found his Lordship's care to hold me back: notwithstanding my Lord SIDNEY had soon made an end of his suit. But my Lord GREY stuck longer to it, and was earnester; insomuch as there passed speeches in heat betwixt him and me.

And yet in the end, such was the favour of the Prince! that I enjoyed both the one and the other charge.

In the same year, 1597, about the latter end of September, I passed into the Low Countries; took and gave the oaths that are usual betwixt those of Holland, the Governor and townsmen of the Brielle; and so was established in that Government.

The Action at Turnhout.

THAT winter, 1597, the enemy laying at Turnhout, an open village, with 4,000 foot and 600 horse. One day, amongst other speeches, I said to Monsieur BARNEVELDT, that "they did but tempt us to beat them!" which it seemeth he marked; for, shortly after, the States resolved to make an attempt upon them; and gave orders to the Count MAURICE to that end, to gather his forces together. Which, at one instant, shipped from their several garrisons, arrived with great secrecy, at Gertruydenburg, in all, to the number of 6,000 foot and 1,000 horse; whereof some 200 [English] came from Flushing, with Sir ROBERT SIDNEY. Which troop, because he desired it should march with the rest of the English; in the love and respect I professed and truly bear to him, I made offer to him to command one of the two troops, the English forces were then divided into: which he refused not.

That evening was spent in consulting and ordering of things.

In the morning, by break of day, the troops began to march; and continued till two hours within night, and there rested, within a league of Turnhout. There we understood by our espial, that the enemy lay still without any manner of intrenchment; having as yet no intelligence of us.

A good part of that night was also spent in debating of matters. In the end, it was resolved, if the enemy abode our coming in the village; with our cannon to batter them and so to dislodge them, or with our troops to force the place upon them.

The Vanguard was given to the English troops, with Count MAURICE's Guard, and some other selected Companies of the Dutch which the Count kept ordinarily in the Vanguard.

The night was very cold, insomuch as the Count MAURICE himself, going up and down the quarters, with straw and such other blazing stuff, made fires in some places, with his own hands, by the *Corps du guard* [*pickets*]. Sir ROBERT SIDNEY and I got us into a barn thronged with soldiers, to rest; because there was no sleeping by the Count MAURICE, who was disposed to watch: whence I was also called, to attend him.

In the morning, we set forward; and by break of day we came within a falcon shot [320 *yards: see Vol. IV. p.* 251] of Turnhout, where the troops were put in battle. Whence sending some light horse towards the town, to discover; word was brought that the enemy had caused his baggage to march all night, and that now the Rereward were going out of the town.

Whereupon the Count MAURICE caused our Vanguard to advance to the town: with which he marched.

By that time we were come to the town, the enemy was clear gone out of it, and some musket shot off, on the way to Herenthals [*which was twelve miles off*] beyond a narrow bridge, over which one man could only go in front. They made a stand with some of their men; and galled our scouts, which followed on the track.

The Count MAURICE made a halt, halfway betwixt the bridge and the town: where I offered to beat the enemy from this passage, if he would give me some men; alleging that this was only a shew of the enemy to amuse us, whilst he withdrew the body of his forces, and therefore this required a speedy execution. Hereupon, he appointed me 200 musketeers of his own Guard and the other Dutch companies, with officers to receive my commands saying that "he would second me, according as occasion should serve."

With which, I went directly towards this bridge. Near to which, I found Count HOLLOCK [*HOHENLO*], who, that Journey, commanded the horse. He told me of an easier passage over that water and offered me guides; but the distance agreed not with the necessity of the haste, and therefore I excused myself of altering my way: which he took in very ill part, insomuch as, not long after, he wrote unto me a letter of expostulation, as if I had failed in the acknowledgement of his authority, which he pretended [*asserted*], by an ancient Commission, to be Lieutenant-General of Holland, and consequently of all the forces; which I answered in good and fitting terms, to his contentment.

And so placing my men in the best places of advantage, to command the bridge, I made them play at the enemy;

who soon forsook the bridge, being so narrow as aforesaid, and of a good length.

I durst not adventure, at the first, to pass my men over it, the rather for that the country on the other side, was very thick of wood: but, after a little pause, I thrust over some few foot; and, by a ford adjoining, though very deep and difficult, I sent some few horse, to discover what the enemy did.

And causing mine own horse to be led through the said ford, I went myself over the bridge; from which, some half a harquebuss shot, I found a small fort of pretty defence, abandoned: into which, I put my footmen which were first passed, and sent for the rest to come with all diligence.

In the meantime, taking my horse, I rode with some few Officers and others, after the enemy; whom we soon espied, some while marching, other while standing as if they had met with some impediment before them; which we thought was caused by the number of their carriages.

The way they marched was through a lane of good breadth, hemmed in with thick underwoods on both sides of it, fit as I thought, to cover the smallness of the number of my men. Whereupon, as also on the opinion the enemy might justly conceive, that the rest of our troops followed at hand, I took the boldness and assurance to follow them with those 200 musketeers: which I put into the skirts of the wood, so as betwixt them and the highway in which the enemy marched, there was a well grown hedge.

Myself, with about some 15 or 16 horsemen, of my own followers and servants, keeping the highway, advanced towards the enemy: giving, in the meantime, the Count MAURICE advice what I saw! what I did! and what an assured victory he had in his hands, if he would advance the troops!

I was not gone two musket shots from this fort, but some choice men of the enemy, whom they appointed to make the retreat [*to act as a rearguard*] discharged on us; and our men again answered them, and pressing upon them, put them nearer to their hindermost body of Pikes: under the favour of which, they and such as, from time to time, were sent to refresh them, maintained the skirmish with us.

When they marched, I followed; when they stood, I stayed: and, standing or marching, I kept within reach, for the most part, of their body of Pikes; so as I slew and galled many of them.

And in this manner, I held them play, at the least four hours, till I came to an open heath, which was from the bridge, about some five or six English miles; sending, in the meantime, messenger upon messenger to the Count MAURICE and the Count HOLLOCK, for more troops. And it pleased Sir ROBERT SIDNEY himself, who also came up to me, and looked on the enemy; when he saw the fair occasion, to ride back to procure more forces.

But all this while, none came, not so much as any principal Officer of the army, to see what I did.

On the left side of this heath, which is little less than three miles over, were woods and enclosed fields coasting the way the enemy were to take, in distance [off] some musket shot and a half. Along these I caused my musketeers to advance; and, as they could from the skirts of the heath to play upon the enemy: which was more to shew them and our men that were behind, by hearing the shot, that we had not forsaken the enemy, than for any great hurt we could do them.

Myself, with some thirty or forty horse that were come up to me to see the sport, following them aloof off.

The enemy, seeing no gross troop to follow them, began to take heart; and put themselves into order in four battalions: their horsemen on their wings advancing their way easily.

When we had, in this manner, passed half the heath, our [1,000] horsemen, in 16 troops (for they were so many), began to appear behind us at the entry of the heath: not the way we had passed, but more to the right hand, coasting the skirts of the heath, at a good round pace.

This sight made the enemy to mend his pace, and gave us more courage to follow them; so as now, we omitted no endeavour which might hinder their way, falling again into skirmish with them. For they fearing more those that they saw far off, than us that followed them at their heels, being a contemptible number to them that might see us and tell [*count*] us, mended still their pace.

I therefore sent messengers to those horsemen, for of our footmen there was no help to be expected, to tell them, that if they came not with all speed possible, the enemy would get into the strait and fast country, in which there could be no good done on them.

They were not above two musket shots from the mouth of the strait [*ravine or pass*], when the Count MAURICE, with six companies of horse, came near unto us, that followed the enemy in the tail. The other horsemen, because they fetched a greater compass, and came more upon the front and right flank of the enemy, were further off. I sent to the Count to desire him to give me those horsemen [*i.e., the six companies*].

And, in the meantime, to give the enemy some stay, I made round proffer [*appearance or shew*] to charge the Rereward: under the countenance of that second [*support*], with those horse and foot I had. Which took good effect. For they, knowing no other but that all the troops were also ready to charge, made a stand; and seeing our horsemen on the right wing to grow somewhat near, put themselves into a stronger order.

My messenger returning from the Count MAURICE, told me, he would speak with me.

To whom I made haste, and as the time required, in few words having delivered my mind; he gave me three [*of his six*] companies of horse to use as I should see cause. With which, I went on the spur: for the enemy were now marching again, and were come even into the entry of the strait.

The other horsemen with the Count HOLLOCK seeing me go to charge, did the like also. So that, much about one instant, he charged on the right corner of their front and on their right flank; and I with my troops, on the rereward and left flank: so roundly, that their Shot, after the first volley, shifted for themselves; and so charged their Pikes, which being ranged in four Battles, stood one in the tail of another, not well ordered (as, in that case, they should have been) to succour the Shot, and abide the charge of the horsemen. And so we charged their Pikes, not breaking through them, at the first push, as it was anciently used by the men-of-arms with their barbed horses: but as the long pistols, delivered at hand, had made the ranks thin, so thereupon, the rest of the horse got within them. So as indeed, it was a victory obtained without a fight.

For till they were utterly broken and scattered, which was after a short time, few or none died by handistrokes.

The footmen defeated; our horsemen disordered, as they had been in the charge and execution, followed the chase of their horsemen and baggage: which took the way of Herenthals.

I foresaw that the enemy's horse, that had withdrawn themselves, in good order and untouched of us, at the beginning of the fight, would soon put to rout those disordered men: and therefore made all the haste that I could, to the mouth of the strait, there to stay them.

Where finding the Count HOLLOCK, I told him he should do well to suffer no more to pass.

So riding forward on to the other end of the strait, where it opened on a champaign, I overtook Sir NICHOLAS PARKER, who commanded the three companies of English horse under me; who had some thirty soldiers with the three cornets [*standards*].

With these, I stayed on a green plot just in the mouth of the strait, having on either hand a road washy way: with purpose to gather unto me, those that came after me; and relieve our men, if the enemy chased them.

I had no sooner placed the troop: but I might see our men coming back as fast and as disordered as they went out; passing the strait on either hand of me, not to be stayed for any intreaty.

The most of our men passed, and the enemy approaching; Sir NICHOLAS PARKER asked me, "What I meant to do?"

I told him, "Attend the enemy, with our troop there!"

"Then," saith he, "you must be gone with the rest!"

And so, almost with the latest, the enemy being upon us, I followed his counsel; and so all of us, great and small, were chased through the strait again: where our troops gathering head, and our foot appearing, we held good; and the enemy, without any further attempt, made his retreat.

There were taken between 40 and 50 ensigns, and slain and taken of the enemy, nearly 3,000: and their general Seigneur DE BALLANCY, and Count DE WARRAS died on the place.

This exploit happily achieved, Count MAURICE with the army, returned that evening, to Turnhout (where the Castle held by some of the enemy, yielded), and the next day, marched to Gertruydenburg: and I, to accompany Sir ROBERT SIDNEY (who took the next [*nearest*] way to his Government [*Governorship*]), went with him to Williamstadt. Where I did, on my part, truly and sincerely, touching the other circumstances of the service; and was very friendly, when I made mention of him.

I gave him my letters to read, and then to one of his Captains to deliver in England: but my letters were held back; and his, that were far more partially written, delivered. Which art of doubleness changed the love I had so long borne him, into a deep dislike that could not be soon digested.

The battle of Nieuport.

IN THE year of our Lord 1600, the enemy's forces being weak and in mutinies, and his affairs in disorder; the States resolved to make an offensive war in Flanders, as the fittest place to annoy the enemy most and to secure their own State, if they could recover the coast towns: which was the scope of the enterprise.

As this action was of great importance, so were the meetings and consultations about it many: to which, though unworthy, I myself was called. Where, amongst other things, the facility of the execution coming in question; it was, by most, affirmed that the enemy was not able nor durst adventure to meet us in the field: which I not only opposed in opinion; but more particularly, made it appear that within fourteen days of our landing in Flanders, they might and would be with us, to offer fight, as afterwards, it fell precisely out.

The army embarked with purpose to have landed at Ostend; but finding the wind contrary when we came to Zealand, upon a new consultation, it was resolved to disembark upon the coast of Flanders, lying on the river Schelde: and accordingly, by a small fort called the Philippines, we ran our vessels, which were flat bottomed after the manner of the country, aground at a high water; which, the ebb coming, lay on dry ground; and so with much ease and readiness, we landed both horse and foot.

Our army consisted of about 12,000 foot and 3,000 horse; and was divided into three parts, committed to several Commanders, viz., the Count EARNEST of NASSAU, the Count SOLMES, and myself.

My troops consisted of 1,600 Englishmen, 2,500 Frisons [*Frisians*], and ten cornets [*squadrons*] of horse: with which troops, I took my turn of Vanguard, Battle, and Rereward, as it fell out.

We marched through the country to Ecloo and Bruges, and so to Oldenburg, a fort of the enemy not far from Ostend, which the enemy had abandoned, as also some others of less strength; by which means, the passage to Ostend was open and free.

The army encamped and rested there [*at Oldenburg*] two or three days, to refresh us with victuals: especially drink, whereof the army had suffered great want, the water of the country we had passed [through], being, for the most part, very troubled [*muddy*] and moorish [*boggy*].

It was again consulted, Where the army should be first employed, whether in taking the forts the enemy held in the low and broken grounds about Ostend, or in the siege of Nieuport?

The latter being resolved on, the States, who had all this while marched and abode with the army, departed to Ostend, as the fittest place to reside in: and the Count SOLMES, with his part of the army, was sent the direct way to Ostend, to take the fort Albertus, and open the passage betwixt that town and Nieuport.

The Count MAURICE, with the rest of the army, leaving the fort of Oldenburg and the others which the enemy had forsaken, well guarded (as was behooveful, because without forcing them, the enemy could not come to us but by fetching a great compass), marched by Hemskerk towards a fort called the Damme, upon the river [*Yperlee*] that goeth to Nieuport: but finding the country weak and moorish, and not able to bear the weight of our carriages and artillery, returned to a small village not far from Hemskerk, and lodged there.

Thence, we crossed through the meadows to the seaside, filling many ditches, and laying bridges to pass the waters, whereof that country is full. And so, with much ado, we got to the downs by the seaside: and encamped, about some cannon shot from the fort Albertus; which was rendered before to the Count SOLMES.

In the morning, early, we marched upon the sea sands towards Nieuport; and, at the ebb, waded the river on that side that maketh the haven of that town: and so encamped.

We spent two or three days in quartering and entrenching ourselves in places of best advantage, for our own safety and the besieging of the town; laying a stone bridge over the narrowest of the haven for our carriages and troops to pass to and fro, at all times, if occasion required.

In the meantime, the Count was advertised from those of Ostend, and those of Oldenburg, that the enemy, with good troops of horse and foot, were come and lodged near the fort [*Oldenburg*]. Whereupon, consulting, the opinions were divers, the most agreeing that it was only a bravado made of RIVAS; who, we had heard before, had gathered between 3,000 or 4,000 together, near the Sluis, to divert us from our enterprise: and that upon our remove towards him, he would make his retreat to the Sluis again.

But this falling out jump with the calculation I had before made, I insisted that it was the gross [*bulk*] of their army; that it was needful for us, without delay, to march thither with our army also, lest that fort and the rest fell into the enemy's hands: who might then come and lodge at our backs, and cut off the passage to Ostend, to the extreme annoyance of the army: that in using diligence to prevent the enemy's taking these forts, we might at once block up and besiege those of the enemy held on the low and drowned lands; which enterprise had been in question and debated as of equal importance with that of Nieuport.

Notwithstanding that my reasons seemed well grounded; the Count MAURICE was (as he is naturally) slow in resolving, so as, for that time, no other thing was done.

The same night came messenger upon messenger, that first, the enemy had cannon; then, that they of the fort were summoned in the Archduke's name; after, that it was yielded upon conditions. And thrice that night was I called from my rest, upon these several alarms, which confirmed me in my former opinion, upon which I insisted, with this change; that whereas my first purpose was to stop the enemy's passage under the favour of those forts: now, that occasion lost, we were to march to the hither mouth of the passage we ourselves had made through the low grounds, and to occupy the same, which was the shortest and readiest way the enemy had to the downs and seaside.

The Count MAURICE liked it well, and resolved to send forthwith the Count EARNEST, with 2,500 footmen and 500 horsemen, with some artillery also and provisions, to entrench upon the same passage; saying: "He would follow and second them, with the rest of the army, in due season." Which course I could not approve nor allow of, shewing my reasons, how this dividing of forces might endanger the whole; for I knew the enemy would, in all likelihood, use all possible diligence to get through this passage, and might well do it with his Vanguard and a part of his forces, before the arrival of these men; which, being so few, would not be able to make resistance: whereas our whole army marching, if the enemy had been fully passed the low grounds, we had our forces united to give them battle according to the resolution taken, if he sought us or came in our way. If part of his army were only passed, which was the likeliest; the shortness of time, the hindrance of the night, and the narrowness of the way considered: then we had undoubted victory. If we were there before him, the passage was ours.

About midnight, the Count [EARNEST] had his despatch and order to take of those troops that were with the Count SOLMES, as readiest for that service. The rest of the army was commanded to march down to the haven's side by the break of day, to pass with the first ebb.

It was my turn then to have the Vanguard, which made me careful not to be wanting in my duty: so as in due time, my troops were at the place appointed.

And because the water was not yet passable, I went myself to the Count MAURICE to know his further pleasure; whom I found by the bridge, with most of the chief Officers of the army: whither not long after, news was brought unto him, that the enemy was passed the downs and marching towards us; which struck him into a dump.

I told him that all possible speed must be used to pass the forces before the enemy were possessed of the other side of the haven: that therefore, I would go to my troops, to take the first opportunity of the tide; desiring him to give me his further orders what I was to do, when I had passed the haven.

He willed me, to do all things, as I saw cause myself. Calling to him the Count LODOWICK of NASSAU, who then commanded the horse as General, he bade him go along with me, and follow my directions.

So I left the Count MAURICE, and went to my troops; and so soon as the tide served, I passed my men as they stood in their battalions.

The soldiers would have stripped themselves to have kept their clothes dry; as I had willed them when I crossed the haven first: but then I thought it not expedient, the enemy being so near; and therefore willed them "to keep on their clothes, and not to care for the wetting of them: for they should either need none, or have better and dryer clothes to sleep in that night."

When the troops of the Vanguard were passed, I left the footmen standing, ranged in their order, betwixt the downs or sand hills and the sea; and with the horse, advanced towards the enemy whom we might discover afar off coming towards us by the seaside. Not to engage a skirmish or fight, but to choose a fit place to attend them in, which was now the only advantage we could by industry get of the enemy: for by the situation of the country, that skill and dexterity we presumed to excel our enemy in (which was the apt and agile motions of our battalions) was utterly taken from us.

For the space betwixt the sea and the sand hills or downs, was commanded by the said hills, which are of many heads reared and commanding one another, containing so much breadth in most places that our troops could not occupy the whole; and were everywhere so confusedly packed together, so brokenly and steeply, that the troops could neither well discern what was done a stone's cast before them, nor advance forward in any order, to second [*support*] if need were. And on the other side of the downs towards the firm land, if the whole breadth were not possessed, the enemy might pass to the haven of Nieuport, where our bridge and most of our shipping yet lay on the dry ground, and spoil and burn them in our view. All which inconveniences, I was to prevent.

Finding therefore, a place where the hills and downs stood, in a manner divided with a hollow bottom, the bottom narrower and the hills higher to the seaside and North than towards the inland and South, which ran clean thwart from the sea sands to the inland; the downs also there being of no great breadth, so that we might conveniently occupy them with our front, and command as well the seashore as the way that lay betwixt the low inland and the foot of the downs: in that place, on the hither side of that bottom, I resolved to attend the enemy. And therefore, having caused my troops to advance, I drew from the whole Vanguard about 1,000 men: *viz.*, 250 Englishmen; the Count MAURICE's Guard, and such other companies as usually marched with it, 250; and of the Frisons, 500, which were all musketeers: the other two troops consisting of Shot and Pikes.

The English and 50 of the Count's Guard [*i.e.*, 300 *in all*], I placed on the top of the hill that lay more advanced than the rest; which being steep and sandy, was not easily to be mounted, and in the top, so hollow that the men lay covered from the hills on the other side, and might fight from it as from a parapet.

Just behind this hill, about 100 paces, was another far more high, on the top of which also, I placed the other 200 of the Troops of the Guard; on which also, with a little labour of the soldier, they lay at good covert.

These two hills were joined together with a ridge somewhat lower than the former hill; which, endwise, lay East and West; and, broadwise, looked towards the South or inland, and commanded all the ground passable. On the outside, it was very steep, loose, sandy, and ill to be mounted; within, it was hollow. In which, I placed the 500 Frison musketeers, giving charge to the Officers to bestow their shot only to the southward, when time should serve; which was directly on our right side and flank, as we then stood turned towards the enemy.

Betwixt those two hills, on the left hand or flank looking towards the sea, I placed in covert in places for the purpose (so near the sea sand, that they might with ease and good order in an instant break into it), two of the four troops of the

English, making about 700 men, ranged with their faces to the northward, looking directly from our left flank. If the enemy adventured to pass by us to the other troops, I meant to leave them [*the* 700] in his eye.

Upon the sands, more easterly than the inmost of the two hills, I ranged in a front, with a space betwixt them, the other two troops [=650 *men*] of the English: and a pretty distance behind them, more to the seaward, the [2,000] Frisons in four battalions; two in front, with a space to receive betwixt them one of the other two battalions that stood behind them, the files and spaces betwixt the troops being as close as might be conveniently, to leave the more space for the ranging the other troops; with a competent distance betwixt each troop, so as one troop shadowed not another, but all might be in the enemy's eye at one instant.

And thus the Vanguard occupied about one-third part of the downs (leaving the rest to be manned as the occasion should serve, by the other troops), and, on the left hand, uttermost to the sea: and more advanced, I placed the horsemen [*i.e.*, *the ten squadrons*].

I had scarce done this work, when the Count MAURICE, with the chief Commanders of the army, came to the head of my troops; where, on horseback, and in the hearing of all standers by (which were many), he put in deliberation, Whether he should advance with his army towards the enemy, or abide their coming?

Those that spake, as in such cases most men will not seem fearful, counselled to march forward: for that they thought it would daunt the enemy, and make the victory the more easy: whereas in attending him, he would gather courage out of the opinion of our fear, or take the opportunity of our stay to fortify upon the passage to Ostend, to cut off our victuals and retreat.

I alleged that their army (that had been gathered in haste, and brought into a country where they intended no such war) could neither have provision of victuals with them for any time, nor any magazines in those parts to furnish them, nor other store in that wasted country, and in that latter end of the year to be expected: so as to fear, there was none, that they should seat themselves there to starve us that had store of victuals in our shipping, and the sea open to supply us, with all sailing winds. And for the vain courage, they should get by our supposed fear, after so long a march with climbing up and down those steep sandy hills, in the extremity of heat, wearied and spent before they could come to us, and then finding us fresh and lusty, and ready to receive them in our strength of advantage, it would turn to their greater confusion and terror.

They persisted, and as it were, with one voice opposed: so as, in the end, I was moved to say that "all the world could not make me change my counsel."

The Count MAURICE was pleased to like of it, resolving not to pass any further towards the enemy; and for the ordering of things, reposed so much trust in me as that he believed they were well, without viewing the places or examining the reasons of my doings: but returned, to give order to the rest of the army, which, as the water ebbed, he enlarged to the seaward, next the which the horsemen were placed; and six pieces of ordnance were advanced into the head [*front*] of the Vanguard.

In this order, we stayed; and the enemy, though still in the eye, moved not forward for the space of two hours, and then, rather turning from us than advancing, they crossed the downs and rested other two hours at the foot of them, towards the land: which confirmed their opinions that held he would lodge.

But we found reasons out of all their proceedings to keep us from wavering. For it was probable to us, that the enemy overwearied and tired with that night and day's travel; and seeing us passed the haven of Nieuport, wherein to have hindered and prevented us was the greatest cause of this haste, whilst he saw us stirring and ordering ourselves, might hope that we (that were fresh, now passed, and engaged to fight) would advance, the rather to have the help of our troops with the Count EARNEST, if perchance he were retired to Ostend, which, the nearer the fight were to that place, might be of most use to us; or else if we had heard of their defeat, we would be drawn on with revenge. But when they saw that we held our place, not moving forward, being out of that hope; and not provided to make any long stay, for the reasons before mentioned: they might resolve to refresh themselves, and then to advance towards us; for which, that side was more convenient than the bare sea sands.

Withal we considered, that their chief trust resting in their footmen (which were old trained soldiers, and to that day, unfoiled in the field); they would rather attend the growing of the tide, which was then at the lowest, that the scope of the sands might be less spacious and serviceable for horsemen.

About half flood, they crossed again the downs to the sea sands, and marched forward, sending some light-horsemen far before the troops. One of which, as we supposed, suffered himself to be taken; who being brought to the Count MAURICE, told him aloud that the Count EARNEST was defeated; and that he should presently have battle, augmenting the number, bravery, and resolution of their men.

The loss of our men we had understood before, and therefore were careful to have but few present at the hearing of the prisoner; whose mouth being stopped by the Count MAURICE's order, the rest that heard it bewrayed it, either in word or countenance, to the soldiers.

The enemy growing nearer and nearer, and their horsemen coming, in the head of their troops, in a competent distance to have been drawn to a fight; I would very willingly have advanced the horsemen of the Vanguard near to them, and with some choice and well-mounted men, have beaten in their carabin[eer]s and skirmishers to their gross [*main body*], with purpose, if they had been charged again, to have retired in haste with the said Vanguard of horse betwixt the sea and the Vanguard of foot: and having drawn them from their foot, under the mercy of our ordnance, and engaged to the rest of our horse, to have charged and followed them resolutely.

This advice could not savour to that young nobleman [*Count LODOWICK of NASSAU*], that was not well pleased with the power that Count MAURICE had given me over his charge; and therefore was not by him put in execution: who chose rather, as the enemy advanced leisurely, so he, in like sort, to recule [*retire*] towards the foot.

This counsel of mine taking no better effect, and their horsemen being now come within reach of our cannon; I made the motion to have them discharged, which was well liked, and so well plied that we made them scatter their troops, and in disorder fly for safety into the downs: which had doubtless given us the victory without more ado, if our horsemen had been ready and willing to have taken the benefit of that occasion.

Their footmen, out of our reach, kept on their way alongst the sands; and the sooner to requite us, advanced their ordnance a good distance before them, and shot roundly at us and did some hurt.

The water now grew very high, so as both we and they were forced to streighten [*narrow*] our front. And the enemy—whether of purpose, as aforesaid, to fight with more advantage (as he took it), with his foot in the downs; or to avoid the shot of our ordnance (for he could not be so careless as to be surprised with the tide, and so be driven to this sudden change)—put all his forces, as well horse as foot, into the downs; which horse crossed to the green way betwixt the lowlands and the downs.

All our horsemen stood with our Rereward. Hereupon our Vanguard altering order, our Battle and Rereward passed into the downs, and (in the same distances, backward and sidewards, as they had been on the sands on my left hand before) ranged themselves. So as the front of the three bodies of foot filled the breadth of the downs: all the horsemen being placed on the green way betwixt the lowland and the foot of the downs; not in any large front, but [*echeloned*] one in the tail of another, as the narrowness of the passage enforced.

I found a fit place on the top of a hill, from whence the green way on the inside of the downs might be commanded with ordnance; on which, by the Count MAURICE his order, two demi-cannon were presently mounted.

The enemy growing very near, I told the Count "It was time for me to go to my charge;" asking him, "Whether he would command me any more service."

He said, "No! but to do as I saw cause." Willing us the Chiefs that stood about him, to advise him in what part of the army he should be personally? Whereunto, we all answered, that for many reasons, he was to keep in the rearward of all: which he yielded unto.

So I went to the Vanguard, and after I had viewed the readiness and order of the several troops, the enemy now appearing at hand; I (the better to discover their proceedings, and for the readier direction upon all occasions, as also with my presence to encourage our men in the abiding of the first brunt), took my place in the top of the foremost hill before mentioned. Where I resolved to abide the issue of that day's service, as well because the advantages of the ground we had chosen were [favourable] to stand upon the defence; as also for that, in that uneven ground, to stir from place to place (as is usual and necessary in the execution and performance of the office of a Captain, where the country is open and plain), I should not only have lost the view of the enemy (upon whose motions, in such cases, our counsels of execution depend), but of my troops, and they of me; which must needs have caused many unreasonable and confused commandments.

The enemy's Forlorn Hope of harquebussiers, having got to the tops of the hills and places of most advantage, on the other side of this bottom before mentioned, began from thence to shoot at us, whilst their Vanguard approached: which now growing near at hand, 500 Spanish Pikes and Shot mingled, without ensigns or precise order, gave upon the place where myself was, and very obstinately, for the space of a great half-hour, laboured to enter and force it; favoured [*covered*] with more store of Shot from the tops of their hills, the gross of their Vanguard standing in some covert from the Shot with me, on the other side of the bottom.

In the meantime, the Vanguard of their horse advanced along the green way (so often mentioned) betwixt the low inland and the downs, towards our horse that stood more backward against the flank of our Battle. Our two pieces of ordnance were discharged from the top of the hill to good effect and well plied; and when they came nearer, and thwart our right flank, the 500 Frison musketeers (who, as I have before said, were destined to bestow their shot that way) did their part, and so galled them, that, upon the first proffer of a charge which our horsemen made, they were put into a disordered retreat, even to their troops of foot: our horsemen following them in the tail; who were fain, there, to give them over. At the same instant, I gave orders that a 100 men should be sent from the foremost troop of foot I had laid, as aforesaid, in the downs, to have given upon the left [? *right*] flank of the enemy, if he attempted to pass by us upon the sands; and as covertly as they could to approach and give upon the right flank of those that were in fight with me.

When they were come up, and at hands with the enemy; I sent from the hill where I was, by a hollow descent, some 60 men to charge them in front; which amazed the enemy, and put them to run, our men chasing and killing them till they had passed the bottom, and came to the gross of their Vanguard: from which were disbanded anew, the like number [500] as before, who followed our men, and seized on some heights that were in the bottom somewhat near us, covering their Pikes under the shadow of the hills, and playing with the Shot, from the tops, upon our disbanded and skirmishing men.

I sent to drive them from thence, being loth they should gain ground upon us, one of the same troops, from whence I had drawn the 100 men before mentioned, with orders only to make that place good.

This was a bloody morsel that we strove for. For whilst our men and theirs were not covered with the hanging of the hills; as they advanced or were chased, they lay open to the shot, not only of those that were possessed of those little hills, but also of the others higher which poured in greater tempests upon them: so as the soldiers that I sent hasted, as for their safety, to get the . . . side of the hill; and the enemy, for like respect, abode their coming with resolution. So as, in an instant (as the hill was round and mountable), the men came to handiblows, upon the whole semicircle of it, with much slaughter on both sides; till in the end, the enemy was forced to retire.

In the meantime, the Battle of the enemy's foot were come up to the gross of the Vanguard: which as it had taken the right hand of the downs so did the Battle, with some distance between them, though even in front. Having been well welcomed with our Shot from the tops of the hills; the Battle stayed in as good covert as the place would afford, sending fresh men to beat ours from those grounds of advantage in the bottom; so as, ours beginning to give back, I sent a new supply to make good the place in this bottom; sometimes getting, and sometimes losing ground.

The fight was still maintained with new supplies on both sides. Wherein I persevered, though with loss of men because the advantage the ground gave me to beat as well upon their gross as on their loose fighting men, made the loss far greater on their side: my design being to engage their whole force upon my handful of men, which I employed sparingly and by piece-meal; and so to spend and waste the enemy, that they should not be able to abide the sight of our other troops, when they advanced.

The horsemen of their Battle and ours encountered, but somewhat more advanced towards the enemy (our men having gotten courage with the first success), so as our forementioned Frison musketeers could not so well favour [*cover*] them. Our horsemen being put to retreat; the enemy in the pursuit, being saluted by them [*the Frisons*], were stopped and drew back.

Their Rereward, having now come up, even with their two bodies (for so I term them, because their Ensigns [*colours*] remain together; though most of the men were drawn from them and in fight, and the Ensigns barely attended), advanced on the left hand of the Battle: and spreading the breadth of the downs, they were to my troops rather on the corner of the right flank than afront; and our Battle and Rereward upon which they directly fronted, were a musket shot behind my troops, towards which it seemed they intended to advance.

First, we gave as much [*fire*] to them as we could spare, from our hills: but when they began to open [*come within sight of*] upon my Frison musketeers (which, as before is said, could only bestow their shot on our right flank; and till that time, had done no service but against their horse), they were exceedingly galled, so as they stayed suddenly: and amazed, or ashamed to go back seeing none to chase them, in a bottom of some small covert, bestowed themselves; sending out some skirmishers along the southermost parts of the downs, against which some loose men were sent from our bodies. But our musketeers that shot, standing and without fear, from their rests, galled them most.

The horsemen of the Rereward shewed themselves on both sides. Some little bickering there was, and so they retired out of the footmen's reach.

This was a strange and unusual sight. For, whereas most commonly in battles the success of the foot dependeth upon that of the horse; here, it was clean contrary: for so long as the foot held good, the horse could not be beaten out of the field; though, as it fell out, they might be chased to them.

All this while, the fight continued, without intermission, hotter and hotter, betwixt the two other troops [*the Archduke's Vanguard and Battle*] of the enemy and me: both of us sending fresh supplies, as occasion required, to sustain the fight. Insomuch as the whole of the English troops [1,600—250 = 1,350 *men*] were engaged to a hand fight in the foresaid bottom, saving those few [250] that were placed on the hills: and on the enemy's part also, few were idle.

And now, I saw was the time to give the enemy a deadly blow: his grosses [*main bodies*] being disbanded, as well in occupying places of height and advantage to annoy us, as by those that were sent to dispute the places in question. For their only strength now consisted in their loose men: which any few horse charging on a sudden in that bottom, would have put to flight; and they being followed pesle-mesle [*pell mell*] with our foot, would never have had means to have rallied and gathered themselves together again. On the other side, I knew that without further succours, their numbers would weary and eat us up in the end.

I therefore at once sent to the [2,000] Frison footmen of the Vanguard to advance; and to the Count MAURICE, to tell him how things stood, and to desire him to send me part of the horse of the Battle. And because I saw the enemy press and gain upon our men more and more, I sent again messenger upon messenger.

In the meantime, to give our men the more courage, I went into the bottom amongst them, where riding up and down, I was in their eyes both doing the office of a Captain and soldier: and with much ado, we entertained the fight, though the enemy encroached and got upon us.

At my first coming [*i.e., unto the bottom*], I got one shot through my leg, and a quarter of an hour after, another through the same thigh; which I then, neither complained nor bragged of, nor so much as thought of a chirurgeon [*surgeon*]: for I knew, if I left the place, my men would instantly quail. I therefore chose, not having been used to have my troops foiled, to try the uttermost, rather than to shew them the way to flee: hoping still for the coming of the Frisons and the horse I sent for.

But their haste was so small, that my men [*i.e., those in the bottom*], overlaid with numbers, forsook the place, notwithstanding my best efforts to stay them; hasting along the sands, towards our cannon; the enemy following them hard.

I was forced, seeing them all going, to go for company, with the last; uneasily and unwillingly, GOD knows! and in the way, my horse fell dead under me and upon me, that I could not stir.

I had neither Officer, Gentleman, nor servant about me, to give me help. Sir ROBERT DRURY by chance came; and a Gentleman, being a servant of his, called HIGHAM [*see p.* 136], drew me from under the horse, and set me up behind his master; which help came very seasonably, for the enemy being near at hand when I fell, by this means, I was saved out of their clutches.

Thus I rode to the ordnance, where I found my brother HORACE [*afterwards Lord VERE*] and the most of the Officers that were living, with some 300 [? *English*] foot.

I made them stand from before the ordnance, and willed the canoneers to discharge upon the enemy that now swarmed upon the sands.

At the same instant, my own company of horse and Captain BALL's coming thither; I willed them to go to the charge; and my brother with the foot to advance and second them home.

This small number of horse and foot made an exceeding great change on a sudden. For the enemy in hope of victory, followed hard; and being upon the sands, where horse might serve upon them, were soon routed and most of them cut in pieces; the rest saving themselves by flight as they could, in the downs. Our men, both horse and foot, followed them.

Their Battles, where their Ensigns remained, began to stir and rouse themselves; rather for defence than to revenge themselves: for they advanced not.

Our men, from the top of the hills, who had kept their places from the beginning, having by this means, a fair mark, plied them with shot. Our English soldiers, on all hands, with new courage resorted to the fight; and finding these

Battles very small and thin (by reason of the men they had sent to supply the fight; especially of Shot, which in these uneven places were of most service), pelted them with our shot, and pressed upon them to make them recule.

The Count MAURICE, seeing things on these terms, caused the Battle to advance, and his horsemen to make a proffer upon the enemies. Upon which sight, without attending any strokes, the enemy routed, and was chased out of the field.

In this Last Charge, I followed not. [*See Sir JOHN OGLE's account of it at pp.* 136–139.] For seeing the success upon the sands, and knowing that my directions in the prosecution of the victory would be executed; I could easily judge that the work of that day was at an end. And therefore I began to care and provide for myself: who, all this while had been undressed, the blood leaking from me at four holes: which, together with a dangerous disease that had long held me, had made me extremely weak and faint.

The enemy lost above 120 Ensigns [*colours*]. Most of his foot were slain: but not many of his horse lost.

On our side, in a manner, the whole loss fell upon the English; of whom, nearly 800 were hurt or slain. Eight [*English*] Captains were slain; of the rest, all but two were hurt, and most of my inferior officers were hurt or slain.

In the rest of the army, there was no loss at all, to speak of: especially among the foot.

I dare not take the whole honour of the victory to the poor English troop of 1,600 men; but leave it to be judged by those that may give their censure, with less suspicion of partiality.

I will only affirm that they left nothing for the rest of the army to do, but to follow the chase: and that it hath not been heard of, that, by so small a number, in a ground so indifferent, whereof the only advantage was the choice and use of the same, without help of spade or other instrument or engine of fortifying, so great and so victorious an army as the Archduke's, had been so long wrestled withal, and so far spent.

Yet this victory had been as assured with less loss, and

touch of reproach (if to give ground to a stronger may be subject to a disgraceful imputation), had the succours of horse or the foot I called for, come sooner to us: wherein I will charge and accuse none, but the messengers of their slackness.

An account of the Last Charge at Nieuport battle,

by Sir JOHN OGLE, Lieutenant-Colonel to Sir FRANCIS VERE.

THE English, who, as that great Captain Sir FRANCIS VERE well noteth, had borne the burthen of the day (overlaid with numbers and wearied with fight, their succour not coming to them in time), were forced to retire themselves in such order as they could, from the downs to the strand: where meeting, but too late, with the [2,000] *Frisons; they, like good fellows, to keep us company* [!] *turned all fairly back again with us, and so we both marched away together in one confused troop.*

Some loose horsemen of the enemy came up close to us, and killed of our men, thrusting divers of them, with their rapiers, under their armour, in at their backs.

Their foot followed leisurely, and were aloof, as not knowing how suddenly we might turn and make head again; for our men kept both their arms, and in troop: which Sir FRANCIS VERE, upon occasion given by some speeches of mine, noted to me for a good sign.

Neither was our retreat or the enemy's pursuit of any extraordinary swift pace; as may be easily gathered by the consideration both of their and our motions. For we had the leisure, though I confess not without danger, to pluck our Captain from under his horse, and mount him again behind another, as he himself hath told in his own Relation [*p.* 132]*: wherein I cannot but wonder that it pleased him not to make any mention of me as well as* HIGHAM*; since his blood, which remained on my clothes so long after as I thought fit to wear them, witnessed clearly that I could not be far from him when that office that came so "seasonably" and in so good a time, as he saith, was performed unto him.*

In this retreat of ours, there wanted no persuasions, as well by Sir FRANCIS VERE *himself as some others, to move our men to stand and turn: for we saw a kind of faintness and irresolution, even in those that pursued us nearest. And it is certain (if we may call anything certain whose effects we have not yet seen) that if then we had turned and stood, we had prevented that Storm of Fortune, wherein we were after threatened; at least, we had saved many of our men's lives. But such apprehensions of fear and amazement had laid hold of their spirits, as no persuasion could, for that time, get any place with them.*

Sir FRANCIS VERE *with his troop formerly mentioned* [p. 132] *took his way towards the cannon, along the sands: where he, by his chirurgeon; they, by their fellows, might hope of succour.*

I being faint and weary through heat and much stirring, took some few with me, and crossed into the downs; there awhile to rest me, till I should see how the succeeding events would teach to dispose of myself, either by direction or adventure.

I was no sooner come thither [in the downs], *but I met with Captain* [CHARLES] FAIRFAX [brother of EDWARD FAIRFAX the Poet], *and young Master* GILBERT *(who soon after was slain near unto us). There we consulted what we should do. But the time and place affording no long deliberation, taught us to resolve that the best expedient for our safety was to endeavour the speedy increase of the little number which we had with us. I think they were* 30 *men. Having brought which to a reasonable competency; our further purpose was to give a charge when we should find it most expedient, that so, with our honours, we might put an end to those uncertainties, the fortune of the day had, to our judgements, then thrown upon us.*

It was not long ere that our little body was multiplied to better than 100 *men. For the loose and scattered began, of themselves, without labour, to rally unto us. So much prevails Union even in a little body: for whilst to it the broken and disbanded ones do willingly offer themselves for safety and protection; they them-*

selves, by adding of strength to that body, not only increase the number thereof, but do give and take the greater security to themselves and others.

We were, all this while, within less than a musket shot of a gross [brigade] *of the enemy, which stood in a hollow or bottom within the downs : the hills about it, giving good shelter against the drops of our shot ; for the showers* [volleys] *of them, as also of the enemy's, were spent and fallen before. But neither were the hills so high, nor so steep, that they could forbid entry and commodious passage of charging, either to our horse or foot.*

The gross had not many wanting of 2,000 *men in it ; and spying, as it should seem, our little handful (which at the first they might peradventure neglect or contemn in regard it was so small a number) now begin to gather some bulk and strength, thought it not unfit to prevent a further growth : and to this end, sent out* 150 *men with colours* [i.e., footmen], *closely and covertly as they could, along the skirt of the downs, next the inland and southward, with purpose to charge on the flank or back of us ; which they might very conveniently do, as we then stood.*

These men advanced very nigh us, ere we descried them : when, lo, just upon the time of their discovery and of our men being ready to fall upon them, comes Sir HORACE VERE on horseback from the strand (it should seem from the pursuit of the enemy, whom the horse had scattered, mentioned by his brother Sir FRANCIS VERE [p. 132]), *with a troop of some* 200 [*foot*] *men, marching along the downs towards us.*

In this troop, there were with him, Captain SUTTON ; his [*Sir HORACE's*] *own Lieutenant Colonel, LOWELL, that commanded Sir FRANCIS VERE's foot company ; and some Lieutenants. MORGAN also came to us, about the same time that FAIRFAX and I* [with the 100 foot] *joined unto him. And these were the Officers that were afoot in the Last Charge.*

The disbanded troops [the above 150 men] *of the enemy, seeing us strengthened with such supplies, thought it their fittest course to hasten them* [*back*] *the same way they came forth towards us.*

Captain FAIRFAX and I would have charged : but Sir HORACE VERE willed us to join our troops [evidently both were footmen] *with his ; and said we should go together and give one good charge for all, upon that great troop which we saw stood firm before us.*

We had now with us, our troops being joined, about some five Ensigns [= about 350 footmen], *amongst which, was mine own; which, after, was lost in the Charge, but recovered again by my Officer.*

The vigilant and judicious eye of His Excellency Prince MAURICE *was, it should seem, upon our actions and motions all this while. For, as I have been informed, he seeing us make head, said to those that stood about him,* Voyez! voyez les Anglais! qui tournent à la charge! *and thereupon gave present order to* DUBOIS, *then Commissary General for the Cavalry, to advance some of the horse, to be ready to attend and fortify the events that might happen upon this growing Charge. This I have not of knowledge; but from such hands as it were ill beseeming me, or any man, to question the credit of one of that rank, quality, and reputation.*

Our troop now, and the disbanded troop of the enemy marched both towards this gross, almost with equal pace, saving that their haste was a little greater according to the proportion of their danger if they had fallen into our clutches, being then too strong for them, ere they recovered the shelter of their own gross.

Yet such haste, they could not make, but that we were with them before they had wholly cast themselves into their friends' arms: who opening to receive them, facilitated not a little the passage of our Charge, as we then fell in pesle mesle together amongst them.

Much about this time, came in the horse, viz., the troops of [Sir FRANCIS] VERE, [Sir EDWARD] CECIL, *and* [Captain] BALL, [see p. 132]; *who rushing in with violence amongst them, so confounded and amazed them, that they were presently broken and disjointed: which being done, the slaughter was as great to them on their side, as the execution was easy to us on ours.*

This rupture also of theirs was not a little furthered by the Archduke's own troop of Harquebussiers; which having advanced somewhat before this gross on the skirt which lay between the inland and the higher downs, was so encountered by CECIL *and his troop (who had as then received orders, by* DUBOIS, *from his Excellency, to charge) that they were forced, with confusion to seek succour amongst their foot:* CECIL *following them in close at their backs.*

VERE *and* BALL, *as I take it, charged at the front, by us; having crossed into the downs from the sands and north side towards the sea. It should seem that having broken and scattered the enemy, who, as Sir* FRANCIS VERE *himself relateth, were by them driven into the downs* [p. 132]; *and seeing Sir* HORACE VERE *also to have taken his way thither: they thought it perhaps convenient to hover thereabouts, and to hold an eye upon our and the enemy's actions; the rather because they might discern Sir* HORACE VERE *now making a new head. And so seeing us charge, charged also with us: which was not disagreeable to the first directions given and mentioned by Sir* FRANCIS VERE.

And this, by all probable conjecture, must also be the cause why Sir FRANCIS VERE, *in his discourse, maketh no mention of Sir* EDWARD CECIL. *For he not having his direction from him to charge, but from his Excellency, as himself* [CECIL] *hath told me; Sir* FRANCIS VERE *(being ignorant thereof; and himself likewise not at the Charge in person, whereby he might take notice of any man's presence) would not, as appears, expose himself to interpretations, by making any further relation touching particulars, than what might receive credit either from his own eyes or commandments.*

This Charge, through the hand and favour of GOD, *gave us the day. What followed is before already set down by that great and worthy Captain, Sir* FRANCIS VERE.

The Siege of Ostend.

IN THE year of our Lord 1601, the States, resolving to send their army, or a good part thereof, into Flanders, to take those forts the enemy held about Ostend, and by that means to open the passage into that country, for the greater annoyance thereof, made choice of myself, though far unfit and unworthy of so great a charge, to command the said forces as General. Of which intent, I had first but only an inkling given me; and was by some principal persons of the State encouraged to accept the same, and to take upon me a journey into England to inform Her Majesty of that purpose; and, with all the necessary circumstances, to frame her liking to the enterprise, and to induce her to the yielding of the succour of 3,000 of her subjects, to be levied, transported, and paid, at their own charge, and to be in the Low Countries by the 10th of May. With these special instructions for the manner of the enterprise:

That for the better diversion of the enemy's forces from the quarter of Flanders, the Count MAURICE should, with the first season of the year, march towards Berg upon Rhine [*Rheinberg*]; and to make shew as if he would, but not to engage his forces in the siege of that town no otherwise but that a good part thereof, especially the English, might be sent towards Ostend, upon the first summons. Which together with 2,000 soldiers to be levied out of the garrisons of Holland and Zealand, and the 3,000 they made account of out of England, should, on a sudden, be transported into Flanders for the said enterprise.

With this errand, I passed into England, delivered the whole plot to Her Majesty, who liked and allowed thereof, and with some difficulty, as her manner was, granted the men to be levied and transported in ten days' warning. For so the States desired, lest the overtimely stirring of them before their other troops were landed in Flanders, might give the enemy an alarm, to the difficulting of the enterprise. Willing me, the grant obtained, to hasten over [back].

Before my coming into the Low Countries, the Count MAURICE was marched towards Berg; and the enemy, that had long threatened to besiege Ostend, with a good part of his forces, was set down before that town: so that it was now question rather of defending, than of gaining more footing in that quarter.

The States therefore dealt with me, to take upon me the charge of the place, for which they gave me Commission, not as Governor, but as "General of the Army employed in and about Ostend," with very ample powers, as aforesaid: whereof I accepted.

And they forthwith gave orders to the Count MAURICE, to send into Holland the 20 English companies he then had in the army. With which troops, I was to go into Ostend.

At the first, he made some difficulty to send any, having engaged himself in the siege of Berg, his works for the defence of the Quarter [*forces covering the siege*] not being finished, and the enemy gathering head in Brabant, to succour and relieve that town: in the end, with importunity, he sent eight companies; with which, my brother [*Sir HORACE VERE*] came.

With these, being by the States put in good hope the rest should follow, and that I should be liberally supplied with forces, ammunition, and all necessaries for such a service: I went into the town, and landed, as I take it, the 11th of July, 1601, on the sands against the middle of the Old Town.

The enemy commanded the haven, so as there was no entering by it; and the use of the [*river*] Geule was not then known: and this place I landed at, was to be subject to their ordnance; and the seege [*rolling*] of the sea such that no shipping could lie there unbroken.

At my landing, Monsieur VANDERNOOD, the Governor, gave me the keys.

In the town, I found about 30 companies of Netherlanders,

which made 1,600 or 1,700 men, newly divided into two regiments; whereof Monsieur VANDERNOOD had the one, and Monsieur DE UTENBURGH had the other: and my eight companies might make 800 men.

The enemy had 30 pieces of cannon placed on the west side, the most within a harquebuss shot off the town; and six on the east side: with which, they shot much into the town, and did great harm to the buildings and men. Their army was judged at 12,000 men. The three parts [thereof] on the west side, quartered near Albertus, a great-cannon shot from the town; were commanded by the Archduke himself. The other part were quartered upon the top of the downs, on the east side, next the Geule.

Those of the town, before my entrance had made a sally on the west approaches: from which they were repulsed with the loss of 300 men slain and hurt.

The town, to the land[ward] was well flanked and high rampiered, but with a sandy and mouldered [*crumbling*] earth.

The Old Town, supposed free from battery, was rather strong against sudden attempts by palisadoes and such helps, than by rampire and flanks [*curtain and side bastions*] to abide the fury of the ordnance and force of approach: which notwithstanding was held to be the strongest part of the town, as well for the reasons abovesaid, as for that it was hemmed in on the one side with the Geule not passable, and on the other with the haven which was passable only some four hours in a tide.

The rest of the town, besides the ditch which was broad and deep, was environed with a royal counterscarp, with ravelins [*half-moons*] of good capacity and defence against the cannon, covering all the Bulwarks of all the town but that which they called the Peckell or East Bulwark [*bastion*], which needed not that help, as lying directly upon the Geule, and not to be assailed by any approach.

Upon the south, south-east, and south-west of the town, there is a plot of ground in the manner of an island, environed on the east side with the Geule, to the southward with a channel that runneth into the Geule, from the said Geule directly westward into the river that (in former times, passed through the Old Haven; and) now had his course in the furthest place from the town not in distance above a harquebuss shot: to the westward, by the old channel of the said river, by which it passed into the Haven; which was now separated from the ditch of the Counterscarp by a low dam near the Poulder Bulwark. This plot of ground, covering the town, from the said Bulwark to the Spanish Bulwark which lieth upon the Geule, had, upon the south-west angle (which is where the channel from the Geule mingleth with that of the river to the haven), a little redoubt, open behind, and of no force to resist the cannon.

To the southward of this Poulder Bulwark, the country is broken by many creeks not passable nor habitable for an army, but by forced means; and in spring tides, for the most part overflown.

On the west side, the ground, for a harquebuss shot from the river (that runneth due west from the said Poulder), lay low, and subject to the like overflowing at the spring tides: but all the waters were more passable, having fewer and shallower creeks. From this bottom, the ground towards the downs goeth higher.

Betwixt these West Downs (which near the town, are more low and level than the East ones) and the *Porcépic* [Porcupine] (which is a Ravelin in the Counterscarp that closeth the New Town on that side, by which the Old Haven passeth into the town), there lieth a down on which the haven beateth on the one side, and the water of the ditch of the counterscarp on the other: being the only place, about that town, by which an approach might be made on firm ground to the wall of the town, and which therefore was held the most weak and dangerous place.

But the cutting of the aforesaid dam, and letting the sea-water into the ditch of the counterscarp was held a sure and sufficient means to prevent the enemy on that side. So as indeed nothing was so much to be doubted [*feared*] as the enemy's passing into this piece of ground before mentioned, called the Poulder: by which means, he might, notwithstanding our best endeavour, in short time, drain the ditches of the counterscarp and the town ditch; and so, make his way to the rampier.

My first care therefore was to fortify and secure the said Poulder against the enemy; and to make a safe place for our shipping to unlade such provisions and commodities as, from time to time, should be brought unto us. Which I readily and easily performed by opening a passage in the counterscarp near the West Poulder of the Spanish Ravelin; by which means, the water from the Geule flowed into the town ditch: in which, with their masts stricken down, I have often seen above one hundred vessels lie safe from the annoyance of the enemy's great shot. Which haven though the entry grew more dangerous by the enemy's approaches, which, in process of time, they, with much cost, labour, and art, advanced, for it lay within the high-water mark (on which they raised new batteries), was used, during the siege, as the better inlet.

Albeit after, to avoid the great harm the enemy did to our shipping at their going out, I made another cut, betwixt the East Ravelin and the mount called the Moses Table, looking northward and directly into the sea: which served the turn, and saved many ships.

When my twelve companies [of English] which I expected from Berg, were arrived; I began, one night, to entrench a piece of ground higher and firmer than the rest about it, lying nearer to the low dam before mentioned, which separated the river that by the old channel had passed into the haven, from the ditch of the counterscarp: which piece of ground, stretched out in the form of a geometrical oblique or oblong, towards the West had a watered ditch, such as in those parts they use for enclosures [*hedges*]: and the whole plot, of continent sufficient to receive 800 or 900 men.

This field, I entrenched; taking the water ditch to advantage, without giving it any other form usual in fortifications; so as, for the form and seat, it was called the West Square: because the westernmost face of it was well flanked from the West Bulwark and the West Ravelin, and the face south-west from the angle of the Poulder where the channel of the Geule and the channel of the old haven met: but chiefly to hold as much room as I could.

For I expecting large numbers of men, doubted [*feared*] more I should want means in that town, hemmed in with so many waters and ditches, to sally and use them abroad, as occasion should require; than bodies to guard that which I entrenched.

The morning after I had begun this work, the enemy

turned divers pieces from the top of the downs upon it; which notwithstanding my best industry, did much hurt amongst my men, till the work was raised and thickened.

This plot put in reasonable defence, and part of the supplies [*the* 3,000 *men*] granted by Her Majesty now arrived; I began to cast up a redoubt upon the like piece of ground for firmness (but not fully half so big as the former) lying about half a harquebuss shot south-west from the angle of the Poulder, close to the river that passeth from the said angle westward, which served well to covert [*protect*] the Poulder on that side, and to flank the west face and south flank of the West Square.

The Poulder thus assured from sudden attempts, I began to raise in the said Poulder a rampier to resist the cannon on the inside of the old channel, from the ditch of the Poulder Ravelin of the counterscarp to the angle aforesaid of the Poulder, which broadways lay due West, and endways North and South. And the redoubt upon the said angle, I raised of a good height, and cannon proof, in the form of a cavallier [*earthwork*] to command over the said rampier of the Poulder.

All this while, the enemy lay still, without making any approaches or intrenchments, or attempting to hinder my works; otherwise than by his cannon shot, of which he was no niggard.

Having, as I supposed, in this manner, well provided for the safe defence of that quarter; I was desirous to draw some of the enemy from the sandhills, to dwell by us in that low watery ground to the south-west and south of the river that runneth from the West to the Poulder: which I knew would cause great expense, great labour, and much loss and consumption of men; on which, besides the plots of ground I had taken, no trench, no approach, nor lodging could be had but such as was forced.

Only about a harquebuss shot westward from my redoubt on that side and upon the same river, there was a pretty round height of ground, on which, sometimes, they of the town of Ostend had held a redoubt to the south-west and south, environed with a plashy moor, into which, by the creeks the water flowed so as, the greatest part of the tide, it was not passable.

From this plot of ground, I could discover the back of their approaches on the downs; and from it, with cannon, could annoy them as well there, as in their shipping and boats by which their army was supplied from Bruges and other ports of the country.

If they suffered me to take this height and fortify it, I had gotten two special advantages; the annoying of them and the securing of my works on that side: which, after, I might have maintained with fewer men. If I were impeached by their sudden planting of ordnance and batteries; I knew they would possess the ground, and piece-meal engage them more and more in those drowned lands: which was the other of my drifts.

This piece of ground, to move and provoke them the more, upon St. James's Day [*July* 25, 1601], being the saint the Spaniards as their Patron do most superstitiously reverence, in the forenoon, I first sent as it were to view and discover: and anon after, I sent for men, and set them on work; and drew down in a readiness, under the favour [*cover*] of my outermost redoubt, 200 soldiers to make head, if the enemy came down to the other side of the river, to hinder my workmen with his shot.

The enemy no sooner perceived my men to work, but he turned certain pieces of ordnance upon them from the downs, and shot at us, as did also those of the Fort of Grootendorst: but being far off, the shot small, and the men (observing the shot), bowing their bodies in the hollowness of the old trench, it did little harm.

Their footmen in a great rage, as it seemed to me, of themselves kindled with zeal, without direction or orders from their chiefs, came down towards the river side amain; not armed men in battle and troop, but shot scatteringly as every one could first and readiliest take his furniture. Others with faggots in their hands, whereof they had store in their approaches, began here and there, in confused manner, to raise a trench from the downs to the river, for other trench and covert they had none: so as they were a fair mark for our artillery from the town, and our musketeers from the West Square and the South-west Redoubt; which spared no powder. Besides, the 200 musketeers I had placed with me, under the favour of small banks on the edge of the river, held them back when they came nearer hand. So as, after much shooting and hurt done, the most of the day being spent, they gave over molesting us.

And that night, I put the place into so good defence against the attempts of handistrokes, that I left a guard in it, and workmen to add more strength to it.

In the morning, betimes, the enemy began to batter it with two cannon, which the same night they had planted on the other side of the plash directly west, and about the fourth part of the way to their Fort called Grootendorst; from whence, also, they shot with a couple of demi-culverin: and thus they continued the whole day, insomuch as our new work to them-ward was laid flat; and our men forced, for safeguard, to make hollow trenches in the said redoubt.

About an hour before sunset, troops were seen to march from Albertus towards Grootendorst: which I gathered was to make an attempt upon the said redoubt in the beginning of the evening, before the breach could be repaired; for which purpose, the water being ebbed, the time served very fitly.

I saw by their earnest proceeding, that there was no striving to keep and maintain that plot; and therefore resolved to give way, but so as I would seem to be forced from the place.

And therefore as I did set men on work in the beginning of the evening, to repair that breach; to confirm the enemy, if he had foreborn his attempt that night, in the opinion that I would maintain the place: so I gave orders to the Officer I left in it, with some 80 men to hold good watch on the side of the plash, if the enemy attempted to pass, to shew himself on the brink of the said plash with his Shot, and discharge upon them, leaving his Pikes by the fort: with orders, if they advanced, to make his retreat to the South-west Redoubt, and there to hold good.

Which directions were not well observed. For the Officer forthwith, when he had sight of the enemy's approach, which was about two hours within night, leaving his Pikes in the redoubt, he with the Shot made for the plash side, and discharged at the enemy: who being strong in numbers and resolved, continued their way; the officer still retiring hard to the redoubt and skirmishing with him, as if his purpose had been rather to have drawn the enemy into some danger, than to save himself and his troops by a timely retreat. Which is an error that many in like cases fall into, to their utter destruction; when fear to have their valour called in question maketh them, against all reason, fight against a stronger enemy, and engage themselves where they have neither purpose nor hope to obtain the victory.

Those of the redoubt stayed the return of their men; whom the enemy pursued so hard after he had gotten footing in the firm ground, that they both at an instant, came to the redoubt; and by the way of the breach, which yet lay open, entered and overthrew soon our men; who so taken at unawares, thought it safer to fight than to run away. Others they overtook before they could get over the palisadoes on the other side of the redoubt. So as most of our Pike men were lost, but few or none of the Shot; who, holpen with the darkness of the night, and their good diligence, escaped.

Upon the alarm, having given orders for some troops to follow, I hasted to the South-west Redoubt: near which, I met with these scattered men; which I stayed, and took with me into the said Redoubt. To which, the enemy even now approached, following their fortune, and hoping of like success: and on the other side of the river towards the northward, from under the favour of the bank to which, of purpose, they had also drawn musketeers, to flank and beat in the back our men as they should shew themselves to resist the attempt of their men on the other side of the water. Of the supplies that came from the town, I reinforced the guard of the said Redoubt: by which means, as also the difficulty they found in passing their gross over the creeks, with some loss to us, yet much more to them, they retired to the redoubt they had gotten.

[The end of the *Commentaries*

of

Sir FRANCIS VERE.]

...WILLIAM DILLINGHAM, D.D.

...inuation of the Siege of Ostend,

...5 July, 1601, as far as 7 Mar. 1602.

Here endeth, or rather here breaks off, Sir FRANCIS VERE'S Commentary. For he continued in his Government of Ostend for many months after [till 7th March, 1602]: but, whether it was because he thought it needless to give the world any further account of it, who were all, by this time, become, as it were, Spectators and Eye-witnesses of what he did; or whether he thought
...so well known to many, some other would carry on the
...he world should think it needful; or whatever else the
... I do not find that his pen ever went any further.
...se there were many things performed by him worthy of
...and because the reader may perhaps have a curiosity to
... of the story; I shall here presume to subjoin a brief
...e chief passages in the sequel of that action, according
...ve met with recorded by others, to my hand, that so
... off Sir FRANCIS VERE with honour from so great an
...and deliver him safe from the exceeding hazard of that
... and this the rather, because I think this was the last
...sequence wherein he embarked.

...RE had no sooner taken a sure footing to himself, and
...e whereon the bloody Tragedy was afterwards to be
...gave a pledge of his resolution to abide by it: refusing
...lgings, notwithstanding that the enemy's cannon had

pierced them through with many a shot, and quite battered a little tower belonging to them.

But though his enemy's cannon could not enforce him to abandon so much as his own lodgings; yet did his own, by a shrewd mishap, constrain him to withdraw himself for a time out of the town. For on the 14th of August [1601], being wounded in the head with the blow of a cannon that split in the discharging, he removed into Zealand to be cured of his hurt. The enemy having gotten intelligence hereof, made no small expressions of joy and triumph; discharging many a peal of cannon.

Whereby if they hoped to fill the hearts of the besieged with terror and consternation, and to beat them from their former resolution; they were much mistaken. For the brave English soldiers observing what storms of great shot came rolling into the town, the besiegers having already discharged little less than 35,000 cannon shot against it; and perceiving by the story, that all the houses were likely, ere long, to be beaten about their ears, and so were likelier to endanger them by their fall, than any way to secure and protect them from the fury of the enemy's artillery: they advised themselves to take this course.

There was a green plot of ground in the town, commonly used for a market-place, which was something higher than the rest of the streets. Here did they earth themselves, by digging it hollow, and fitting themselves with cabins and lodgings within the ground. The like did they, by another void piece of ground upon the south-west.

Whereby, as they thought themselves secure from the enemy's battery, being confident they would not shoot mattocks and pickaxes; so did they sufficiently testify their own resolution, rather to inter themselves in the graves which they had digged, than to quit their possession of the place unto the enemy.

Hereupon, the besiegers shifted sails, and suiting their counsels to the disposition of the English soldiers (who are sooner won by fair means than foul), shot arrows with letters into the English Quarters, promising ten stivers [=1*s.* 2*d.* (=5*s.* *now*)] a day to such as would serve the Archduke against the town.

But these offers were slighted by the English, who hated falseness as much as they contemned danger: and this device was looked upon by those of the town, as the product of languishing counsels; which having already spent all their powder, came a begging for the conclusion.

And if the Archduke had then given over the siege, I question not but the world would generally have excused him. For what should he do?

He had made his approaches as near unto Sand Hill as was

possible for the Haven; which was the most probable place of doing any good upon the town. And therefore he had, ever since the beginning of the siege, bent the most of his great shot upon it, if it were possible to have made a breach; but all had hitherto produced no other effect than the fortifying of the Sand Hill Bulwark, instead of beating it down. For by this time, it was so thickly studded with bullets, that the ordnance could scarcely shoot without a tautology and hitting its former bullets; which, like an iron wall, made the later fly in pieces up in the air. Yea, the bullets in it were so many, that they left not room to drive in palisadoes, though pointed with iron: and some there were, that would have undertaken to make the Bulwark [a]new, if they might have had the bullets for their pains.

Besides, whenever they meant to assault it, they must resolve to force seven Palisadoes made of great piles, within the haven, before they could come to the foot of the Bulwark: and if they were not intercepted by the springing of a mine or two, yet was the Bulwark itself unmountable by armed men. And it might easily have been conceived they had gotten intelligence that there were thirteen cannon in the Counterscarp and other convenient places, charged with chained shot and rusty iron to scour the Sand Hill, if need should require.

Besides all this, all was to be done at a running pull. For when the coming in of the tide should sound a retreat, off they must! or be utterly lost. And they easily saw that the musketeers in the Half-moon of the Counterscarp were likely to give them such a welcome as would make many of them forget to return to the camp.

Notwithstanding all these great difficulties, no advice of old Captains could prevail against the obstinacy of the States of Flanders: who, to keep life in the siege, spared not to undertake the payment of a million of crowns [=£300,000 (=£1,300,000 *now*)] to the Archduke, rather than he should draw off from the town.

So that he took up a resolution not to stir, and, as his fugitives [*deserters*] reported, once he swore that "he would not rise from the table at which he sat, before they of the town were made to serve him." But then they, on the other side, laid a wager that they "would give it him so hot, that it should burn his fingers."

Not long after, the Lord of CHATILLON met with an unhappy mischance. For being upon the high Bulwark of Sand Hill, with Colonel UTENBRUCH and other Gentlemen and men of Command; he had his head struck off, above the teeth, with a cannon shot; and his brains dashed upon the Colonel's left cheek. Which possibly might receive its direction from the self-same hand, that did, more than once during this siege, shoot a bullet into the mouth of a charged cannon; which,

because it would not be too lo
fire with the blow, returned th
with another of its own.

As good a marksman was
soldier of the town, having bo
in a boasting way, with a shot
leaving the other in the sold
received no hurt, said, "It wa
left him the better half behind
have been contented with th
dividing again.

On the 19th of September
his hurt, returned from Zealan
English and 20 Ensigns [=c
and Frisons, that had arrived

Soon after his arrival, he to
ening of divers of the works,
the south and west, the better
serve them from the injury of

Which the enemy perceivin
and stronger, resolved to att
verse—

dolus an virtu

To that purpose, an Englis
Diary [*i.e.*, of the Siege; ? that
du Siege d'Ostende en Fland
1615] relates, who had served
of foot in their army, returned
he prevailed so much, by m
letters of recommendation to
senting himself, he desired t
which the General could not
effectually recommended.

This traitor having thus s
began his practice. For he r
from the enemy, and gave the
the town, and of the best mea
and projects according to the
them.

For the better conveyance o
them into a broken boat, wh
been sunk by the enemy, and
town and the camp, under the

and there disposed them in a place appointed: whence the enemy fetched them by night, with the help of a little boat; and, upon certain days, brought him answers, and sometimes money for his reward, which he failed not to fetch at the place appointed.

When he was discovered, he had drawn four men into his conspiracy: among others a Sergeant, who was the means of revealing it.

This Sergeant coming out of prison, where his Captain had caused him to be laid some days in irons, being all malcontent, chanced to meet with CONISBY: who told him he was glad to see him out of prison; withal asking him the reason of his so great and grievous punishment.

To whom, the Sergeant railing upon his Captain, sware earnestly, that he would be revenged for the wrong he had received, though it cost him his life.

CONISBY, supposing he had found a man fit for his purpose, told him he might easily find the means to be revenged, without losing his life, and with his own profit and advancement; and that if he would follow his counsel, he should want no money.

The Sergeant began to listen to his words, and seemed inclinable enough to so advantageous a design, and ready to follow his advice. Whereupon CONISBY, having first made him swear secrecy, discovered himself: and presently asked him if he had the resolution to set fire on one of the Magazines; for which purpose, he himself had prepared a certain invention of powder, lead, and match.

This, the Sergeant undertook to perform; which he said, "could not be difficult for him to do, being often sent to fetch powder for the soldiers."

CONISBY assured him that he had practised [with] more associates; and that when he should have made the number up to twenty, he would then put the design in execution: which was, that one of the Magazines being set on fire, he would so work it, as to have the guard of a Sluice in a Bulwark near the enemy, who should then give on, and be admitted into the town.

The Sergeant seemed to hug the device, demanding only of CONISBY some assurance, under his hand, that he should have his recompence when the work should be performed. Which having once obtained, away he goes to the General, and discovers the practice to him.

Whereupon CONISBY being apprehended and put to the rack, confessed all, and that he came to Ostend with that purpose and intent: as also what instructions and promises he had received; and what [ac]complices he had made, who were likewise apprehended and put in prison.

This plot failing, the enemy's only hope of taking the town was by stopping up the haven, and so hindering the coming in of supplies.

To this purpose, the Old Haven on the west of the town, having been made dangerous and useless, and the defendents constrained to make a new one out of the Geule on the east side: the enemy had now so straitened this also, by their float [*raft*] of great planks bearing ordnance, on the Geule; that they of the town were fain to make a second new haven against the midst of the Old Town, by which means the enemy's designs were eluded, and the ships of supplies admitted into the town at pleasure.

This dangerous thrust being so handsomely put by, the enemy had no other play left but to storm: which he resolved upon, and prepared himself accordingly.

But in the meanwhile, it will not be amiss to take notice of a passage which happened in the town. A French Gentleman, disobeying his Sergeant, and thereupon causing a great tumult, was committed to prison; and, eight days after, condemned by a Council of War, to be shot to death: but because he was descended of a good house, all the French Captains interposed their earnest entreaties to General VERE, and begged his life; which was granted, upon condition that he should ask the Sergeant forgiveness. This, when he could not, by any means or persuasion be brought unto; he had eight days' respite granted him to resolve himself: which being past, and he continuing still as obstinate as ever, he was brought forth unto the place of execution, and tied to a stake. But when once he saw the harquebussiers ready to discharge; he began to be apprehensive of the horror of death, and promised to perform the sentence, and ask the Sergeant's forgiveness: which he forthwith did, and thereupon was released. So much easier it is for pride and rashness to commit a fault, than heartily to acknowledge it.

A truer courage was that of another in the town during the siege. An English Gentleman of about 23 years of age, in a sally forth, had one of his arms shot off by a cannon: which taking up, he brought back with him into the town, unto the chirurgeon; and coming to his [*the surgeon's*] lodging, shewed it, saying, "Behold the arm, which but at dinner helped its fellow!" This he did and endured, without the least fainting, or so much as reposing upon his bed.

Not long after, on the 4th of December [1601], early in the morning, the besiegers gave a fierce and sharp assault on the English trenches: which take in the words of one present at it [*evidently Sir* FRANCIS VERE'*s Page*, HENRY HEXHAM, *see pp.* 171, 174].

SIR FRANCIS VERE having been abroad the most part of that night, was laid down to take his rest: but hearing the alarm that the English trenches were assaulted, and knowing of how great import that work was for the defence of the town, pulling on his stockings, with his sword in his hand; he ran in all haste, unbraced, with some soldiers and Captain COULDWELL and myself [*HENRY HEXHAM*], into the works: where he found his own Company at push of pike, upon a turnpike [*barrier*] with the enemy; who crying in French, *Entrez! entrez! advancez! advancez!* strove to enter that way; and sought to overturn the turnpike with their pikes.

Some of his Gentlemen were slashing off the heads of their pikes: among the rest, Lieutenant-Colonel PROUD (who was afterwards slain at Maestricht), which he took notice of, and shortly after made him a Lieutenant.

The enemy being repulsed and beaten off; Sir FRANCIS VERE (to the end our men might give fire the better upon them, from the town and Bulwarks that flanked these works, both with our ordnance and small shot) commanded the soldiers to take some straw from the huts within the works, and making wisps of it, to set it on fire, upon the parapet of the work, and upon the heads of their pikes: by which light the enemy were discovered, so that our men gave fire bravely upon them from the town and works; and shot into their battalions which had fallen on, and their men that were carrying off their dead. So that upon this attempt, the enemy lost a matter of 500 men, which lay under our works and between their trenches.

The enemy being retreated into his works, Sir FRANCIS VERE called me to him, and said, "Boy, come now, pull up my stockings, and tie my points!" and so returned home again to his rest.

The next Remarkable in the series of this famous siege was that memorable Treaty which General VERE entertained with the Archduke: of which I know none better able to give an account than Sir JOHN OGLE, who had much at stake in the business, and was well acquainted with the several passages thereof; of which he hath left behind him the following account.

Sir FRANCIS VERE's *Parley at Ostend*: written by Sir JOHN OGLE, there present.

AFTER the battle of Nieuport, the Archduke CHARLES, desirous to clear Flanders, in the year following [1601], sat down with his army before Ostend: unto which, the Lords the States sent Sir FRANCIS VERE, their General to defend it.

He having good numbers of men, thought it most serviceable for the States, to employ them so, as he might keep the enemy at arm's end, and a fair distance from the town. To this purpose, he possessed himself of several advantageous pieces of ground, fortifying upon them so well as the time would give him leave. But they were morsels as well for the enemy's tooth as his, and therefore cost both bickering and blood on both sides, till at the last, what with numbers, artillery, and better commodity of access, he was forced to quit the most of them; and that, ere he brought them to any perfection of strength whereby to make any resistance.

Such as were nearest the town, and under the succour of his own power, as the three Quarriers or Squares, with some few others, he kept and maintained as long as he stayed there. Yet when, by protract of time and casualties of war, he found his numbers wasted, and himself (the enemy creeping upon him) so straitened as he was thrust merely upon the defence; he saw he was not in his proper element. Nor indeed, was he: for the truth is, his virtues, being great, strong, and active, required more elbow room; having their best lustre where they had the largest foil to set them off.

The works of Battle, Invasion, and the like were the proper objects of his spirit. The limits of Ostend were much too narrow for him: yet did he, there, many things worth the observation and reputation of so great a Captain as he was. Amongst the rest, that of his Parley [*negotiations with the Archduke ALBERT*] was of most eminent note; and as most noted, so most and worst censured, and that as well by Sword- as Gown-men. Yea, his judgement (which even by his enemies hath often been confessed to be one of the most able that ever our nation delivered to the world, in matters of his profession) was in the action taxed [*censured*], and that in print, too, for his manner of carriage in this business.

Now because I was, in some sort, the only instrument he used in the managing thereof, and best acquainted with all passages: I have (for the love I owe to Truth, and his memory) thought good to set down in writing, what I have hitherto delivered to the Lords the States General in their council chamber; as also, some time after that, to the Prince MAURICE of Nassau, and the Earl WILLIAM his cousin, concerning this matter.

Yet ere I come to the Relation, it shall not be amiss to wipe away two main aspersions which I have often met withal, by way of objection; and are as well in every man's mouth, as in EMANUEL DE METEREN's book.

The first, and that is the word, *it lucked well!* judging the fact by the event; but reservedly condemning the purpose, *for had not the shipping come*, say they, *as it did, what would have become of the town? He would have given it up!*

Colonel UTENHOVEN, a man of note and yet living, one of their own nation, a Governor of a town, knows better: and the following treatise shall also make it appear otherwise; and that he had not the least thought of rendering the town, though succour had not come to him at all. This point therefore shall here need no further enlargement.

The second is that *he might have carried the matter otherwise, and have drawn less jealousy upon himself, by acquainting the Captains with it sooner; considering it was done without the privity of the Lords the States: nor was it fitting, to bring an enemy through such secret passages.*

This, at the first view, seems to say somewhat, as borrowing strength from the common proceedings in other ordinary Governors; who, upon the point as well of Parley as *Article*, ere they enter into either with an enemy, consult first, as it is fit, with the Captains of the garrison; and this, it seems, was likewise expected here. But upon what reasons? Was he such a Governor? He was a General! He had Governors under him! Did he intend, as commonly do others, to deliver the town? He meant nothing less! as is partly before, and shall be hereafter largely proved. What account did the States ever require of him? What disgrace was there given him, more than a free acknowledgement of his singular carriage and judgement in the managing of a business of so great importance!

True it is, there was at first a kind of staggering, among the best; which the mist of some partial information from some malevolent person in Ostend had brought them to: but this was soon cleared (first, by his own letters in brief, and after by me more at large), if not to the most of them; yet I dare say to the most discreet and judicious amongst them.

But let us now see whether it had been either necessary or convenient that the secret of this stratagem should have been revealed sooner, either to the Lords the States, or Captains of the garrison?

To me it seems, that it had been, to the States, preposterous! to the Captains, dangerous! nay more, repugnant to sense and common reason! and that for these reasons following.

The project itself was but an *embryo*; and had been a mere abortive, had he delivered himself of it, before the attempt of the enemy: for from thence, it must receive both form and being. Now that, was uncertain and unknown to him, especially the time. He could therefore have no certain befitting subject to write to the Lords the States of this matter till the deed were done, and the project put in practice: which so soon as it was, he presently despatched a messenger, giving them a due account of the cause of his proceedings; and that, to their contentment.

It was a stratagem, whose power and virtue consisted wholly in secrecy. It was also a thread whereon hung no less than the States' town, his own honour, and the lives of all them that were with him; and therein reason did not admit of the last communication. *For the best pledge you can have of a man's secrecy, is not to open your thoughts unto him.*

Lastly, if he would have forgot himself so much as to have committed a secret to the trust of many; could he yet promise himself that he should not meet with opposition? Would they, instantly, have been, all, of his mind? Would no man suspect the handling? Why did they then after? and that, when it was consummated and finished?

I have heard Colonel UTENHOVEN say, that "if the General should have made the proposition, he had broken the enterprise!" and he knew best the Captains' inclinations: for he was the mouth betwixt the General and them, to clear those jealousies he saw them apprehend in him. It was therefore the safest and best way that could be taken, to set this business abroach, rather without their knowledge than flatly against it; and to hazard the interpretation of the action rather than the action itself.

Besides, whoever yet knew the General VERE so simple or so weak, as to avoid military forms where they were necessary or expedient? Wanted he judgement? His enemies will not say it! Had he not will? He had too many of them too Great, to lay himself open to their malice! He was a better manager of his reputation than to give them so palpable, so gross an advantage to build their scandal on.

It was the Public Service and his own judgement that led him into this course: wherein, if there were any danger for his part, it lay on my head, which he ventured for the safety of all.

It seems, then, that as it was not necessary, so had it been exceedingly inconvenient that the book of this secret should have been sooner unclasped before it was set on foot; or to the Lords the States, before it was accomplished.

I come now to the Relation, leaving the branch in the objection, touching *the bringing in of the enemy*, as not worthy to receive an answer [*see p.* 163].

About the 12th of November [1601], it began to freeze exceedingly, the wind being North-west; where it remained till Christmas or after, blowing for the most [part] a stiff gale, and often high and stormy.

In this time, came no shipping unto us, or succour out of Holland or Zealand; nor could they for the wind: nor had we any, for some few weeks after. Our men, munition, and materials wasted daily. The sea and our enemy both grew upon us.

At the spring-tide, we look still when that would decide the question touching the town, betwixt us and our adversaries: so exceedingly high and swelling it was, through the continuance of the north-west wind; which beat flat upon us, and brought extraordinary store of waters from the ocean into those narrow parts. Hands, we could set very few on work: our places of Guard were so many, our numbers so small, and those over-watched. 2,100 men was our strength; but the convenient competency for the town was at least 4,000. For workmen, our need was more than ever: for the whole town, with the new forts therein, lately begun by the General (who foresaw the storm), lay more than half open; insomuch that, in divers places, with little labour, both horse and foot might enter. The North-west Ravelin, our champion against the sea, was almost worn away. The Porcupine or *Porcépic* was not well defensible. At all these places, could the enemy come to push of pike with us, when they list, at low water.

This was our condition: neither was the enemy ignorant thereof, nor unmindful to lay hold on his advantage; preparing all things from all parts, fitting for the advancement of his purpose, that was to assault the town.

Our General saw their provision and power, and his own weakness; but could prevent none of them otherwise than by practice [*craft*]. His industry slept not. His vigilancy appeared by the daily and nightly rounds he made about the town and works. His courage was the highest, when his forces were the lowest: for even then, he manifestly made it known so much, that of his store, he furnished plenty to others.

One day, going about the walls, he began to discourse of our being pressed, and said, "He cared not what the enemy could attempt upon him!" He was in one of the strongest quarters of the town, when he spake this; and not unwilling that such, as of themselves saw it not, should be kept ignorant of the danger that hung over their heads. The Captains and the Officers, he commended for their care and industry in their watch and guard: more to stir them up unto it, than really to congratulate that virtue in them. He said, "A Captain could receive no greater blow in his reputation, than to be surprised." Divers other speeches he used, tending to encouragement, and dissuading from security; and often, amongst them, interlaced the strength of the town.

I, at the first perceiving not his mask, began to put him in mind of some of the former particulars; the whole town's weakness, and the Archduke's opportunity: but he told me quickly by his eye, he would not have their strength touched in such an audience; so, slighting my speeches, he continued his pace, and *à la volée* his discourse, till he came to his lodging.

There, he called to me alone, and brake to me in these terms, "I perceive you are not ignorant of our estate; and therefore I will be more open and free with you! What think you? Are we not in a fine taking here! ha! I will tell you, Captain OGLE, there was never man of my fortunes and reputation, both of which have been cleared hitherto, plunged in greater extremity than I am now."

Here, we discoursed of our condition before mentioned. Whereupon, he inferred that "he was like a man that had both courage and judgement to defend himself; and yet must sit with his hands bound, whilst boys and devils came and boxed him about the ears. Yet this will I tell you too," said he, "rather than you shall ever see the name of FRANCIS VERE subscribed in the delivery of a town committed to his custody, or this hand to the least *Article* of Treaty, though with the Archduke's own person, had I a thousand lives, I would first bury them all in the rampire! Yet, in the meanwhile, judge you of the quality of this our being!"

I told him, that I thought "if he were in his former liberty; he would bethink himself ere he suffered himself to be penned up in such a cage again."

He made no reply; but addressed himself to his business, and I to mine. What his thoughts now were, I will not enter into; unless I had more strength to reach them. Sure I am, they want no stuff to work on. For the bone he had to gnaw upon, required as good teeth as any that were in HANNIBAL's head, to break it; and had not this been such, all the hands we had there, could not have plucked it out of our own throats.

Not long after this, the General called a Council of the Colonels and chief Officers. There he propounded these two points.

First, Whether, with the numbers formerly mentioned, we could, in time of assault, sufficiently furnish all parts?

Secondly, or if not, Whether, in such an extremity, we ought not to borrow the troops employed for the guard of the Quarriers, to the preservation of the Town?

This was more to sound our judgements than of any necessity for him to seek allowance of his actions from them, for Generals use not [*are not accustomed*] to ask leave of their Captains to dispose of their guards; what they are to quit, and what they are to keep.

Our numbers, they confessed, were too few; yet must the Quarriers at no hand be abandoned: but how to hold them sufficiently, and to provide for those places on which the fury of the storm was likely to pour itself forth, no man gave expedient. The voices were severally collected.

When it came to me, I said that "seeing our case standeth as it doth, our breaches many and great, our numbers few to defend them; my opinion is that, when we should see the cloud coming, we quit the Quarriers: for I know they were ordained for the custody, not to endanger the loss of the town:" that "of inconveniences, the least must ever be chosen"; that "it were ill husbandry to hazard the Principal, to save the Interest; and as little discretion to let the fire run on to burn the palace, whilst we were preserving the lodge."

The two Colonels, ROONE and Sir HORACE VERE, who spake after me, for the Chief spake last, were of the same mind; differing only in some circumstances, not in substance of opinion.

That the others were so scrupulous in this point is to be

thought to have proceeded rather from ignorance of our estate and danger, or else an apprehension grounded upon common opinion which was "lose the Quarriers, lose the town!"; or, it may be, the fear of the interpretation that the Lords the States would make of such an advice: and that fear was likely to be the greater, because perhaps they were not furnished with strength of reason to maintain their opinion; or else they might find it fittest to lay the burden on his shoulders that was best able to bear it, the General himself.

After this Council, there passed some few days till it was near Christmas. The Archduke was himself in person in the camp, the assault resolved on, and the time; the preparations brought down to the approaches: and the army, they only stayed for low water to give on.

Here began the General's project to receive being. Till now, it had none. Neither was it now time to call the Captains to a new Council, either to require their advice, or to tell them his own. He had his head and hands full: ours had not ached now, had not his waked then more for our safeties than ours could do for our own.

He bestirred him on all sides. His powers were quick and strong within him; and those without, he disposed of thus:

His troops, he placed mostly on Sand Hill, Porcupine or *Porcépic*, the North-east Ravelin, and the Forts and Curtain of the Old Town. These were the breaches. The other Guards were all furnished as was then fitting, according to our numbers.

The Quarriers held their men till a Parley was commenced: and by it, they were secured. The False Bray was abandoned by order, as not tenable in time of assault. The cannon in it were dismounted, lest it should be spoiled by our own in Helmont, which flanked it and the whole face of Sand Hill.

This False Bray [*a space at the bottom of the wall outside, defended by a parapet or breastwork defending, from the inner side of it, the moat*] was that dangerous *passage* mentioned in the objection going before [*pp.* 157, 159]; which I thought to have passed over, but am since otherwise advised.

It lay at the foot of Sand Hill, in the eye of the enemy, and was therefore as well known to them as to ourselves: and so was the way to it, for they saw daily our entry to the Guard, to be through a covert gallery forced through the bottom of the said hill. It [*the gallery*] was so narrow that two men armed were the most that could pass in front [*in a row*]. When you were come out of it, you were presently at the haven's side and the New Town, without discovering any Guard, Passage, or Place of importance, such as might any ways give the least advantage to the enemy's observation. It was, in truth, in nothing else secret but that it was covered overhead from the eye of the heavens: otherwise there was no passage about the whole town less prejudicial than that.

There is a bolt of the same quiver likewise fallen into EMANUEL DE METEREN's book. There, the General's judgement is, forsooth! controlled; and by the providence of Captain SINKLYER [? *SINCLAIR*] and some others, as they think, much bettered. The General, there, is said to have neglected the False Bray, and that, in a time when it was needful to have defended it: but Captain SINKLYER with other Captains provided for it. But how provided for it? SINKLYER with six musketeers undertook it! The Captains promised him two companies: the place could contain one good one! But why Musketeers alone, and not Pikes? Since they could make it good, why but six? and that against the fury of an army! What knowledge would they teach our cannon to spare the Scots and kill the Spaniards, being pesle mesle?

It is ridiculous. Captain SINKLYER, if he lived, would be angry to have his judgement thus wronged and printed so small, as to undertake the defence of the False Bray, when the Bulwark [*i.e., the Sand Hill*] itself was assaultable. But I leave these poor detractions that betray only the detractors' weakness: and so to return to the matter.

On the two Bulwarks formerly mentioned, Helmont and Sand Hill, with the mount Flamenburg, he placed store of artillery and mortars: the mortars most of all at Helmont with much ordnance; for that, as I said before, scoured the avenue of the enemy's coming upon the Sand Hill and the Old Town.

When he had thus ordered his affairs for defence, he began to betake him to his stratagem: which, indeed, was our best shelter against that storm.

He sent Captain LEWIS COURTIER, who spake good Spanish, into the Porcupine or *Porcépic,* the nearest place of Guard to the enemy, with orders to desire speech with some of them. He called twice or thrice, or more; but none answered him. So he effected nothing.

The General displeased thereat, sent me to the place on the same errand. I called, but no man answered. I beat a drum, but they would not hear. Upon that, I returned to the General, and told him, "they expected form. If he would speak with any of them, I must go without the limits of our works."

He desired it: but feared they would shoot at me. I put it to an adventure.

Coming to the haven's side, I caused the drummer to beat: and at the second call, one answered me.

After a little stay, the Governor of Sluis, MATTHEO CERANO, came to me. Each made his quality known to the other, and I, my errand to him that "the General VERE desired to have some qualified person of theirs, sent into the town to speak with him."

He made this known to the Archduke. I attended his return; which was speedy, and with acceptance. He told me of his affection to our nation, bred and nourished through the good correspondency and neighbourhood betwixt the Lord Governor of Flushing Sir ROBERT SIDNEY, and him. He would take it as a courtesy that the General VERE would nominate and desire him of the Archduke, to be employed in this business.

This was performed: and at our next meeting, it was agreed that I should be a pledge for him; that each should bring a companion with him; that he with his, should have General VERE's, I and mine, Don AUGUSTINO's word for our safety; that during the treaty, no hostility should be used on land; and that against low water, we should find ourselves there again at the same place. This done, we parted each to his home.

I told the General what had passed. He persuaded, and that earnestly, with the Netherlandish, French, and Captains of other nations, to have some one of them accompany me in this action; the rather to avoid that interpretation which he foresaw would follow, being managed by him and his English only: but they all refused, notwithstanding he assured several of them, his purpose was no other than to gain time.

Where, myself can testify, that coming to him almost at low water, to know his further pleasure; I found him very earnest in persuading with an old Captain, called NICHOLAS DE LEUR: to whom I heard him say, *Je vous assure ce n'est que pour gaigner temps.* I was not then so good a Frenchman as that I durst say I well understood him, neither the purpose he had with him. Since, I have learned both better.

This man refused as well as the rest. Whereupon the General, in a choler, willed me, to take with me whom I would myself; for he would appoint none!

I took my old companion, and then familiar friend, Captain FAIRFAX.

CERANO and OTTANES were then at the water side, when we came. SIMON ANTHONIO and GAMBOLETTI, both Colonels [*of Horse*] or *Maestros del Campo*, brought them over on horseback to us.

On the other side, Don JUAN DE PANTOCHI, *Adjudante*, received us; and Don AUGUSTINO DE MEXIA, at the battery: behind which, was the army ranged ready for the assault.

These two brought us to the Archduke [ALBERT], who was then come to the approaches [*trenches*], accompanied as became so great a Prince.

We performed those respects that were fitting.

He vouchsafed us the honour to move his hat.

Being informed by one HUGH OWEN, an Englishman, but a fugitive, of our names and families; as also that I could speak Spanish: he conjured me "as I was a Gentleman, to tell him if there were any deceit in this handling or not?"

I told him, "If there were, it was more than I knew of: for, with my knowledge, I would not be used as an instrument in a work of that nature."

He asked me then, "What instructions I had?"

I told him, "None! For we were come hither only as

pledges to assure the return of them, to whom he had given his instructions."

He asked me again, "Whether I thought the General meant sincerely or not?"

I told him, "I was altogether unacquainted with his purpose: but for anything I knew, he did."

Upon this, we were dismissed; and were by Don AUGUSTINO [DE MEXIA], whom Don JUAN DE PANTOCHI ever attended, brought to his lodging: and there honourably and kindly entertained; and visited by most of the chiefs of the army, and also by some ecclesiastical persons.

There came an advertisement from the approaches [*trenches*], of working in the town. This was occasioned, as they thought, by noise of knocking in palisadoes.

To give orders to the contrary; we were, after, carried on horseback thither. We having received answer that "it was only a cabin of planks set up to keep beer in": the noise of that work, and their suspicion ceased together. Yet we stayed some hours at the Guard of GAMBOLETTI, the Italian Colonel, who at that time had the Point [*the advanced post or entrenchment*]; and the Conde THEODORO TRIVULCI and some others of the cavalry accompanied us some hours: after which, we returned to the camp, and to the Don AUGUSTINO, and our rest.

In the morning, we found our lodging environed with a strong guard: and understood of the discontentments of CERANO and OTTANES, who had returned; and how they had not any speech with the General.

This startled me and FAIRFAX, who dreamt of no such matter; nor of any such manner of proceedings: FAIRFAX thought I had some secret instructions in particular; and desired me to tell "what the Fox meant to do?"

I told him, and it was truth, "I knew as little as he": but calling then to mind the discourse he [*VERE*] had in his lodging, and mentioned formerly in this [*p.* 161], and comparing it with the action; I said to FAIRFAX, "I verily believed that he meant to put a trick upon them."

"But," quoth he, "the trick is put upon us, methinks! For we are prisoners and in their power; they, at liberty, and our judges."

Don AUGUSTINO coming to us, gave an end to this discourse; and beginning another with me, apart in his own chamber, where, with a grave and settled countenance, he told me of the Commissioners' return, their entertainment and discontentment; as also the Archduke's towards me, for abusing him. And especially he urged these two points, That I told CERANO that "the General desired speech with some from His Highness;" which seemed not to be so, for he flatly refused: and that I had said to His Highness himself that "I was not an instrument of deceit," which also appeared otherwise, and would not, I must account, be so slightly passed over.

Hereunto, I answered, "That the Commissioners are returned without speech with the General is as strange to me as unexpected to them; and I am the more sensible of this discourtesy towards them, through the kind usage I receive here of you! but as I am not of counsel in this manner of proceedings, so I know as little how to help it as I can reach the drift. Touching the other point of His Highness's displeasure towards me, I hope so noble a Prince will admit no other impression of my person or actions than the integrity of both shall fairly deliver him. For if I have deceived him, it is more than probable I am deceived myself: nor do I believe that His Highness or any of you judge me so flat or so stupid as, upon knowledge of such a purpose, in irritating His Highness, I would deliver myself and friend as sacrifices to make another man's atonement. It is certain then, if the General hath fraud in this action, he borrows [*pledges*] our persons, not our consents to work it by; which though you have now in your power, yet I will not fear the least ill measure, so long as I have the word of Don AUGUSTINO for my safety."

The noble Gentleman, moved with my confidence, took me in his arms, assured me it again; as also any courtesy during my stay there: and was indeed as good as his word.

This thus passed, he told me, "He would relate faithfully to the Archduke, what I had said:" but yet, ere he went, he desired to know of me, what I thought was to be further done.

I told him, "It could not be, but there must be a mistaking on the one side or the other. That therefore, to clear all doubts, I held it expedient for me to write to the General, to let him know our present condition, His Highness's discontentment upon this manner of proceeding, the danger he exposed me unto; and to understand his further purpose for our enlargement."

This answer he carried presently to His Highness, and was interpreted by OWEN; and then sent by a messenger into the town. And thus was this rub removed, the Commissioners required and sent in, and the Parley brought upon the former foot again.

The General was not a little glad of their return, for it redeemed the fear he had of ours: who, as Captain CHARLES RASSART told me after, was not a little perplexed for me. He would often say, "What shall I do for my Lieutenant Colonel?" and wished he had me back again, though he paid my ransom five times over. He would sometimes comfort himself with hope of their civility and my demeanour: fearing the worst, he said, "I could not suffer better than for the public cause."

The reason he hazarded us, and handled them, was to gain so much more time. For that was precious to him, for the advancement of his works in the Old Town: to which, through the benefit of this occasion of cessation of hostility, he had now drawn most of the hands that could labour, giving them spades to work, and orders to have their weapons by them ready, upon occasion to fight.

He handled the matter so, that ere the Commissioners returned again, the Old Town and works were stronger by [the value of] a thousand men. He could not have done this, at least so conveniently, had he begun conference with them at their first entry; nor avoided that first conference, had he stayed them in the town: at least, (every man hath his own ways) he understood it so; and it was a sure and safe course for him and his designs.

For causing EDWARD GOLDWELL, a Gentleman that then waited on him in his chamber, to make an alarm at their entry: he pretended thereupon, treachery on their part, and made it the cause why he would neither let them stay in the town, nor return the way they came.

This bred disputes, and messengers passed to and fro betwixt them and the General. In the meantime, the flood [tide] came in, and the water waxed so high that there was no passage that way, without a boat: whereof there was none on that side of the town, nor any brought; for that had been to cross his own purpose.

The Commissioners desired earnestly to be suffered to stay, though it were upon the worst Guard [*the most destroyed fort*] of the town; but it was denied. For he must rid himself of them. He could not do his business so well, if their eyes and ears were so near him.

He sent them therefore to their friends on the *east* side, forecasting wisely that ere they could come there, and thence by the south to the west side again there to have admittance to His Highness, and there to have the matter debated in Council, he should not only gain the whole winter's night, but also the most part of the next day, for his advantage. Which fell out according to that calculation; and, beyond his expectation, it continued longer.

At the Commissioners' return, his latter entertainment to them was better than the first. He feasted with them, drank and discoursed with them; but came to no direct overture of *Article*, though they much pressed him. That part of the day and the whole night was so spent, and in sleep.

The like had we in the camp; except drinking, whereof there was no excess; but of good cheer and courtesy abundance.

In the morning, were discovered five ships out of Zealand riding in the road. They brought 400 men, and some materials for the sea works. The men were landed on the strand with long-boats and shallops. The enemy shot at them with their artillery, but did no hurt.

The pretext of succour from the States, the General took to break off the treaty: which he had not yet really entered into.

The Commissioners were, on both sides, discharged in this order. CERANO came first into the army. It was my right to have gone [back] for him; but I sent Captain FAIRFAX, at the earnest entreaty of Don JUAN DE PANTOCHI [*pp.* 166, 167] and some others: who said, "They desired my stay, only to have my company so much the longer;" making me believe it was agreeable to them, the rather for that I spake their language. I was the more willing to yield, because I would not leave any other impression than that I saw they had received of my integrity in the negotiation. FAIRFAX being in the town, OTTANES made not long stay; nor I, after him.

The General was not pleased that I stayed out of my turn; but when I gave him my reasons for it, he seemed to be well contented.

Concerning what was done within the town during the treaty; HENRY HEXHAM [*Sir F. VERE's Page*] gives us this further account upon his own knowledge.

THE next day, towards evening, the enemy's Commissioners, CERANO and OTTANES, returned again. General VERE's last entertainment of them, was better than his first. For he then feasted them, made them the best cheer he could, drank many healths as the Queen of England's, the King of Spain's, the Archduke's, Prince MAURICE's, and divers others; and discoursed with them at the table, before his brother Sir HORACE VERE and the chief Officers of the town, whom he had invited to keep them company: and having drunk freely, led them into his own chamber, and laid them in his own bed, to take their rests.

The Commissioners going to bed, the General took his leave of them; and presently after, went to the Old Town: where he found Captain DEXTER and Captain CLARK with their men, silently at work. Having been with them an hour or two, to give them directions what they should do, returning to his lodging, he laid him down upon his quilt, and gave me charge that, an hour before day, I should go to RALPH DEXTER, and command him from him, "not to draw off his men till the dawning of the day, but that they should follow their work lustily."

And coming to him, at the time appointed, according to my Lord's command; after the break of day, we looked out towards the sea, and espied five men-of-war, come out of Zealand, riding in the road, which had brought 400 men and some materials for the sea works.

Coming home, I wakened my Master, and told him the first news of it. He presently sent for our Captain of the Shallops and Long-boats, which la[u]nc[h]ing out, landed them on the strand, by our new Middle Haven.

And notwithstanding the enemy shot mightily upon them, with their cannon from their four batteries on the east and west side, to sink them, and hinder their landing: yet did they no other harm but only hurt three mariners.

These pieces of ordnance roused CERANO from "his naked bed": who knocking, asked me, "What was the reason of this shooting?"

I answered him in French, *Il y avait quelque gens d'armes de notres entrés dans la ville*: whereat he was much amazed; and would hardly give credit to it, till Captain POTLEY (who came with these ships, and whom he knew well) was brought before him, and assured him it was so.

General VERE, having now received part of the long-expected supplies, together with the assurance of more at hand, straightways broke off the Treaty: which, though ending somewhat abruptly, had, it seems, finished the part which was by him allotted to it.

Whereupon, he sent the Archduke the following acquittance.

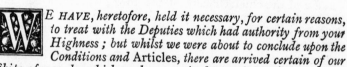

WE HAVE, heretofore, held it necessary, for certain reasons, to treat with the Deputies which had authority from your Highness; but whilst we were about to conclude upon the Conditions and Articles, *there are arrived certain of our Ships of war, by which we have received part of that which we had need of: so that we cannot, with our honour and oath, continue the Treaty, nor proceed in it, which we hope that your Highness will not take in ill part; and that, nevertheless, when your power shall reduce us to the like estate, you will not refuse, as a most generous Prince, to vouchsafe us again a gentle audience.*

From our town of Ostend,
the 25th of December, 1601.

(*signed*) *FRANCIS VERE.*

Now, whosoever shall but consider how many, and how great difficulties the Archduke had struggled with, to maintain the siege; how highly concerned he was in point of honour, and how eagerly engaged in his affections; and what assured hopes he had of taking the town, will easily conceive that he must needs find himself much discomposed at so unexpected a disappointment. He had already taken it with his eyes: and as if he had bound the Leviathan for his maidens to sport withal, under the assurance of the truce, he walked the Infanta before the town, with twenty Ladies and Gentlewomen in her train; as it were valiantly to stroke this wild beast which he had now laid fast in the toils, and to look upon the outside of the town before they entered into it.

Now, to have his hopes thus blown up, and to be thrown from the top of so much confidence; wonder not if we find him much enraged at it! and what can we now expect but that he should let fly his rage in a sudden and most furious assault upon the town? especially considering that, before the Treaty began, all things were in readiness for such a purpose. But whether it were, that the Treaty had unbended the soldiers' resolution, or the unexpected breaking off had astounded the Archduke's counsels, or whether his men were discouraged at their enemy's increased strength, or whatsoever the cause were: certain it is, that there was no considerable assault made upon the town, for many days after.

And we have cause to believe that General VERE was never a whit sorry for it; who had by this means, opportunity, though no leisure, to repair his works: wherein he employed above 1,200 men for at least eight days together. During which time, he stood in guard in person, at the time of low water in the night, being the time of greatest danger; which conduced much to the encouragement of his men. Having received intelligence, by his scouts, of the enemy's preparations and resolutions, within a few days, to give them a general assault: he was careful to man the chief places, Helmont, Sand Hill, and the rest; and to furnish them with cannon and stones, and what else might be useful for their defence.

Meanwhile, the besiegers spared no powder; but let fly at the ships, which notwithstanding, daily and nightly, went into the town: and many a bullet was interchanged between the town and the camp, which lay, all this while, pelting at one another; some small hurts on both sides being given and received.

But the 7th of January [1602] was the day designed by the besiegers wherein to attempt something extraordinary.

All the day long without intermission, did the Archduke batter the Bulwark of Sand Hill, Helmont, *Porcépic*, and other places adjoining, with 18 cannon from two of his batteries: the one at the foot of the downs upon the Catteys, and the other on the south side thereof. From whence were discharged, which the cannoneers counted, above 2,000 shot on that side of the town: all the bullets weighing 40lbs. or 46lbs. apiece.

After I was thus far engaged, I happily [*by hap*] met with an account of this bloody assault, by HENRY HEXHAM, who was present at it. To him, therefore, I shall willingly resign the story.

[Henry Hexham, Sir Francis Vere's Page.

Account of the Assault on Ostend, 7th January, 1602.]

HIs Highness the Archduke then seeing himself thus deluded by General VERE's Parley, was much vexed thereat; and was very angry with the chief of his Council of War, who had diverted him from giving the assault upon that day [*23rd December*, 1601] when the Parley was called for: insomuch that some of them, for two or three days after, as it was credibly reported, durst not look him in the face.

Others, to please him, persuaded him to give an assault upon the town. Hereupon, His Highness took a resolution to revenge himself of those within the town, saying "he would put them all to the sword!" his Commanders and soldiers taking likewise an oath that, if they entered, "they would not spare man, woman, nor child in it!"

Till that, the enemy had shot upon and into the town, above 163,200 cannon shot, to beat it about our ears; scarcely leaving a whole house standing: but now, to pour out his wrath and fury more upon us, on the 7th of January [1602] above-said, very early in the morning, he began with 18 pieces of cannon and half-cannon, carrying bullets of 48lbs and 40lbs apiece [*See Vol. IV. p.* 251], from their Pile Battery, and that which stood under their Cattey upon the foot of the downs, to batter Sand Hill, the *Porcépic*, and Helmont. And that day till evening, he shot upon Sand Hill and the Curtain of the Old Town, above 220 cannon shot; insomuch that it might rather have been called Iron Hill than Sand Hill: for it stuck so full of bullets, that many of them tumbled down into the False Bay; and others striking on their own bullets, broke in pieces, and flew up into the air as high as a steeple.

During this furious battery, the enemy, all the day long, made great preparations to assault us against night: and to that end, brought down scaling ladders, great store of ammunition, hand grenades [*small shells thrown with the hand*], and divers other instruments and materials of war fitting thereunto; and withal, towards evening, drew down his army, and ordered his men in this manner:

Count FARNESE, an Italian, should first give on, with 2,000 Italians and Spaniards, upon Sand Hill, the breach, and the Curtain of the Old Town: and the Governor of Dixmunde, with 2,000 Spaniards and other nations, upon the *Porcépic* and Helmont. Another Captain, with 500 men, was to fall on upon the West Ravelin; and another Captain, with 500 men more, upon the South Quarriers: and the Spanish Sergeant-Major General [? *OTTANES*] which was an hostage in Ostend, upon the West Quarriers. Making in all 8,000 men to assault the west side.

And the Count of BUCQUOY was to have assaulted the east side, the East Ravelin and the New Haven; as a second [*support*] for them which fell on upon the Sand Hill and the Old Town on the west side. And thus their men, time, and place were ordered.

General VERE knowing the enemy's intent, that he would assault us at low water, slept not; but was exceedingly careful and vigilant, all the day, to prepare the things necessary to defend the town and withstand the enemy. And because there were no spars, beams, and palisadoes in the Magazine, he caused divers houses that were shot [through], to be pulled down; and taking the beams and spars from off them, he made the carpenters make palisadoes and stockadoes of them. At a high water, he shut the West Sluices, and engrossed as much water as he possibly could into the Old and New Town.

Towards evening, he drew all the men in the town that were able to fight, into arms: and disposed of them, as followeth:

To maintain Sand Hill, and defend the breach, he placed his brother Sir HORACE VERE, and Sir CHARLES FAIRFAX [*pp.* 136, 166] with 12 weak companies, whereof some were not above 10 or 12 strong; giving them double arms, a pike and a musket, and a good store of ammunition.

Upon the Curtain [*i.e., the plain wall*] of the Old Town between Sand Hill and a redoubt called Schottenburch (a most dangerous place, which he feared most; being torn and beaten down with the sea and the enemy's cannon), Sir FRANCIS VERE stood himself, with Captain ZEGLIN with 6 weak companies, to help to defend it.

Within the redoubt of Schottenburch itself, he appointed Captain UTENHOVEN [*pp.* 157, 159] and Captain HAUGHTON, with their 2 companies.

From Schottenburch along the Curtain to the Old Church (which the enemy had shot down); he placed Colonel LONE with his 300 Zealanders that came in to the town [*in the five ships, pp.* 170, 172] the day [25*th Dec.*, 1601] the Parley brake off.

From the Old Church along the Curtain and the Flanks to the north part; Captain ZITHAN commanded over 6 weak companies.

Upon the redoubt called Moses Table, was Captain MONTESQUIRE DE ROQUES, a worthy French Captain, whom Sir FRANCIS VERE loved entirely for the worth and valour that was in him, with 2 French companies.

For the guarding of the North Ravelin; he appointed Captain CHARLES RASSART with 4 weak companies.

The rest of the Curtain, by reason of the Flanks upon the cut of the New Haven, being reasonably well defended, were left unmanned.

Upon the Curtain of the New Town, under Flamenburg, were placed 5 weak companies; to second [*support*] Moses Table, if need did require.

Upon Flamenburg, 2 whole-cannon and 2 field pieces were planted, to scour the Old Town.

Upon the West Ravelin, 2 companies were likewise placed, and a whole-cannon and 2 half-cannon planted upon it.

For the defending of the *Porcépic*, a place of great importance, lying under the Helmont; Sir FRANCIS VERE placed four of the strongest companies that could be found in the town.

Upon the Bulwark called Helmont, which flanked directly the breach and Sand Hill, and scoured along the strand, between the enemy's Pile Battery, the Old Haven, over which they were to pass to come to Sand Hill, and the Curtain of the Old Town, which also did help to defend the *Porcépic*: he placed 10 weak companies, whereof the General's company was one. And it had upon it 9 brass and iron pieces, ladened with chained bullets, boxes with musket bullets, and cartridge shot. These 10 companies were kept as a reserve, to be employed as a second [*reinforcement*] where most occasion required. They were commanded by Captain METKIRCK and Sergeant-Major [= *the present Major of a foot regiment: see Vol. I. p.* 463] CARPENTER.

The rest of the bulwarks and rampires, and the Counterscarp about the town were but slightly manned, with a few men; in regard that the enemy could come to attempt none of them, till he became master of the former.

Here you see a great many companies thus disposed of; but all, or most of them, were exceedingly weak, and some of them not above 7 or 8 men strong: which in all, could not make above 1,200 able fighting men, to resist an army of 10,000 men, that stood ready to assault them.

The ordnance and other instruments and materials of war the General disposed of in this sort:

Upon the casement of the West Bulwark, he planted two whole and two half-cannon, which flanked Helmont and the *Porcépic*, and scoured along the Old Haven down as far as the Ton Beacon, beyond their Pile Battery, next to that place where they were to pass over the haven at a low water. This ordnance was likewise charged with musket bullets, chain bullets, and iron bullets.

Upon all these batteries, especially those which flanked the breach and played directly upon the strand; Sir FRANCIS VERE disposed of the best cannoneers in the town: among the rest, FRANCIS the GURMER, an excellent cannoneer, who had been the death of many a Spaniard. And because they should be sure to take their mark right upon their cog [*mark*], before it grew dark, he commanded them to let fly two or three cannon bullets upon the strand and towards the New Haven, to see for a trial where their bullets fell, that they might find their ground the better in the night, when the enemy was to fall on.

Moreover, on the top of the breach, and along the Curtain of the Old Town, were set firkins of ashes, to be tumbled down the wall upon the enemy to blind them: also little firkins with *frize-ruyters* or quadrant tenternails, three sticking in the ground and one upright; which were likewise to be cast down the rampire to prick them, when they sought to enter. Then there were many great heaps of stones and brickbats (brought from the Old Church they had shot down) to throw amongst them. Then we had ropes of pitch, hoops bound about with squibs and fireworks to throw among them, great store of hand grenades; and clubs, which we called "Hercules Clubs," with heavy heads of wood and nails driven into the squares of them. These and some others, because the enemy had sworn all our deaths, the General provided to entertain and welcome them.

When it began to grow darkish, a little before low water, in the interim while the enemy was a cooling of his ordnance, which had played all the day long upon the breach and the Old Town: the General taking advantage of this precious time, commanded Captain DEXTER and Captain CLARK with some 50 stout workmen, who had a rose-noble [=16*s.* 8*d.*=£4 *now*] a piece, for a quarter of an hour's work, to get up to the top of the breach which the enemy's cannon had made very mountable, and then, with all expedition, to cast up a small breastwork and drive in as many palisadoes as possibly they could: that his brother Sir HORACE VERE, and the rest of the Captains and soldiers which he commanded, might have some little shelter, the better to defend the breach and repulse the enemy, when he strove to enter. Which, blessed be GOD! with the loss of a few men, they performed.

This being done, Sir FRANCIS VERE went through the Sally Port, down into the False Bray. And it being twilight, called for an old soldier, a Gentleman of his company, to go out *sentinel-perdu* [*i.e.*, *in a hazardous position*], and to creep out to the strand between two gabions; giving him express command that if he saw an enemy, he should come in unto him silently, without giving any alarm at all.

He crept upon his belly as far as he could; and, at last, discovered Count FARNESE above mentioned, wading and put over the Old Haven, above their Pile Battery, with his 2,000 Italians, which were to fall on first: and, as they [had] waded over, he drew them up into battalions and divisions: which this Gentleman having discovered, came silently to Sir FRANCIS VERE, as he had commanded him. Who asked him, "What news?"

"My Lord," says he, "I smell good store of gold chains, buff jerkins, Spanish cassocks [*long military cloaks*], and Spanish blades."

"Ha!" say Sir FRANCIS VERE, "sayest thou me so! I hope thou shalt have some of them anon!" and giving him a piece of gold, he went up again through the Sally Port to the top of Sand Hill. Where he gave express order to Sergeant-Major CARPENTER to go to Helmont, and every man to his charge; and not to take any alarm, or shoot off either cannon- or musket-shot till he himself gave the signal: and then to give fire, both with the ordnance and small shot, as fast as ever they could charge and discharge.

When the enemy had put over his 2,000 Italians; he had also a signal, to give notice thereof to the Count of BUCQUOY, that they were ready to fall on: whose signal was the shot of a cannon from their Pile Battery into the sea towards his quarters, with a hollow-holed bullet, which made a humming noise.

When General VERE had got them under the swoop of his cannon and small shot, he poured a volley of cannon- and musket-shot upon them, raking through their battalions, and makes lanes through them upon the bare strand; which did so amaze and startle them, that they were at a *non-plus* whether they should fall on or retreat back again. Yet at last taking courage, and tumbling over the dead bodies, they rallied themselves and came under the foot of Sand Hill and along the foot of the Curtain of the Old Wall, to the very piles that were struck under the wall, where they began to make ready to send us a volley.

Which Sir FRANCIS VERE seeing they were a presenting, and ready to give fire upon us, because indeed all the breastwork and parapet was beaten down flat to the rampire that day, with their ordnance, and we standing open to the enemy's shot, commanded all the soldiers to fall flat down upon the ground, while the enemy's shot flew like a shower of hail over their heads: which, for the reasons above said, saved a great many men's lives.

This being done; our men rising, saw the enemy hasting to come up to the breach, and mounting up the wall of the Old Town. Sir FRANCIS VERE flourishing his sword, called to them in Spanish and Italian, *Vienneza!*; causing the soldiers, as they climbed up, to cast and tumble down among them, the firkins of ashes, the barrels of *frize-ruyters*, the ropes, stones and brickbats which were provided for them.

The alarm being given, it was admirable to see with what courage and resolution our men fought. Yea, the LORD did, as it were, infuse fresh courage and strength into a company of poor snakes [? *sneaks or hideaways*] and sick soldiers, which came running out of their huts up to the wall to fight their shares; and the women with their laps full of powder, to supply them, when they had shot away all their ammunition.

Now were all the walls of Ostend all on a light fire, and our ordnance thundering upon them, from our Bulwarks. Now was there a lamentable cry of dying men among them: for they could no sooner come up to the top of the breach to enter it, or peep up between Sand Hill and Schottenburch but they were either knocked on the head with the stocks of our muskets or our Hercules Clubs, or run through with our pikes and swords. Twice or thrice, when they strived to enter, they were beaten off, and could get no advantage upon us.

The fight upon the breach and the Old Town continued, hotter and hotter, for the space of above an hour. The enemy fell on, at the same instant, upon the *Porcépic*, Helmont, the West Ravelin, and Quarriers; but were so bravely repulsed, that they could not enter a man.

The enemy fainting, and having had his belly full; those on the west side beat a doleful retreat: while the Lord of Hosts ended our dispute for the town, and crowned us with victory: and the roaring noise of our cannon rending the air and rolling along the superficies of the water, the wind being South and with us, carried that night the news thereof, to our friends in England and Holland.

General VERE perceiving the enemy to fall off, commanded me to run, as fast as ever I could, to Sergeant-Major CARPENTER and the Auditor FLEMING, who were upon Helmont, that they should presently [*at once*] open the West Sluice: out of which there ran such a stream and torrent, through the channel of the West Haven, that, upon their retreat, it carried away many of their sound and hurt men into the sea. And besides, our men fell [*went*] down our walls after them, and slew a great many of their men as they retreated. They took some prisoners, pillaged and stript a great many [of the killed], and brought in gold chains, Spanish pistols, buff jerkins, Spanish cassocks, blades, swords, and targets [*shields*] (among the rest, one wherein was enamelled in gold, the Seven Worthies worth 700 or 800 guilders [=£70 or £80= £350 or £400 *now*]).

Among the rest, was that soldier which Sir FRANCIS VERE had sent out to discover; who came with as much booty as ever he could lug, saying, "Sir FRANCIS VERE was now as good as his word."

Under Sand Hill and all along the walls of the Old Town, the *Porcépic*, and West Ravelin, lay whole heaps of dead carcases, 40 or 50 upon a heap, stark naked; goodly young men, Spaniards and Italians: among which, some, besides other marks to know them by, had their beards clean shaven off. There lay also upon the sand some dead horses; ladened with baskets of hand grenades. They left also behind them their scaling ladders, great store of spades and showels [*shovels*], bills, hatchets and axes, with other materials.

Here the French *Diary* adds, that those who gave the assault on the Old Town, were furnished with two or three day's victuals, which they had brought in sacks: intending to have intrenched themselves, and maintain the place against the besieged, if their enterprise had succeeded. Also that, among the heaps of the slain was found, in man's apparel, the body of a young Spanish woman, near unto Sand Hill: who, as was conjectured by her wounds, had been slain in the assault; having under her apparel, a chain of gold set with precious stones, besides other jewels and silver. And also that, during this assault, the Archduke disposed of himself behind the battery of the Catteys; and the Infanta remained at the Fort Isabella.

Upon the east side also, they stood in three great battalions before the town, upon the Gullet; but the tide coming in, they came too late: so that they could not second those on the west side, and fall on where they were appointed; to wit, upon our New Haven, which lay upon the north-east side of the town. For the water beginning to rise, it did amaze the soldiers; and they feared, if they stayed any longer, they could not be relieved by their fellows.

However, for their honour, they would do something: and resolved to give upon our Spanish Half-Moon, which lay over the Gullet [*i.e.*, *on the other side the Geule from the town*], on the south-east part of the town.

A soldier of ours falling out of it (a policy of Sir FRANCIS VERE's); disappointed this design [*i.e.*, *of supporting the western attack*], and yielding himself prisoner unto them, told them that there were but 40 soldiers in the Half-Moon; and offered to lead them to it. Which he did, and they took it. For General VERE, with great judgement, had left it thus ill-manned; to draw the enemy on the east side thither, to separate them from their fellows on the west side, and to make them lose time: contenting himself to guard the places of most importance; and assuring himself that he should soon recover the other at his pleasure.

The Archduke's men, having thus taken the Half-Moon, and being many therein; they began with spades, shovels, pickaxes, and other instruments, to turn it up against the town: but all prevailed not, for it lay open towards the town. And those of the town began to shoot at them, from the South and Spanish Bulwarks, both with cannon- and musket-shot, with such fury, that they slew many of them; and withal seeing the tide come in more and more, they began to faint. Whereupon General VERE sent Captain DAY with some troops, to beat them out of it; who, with great courage, chased them out of it, with the effusion of much blood: for, the next day, they told [*counted*] 300 men slain in the Half-Moon, besides those that were drowned and hurt.

In this general assault, which, on both sides of the town, continued above two hours upon all the places above mentioned; the Archduke, besides some that were carried into the sea, lost above 2,000 men. Among the which, there were a great number of noblemen, chiefs and commanders: among the rest, the Count D'IMBERO, an Italian (who offered as much gold as he did weigh for his ransom, yet he was slain by a private soldier); Don DURANGO, *Maistro del Campo*, or Colonel; Don ALVARES SUARES, Knight of the Order of St. James; SIMON ANTHONIO, Colonel; the Sergeant-Major-General [? OTTANES], who had been hostage in Ostend, on the 24th and 25th of December, 1601 [*see pp.* 166, 171]; and the Lieutenant-Governor of Antwerp, and divers others.

On our side, there were slain between 30 and 40 soldiers, and about 100 hurt. The men of Command slain were, Captain HAUGHTON, Captain VAN DEN LIER a Lieutenant of the new *Geux*, 2 English Lieutenants, an Ancient [*Ensign-bearer*], Captain HAUGHTON'S two Sergeants: and Master TEDCASTLE, a Gentleman of Sir FRANCIS VERE'S horse, who was slain between Sir FRANCIS VERE and myself, his Page, with two musket-bullets chained together. Who calling to me, bade me pull off his gold ring from off his little finger, and send it to his sister, as a token of his last "Good night:" and so, commending his spirit into the hands of the LORD, died. Sir HORACE VERE was likewise hurt in the leg, with a splinter that flew from a palisado.

And thus much, briefly, of the assault and the repulse they received in Ostend, that day and night; in memory of the heroic actions of Sir FRANCIS VERE, of famous memory, my old Master.

After this bloody shower was once over, the weather cleared up into its usual temper: and so continued, not without good store of artificial thunder and lightning on both sides daily; but without any remarkable alterations, until the 7th of March then next ensuing, which was in the year 1602.

Then did General VERE, having lately repaired the Poulder and West Square, resign up his government of Ostend unto others appointed by the States to succeed him: having valiantly defended it, for above eight months, against all the Archduke's power; and leaving it much better able to defend itself, than it was at his first coming thither.

So the same night, both he and his brother, Sir HORACE VERE, embarked themselves, having sent away their horses and baggage before them; both carrying with them, and leaving behind them, the marks of true honour and renown.

FINIS.

Sir THOMAS OVERBURY

HIS

OBSERVATIONS,

IN HIS TRAVELS,

UPON THE STATE OF THE SEVENTEEN PROVINCES,

AS THEY STOOD ANNO DOMINI 1609;

THE TREATY OF PEACE BEING THEN ON FOOT.

Printed. M.DC.XXVI.

Sir THOMAS OVERBURY's *OBSERVATIONS*, IN HIS TRAVELS, *UPON THE STATE OF THE SEVENTEEN PROVINCES*, *AS THEY STOOD ANNO, DOMINI 1609; THE TREATY OF PEACE BEING THEN ON FOOT.*

And first, Of the Provinces United.

ALL things concurred for the rising and maintenance of this State: the disposition of the people, being as mutinous as industrious and frugal; the nature of the country, everywhere fortifiable with water; the situation of it, having behind them the Baltic sea, which yields them all materials for ships, and many other commodities; and for men, hard before them France and England, both fearing the Spanish greatness, and therefore both concurring for their aid; the remoteness of their Master from them; the change of religion, falling out about the time of their Revolt; and now the Marquis of BRANDENBURGH, a Protestant, like[ly] to become [the] Duke of CLEVE.

The discontentments of the Low Countries did first appear soon after the going away of the Kings of Spain, while the Duchess of PARMA governed. To suppress which beginnings, the Duke of ALVA being sent, inflamed them more upon attempting to bring in the Inquisition, and Spanish decimation; upon the beheading [of] Count HORN and Count EGMONT, persecuting those of the Religion: and undertaking to build citadels upon all their towns; which he effected at Antwerp, but enterprising the like at Flushing, that town revolted first, and under it began the war.

But the more general Revolt of the Provinces happened after the death of Don LOUIS DE REQUIESCENS, and upon the coming down of Don JOHN of Austria: when all the Provinces, excepting Luxemburg (upon the sack of Antwerp and other insolences), proclaimed the Spaniards "rebels, and enemies to the King." Yet the abjuring of their obedience from the Crown of Spain, was not in a year or two after.

Holland and Zealand (upon their first standing out) offered the Sovereignty of themselves to the Queen, then the Protection, both which she neglected; and that, while the French sent greater aid, and more men of quality than we: but after the Civil War began in France, that kept them busy at home; and then the Queen, seeing the necessity of their being supported, upon the pawning of Brill and Flushing, sent money and men. And since that, most part of the great exploits there, have been done by the English, who were commonly the third part of their army; being four regiments, besides 1,100 in Flushing and the Ramekins, and 500 in the Brill. But, of late, the King of France appearing more for them than ours, and paying himself the French [soldiers] that are there; they give equal, if not more countenance to that nation. But upon these two Kings, they make their whole dependency: and though with more respect to him that is stronger for the time; yet so, as it may give no distaste unto the other.

For the manner of their Government. They have, upon occasion, an Assembly of the General States, like our Parliament; being composed of those which are sent from every Province upon summons; and what these Enact, stands for Law. Then is there besides, a Council of State, residing, for the most part, at the Hague: which attends [to] daily occasions; being rather employed upon Affairs of State than particular [*individual*] justice. The most potent in this Council was BARNEVELD, by reason of his Advocates of Holland. And besides both these, every Province and great

Town have particular Councils of their own. To all which Assemblies, as well of the General States as the rest, the gentry is called for order sake, but the State indeed is democratical: the merchant and the tradesman being predominant, the gentry, now, but few and poor; and, even at the beginning, the Prince of ORANGE saw it safer to rely upon the towns than [upon] them. Neither are the gentry so much engaged in the Cause: the people having more advantages in a Free State; they, in a Monarchy.

Their care in Government is very exact and particular, by reason that every one hath an immediate interest in the State. Such is the equality of justice, that it renders every man satisfied; such is the public regularity, as a man may see [that] their laws were made to guide, and not to entrap; such their exactness in casting the expense of an army, as that it shall be equally far from superfluity and want; and as much order and certainty in their acts of war, as in ours of peace; teaching it to be both civil and rich. And they still retain that sign of a Commonwealth yet uncorrupted, "Private poverty, and public weal!" for no one private man there is exceeding rich, and few very poor; and no State more sumptuous in all public things. But the question is, whether this, being a free State, will, as well subsist in peace, as it hath hitherto done in war. Peace leaving every one to attend [to] his particular wealth: when fear, while the war lasts, makes them concur for their common safety. And Zealand, upon the least security, hath ever been envious at the predominancy of Holland and Utrecht; ready to mutiny for religion: and besides, it is a doubt, whether the same care and sincerity would continue if they were at their Consistence, as appears yet, while they are but in Rising.

The Revenue of this State ariseth chiefly from the Earl of HOLLAND's domains; and confiscated church livings; the rising and falling of money, which they use with much advantage; their fishing upon our coasts, and those of Norway; contributions out of the enemy's country, taxes upon all things at home, and impositions [*import duties*] upon all merchandise from abroad.

Their Expenses upon their Ambassadors, their shipping, their ditches, their rampiers [*dykes*] and munition; and commonly they have in pay, by sea and land, 60,000 men.

For the strength. The nature of the country makes them able to defend themselves long by land. Neither could anything have endangered them so much as the last great frost [*of* 1608, *see Vol. I. p.* 77], had not the Treaty been then on foot: because the enemy, being then master of the field; that rendered their ditches, marshes, and rivers as firm ground.

There belongs to that State, 20,000 vessels of all sorts. So that if the Spaniard were entirely beaten out of those parts; the Kings of France and England would take as much pains to suppress, as ever they did to raise them. For being our enemies, they are [*would be*] able to give us the law at sea; and eat us out of all trade, much more the French: having at this time three ships for our one, though none so good as our best.

Now that whereupon the most part of their Revenue depends is their traffic, in which mystery of State they are, at this day, the wisest. For all the commodities that this part of the world wants, and the Indies have (as spice, silk, jewels, gold), they are become the conveyers of them for the rest of Christendom, except[ing] us: as the Venetians were of old. And all those commodities that those Northern countries abound with, and these Southern countries stand in need of: they likewise convey thither; which was the ancient trade of the Easterlings [*Baltic cities*]. And this they do, having little to export of their own, by buying of their neighbour-countries the former; and selling them again what they bring back, at their own prices: and so consequently, live upon the idleness of others. And to this purpose, their situation serves fitly. For the rivers of the Rhine, the Maas, and [the] Scheldt all end in their dominions; and the Baltic sea lies not far from them: all which afford them whatever the great continent of Germany, Russia, and Poland yields.

Then they, again, lying between Germany and the sea, do furnish it back, with all commodities foreign.

To remember some pieces of their discipline, as patterns of the rest. The Watches at night are never all of one nation [*race*], so that they can hardly concur to give up any one town. The Commissaries are nowhere so strict upon Musters, and where he finds a company thither, he reduceth them: so that, when an army marcheth, the List and the Poll are never far disagreeing. The army is ever well clothed, well armed; and had never yet occasion to mutiny for pay or victuals. The soldiers commit nowhere fewer insolences upon the burghers, few robberies upon the country; nor the Officers fewer deceits upon the soldiers. And lastly, they provide well that their General shall have small means to invade their liberties. For first, their Army is composed of many nations, which have their several Commanders; and the commands are disposed by the States themselves, not by the General. And secondly, he hath never an implicit commission left to discretion: but, by reason their country hath no great bounds, receives daily commands what to do.

Their territory contains six entire Provinces; Holland, Zealand, Utrecht, Groningen, Overyssel, and Friesland, besides three parts of Guelderland, and certain towns in Brabant and Flanders: the ground of which is, for the most part, fruitful; the towns nowhere are so *equally* beautiful, strong, and rich: which equality grows by reason that they appropriate some one staple commodity to every town of note; only Amsterdam not only passeth them all, but even Seville, Lisbon, or any other Mart Town in Christendom. And to it, is appropriated the trade of the East Indies, where they maintain commonly forty ships; besides which, there go, twice a year, from it and the adjoining towns, a great fleet to the Baltic sea. Upon the fall of Antwerp, that [town of Amsterdam] rose, rather than Middleburgh; though it [*that*] stands at the same river's mouth, and is the second Mart Town; to which is appropriated our English cloth.

Concerning the people. They are neither much devout, nor much wicked; given all to drink, and, eminently, to no other vice; hard in bargaining, but just; surly, and respectless, as in all democracies; thirsty [? *thrifty*], industrious, and cleanly; disheartened upon the least ill-success, and insolent upon good; inventive in manufactures; cunning in traffic. And generally, for matter of action, that natural slowness of theirs suits better (by reason of the advisedness and perseverance it brings with it) than the rashness and changeableness of the French and Florentine wits. And the equality of spirits which is among them and the Swiss, renders them so fit for a Democracy; which kind of Government, nations, of more unstable wits, being once come to a Consistent Greatness, have seldom long endured.

Observations upon the State of the Archduke's Country, 1609.

By Sir THOMAS OVERBURY.

AS SOON as I entered into the Archduke's country, which begins after Lillow; presently, I beheld [the] works of a Province, and those of a Province distressed with war. The people heartless; and rather repining against their Governors than revengeful against their enemies. The bravery of that gentry which was left, and the industry of the merchant, quite decayed. The husbandman labouring only to live, without desire to be rich to another's use. The towns (whatsoever concerned not the strength of them) ruinous. And, to conclude, the people here growing poor with less taxes, than they flourish with on the States' side.

This war hath kept the King of Spain busy ever since it began, which [is] some thirty-eight years ago: and, spending all the money that the Indies, and all the men that Spain and Italy could afford, hath withdrawn him from persevering in any other enterprise. Neither could he give over this, without foregoing the means to undertake anything hereafter upon France or England; and, consequently, the Hope of the Western Monarchy. For without that handle [*i.e., that hope*] the mines of Peru had done little hurt in these parts, in comparison of what they have. The cause of the expensefulness of it, is the remoteness of those Provinces from Spain; by reason of which every soldier of Spain or Italy, before he can arrive there, costs the King a 100 crowns [=£30 *then* = £135 *now*], and not above one in ten that arrive, proves good. Besides, by reason of the distance, a great part of the money is drunk up betwixt the Officers that convey it, and pay it.

The cause of the continuance of it, is not only the strength of the enemy; but partly, by reason that the Commanders themselves are content [that] the war should last, so to maintain and render themselves necessary; and partly, because the people of those Countries are not so eager to have the other reduced, as willing to be in the like state themselves.

The usual revenue of those Provinces which the Archduke hath, amounts to 1,200,000 crowns [=, *at* 6*s. the Crown*, £360,000 *then=about* £1,600,000 *now*] a year. Besides which, there come from Spain every month, to maintain the war, 150,000 crowns [=£45,000 *a month, or* £540,000 *a year, then*; =£2,430,000 *annually now*]. It was, at the first, 300,000 crowns a month [*or, in present annual value, about* £5,000,000]; but it fell by fifties [*i.e.*, 50,000] to this, at the time when the Treaty began. Flanders pays more towards the war, than all the rest; as Holland doth, with the States. There is no Spaniard of [*belonging to*] the Council of State, nor Governor of any Province: but of the Council of War, which is only active; there [*in which*] they only are, and have in their hands all the strong towns and castles of those Provinces, of which the Governors have but only the title.

The nations of which their army consists are chiefly Spaniards and Italians, emulous one of another there; as on the other side, [are] the French and English: and of the country, chiefly Burgundians and Walloons. The Pope's Letters, and SPINOLA's inclination keep the Italians there; almost in equality of command with the Spaniard himself.

The Governors for the King of Spain there, successively, have been the Duke of ALVA, Don LOUIS DE REQUIESCENS, Don JOHN of Austria, the Prince of PARMA, the Archduke EARNEST, the Cardinal ANDREW of Austria, and the Cardinal ALBERT till he married the Infanta.

Where the dominion of the Archduke and the States

part, there also changeth the nature of the country; that is, about Antwerp. For all below, being flat, and betwixt meadow and marsh; thence, it begins to rise and become champion [*open country*]: and consequently, the people are more quick and spiritful, as the Brabanter, Fleming, and Walloon.

The most remarkable place on that side is Antwerp, which rose upon the fall of Bruges; equally strong and beautiful; remaining yet so upon the strength of its former greatness: twice spoiled by the Spaniards, and the like attempted by the French. The Citadel was built there by the Duke of ALVA, but renewed by the Prince of PARMA, after his eighteen months' besieging it; the town accepting a castle, rather than a garrison to mingle among them. There are yet in the town, of citizens 30,000 fighting men, 600 of which keep watch nightly; but they [are] allowed neither cannon upon the rampier [*ramparts*], nor magazines of powder. In the Castle are 200 pieces of ordnance, and commonly 700 or 800 soldiers.

Flanders is the best of the Seventeen Provinces, but the havens thereof are naught [*worthless*].

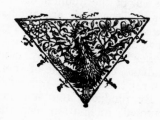

Observations on the State of France, 1609, *under* HENRY *IV.*

By Sir THOMAS OVERBURY.

HAVING seen the form of a Commonwealth, and a Province, with the different effects of wars in them; I entered France, flourishing with peace; and of Monarchies, the most absolute. Because the King there, not only makes peace and war, calls and dissolves Parliaments, pardoneth, naturaliseth, ennobleth, names the value of money, [im]presseth to the war; but even makes laws, and imposes taxes at his pleasure. And all this he doth alone. For, as for that form that his Edicts must be authorised by the next Court of Parliament, that is, the next Court of Sovereign Justice: first, the Presidents thereof are to be chosen by him, and to be put out by him; and secondly, when they concur not with the King, he passeth anything without them, as he did the last Edict [? *of Nantes*] for the Protestants. And for the Assembly of the Three Estates, it is grown now almost as extraordinary as a General Council [of the Church]; with the loss of which, their liberty fell: and when occasion urgeth, it is possible for the King to procure that all those that shall be sent thither, shall be his instruments. For the Duke of GUISE effected as much, at the Assembly of Blois.

The occasion that first procured the King that supremacy, that his Edicts should be Laws, was the last invasion of the English. For, at that time, they possessing two parts of France, the Three Estates could not assemble: whereupon they did then grant that power unto CHARLES VII. during the war. And that which made it easy, for LOUIS XI. and his successors to continue the same, the occasion ceasing; was that the Clergy and the Gentry did not run the same fortune with the People there, as in England. For most of the taxes falling only upon the people; the Clergy and Gentry, being foreborne [*exempt*], were easily induced to leave them to the King's mercy. But the King having got strength upon [*subverted*] the peasants, hath been since the bolder to invade part of both their [*the Clergy's and Gentry's*] liberties.

For the succession of this monarchy. It hath subsisted, without intermission, these 1,200 years, under three Races of Kings. No nation hath, heretofore, done greater things abroad, in Palestine and Egypt, besides all parts of Europe; but, for these last four hundred years, they have only made sallies into Italy, and [have] often suffered at home. Three hundred years the English afflicted them, making two firm invasions upon them, and taking their King prisoner: the second greatness of Christendom (next [to] the Emperor) being then in competition betwixt us and them. And to secure themselves against us, rather than the House of Austria, as it then stood; they chose to marry the heir of Brittany before that of Burgundy. And for this last hundred years, the Spaniard undertaking [*attacking*] them, hath eaten them out of all but France, and endangered that too!

But for this present, France had never, as France, a more entire greatness; though it hath often been richer. For since the war; the King has only [*simply*] got aforehand, the country is but yet in recovering; the war having lasted, by spaces, thirty two years; and so generally, that [as there was] no man but had an enemy within three miles, so the country became frontier all over. Now that which hath made them, at this time, so largely great at home, is their adopting into themselves the lesser adjoining nations, without destruction or leaving any mark of strangeness upon them: as the Bretons,

Gascons, Provençals, and others which are not French. Towards which unions, their nature, which is easy and harborous [*receptive*] to strangers; hath done more than any laws could have effected but with long time.

The King, as I said, enjoying what LOUIS XI. did gain, hath the entire Sovereignty in himself; because he can make the Parliament do what he pleases, or else do what he pleases without them.

For the other Three Estates. The Church is there very rich, being estimated to enjoy the third part of the revenue of France, but otherwise is nothing so potent as elsewhere; partly because the Inquisition is not admitted in France: but principally because the Pope's ordinary power is much restrained there, by the liberties which the French Church claimeth; which liberties do not so much enfranchise the Church itself, as confer the authority the Pope loseth upon the King, as Firstfruits and the Disposing of all spiritual preferments. And by reason of this neutrality of authority, the church men [*clergy*] suffer more there, than either in England, where they wholly depend upon the King; or in Spain and Italy, where they wholly subsist by the Pope: because the Pope is not able totally to support them, and the King takes occasion ever to suppress them, as being not entirely his subjects; and to him, they pay, yearly, both the tenth of all their tithe, and of all their temporal land.

The Gentry are the only entire Body, there, which participate with the prerogatives of the Crown. For from it, they receive privileges above all other men and a kind of limited regality upon their tenants; besides [a] real supply to their estates by governments and pensions, and freedom from tallies [*taxations*] upon their own lands, that is, upon their domains and whatsoever they manure by their servants: but so much as they let to tenants is, presently, tallieable [*taxable*] which causeth [a] proportionate abatement in the rent. And in recompense of this, they owe to the King the Ban and the Arrière Ban; that is, to serve him and his Lieutenant, three months within the land, at their own charges. And as in war, they undergo the greatest part of the danger, so then is their power most peremptory above the rest: whereas in the time of peace, the King is ready to support inferior persons against them, and is glad to see them to waste one another by contention at law for fear they grow rich; because he forsees that, as the Nobility, only, can do him service, so they only, misapplied, can do him harm.

The ancient Gentry of France was most of it consumed in the wars of GODFREY DE BOULOGNE, and some in those of St. LOUIS; because on their setting out they pawned all their fiefs to the Church, and few of them were after[wards] redeemed: by reason, whereof the Church possesseth at this day the third part of the best fiefs in France. And that Gentry was afterwards made up by advocates, financiers, and merchants ennobled, which are now reputed ancient; and are daily eaten out again, and repaired by the same kind of men.

For the people. All those that have any kind of profession or trade, live well; but for the mere peasants that labour the ground, they are only sponges to the King, to the Church, and to the Nobility! having nothing to their own, but to the use of them: and are scarce allowed, as beasts, enough to keep them able to do service; for besides their rent, they pay usually two-thirds to the King.

The manner of Government in France is mixt between Peace and War; being composed as well of military discipline as [of] civil justice: because having open frontiers and strong neighbours, and therefore obnoxious [*liable*] to sudden invasions; they cannot, as in England, join ever peace and security together.

For the Military Part, there is ever a Constable and a Marshal in being, troops of horse and regiments of foot in pay, and in all Provinces and places of strength, Governors and garrisons distributed: all which are means for the preferment of the Gentry. But those, as they give security against the enemy, so when there is none, they disturb the enjoying of peace, by making the countries taste somewhat of a Province. For the Gentry find a difference betwixt the Governor's favour and disfavour; and the soldiers often commit insolences upon the people.

The Governments there, are so well disposed by the King, as no Governor hath means to give over a Province into the enemy's hands; the commands thereof are so scattered. For the Governor commands the country, and, for the most part, the chief town: then there is a Lieutenant to the King, not to him! of the same; and betwixt these two there is ever jealousy nourished. Then hath every town and fortress particular Governors, which are not subaltern [*subordinate*] to that of the Province; but hold immediately from the Prince: and many times the Town hath one Governor, and the Castle another.

The advantages of the Governors, besides their pay from the King, are presents from the country, dead payes [?*pay drawn for dead men*], making their magazines of corn and powder more than they need, at the King's price; and, where they stand upon the sea, overseeing of unlawful goods: thus much in peace. In war, they are worth as much as they will exact. Languedoc is the best, then Brittany: Provence is worth, by all these means, to the Duke of GUISE, 20,000 crowns [=£6,000 *or about* £25,000 *in present value*] a year; but Provence only, he holds without a Lieutenant.

Concerning the Civil Justice there: it is nowhere more corrupt or expenseful. The corruptness of it proceeds, First, by reason that the King sells the places of justice at as high a rate as can honestly be made of them: so that all thriving is left to corruption; and the gain the King hath that way, tempts him to make a multitude of officers, which are another burden to the subject. Secondly, the Presidents are not bound to judge according to the written Law, but according to the equity drawn out of it; which liberty doth not so much admit Conscience, as leave Wit without limits. The expensefulness of it ariseth from the multitude of laws, and multiplicity of forms of processes; the which too doth beget doubt, and make them long in resolving. And all this *chicanery*, as they call it, was brought into France from Rome, upon the Popes coming to reside at Avignon.

For the strength of France. It is at this day, the greatest united force of Christendom. The particulars in which it consists, are these. The shape of the country; which being round, no one part is far from succouring another. The multitude of good towns and places of strength therein are able to stay an army, if not to waste it; as Metz did the

Emperor's. The mass of treasure which the King hath in the Bastille. The number of arsenals distributed upon the frontiers, besides that of Paris: all which are full of good arms and artillery. And for ready men, the five Regiments bestowed up and down in garrisons, together with the 2,000 of the Guard [and] the troops of Ordinary and Light Horse: all ever in pay. Besides their Gentry, all bred soldiers; of which they think there are, at this present, 50,000 fit to bear arms. And to command all these, they have, at this day, the best Generals of Christendom; which were the only commodity the Civil Wars did leave them.

The weaknesses of it are, First, the want of a sufficient Infantry, which proceeds from the ill distribution of their wealth: for the peasant having no share allowed him, is heartless and feeble; and consequently unserviceable for all military uses. By reason of which, they are, first, forced to borrow aid of the Switzers at a great charge; and secondly, to compose their armies, for the most part, of Gentlemen: which makes the loss of a battle there almost irrecoverable. The Second, is the unproportionable part of the land which the Church holds, all which is likewise dead to military uses: for as they say there, "The Church will lose nothing, nor defend nothing." The Third, is the want of a competent number of ships and galleys: by reason of which defect, first, the Spaniard overmasters them upon the Mediterranean, and the English and Hollander upon the Ocean; and secondly, it renders them poor in foreign trade; so that, all the great actions of Christendom for these fifty years having been bent upon the [*West*] Indies, they, only, have sat idle. The Fourth, is the weakness of their frontiers: which is so much the more dangerous because they are possessed, all but the Ocean, by the Spaniard; for Savoy hath been always as his own, for all uses against France. The Last, is the difference of religion among themselves; which will ever yield matter of civil dissension, and consequently cause the weaker to stand in need of foreign succours.

The ordinary revenue of the King is, as they say now, some 14,000,000 of crowns [= £4,200,000 *sterling, or in present value, about* £18,000,000]; which arise principally from the domains of the Crown, the *gabel* of salt, tallies [*taxes*] upon the country, customs upon the merchandise, sale of offices, the yearly tithe of all that belongs to the Church, the rising and falling of money, fines and confiscations cast upon him by the law: but as for Wardships, they are only known in Normandy.

His expense is, chiefly, Ambassadors, munition, building, fortifying, and maintaining of galleys, (as for ships when he needs them, he makes an embarque [*embargo*]); in pay for soldiers, wages for officers, pensions at home and abroad; upon the entertaining his House, his State, and his private pleasures. And all the first, but the domains, were granted in the beginning upon some urgent occasion; and afterwards by Kings made perpetual, the occasion ceasing: and the domains themselves granted because the King should live upon his own without oppressing his subjects. But at this day, though the revenue be thus great, and the taxes unsupportable; yet do they little more than serve for necessary public uses. For the King of Spain's greatness and neighbourhood forceth the King there to live continually upon his guard: and the treasure which the Spaniard receives from his Indies, constrains him to raise his revenue thus by taxes, so to be able, in some proportion, to bear up against him; for fear, else, he should be bought out of all his confederates and servants.

For the relation of this State to others. It is first to be considered that this part of Christendom is balanced betwixt the three Kings of Spain, France, and England; as the other part [is] betwixt the Russian, the Kings of Poland, Sweden, and Denmark. For as for Germany, which if it were entirely subject to one Monarchy, would be terrible to all the rest: so being divided betwixt so many Princes and those of so equal power, it serves only to balance itself, and entertain easy war with the Turk; while the Persian withholds him in a greater. And every one of those first three hath his particular strength, and his particular weakness. Spain hath the advantage of both the rest in treasure, but is defective in men: his dominions are scattered and the conveyance of his treasure from the Indies lies obnoxious to [*at the mercy of*] the power of any nation that is stronger by sea. France abounds with men, lies close together, and hath money sufficiently. England, being an island, is hard to be invaded, abounds with men, but wants money to employ them. For their particular [*several*] weakness, Spain is to be kept busy in the Low Countries, France to be afflicted with the Protestants, and England, in Ireland. England is not able to subsist against any [*either*] of the other [two] hand in hand; but joined with the Low Countries it can give law to both by sea: joined with either of them two, it is able to oppress the third, as HENRY VIII. did.

Now the only entire body in Christendom that makes head against the Spanish Monarchy is France: and therefore they say in France, that, "The day of the ruin of France is the eve of the ruin of England." And thereupon England hath ever, since the Spanish greatness, inclined rather to maintain France, rather than to ruin it: as when King FRANCIS [I.] was taken prisoner, the King of England lent money towards the payment of his ransom; and the late Queen [*ELIZABETH*], when the Leaguers, after the Duke of GUISE's death, had a design to Cantonize France, though offered a part of that country, would not consent. So then, this reason of State, of mutual preservation, conjoining them; England may be accounted a sure confederate of France; and Holland, by reason it partly subsists by it; the Protestant Princes of Germany, because they have countenance from it, against the house of Austria; the Protestant Switzers, for religion and money; and the Venetians, for protection against the Spaniard in Italy. So that all their [*the French's*] friends are either Protestants or inclining thereto; and whosoever is extremely Catholic is their enemy, and factor for the Spanish Monarchy: as the Pope and Cardinals, for the most part; and totally, the Jesuits, the Catholic Princes of Germany, and the Catholics of England and Ireland. For the Jesuits, which are the Ecclesiastical Strength of Christendom, France—notwithstanding the many late obligations—hath cause to despair of them. For they intending as "one Pope, so one King" to suppress the Protestants; and for the better support of Christendom against the Turks: and seeing Spain the likelier to bring this to pass, they follow the nearer probability of effecting their end.

No addition could make France so dangerous to us, as that of our Low Countries; for so it were worse, than if the

Spaniard himself had them entirely. As for their hopes of regaining Italy; it concerns the Spaniard immediately, rather than us.

Concerning the state of the Protestants in France. During peace, they are protected by their Edict [*of Nantes*]. For their two Agents at Court defend the general from wrong; and their *chambres impartis* every particular person. And if troubles should arise, some scattered particulars might be in danger; but the main body is safe. Safe to defend themselves, though all France join against them! and if it break out into factions, the safest; because they are both ready and united.

The particulars of their strength are, First, their Towns of Surety, two of which command the river of the Loire. Secondly, their situation. The greatest part of them lying near together, as Poitou, Saintonge, High [*Upper*] Gascony, Languedoc, and Dauphiny: near the sea, so consequently fit to receive succours from abroad; and remote from Paris, so that the quality of an army is much wasted, before it can approach them. The Third, is the sufficiency of their present Governors, BOULOGNE and DESDEGUIERS, and other second Commanders. And for the Princes of the Blood, whom the rest may, in shew, without emulation, obey; when they come once to open action, those which want a party, will quickly seek them. The Last, is the aid they are sure of from foreign Princes; for whosoever are friends to France in general, are more particularly their friends: and besides, the Protestant party being grown stronger of late, as the Low Countries; and more united, as England and Scotland, part of that strength reflects upon them. And even the King of Spain himself, who is [the] enemy of France in general, would rather give them succour than see them utterly extirpated. For as soon as they get an Edict with better conditions, they turn head against him that now succoured them; as they did against us, at Newhaven [*Hâvre in* 1562].

Concerning the porportion of their number, they are not above the Seventeenth or Eighteenth part of the People: but of the Gentlemen, there are 6,000 of the [Protestant] Religion. But since the peace [? *in* 1602] they have increased in People, as principally in Paris, Normandy, and Dauphiny, but lost in the Gentry: which loss cometh to pass by reason that the King when he finds any Gentleman that will but hearken, he tempts him with preferment; and those that he finds utterly obstinate, he suppresseth. And by such means, he hath done them more harm in peace; than both his predecessors in war. For in all their Assemblies, he corrupts some of their Ministers to betray the counsel in hand. Of the 106,000 crowns [=£31,800, *or in present value* £140,000] a year which he pays the Protestants to entertain their Ministers and pay their garrisons, he hath gotten the bestowing of 16,000 of them, upon what gentleman of the [Protestant] Religion he pleaseth; whom by that means he moderates, if not gains. And besides, they were wont to impose upon him their two Deputies, which are to stay at Court: but now he makes them propose six, out of which he chooseth the two, and by that, obligeth those; and yet notwithstanding all this, in some occasions he makes good use of them too. For as towards England, he placeth none in any place of strength but firm Catholics; so towards Spain and Savoy, he often gives charge to Protestants, as to LA FORCE in Bearn, DESDEGUIERS and BOISSE in Bresse.

Concerning the King himself. He is a person wonderful, both in war and peace. For his acts in War, he hath manumized [*manumitted*] France from the Spaniard: and subdued the League, being the most dangerous plot that hath been laid; weakening it by Arms, but utterly dissolving it by Wit. That is, by letting the Duke of GUISE out of prison, and capitulating with the heads of it, every one apart; by which means, he hath yet left a continual hatred among them. Because every one sought by preventing [*anticipating*] other, to make his conditions the better. So that now there remains little connection of it, amongst the Gentry: only there continue some dregs still among the Priests, and consequently the People; especially when they are angered with the increase and prosperity of the Protestants.

For his acts of Peace. He hath enriched France with a greater proportion of wool and silk, erected goodly buildings, cut passages [*canals*] betwixt river and river, and is about to do the same betwixt sea and sea, redeemed much of the mortgaged domains of the Crown, better husbanded the money (which was wont to be drunk up, two parts of it, in the officers' hands), got aforehand in treasure, arms, and munition, increased the infantry and suppressed the unproportionable cavalry, and left nothing undone but the building of a navy.

And all this may be attributed to himself, only: because in a Monarchy, officers are active or careless, as the Prince is able to judge and distinguish of their labours; and withal to participate of them somewhat, himself.

Sure it is, that the peace of France, and somewhat that of Christendom itself, is secured by this Prince's life. For all titles and discontents, all factions of religion there suppress themselves till his death: but what will ensue afterwards? What the rest of the House of BOURBON will enterprise upon the King's children? What the House of GUISE, upon that of BOURBON? What the League? What the Protestants? What the Kings of Spain and England, if they see a breach made by civil dissension? I choose rather to expect, than conjecture! Because GOD hath so many ways to turn aside from human foresight; as He gave us a testimony upon the death of our late Queen [*ELIZABETH*].

This country of France, considering the quantity, is the fairest and richest of all Christendom; and contains in it, most of the countries adjoining. For Picardy, Normandy, and Brittany resemble England; Languedoc, Spain; Provence, Italy; and the rest is France.

Besides, all the rivers that pass through it, end in it. It abounds with corn, wine, and salt, and hath a competency of silk; but is defective in wool, leather, metals, and horses: and hath but few very good havens, especially on the north side.

Concerning the people. Their children, at first sight, seem men, and their men, children; but whoso, in negotiating, presumes upon appearances shall be deceived! compassionate towards their own nation and country; loving to the Prince, and so they may have liberty in ceremony and free access to him, they will be better content that he shall be absolute in matter of substance: impatient of peace any longer than while they are in recovering the ruins of war: the presentness [*presence*] of danger inflames their courage, but any expectation makes it languish. For the most part, they are all Imagination and no Judgement; but those that prove solid, excel!

Their Gentlemen are all good outward men, good Courtiers, good soldiers, and knowing enough in men and business; but merely [*simply*] ignorant in matters of Letters, because at fifteen they quit books and begin to live in the world: when indeed a mediocrity [*medium*] betwixt their form of education and ours, would do better than either. No men stand more punctually [*punctiliously*] upon their honour in matter of valour; and, which is strange, in nothing else: for otherwise, in their conversation, the custom, and shifting, and overspeaking, hath quite overcome the shame of it.

FINIS.

THE

INTERPRETER.

Wherein three principal Terms of State,

much mistaken by the vulgar,

are clearly unfolded.

Qui vult decipi, decipiatur.

Anno 1622.

To such as understand not the English tongue perfectly.

THAT the unwise may learn to understand
How certain Words are usèd in our land;
And that they may write sense, whilst they remain
In foreign parts, or shall return again;
(For idioms, fashions, manners alter here,
As friendship and religion everywhere):
I have some elegancies for our tongue
Observed, as they are usèd now, among
Our ablest linguists, who mint for the Court
Words fit to be proclaimed; and do resort
Where lords and ladies couple and converse,
And trade lip learning, both in prose and verse.
And by these few, the docible may see
How rich our language is! religious, we!
Time was, a PURITAN was counted such
As held some Ceremonies were too much
Retained and urged; and would no Bishops grant,
Others to rule, who government did want.
Time was, a PROTESTANT was only taken
For such as had the Church of Rome forsaken;
Or her known falsehoods in the highest point:
But would not, for each toy, true peace disjoint.
Time was, a PAPIST was a man who thought
Rome could not err, but all her *Canons* ought
To be canonical; and, blindly led,
He from the Truth, for fear of Error, fled.
But now these words, with divers others more,
Have other senses than they had before:
Which plainly I do labour to relate,
As they are now accepted in our State.

A Puritan.

(So nicknamed, but indeed the sound Protestant.)

A PURITAN is such another thing
As says, with all his heart, "GOD save the King
And all his issue!" and to make this good,
Will freely spend his money and his blood;
And in his factious and fond mood, dare say,
"'Tis madness, for the Palsgrave, thus to stay
And wait the loving leisure of kind Spain!
Who gets at first, only to give again
In courtesy, that faithless heretics
May taste the Faith and Love of Catholics.
And Hope too!" For a Puritan is he
That doth not hope these Holy Days to see;
And would a wasted country, on condition
Scorn to receive! although the High Commission
Of England, Spain, and Rome would have it so.
False favours he'd not take from a true foe!
A Puritan is he, that rather had
Spend all, to help the States (he is so mad!),
Than spend one hundred thousand pounds a year
To guard the Spanish coasts from pirates' fear:
The whilst, the Catholic King might force combine
Both Holland, Beame, and Palz to undermine;
And by his cross-curse-Christian counterwork
To make Rome both for Antichrist and Turk

Right Catholic. So th' Empire first divided,
By Holy Mother's pious plots (who sided
The East, and West; that she might get between,
And sit aloft, and govern like a Queen);
The Turk did great Constantinople gain,
And may win Rome too, by the help of Spain.
A Puritan is he that would not live
Upon the sins of other men; nor give
Money for Office in the Church or State,
Though 'twere a Bishopric: he so doth hate
All ceremonies of the Court and Church,
Which do the coffer and the conscience lurch
Of both the[ir] treasures. So that (covetous!) he
Would not have such as want both, better be!
A Puritan is he that thinks, and says
He must account give of his works and ways:
And that whatsoever calling he assumes,
It is for others' good. So he presumes
Rashly to censure such as wisely can
(By taking timely bribes of every man),
Enrich themselves: knowing to that sole end,
GOD and the King did, them their honours send;
And that Simplicity hath only mounted
By virtue; but such fools, they'll not be counted!
A Puritan is he, that, twice a day,
Doth, at the least, to GOD devoutly pray,
And twice a Sabbath, he goes to church to hear,
To pray, confess his sins, and praise GOD there
In open sight of all men: not content
GOD knows his heart, except his knee be bent,
That men, and angels likewise, may discern
He came to practise there, as well as learn;
And honour GOD with every outward part,
With knee, hand, tongue, as well as with the heart.
A Puritan is he, which grieves to think
Religion should in France shipwreck and sink;
Whilst we give aim! and that those men should sway
The kingdom there, who made the King away
The whilst all such as helped to crown the father* [* HENRY IV.]
Should by the son † be now proscribed the rather. [† LOUIS XIII.]
A Puritan, in unadvised zeal,

Could wish that huntsmen ruled the Common weal:
And that the King's hounds were the only spies,
For they would tell truth! as the others, lies.
He wisheth beasts were men, as men resemble
Beasts: for surely they would not dissemble!
But would tell where the fault lies, and hunt home
The subtle Fox, either to Spain or Rome.
A Puritan is he, that speaks his mind
In Parliament: not looking once behind
To others' danger; nor yet sideways leaning
To promised honour, his direct true meaning.
But for the Laws and Truth doth firmly stand:
By which, he knows, Kings only do command;
And Tyrants otherwise. He crosseth not
This man, because a Courtier or a Scot;
Or that, because a Favourite, or soe:
But if the State's friend, none can be his foe!
But if the State's foe (be he what he will,
Illustrious, wise, great, learned), he counts him ill.
He neither sides with that man nor with this,
But gives his voice just as the reason is,
And yet, if Policy would work a fraction
To cross Religion by a foreign faction
Pretending public good; he'll join with those
Who dare speak Truth, not only under the rose,
But though the White Rose and the Red do hear!
And though the pricking Thistle too be there!
Yea, though the stars,* the moon,* the sun,* look on,
[* The Nobility, Prince CHARLES, and King JAMES.]
And cast, through clouds, oblique aspects upon
His clear and free intentions; he's as bold
And confident as the bright marigold! † [† BUCKINGHAM.]
That flatterer, that favourite of the sun,
Who doth the self-same course observe and run;
Not caring though all flowers else wax sear,
So he, the golden livery may wear!
But our free, generous, and noble spirit
Doth from his ancient English stock, inherit
Such native worth and liberty of mind,
As will omit no slavery of his kind;
Yet he is ready to obey wheresoe'er

He may not prejudice the Truth by fear,
Nor faintly seem to shrink, withdraw, give way,
Whilst other mushrumpes * do the State betray.
He'll not a traitor, be unto the King, [* Mushrooms.]
Nor to the Laws (for that's another thing
Men dream not of, who think they no way can
Be traitors unto many, for *one* man),
But his chief error is to think that none
Can be a traitor, till Law calls him one ;
And that the Law is what the State decrees
In Parliament : by which, whilst that he sees
His actions and intentions justified,
He counts himself a martyr glorified,
If, in this cause, he suffers ; and contemns
All dangers in his way. Nay, he condemns
All such as traitors be to Church and State,
Who for the love of one, all others hate !
And for particular ends and private aims,
Forsake their Country ! and their conscience maim !
His Character abridged, if you would have,
HE'S ONE, THAT WOULD A SUBJECT BE, NO SLAVE !

A Protestant.

(So will the Formalist be called.)

A PROTESTANT is such an other thing
As makes, within his heart, God of the King;
And (as if he did, with his Crown inherit
A never-erring and infallible spirit),
Labours to blow him up by praise of wit,
And by false flatteries cosen him of it.
A Protestant is one that shakes his head
And pities much the Palsgrave was misled
To meddle with Bohemia, and incense
The Spanish wrath; 'gainst which, there is no fence!
That his revenues in the Palz again
Were well restored, he wishes; so that Spain
Would take the honours of that house, and give
MENTZ his demands, letting the Palsgrave live:
For such a favour as his lands and life,
Not one, except the father of his wife
(That King of Peace and Love!) dares boldly crave
But what is it he may despair to have
By means of th'English and the Scottish Saint,
Who, at their pupils' suit, doth still acquaint
The Spanish Patron, how, the first of May,
PHILIP and JAMES make one Holy Day;
What therefore's given to one, the other must
Be shares in; for JAMES is surnamed "Just."
And so, this year, by Holy Church's count,

The Calendar reformed hath singled out,
These two most sacred Saints to wait upon
Our Saviour's feast of Resurrection,
Which by the English heathen computation
Meets with May Day among the Catholic nation;
And may be such a day, as that, for goodness,
Which some called "Ill May Day" from people's woodness,
A day of feasting, and a day of pleasure,
A day of marriage, and withal of treasure,
A day of Catholic unity and love
Which may a kind of resurrection move
In our State, Union; almost now forgot,
Being buried both by th'English and the Scot.
Spain strikes betwixt, and like a Lord commands,
They join their Laws together with their Lands:
And join they will! but in despite of Spain,
Making his Holy Day of hope but vain.
  A Protestant is he, that fain would take
Occasion from the East or West, to shake
Our League with the United Provinces:
To which end, he hath many fair pretences.
Our Honour first, for in the Greenland, they,
And the East Indies, beat our ships away.
Our Profit likewise, for in both those places
We do great loss sustain, besides disgraces:
And in the Narrow Seas, where we are masters;
They will presume to be our herring-tasters!
But we should have white herrings wondrous plenty,
If they would give us two of every twenty;
Or stay our idle leisure, till that none
Remained for them or us, but all were gone.
And if they will not thus, our humours serve,
"That we," saith he, "should leave them, they deserve!"
A herring cob, we see, will make him quarrel;
What would the man do, think you! for a barrel?
Well could I wish these things were all amended;
But greater business, now, is to be 'tended.
Our Lives, Religions, Liberties, and Lands
Upon this nice and tickle quarrel stand;
And we must for a fitter time attend,
Else Spain will soon this controversy end!

A Protestant is he, that, by degrees,
Climbs every Office; knows the proper fees
They give and take, at entrance of the Place,
And at what rate again, they vent that grace;
Knows in how many years a man may gather
Enough to make himself a reverend father,
Or from the lowest civil step arise
To sit with honour in the starry skies:
For he hath gone that Progress, step by step,
As snails creep up where safely none can leap;
For snails do leave behind their silver slime,
And guild the way for falling as they climb.
A Protestant is he that with the stream
Still swims, and wisely shuns every extreme;
Loves not in point of faith to be precise;
But to believe as Kings do, counts it wise:
If CONSTANTINE the Great will christened be;
This will the white robe wear as well he!
And in the hallowed fountain plunge amain
His naked body, as if every stain
Were now washed off, and his inflamèd zeal
Thirsted these waters, which soul's sin doth heal.
Again, if JULIAN will renounce his faith;
This man will say, just as his Sovereign saith.
If he intend Religion to betray,
And yet will walk a close and covert way,
Corrupting men by office, honour, bounty,
You shall find this man will deserve a County;
By double dealing and by broking so,
That none shall think him ere they find him too
Apostated: for no way so doth work
To make a man an Atheist, Jew, or Turk,
As do corrupted manners, which let in
A deluge of impiety and sin.
These, backed by favour and preferment, may
Have power to make all error open way;
And every man will censure opposition,
When gilden flattery kills without suspicion.
This poisoned vial then was poured in
When, first, the Church got means to maintain sin;
And now the means withdrawn or misemployed,

Makes all religion and all conscience void.
For man that hunts for honour, wealth, or fame,
Will be as those be, who dispose the same.
So that no readier way there can be found
To conquer us, than to corrupt the sound
By bribes; the worst assault that can befall
To Bodies Politic, confounding all.
Gifts blind the wise. And though the Chequer be
Open and empty, as erst full and free;
Yet other bribes can work the same effect
That Mammon would. The favour and respect
Of Favourites, a nod or wink from Kings,
Employment, Office, Grace are able things!
  Besides, the honoured style of Viscount, Lord,
Earl, Marquess, Duke can work, at every word,
Strange alterations, more than CIRCE's cup,
In such as can, no other ways get up.
  Will he speak truth directly? Make him then
A Dean, or Bishop! they are no such men!
The wolf hath seen them first! Their throat is furred,
You shall not hear from them, a factious word!
  Stands he for Law, and custom of the land?
Make him an Officer! Give him command!
Command, where he may gain! this will bewitch
DEMOSTHENES, who labours to be rich.
  What, is he bold and forward? Send him out
On some embassage! or employ the stout
At sea or land! some desperate voyage, where
They may be lost! Then leave them helpless there!
Undo them thus! Before, they had too much;
But being poor, they'll nothing dare to touch!
This ostracism will, sure, abate their pride;
And they shall give great thanks for it beside!
  If he be poor, oppress him! shut him out
In forlorn banishment, where round about
The faithless world, he may his living seek!
Then no man, after him, will do the like.
  If he be faint, check him! or do but chide,
He'll hold his tongue, and his tail closely hide!
  Is he free-tongued, though serious and discreet?
Proclaim him silent! Whip him through the street!

Thus, whatsoe'er is done, nor bird shall dare
To warn the rest, till all be in the snare.
Is he a rich man? Then, the Fleet and fine
Will make him seem, although he be not, thine.
Briefly, whatsoe'er he be, except alone
Directly honest (of which few or none
Remain alive) a Statist, ways can find,
By policy to work him to his mind.
And thus the Common wealth may conquered be,
The Church deflowered, beslaved our Liberty,
Without all bloodshed; under the pretence
Of Peace, Religion, Love, and Innocence.
A Protestant is an indifferent man,
That with all faiths, or none, hold quarter can;
So moderate and temperate his passion
As he to all times can his conscience fashion.
He at the Chapel, can a Bishop hear;
And then in Holborn a religious Freer.
A *Mass* ne'er troubles him more than a Play;
All's one: he comes all one, from both away.
A Protestant, no other fault can spy
In all Rome's beadroll of iniquity,
But that, of late, they do profess King-killing;
Which Catholic point, to credit he's unwilling.
Only because he gains by Kings far more,
Than he can hope for, by the Romish whore.
He saith, "This only, doth the Pope proclaim
For ANTICHRIST, because that Greekish name
Doth signify *Against the LORD's Anointed*";
As if it only, 'gainst this doctrine pointed.
And therefore leaving this out of their *Creed*;
He in the rest, with them is soon agreed.
And so the King's part may be safe from fear:
Let GOD Himself, for His own part, take care!
A Protestant is he, that guards the ear
Of Sovereign Justice, so that Truth to hear
He's not permitted; nor to know the danger
He stands in, 'twixt the Subject and the Stranger;
The plots which strangers have, grief of his own;
Which may too late be prevented, known.
For though his foes be wily wolves and foxes,

His subjects shackled asses, yokèd oxes:
Yet time will show them not to be such daws
As will look on, whilst others change the Laws,
And rob the State, Religion do deflower;
Having their Prince imprisoned in their power!
As Princes have been prisoners to their own;
And so may ours too, if the truth were known:
The liberty of will by strong affection
May be restrained; which is the worst subjection!
For then the understanding will not see,
But rusheth on whatsoe'er the danger be.
A Protestant is he, whose good intention
Deserves an English and a Spanish pension,
Both for One service; and obtains it too
By winning Spain, more than their arms could do,
With long delays: and losing us and ours;
What lost, to get again we want both powers,
And perhaps will.
Others by treaties and disputes may gain;
But we by blows: else old said saws be vain!
A Protestant is he, that hath no eye
Beyond his private profit; but doth lie
In wait to be the first that may propound
What he foresees Power plots. The solid ground
He ne'er examines: be it right or wrong,
All's one! since it doth to his part belong.
For to his part belongs to sooth and flatter
The greatest Man, though in the foulest matter;
And him, he holds a rebel, that dare say
"No man against the Laws, we must obey!"
His character abridged, if you will have,
HE'S ONE THAT'S NO TRUE SUBJECT, BUT A SLAVE!

A Papist.

A ROMANIST is such an other thing
As would, with all his heart, murder the King;
That saith, "The House of Austria is appointed
To rule all Christians; and for this anointed
By CHRIST's own Vicar: and they, rebels are;
Who dare against this House make any war,
Invasive or defensive." Jesuits' wit
And Indian gold do both attend on it;
And all Rome's hierarchy do plot, pray, curse,
And spend the strength of body, soul, and purse
To this sole end, that every State besides,
May be the vassals to the Austrian pride.
And so Rome may, of both the Empiries,
Keep still the Civil and Religious keys.
A Romanist is he, that sows debate
'Twixt Prince and People; and 'twixt every State
Where he remains: that he, by the division,
May work himself some profit in decision;
Or bring in Rome and Spain to make all friends
Who, having footing once, have half their ends.
For as the Devil, since first he got within
Man's heart, keeps still there by Original Sin;
So those wheresoe'er once they Interest gain
Keep all; or such a party let remain
Behind, assured to them, as may procure
A relapse, when men think themselves secure.

Thus each disease, though cured, remains in part:
And thus the frail flesh oft betrays the heart.
Now, for the rest, no Romish false opinion
Can make a Papist in the King's dominion;
Nor absence from the Church: for, at this season,
He is no Papist that *commits not treason*!
Let him to Church resort, or be Recusant;
All's one! he's counted a good Protestant.
Nay, 'tis a question, if GUY FAWKES were one!
But 'tis resolved that Papist, he was none.
His Character abridged, if you will have,
HE IS SPAIN'S SUBJECT, AND A ROMISH SLAVE!

THE
FAMOUS AND WONDERFUL RECOVERY
of a Ship of Bristol, called the *Exchange*, from the Turkish Pirates of Argier.

WITH THE UNMATCHABLE attempts and good success of JOHN RAWLINS, Pilot in her, and other slaves: who, in the end (with the slaughter of about forty of the Turks and Moors), brought the ship into Plymouth, the 13th of February [1622] last, with the Captain a *Renegado*, and five Turks more; besides the redemption of twenty-four men and one boy from Turkish slavery.

LONDON:
Printed for NATHANIEL BUTTER, dwelling at the *Pied Bull*, at Saint Austen's Gate.
1622.

To the Right Honourable

GEORGE, Marquis of BUCKINGHAM,

Viscount VILLIERS, Baron of WHADDON, Lord High Admiral of England; Justice in Eyre of all His Majesty's Forests, Parks, and Chases beyond Trent; Master of the Horse to His Majesty, and one of the Gentlemen of His Majesty's Bed Chamber; Knight of the most noble Order of the Garter, and one of His Majesty's most honourable Privy Council of England and Scotland.

RIGHT HONOURABLE,

SEEING it hath pleased GOD by so weak means as my poor self, to have His power and goodness made manifest to the World, as by this following Relation may appear: I thought it my duty to present the same unto you; whom the Majesty of England hath presented unto us, as our Patron, and Chief Commander of our sea affairs. Accept it then, I humbly beseech you! as the unpolished work of a poor sailor; and the rather, for that it exemplifies the glory of GOD. For by such men as myself, your Honour must be served, and England made the happiest of all nations.

For though you have greater persons, and more braving spirits to be over our heads, and hold inferiors in subjection; yet are we the men that must pull the ropes, weigh up the anchors, toil in the night, endure the storms, sweat at the helm, watch the biticle [binnacle], *attend the compass, guard the ordnance, keep the night hours, and be ready for all impositions.*

If, then, you vouchsafe to entertain it! I have my desire. For, according to the oath of Jurors, it is "the truth, and the very truth." If otherwise, you suppose it trivial! it is only the prostitution of my service; and Wisdom is not bought in the market!

Your Honour's humbly to be commanded,

JOHN RAWLINS.

THE FAMOUS and Wonderful Recovery of the *Exchange* of Bristol from the Turkish pirates of Argier.

THE Psalmist saith, that "He that goeth to sea, shall see the wonders of GOD!" and I may well say, that he that converseth with mariners and sailors shall hear of the wonders of men! as by this following Discourse shall appear.

Not that I am willing to be the author of novelty, or amaze you with incredible reports; but because I would not let slip so remarkable an accident, and so profitable a relation. Remarkable, as extending to manifest the power and glory of GOD, who hath variety of supportation in store to sweeten affliction, and make all endurances subject to fortitude and patience: profitable, as being thus far exemplary, to teach all men of action and employment, not to despair in distress; and to know thus much, that brave attempts are compassed by resolution and industrious employment, and whether they thrive or not, yet shall the enterprise be Charactered with a worthy exploit. And if it end with success; O how shall the Actors be remembered to posterity! and make their fame immortal that, either purchased their liberty, even out of fire; or delivered themselves (though by death itself) from slavish captivity, or the thraldom of barbarous Infidels; who glory in nothing more than the perdition of our souls, and the derision of our CHRIST.

Hearken, then, I pray you! to this following Relation! and

learn thereby, as I said, both to give GOD the praise of all deliverances; and to instruct one another in the absolute duties of Christianity. By the one, the Power and Providence, with all the attributes belonging to so immense a Deity, shall be made manifest; by the other, the weak brother shall be comforted, the strong confirmed, the wavering reduced, the faint-hearted erected, and the presumptuous moderated. By both, Religion shall have a sweet passage in the consciences of men; and men made the happy instruments of GOD's glory, and their own increases of good example and imitation.

And thus much for Preamble or Introduction. Now, to the matter itself!

In the year 1621, the 1st of November, there was one JOHN RAWLINS (born in Rochester, and dwelling three and twenty years in Plymouth) employed to the Straits of Gibraltar, by Master[s] RICHARD, and STEVEN TREVILES, Merchants of Plymouth; and freighted in a bark called the *Nicholas* of Plymouth, of the burden of 40 tons: which had also in her company, another ship of Plymouth, called the *George Bonaventure*, of 70 tons burden or thereabouts; which, by reason of her greatness beyond the other, I will name the Admiral [*flag-ship*], and JOHN RAWLINS's bark shall, if you please, be the Vice-Admiral.

These two, according to the time of the year, had a fair passage; and, by the 18th of the same month, came to a place at the entering of the Straits, named Trafalgar; but the next morning [19*th November*, 1621], being in the sight of Gibraltar, at the very mouth of the Straits, the watch descried five sail of ships. Who, as it seemed, used all the means they could to come near us; and we, as we had cause, used the same means to go as far from them; yet did their Admiral take in both his topsails, that either we might not suspect them, or that his own company might come up the closer together. At last, perceiving us [to be] Christians, they fell from devices, to apparent discovery of hostility, and making out against us. We again suspecting them [to be] pirates, took our course to escape from them; and made all the sails we possibly could for Terriff or Gibraltar: but all we could do, could not prevent their approach. For, suddenly, one of them came right over against us to windward; and so fell on our quarter. Another came up on our luff, and so threatened us there. And, at last, all five chased us; making great speed to surprise us.

Their Admiral was called *Callfater*; having upon her main-topsail, two topgallant sails, one above another. But whereas we thought them all five to be Turkish Ships of War; we afterwards understood that two of them were their prizes (the one, a small ship of London, the other of the West Country), that came out of the Quactath, laden with figs and other merchandise, but now [were] subject to the fortune of the sea, and the captivity of pirates. But to our business!

Three of these ships got much upon us; and so much, that, ere half the day was spent, the Admiral, which was the best sailer, fetched up the *George Bonaventure*, and made booty of it.

The Vice-Admiral again, being nearest unto the lesser bark whereof JOHN RAWLINS was Master, shewed him the force of a stronger arm; and by his Turkish name, called VILLA RISE, commanded him, in like sort, to strike his sails, and submit to his mercy: which, not to be gainsaid, nor prevented, was quickly done. And so RAWLINS, with his bark, was as quickly taken; although the Rear-Admiral, being the worst sailer of the three, called *Riggiprise*, came not in, till all was done.

The same day, before night, the Admiral (either loath to pester himself with too much company, or ignorant of the commodity [which] was to be made by the sale of English prisoners, or daring not to trust them in his company for fear of mutinies, and exciting others to rebellion) set twelve persons who were in the *George Bonaventure*, and divers other English whom he had taken before, on the land, to try their fortunes in an unknown country.

But VILLA RISE, the Vice-Admiral, that had taken JOHN RAWLINS, would not so dispense with his men; but commanded him, and five more of his company to be brought aboard his ship: leaving in his bark, three men and his boy, with thirteen Turks and Moors, who were, questionless, sufficient to overmaster the others, and direct the bark to harbour.

Thus they sailed direct for Argier [*Algiers*]. But, the night following followed them with great tempest and foul weather, which ended not without some effect of a storm: for they lost the sight of RAWLINS's bark, called the *Nicholas*; and, in a manner, lost themselves (though they seemed safe a shipboard) by fearful conjecturing what should become of us?

At last, by the 22nd of the same month, they, or we (choose you whether! for I would not be mistaken in altering the persons, by either naming the first for the third, or the third for the first; but only make the discourse equal, by setting down the business honestly and truly as it chanced) arrived in Argier; and came in safety within the Mole: but found not our other bark there; nay, though we earnestly inquired after the same.

Yet heard we nothing to our satisfaction; but much matter was ministered to our discomfort and amazement. For although the Captain and our Overseers were loath we should have any conference with our countrymen; yet did we adventure to inform ourselves of the present affairs, both of the town and of the shipping. So that finding many English at work in other ships, they spared not to tell us the danger we were in, and the mischiefs we must needs incur; as being sure, "If we were not used like slaves, to be sold as slaves: for there had been five hundred brought into the market for the same purpose, and above a hundred handsome youths compelled to turn Turks; all English!" Yet, like good Christians, they bade us "Be of good cheer! and comfort ourselves in this! That GOD's trials were gentle purgations; and these crosses were but to cleanse the dross from the gold, and bring us out of the fire again, more clear and lovely."

Yet, I must needs confess, that they afforded us reason for this cruelty; as if they determined to be revenged of our last attempt to fire their ships in the Mole [*by Sir* ROBERT MANSELL'*s fleet in May*, 1621. *See J. B's.* Algiers Voyage. 1621], and therefore protested "to spare none! whom they could surprise, and take alone; but either to sell them for money or to torment them to serve their own ends."

Now their customs and usages, in both these, were in this manner.

First, concerning the first. The Bashaw [*Pasha*] had the overseeing of all prisoners who were presented unto him, at their first coming into the harbour; and so chose one out of every eight, for a present or fee to himself. The rest were rated by the Captains, and so sent to the market to be sold: whereat, if either there were repining, or any drawing back; then certain Moors and Officers attended, either to beat you forward, or thrust you in the sides with goads. And this was the manner of the selling of slaves.

Secondly, concerning their enforcing them, either to turn Turk or to attend their impieties: although it would make a Christian's heart bleed to hear of the same; yet must the truth not be hid, nor the terror left untold. They commonly lay them on their naked backs or bellies, beating them so long till they bleed at the nose and mouth: and if yet they continue constant, then they strike the teeth out of their heads, pinch them by their tongues, and use many other sorts of tortures to convert them. Nay, many times, they lay them, their whole length, in the ground, like a grave; and so cover them with boards, threatening to starve them, if they will not turn. And so, many, even for fear of torment and death, make their tongues betray their hearts to a most fearful wickedness: and so are circumcised with new names, and brought to confess a new religion. Others again, I must confess, who never knew any gód but their own sensual lusts and pleasures, thought that any religion would serve their turns: and so, for preferment or wealth, very voluntarily renounced their faith, and became Renegadoes; in despite of any counsel which seemed to intercept them.

And this was the first news we encountered with, at our coming first to Argier.

The 26th of the same month, JOHN RAWLINS' bark, with his other three men and a boy, came safe into the Mole; and so were put all together, to be carried before the Bashaw; but that they took the Owner's Servant [? *Supercargo*] and RAWLINS's boy, and, by force and torment, compelled them to turn Turks.

Then were they in all, seven English, besides JOHN RAWLINS: of whom the Bashaw took one; and sent the rest to their Captains, who set a valuation upon them. So the soldiers hurried us, like dogs, into the market; where, as men sell hackneys in England, we were tossed up and down, to see who would give most for us. And although we had heavy hearts, and looked with sad countenances; yet many came to behold us; sometimes taking us by the hand, sometimes turning us round about, sometimes feeling our brawns and naked arms: and so beholding our prices written in our breasts, they bargained for us accordingly; and, at last, we were all sold, and the soldiers returned with their money to their Captains.

JOHN RAWLINS was the last that was sold, by reason of his lame hand. He was bought by the Captain that took him, even that dog VILLA RISE! who (better informing himself of his skill fit to be a Pilot, and his experience to be an Overseer) bought him and his Carpenter at very easy rates. For, as we afterwards understood by divers English Renegadoes, he paid for RAWLINS but 150 Doublets, which make, of English money, £7 10s.

Thus was he and his Carpenter, with divers other slaves, sent into his ship to work; and employed about such affairs as belonged to the well rigging and preparing the same.

But the villainous Turks perceiving his lame hand, and that he could not perform so much as other slaves, quickly complained to their Patron: who as quickly apprehended the inconvenience; whereupon he sent for him, the next day, and told him, "He was unserviceable for his present purpose! and therefore unless he could procure £15 of the English there, for his ransom: he would send him up into the country, where he should never see Christendom again, and endure the extremity of a miserable banishment."

But see how GOD worketh all for the best for His servants! and confoundeth the presumption of tyrants, frustrating their purposes, to make His wonders known to the sons of men! and relieves His people, when they least think of succour and releasement!

Whilst JOHN RAWLINS was thus terrified with the dogged answer of VILLA RISE, the *Exchange* of Bristol, a ship formerly surprised by the pirates, lay all unrigged in the harbour, till, at last, one JOHN GOODALE, an English Turk, with his confederates (understanding she was a good sailer, and might be made a proper Man of War) bought her from the Turks that took her; and prepare her for their own purposes.

Now the Captain that set them on work, was also an English Renegado, by the name of RAMMETHAM RISE, but by his Christian name HENRY CHANDLER: who resolved to make GOODALE, Master over her.

And because they were both English Turks (having the command, notwithstanding, of many Turks and Moors) they concluded to have all English slaves to go in her; and for their gunners, English and Dutch Renegadoes: and so they agreed with the Patrons of nine English slaves and one

French for their ransoms; who were presently employed to rig and furnish the ship for a Man of War.

And while they were thus busied, two of JOHN RAWLINS's, men (who were taken with him), were also taken up to serve in this Man of War: their names, JAMES ROE and JOHN DAVIES, the one dwelling in Plymouth; and the other in Foy, where the Commander of this ship was also born, by which occasion they became acquainted. So that both the Captain and the Master promised them good usage, upon the good service they should perform in the voyage; and withal, demanded of DAVIES if he knew of any Englishman to be bought, that could serve them as a Pilot; both to direct them out of harbour, and conduct them in their voyage. For, in truth, neither was the Captain a mariner, nor any Turk in her of sufficiency to dispose of [*navigate*] her through the Straits in security; nor oppose any enemy that should hold it out bravely against them.

DAVIES quick replied that, "As far as he understood, VILLA RISE would sell JOHN RAWLINS, his Master, and Commander of the bark which was taken. A man every way sufficient for sea affairs, being of great resolution and good experience; and for all he had a lame hand, yet had he a sound heart and noble courage for any attempt or adventure."

When the Captain understood thus much, he employed DAVIES to search for RAWLINS; who, at last lighting upon him, asked him, "If the Turk would sell him?"

RAWLINS suddenly answered, that "By reason of his lame hand he was willing to part with him; but because he had disbursed money for him, he would gain something by him; and so priced him at 300 doublets, which amounteth to £15 English; which he must procure, or incure sorer indurances."

When DAVIES had certified thus much, the Turks a shipboard conferred about the matter; and the Master, whose Christian name was JOHN GOODALE, joined with two Turks who were consorted with him, and disbursed 100 doublets a piece, and so bought him of VILLA RISE: sending him into the said ship called the *Exchange* of Bristol; as well to supervise what had been done, as to order what was left undone; but especially to fit the sails, and to accommodate [*fit out*] the ship. All which, RAWLINS was very careful and indulgent in; not yet thinking of any particular plot of deliverance, more than a general desire to be freed from this Turkish slavery, and inhuman abuses.

By the 7th of January [1622], the ship was prepared, with twelve good cast pieces, and all manner of munition and provision which belonged to such a purpose: and, the same day, hauled out of the Mole of Argier, with this company, and in this manner.

There were in her sixty-three Turks and Moors, nine English slaves and one French, four Hollanders that were free men (to whom the Turks promised one prize or other, and so to return to Holland; or if they were disposed to go back again for Argier, they should have great reward, and no enforcement offered, but continue, as they would, both their religion and their customs): and for their gunners, they had two of our soldiers, one English and one Dutch Renegado. And thus much for the company.

For the manner of setting out, it was as usual, as in other ships; but that the Turks delighted in the ostent[ati]ous bravery of their streamers, banners, and topsails: the ship being a handsome ship, and well built for any purpose. The slaves and English were employed under hatches, about the ordnance and other works of order, and accommodating [*berthing*] themselves.

All which, JOHN RAWLINS marked, as supposing it an intolerable slavery to take such pains, and be subject to such dangers; and still to enrich other men, and maintain their voluptuous lives; returning themselves as slaves, and living worse than dogs amongst them. Whereupon, after he had conceited the indignity and reproach of their baseness, and the glory of an exploit that could deliver himself and the rest from this slavish captivity; being very busy among the English in pulling of ropes, and placing of ordnance, he burst into these, or such like abrupt speeches: "O hellish slavery! to be thus subject to dogs! to labour thus to enrich infidels, and maintain their pleasures! to be ourselves slaves, and worse than the outcast of the world! Is there no way of releasement? no device to free us from this bondage? no exploit, no action of worth to be put in excution, to make us renown in the world, and famous to posterity? O GOD! strengthen my heart and hand, and something shall be done to ease us of these mischiefs, and deliver us from these cruel Mahomedan dogs!"

The other slaves pitying his distraction, as they thought, bade him, "Speak softly! least they should all fare the worse for his distemperature!"

"The worse!" quoth RAWLINS, "what can be worse? Death is the determiner of all misery! and torture can last but a while! But to be continually a dying, and suffer all indignity and reproach; and, in the end, to have no welcome but into the House of Slaughter or Bondage, is insufferable! and more than flesh and blood can endure! And therefore, by that salvation which CHRIST hath brought, I will either attempt my deliverance at one time or another, or perish in the enterprise! but if you would be contented to hearken after a release, and join with me in the action; I would not doubt of facilitating the same, and shew you a way to make your credits thrive by some work of amazement, and augment your glory in purchasing your liberty!"

"Ay, prithee, be quiet!" said they again, "and think not of impossibilities! Yet, if you can but open such a door of reason and probability that we be not condemn for desperate and distracted persons, in pulling the sun (as it were) out of the firmament; we can but sacrifice our lives! and you may be sure of secrecy and taciturnity!"

"Now, blessed be my genius!" said RAWLINS, "that ever this motive was so opportunely preferred! and therefore we will be quiet a while, till the iron be hotter, that we may not strike in vain."

The 15th January, the morning water [*tide*] brought us near Cape de Gatte, hard by the shore; we having in our company, a small Turkish Ship of War that followed us out of Argier, the next day: and now joining us she gave us notice of seven small vessels, six of them being Sattees and one a Polacca; who very quickly appeared in sight, and so we made towards them.

But having more advantage of the Polacca than the rest, and loath to lose all, we both fetched her up, and brought her past hope of recovery; which when she perceived, rather than she would voluntarily come into the slavery of the Mahomedans, she ran herself ashore; and so all the men forsook her.

We still followed as near as we durst, and for fear of splitting [*i.e., on the rocks*], let fall our anchors; making out [*sending*] both our boats, wherein were many musketeers and some English and Dutch Renegadoes: who came aboard home at their *congé* [*entered the vessel, without opposition*], and found three pieces of ordnance, and four murtherers [*see Vol. I. p.* 500], but straightway threw them all overboard, to lighten the ship. So they got her off, being ladened with hides, and logwood for dyeing: and presently sent her to Argier, taking nine Turks and one English slave out of one ship, and six out of the lesser; which, we thought, sufficient to man her.

But see the chance! or, if you will, how fortune smiled on us. In the rifling of this *Cataleynia* [? Catalonian], the Turks fell at variance, one with another; and in such a manner that we divided ourselves [*parted company*]: the lesser ship returned to Argier and our *Exchange* took the opportunity of the wind, and plied out of the Straits; which rejoiced JOHN RAWLINS very much, as resolving on some stratagem, when opportunity should serve.

In the meanwhile, the Turks began to murmur, and would not willingly go into the *Marr Granada*, as the phrase is amongst them; notwithstanding the Moors, being very superstitious, were contented to be directed by their *Hoshea*, who, with us, signifieth a Witch [*or rather Wizard*]: and is of great account and reputation amongst them, as not going in any great vessel to sea without one; and observing whatsoever he concludeth, out of his divination.

The ceremonies he useth are many; and when they come into the ocean, every second or third night, he maketh his conjuration. He beginneth, and endeth with prayer, using many characters, and calling upon GOD by divers names.

Yet, at this time, all that he did, consisteth in these particulars. Upon the sight, and, as we were afraid, the chasing of two great ships, being supposed to be Spanish Men of War, a great silence is commanded in the ship; and when all is done, the company giveth as great a screech; the Captain still coming to JOHN RAWLINS and sometimes making him to take in all his sails, and sometimes causing him to hoist them all out, as the Witch findeth by his book and presages.

Then have they two arrows and a curtleaxe lying on a pillow, naked. The arrows are, one for the Turks, and the other for the Christians. Then the Witch readeth, and the Captain or some other, taketh the arrows in their hand by the heads, and if the arrow for the Christians cometh over the head of the arrow for the Turks, then do they advance their sails, and will not endure the fight, whatsoever they see; but if the arrow of the Turks is found, in the opening of the hand, upon the arrow of the Christians, they will then stay and encounter with any ship whatsoever.

The curtleaxe is taken up by some child that is innocent, or rather, ignorant of the ceremony; and so laid down again. Then they do observe whether the same side is uppermost, which lay before: and so proceed accordingly.

They also observe lunatics and changlings, and the Conjurer writeth down their sayings in a book, grovelling on the ground, as if he whispered to the Devil, to tell him the truth: and so expoundeth the Letter, as it were, by inspiration.

Many other foolish rites they have, whereon they do dote as foolishly; and whereof, I could entreat more at large, but this shall suffice at this time.

Whilst he was thus busied, and made demonstration that all was finished; the people in the ship gave a great shout, and cried out "A sail!" "a sail!": which, at last, was discovered to be another Man of War of Turks. For he made towards us, and sent his boat aboard us; to whom, our Captain complained that being becalmed by the Southern Cape [? *of Portugal, i.e., Cape St. Vincent*]; and having "made" no voyage, the Turks denied to go any further northward; but the Captain resolved not to return to Argier, except he could obtain some prize worthy his endurances; but rather to go to Salle, and sell his Christians to victual his ship. Which the other Captain apprehended for his honour; and so persuaded the Turks to be obedient unto him: whereupon followed a pacification amongst us; and so that Turk took his course for the Straits, and we put up northward, expecting the good hour of some beneficial booty.

All this while our slavery continued; and the Turks, with insulting tyranny, set us still on work in all base and servile actions; adding stripes and inhuman revilings, even in our greatest labour. Whereupon JOHN RAWLINS resolved to obtain his liberty and surprise the ship, providing ropes with broad specks of iron, and all the iron crows, with which he knew a way, upon the consent of the rest, to ram up or tie fast their scuttles, gratings, and cabins; yea, to shut up the Captain himself with all his consorts: and so to handle the matter, that, upon the watchword given, the English being masters of the Gunner Room, ordnance and powder, they would either blow them into the air; or kill them, as they adventured to come down, one by one, if they should, by any chance, open their cabins.

But because he would proceed the better in his enterprise, as he had somewhat abruptly discovered himself to the nine English slaves, so he kept the same distance with the four Hollanders that were free men: till finding them coming somewhat towards them; he acquainted with them the whole conspiracy; and they affecting the plot, offered the adventure of their lives in the business.

Then, very warily, he undermined the English Renegado which was the Gunner; and three more, his associates: who, at first, seemed to retract.

Last of all, were brought in the Dutch Renegadoes, who were also in the Gunner Room; for always there lay twelve there, five Christians, and seven English and Dutch Turks.

So that, when another motion had settled their resolutions, and JOHN RAWLINS's constancy had put new life, as it were, into the matter: the four Hollanders very honestly, according to their promise, sounded the Dutch Renegadoes; who, with easy persuasion, gave their consent to so brave an enterprise.

Whereupon JOHN RAWLINS, not caring whether the English Gunners would yield or not, resolved, in the Captain's morning watch, to make the attempt.

But, you must understand that where the English slaves lay [*in the Gun Room*], there hung up always four or five crows of iron; being still under the carriages of the pieces. And, when the time approached, being very dark: because JOHN RAWLINS would have his crow of iron ready, as other things were, and other men prepared, in their several places; in taking it out of the carriage, by chance, it hit on the side of the piece, making such a noise, that the soldiers hearing it, awaked the Turks, and bade them come down. Whereupon, the Boatswain of the Turks descended, with a candle, and presently searched all the slaves' places, making much ado of the matter: but finding neither hatchet, nor hammer, nor anything else to move suspicion of the enterprise more than the crow of iron, which lay slipped down under the carriages of the pieces; they went quietly up again, and certified the Captain, what had chanced, who satisfied himself that it was a common thing to have a crow of iron slip from his place.

But by this occasion, we made stay of our attempt; yet were resolved to take another or a better opportunity.

Only I must tell you, what JOHN RAWLINS would have done, if this accident had not happened. He was fully minded, with some others, with their naked knives in their hands, to press upon the Gunner's breast and the other English Renegadoes, and either force them to consent to their designs, or to cut their throats; first telling them plainly that "They had vowed to surprise the ship, and, by GOD's assistance, to obtain their liberty; and therefore Die! or Consent (when you hear the watchword given, *For GOD! and King JAMES!* and *St. GEORGE for England!*) [that] you presently keep your places! and advise to execute what you are commanded!"

But as you have heard, GOD was the best physician to our wounded hearts; and used a kind of preventing physic, rather than to cure us so suddenly. So that, out of His Providence, perceiving some danger in this enterprise, He both caused us to desist; and, at last, brought our business to a better period, and fortunate end.

For we sailed still more northward, and RAWLINS had more time to tamper with his Gunners, and the rest of the English Renegadoes: who very willingly, when they considered the matter, and perpended the reasons, gave way unto the project; and with a kind of joy seemed to entertain the motives. Only they made a stop at [*as to*] the first onset, who should begin the enterprise, which was no way fit for them to do; because they were no slaves, but Renegadoes, and so had always beneficial entertainment amongst them: but when it was once put in practice, they would be sure not to fail them; but venture their lives for GOD and their country.

When RAWLINS had heard them out, he much liked their contradiction [*reservation*]; and told them plainly, "He did require no such thing at their hands! but the slaves and himself would first sound the channel, and adventure the water." And so, after reciprocal oaths taken, and hands given; RAWLINS, once again, lay in wait for the fittest opportunity. But once again he was disappointed; and a suspicious accident brought him to re-collect his spirits anew, and study on the danger of the enterprise: and thus it was.

After the Renegado Gunner had protested secrecy, by all that might induce a man to bestow some belief upon him; he presently went up the scottle [*scuttle*]; but stayed not aloft a quarter of an hour. Nay, he came sooner down; and in the Gunner Room sat by RAWLINS, who tarried for him, where he left him.

He was no sooner placed, and entered into some conference, but there entered into the place, a furious Turk, with his knife drawn, and presented it to RAWLINS's body: who verily supposed he intended to kill him; as suspicious that the Gunner had discovered something. Whereat RAWLINS was much moved; and so hastily asked, "What the matter meant? or whether he would kill him or not?" observing his countenance; and (according to the nature of jealousy) conceiting that his colour had a passage of change, whereby his suspicious heart condemned him for a traitor; but that, at more leisure, he sware the contrary, and afterwards proved faithful and industrious in the enterprise. And for the present, he answered RAWLINS, in this manner, "No, Master! be not afraid! I think, he doth but jest!"

With that, JOHN RAWLINS gave back a little, and drew out his knife; stepping also to the Gunner's sheath, and taking out his, whereby he had two knives to one: which, when the Turk perceived, he threw down his knife, saying, "He did but jest with him!"

But, as I said, when the Gunner perceived, RAWLINS took it so ill, he whispered something in his ear, that, at last, satisfied him: calling heaven to witness that "He never spake a word of the enterprise, nor ever would! either to the prejudice of the business, or danger of his person."

Notwithstanding, RAWLINS kept the knives in his sleeve, all night, and was somewhat troubled; for that he had made so many acquainted with an action of such importance: but, the next day, when he perceived the coast clear, and that there was no further cause for fear, he somewhat comforted himself; and grew bolder and bolder in disposing the affairs of the ship. Only it grieved him that his enterprises were thus procrastinated: whereby the Mahomedan tyranny increased, and the poor slaves even groaned again under the burden of their bondage; and thought every day a year, till something was put in execution for their deliverance. For it was now full five weeks, since RAWLINS first projected the matter.

All this while, RAWLINS drew the Captain to lie for the Northern Cape [? *Cape Finisterre*], assuring him, that thereby he should not miss purchase; which accordingly fell out, as a wish would have it: but his drift was, in truth, to draw him from any supply or second [*reinforcement*] of Turks, if GOD should give way to their enterprise, or success to the victory.

Yet, for the present, the 6th of February, being twelve leagues from the Cape, we descried a sail; and presently, took the advantage of the wind in chasing her, and at last fetched her up, making her strike all her sails: whereby we knew her to be a bark belonging to Torbay, near Dartmouth, that came from Averare, laden with salt.

Ere we had fully despatched, it chanced to be foul weather; so that we could not, or at least would not make out our boat; but caused the Master of the bark to let down his, and come aboard with his company; there being in the bark but nine men, and one boy.

And so the Master, leaving his Mate with two men in the same, came himself, with five men and the boy unto us; whereupon our Turkish Captain sent ten Turks to man her: amongst whom, were two Dutch and one English Renegado, who were of our confederacy, and acquainted with us.

But when RAWLINS saw this partition of his friends, before they could hoist out their boat for the bark; he made means to speak with them, and told them plainly that "He would prosecute the matter, either that night, or the next: and therefore, whatsoever came of it, they should acquaint the English with his resolution, and make towards England; bearing up the helm, whiles the Turks slept and suspected no such matter. For, by GOD's grace, in his first watch, about midnight, he would shew them a light; by which they might understand that the enterprise was begun, or, at least, in a good forwardness for the execution."

So the boat was let down, and they came to the bark of Torbay; where the Master's Mate being left, as before you have heard, apprehended quickly the matter, and heard the discourse with amazement.

But time was precious, and not to be spent in disputing or casting of doubts, whether the Turks that were with them were able to master them or not; being seven to six: considering they had the helm of the ship, and the Turks being soldiers, and ignorant of sea affairs, could not discover whether they went to Argier or not; or, if they did, they resolved, by RAWLINS's example, to cut their throats, or cast them overboard. And so I leave them to make use of the Renegadoes' instructions: and return to RAWLINS again.

The Master of the bark of Torbay and his company were quickly searched, and as quickly pillaged, and dismissed to the liberty of the ship; whereby RAWLINS had leisure to entertain him with the lamentable news of their extremities, and the adventure of their voyages: whereby he understood of his first setting out from the West country, of his taking and surprising at sea by VILLA RISE; of his twice being sold as a slave, and so continuing to his heart-burning and excruciation; of the making [of] the *Exchange* of Bristol, a Man of War, which they were now in; of the Captain and Master, who were both English Renegadoes; of the cruelty of the Turks in general, and his own fortunes in particular; of his admission into the ship as a Pilot; of the friendship which passed between him and the Hollanders; of the imparting of the secret of surprising the ship, both to the slaves and Christian Renegadoes; of their consent and courageous apprehension of the matter; of the first attempt, and their twice disappointing; of his still resolution presently [*at once*] to put it in practice; of his last acquainting [of] the Dutch Renegadoes who went aboard his bark; and in a word, of every particular which was befitting to the purpose.

"Yea," he told him, that "that night, he should lose the the sight of them, for they would make the helm for England;" and that he "would, that night, and evermore, pray for their good success and safe deliverance."

When the Master of the Bark of Torbay had heard him out, and that his company were partakers of his story; they all became silent: not either diffident of his discourse or afraid of the attempt; but as wondering at the goodness of GOD, and His mercy in choosing out such weak instruments to set forth His glory.

"True," quoth Rawlins, when he found them coming towards him, "it is so! For mark but the circumstance of the matter! and you shall see the very finger of GOD to point us out our deliverance! When we came into the main ocean to hunt after prizes, according to the nature of pirates, and that I resolved on the enterprise, there were sixty-five Turks in our ship, and only seventeen of our confederacy. Then it pleased GOD to abate us ten of the Turks, who were sent with the Polacca before recited. And when we were disappointed again of our purposes; you see now what hath chanced! We are rid of more Turks, and welcome you, as a new supply! so that, if you please, we shall be twenty-four strong; and they, in all, are but forty-five. Be therefore courageous! and let us join heart, hand, and foot together that we may execute this brave attempt for GOD's glory, our country's honour, the good example to others, our own deliverance, and (if we may not be counted vainglorious) our everlasting memory."

By that time he had finished this discourse also, the Master of the Bark and his company resolved to assist him: as projecting[*foreseeing*] the misery and wretchedness they should endure by being slaves to the Turks, and the happiness of their liberty besides the reputation of the enterprise. As for death, it was in community to all men: and so in the hands of GOD to dispose, at His pleasure; and either could not happen before the hour of limitation, or could not be prevented. For human policy must submit to Divine Providence.

Yet to shew himself an understanding man, he demanded of RAWLINS, "What weapons he had? and in what manner he would execute the business?"

To which, he answered, that "He had ropes and iron hooks, to make fast the scottels, gratings, and cabins. He had also in the Gunner Room two curtleaxes, and the slaves had five crows of iron before them. Besides, in the scuffling, they made no question [of taking] of some of the soldiers' weapons."

Then for the manner, he told them, "They were sure of the ordnance, the Gunner Room, and the powder: and so blocking them up, would either kill them, as they came down; or turn the ordnance against their cabins, or blow them into the air by one stratagem or other." Thus were they contented, on all sides; and resolved to the enterprise.

The next morning, being the 7th of February, the prize of Torbay was not to be seen or found; whereat the Captain began to storm and swear, commanding RAWLINS to search the seas up and down for her: who bestowed all that day in that business, but to little purpose; whereupon, when the humour was spent, the Captain pacified himself, as conceiting he should be sure to find her at Argier. But, by the permission of the Ruler of all actions, that Argier was England! and all his wickedness frustrated.

For RAWLINS being now startled, lest he should return in this humour, for the Straits; the 8th of February went down into the hold, and finding a great deal of water below; told the Captain of the same: adding that "It did not come to the pump!" which he did very politicly, that he might remove the ordnance.

For when the Captain asked him the reason, he told him, "the ship was too far after the head."

Then, he commanded to use the best means he could, to bring her in order.

"Sure, then," quoth RAWLINS, we must quit our cables, and bring four pieces of ordnance after [*abaft*]; and that would bring the water to the pump." Which was presently put in practice.

So the pieces being usually made fast thwart the ship, we brought two of them, with their mouths right before the biticle [*binnacle*]. And because the Renegado Flemings would not begin [*i.e., the fight*]; it was thus concluded.

That the ship having three decks; we that did belong to the Gunner Room should be all there, and break up the lower deck. The English slaves, who always lay in the middle deck should do the like, and watch the scuttles. RAWLINS himself prevailed with the Gunner, for so much powder as should prime the pieces: and so told them all, there was no better watchword, nor means to begin, than, upon the report of the piece, to make a cry and screech [*shout*], "For GOD, and King JAMES!" and "St. GEORGE for England!"

When all things were prepared, and every man resolved, as knowing what he had to do; and the hour when it should happen, to be two in the afternoon: RAWLINS advised the Master Gunner to speak to the Captain, that the soldiers might attend on the poop, which would bring the ship after [*more aft*]. To which the Captain was very willing; and upon the Gunner's information, the soldiers gat themselves to the Poop to the number of twenty; and five or six went into the Captain's cabin, where always lay divers curtleaxes and some targets [*shields*].

And so we fell to work to pump the water; and carried the matter fairly till the next day, which was spent as the former;

being the 9th of February, and, as GOD must have the praise! the triumph of our victory.

For by that time, all things were prepared, and the soldiers got upon the Poop as the day before. To avoid suspicion, all that did belong to the Gunner Room went down; and the slaves in the middle deck, attended [to] their business. So that we may cast up our account in this manner.

> First, nine English slaves, besides JOHN RAWLINS; five of the Torbay men and one boy; four English Renegadoes and two Dutch; four Hollanders: in all, four and twenty and a boy.

So that lifting up our hearts and hands to GOD, for the success of the business; we were wonderfully encouraged, and settled ourselves till the report of the piece gave us warning of the enterprise.

Now, you must consider that, in this company, were two of RAWLINS's men, JAMES ROE and JOHN DAVIES, whom he brought out of England; and whom the fortune of the sea brought into the same predicament with their Master.

These were employed about noon, being, as I said, the 9th of February, to prepare their matches; while all the Turks, or at least most of them, stood on the Poop, to weigh down the ship as it were, to bring the water forward to the pump, the one brought his match lighted between two spoons, the other brought his, in a little piece of a can. And so, in the name of GOD! the Turks and Moors being placed as you have heard, and five and forty in number; and RAWLINS having proined the touchholes: JAMES ROE gave fire to one of the pieces, about two o'clock in the afternoon; and the confederates, upon the warning, shouted most cheerfully.

The report of the piece did tear and break down all the biticle and compasses; and the noise of the slaves made all the soldiers amazed at the matter: till seeing the quarter of the ship rent and feeling the whole body to shake under them; understanding the ship was surprised, and the attempt tended to their utter destruction, never bear robbed of her whelps was so fell and mad!

For they not only called us "Dogs!" and cried out "*Usance de la mar*," which is as much as to say, "The fortune of the wars!" but attempted to tear up the planks, setting a work hammers, hatchets, knives, the oars of the boat, boat-hook, their curtleaxes, and what else came to hand; besides stones and bricks in the Cook Room: all which they threw amongst us; attempting still and still, to break and rip up the hatches and boards of the steering, not desisting from their former execrations, and horrid blasphemies and revilings.

When JOHN RAWLINS perceived them so violent, and understood how the slaves had cleared the decks of all the Turks and Moors beneath; he set a guard upon the powder, and charged their own muskets against them: killing them from divers scout holes, both before and behind; and so lessened their number, to the joy of all our hearts.

Whereupon they cried out, and called for the Pilot: and so RAWLINS, with some to guard him, went to them; and understood them, by their kneeling, that they cried for mercy and to have their lives saved; and they would come down; which he bade them do. And so they were taken one by one, and bound; yea, killed with their own curtleaxes. Which, when the rest perceived, they called us, "English dogs!" and reviled us with many opprobrious terms; some leaping overboard, saying, "It was the chance of war!" Some were manacled, and so thrown overboard: and some were slain and mangled with the curtleaxes; till the ship was well cleared, and ourselves assured of the victory.

At the first report of our piece, and the hurly burly in the decks; the Captain was writing in his cabin: and hearing the noise, thought it some strange accident; and so, came out with his curtleaxe in his hand, presuming by his authority to pacify the mischief.

But when he cast his eyes upon us, and saw that we were like to surprise the ship; he threw down his curtleaxe, and begged to save his life: intimating to RAWLINS, "how he had redeemed him from VILLA RISE; and ever since admitted him to place of command in the ship; besides honest usage in the whole course of the voyage."

All which RAWLINS confessed; and at last, condescended [*agreed*] to mercy: and brought the Captain and five more into England.

The Captain was called RAMTHAM RISE; but his Christian name, HENRY CHANDLER: and, as they say, a chandler's son in Southwark. JOHN GOODALE was also an English Turk. RICHARD CLARKE, in Turkish, JAFAR; GEORGE COOKE,

RAMEDAM; JOHN BROWNE, MAMME; WILLIAM WINTER, MUSTAPHA: besides all the slaves and Hollanders; with other Renegadoes, who were willing to be reconciled to their true Saviour, as being formerly seduced with the hopes of riches, honour preferment, and such like devilish baits to catch the souls of mortal men and entangle frailty in the tarriers of horrible abuses and imposturing deceit.

When all was done, and the ship cleared of the dead bodies; JOHN RAWLINS assembled his men together, and with one consent gave the praise to GOD: using the accustomed Service on ship board; and, for want of books, lifted up their voices to GOD, as He put into their hearts or renewed their memories. Then, did they sing a *Psalm*; and, last of all, embraced one another, for playing the men in such a deliverance, whereby our fear was turned into joy, and trembling hearts exhilarated; that we had escaped such inevitable dangers, and especially the slavery and terror of bondage, worse than death itself!

The same night, we washed our ship, put everything in as good order as we could, repaired the broken quarter, set up the biticle, and bore up the helm for England: where, by GOD's grace and good guiding, we arrived at Plymouth, the 13th of February [1622]; and were welcomed like the recovery of the lost sheep, or as you read of a loving mother that runneth, with embraces to entertain her son from a long voyage and escape of many dangers.

Not long after, we understood of our confederates that returned home in the bark of Torbay, that they arrived in Penzance in Cornwall, the 11th of February.

And if any ask after their deliverance, considering there were ten Turks sent to man her, I will tell you that too.

The next day after they lost us [*i.e.*, *7th*], as you have heard, the three Renegadoes had acquainted the Master's Mate and the two English in her, with RAWLINS' determination; and that they themselves would be true to them, and assist them in any enterprise: then, if the worst came, there were but seven to six.

But, as it fell out, they had a more easy passage than turmoil and manslaughter. For they made the Turks believe the wind was come fair, and that they were sailing to Argier, till they came within sight of England: which one of them amongst the rest discovered, saying plainly, "that land was not like Cape St. Vincent!"

"Yes!" saith he that was at the helm, "and [*if*] you will be contented, and go down into the hold; and turn the salt over to windward, whereby the ship may bear full sail: you shall know and see more to-morrow!"

Whereupon five of them went down very orderly, the Renegadoes feigning themselves asleep; who presently start up, and with the help of the two English, nailed down the hatches. Whereat the principal amongst them much repined; and began to grow into choler and rage, had it not quickly been overpassed. For one stepped to him, and dashed out his brains; and threw him overboard.

The rest were brought to Exeter: either to be arraigned according to the punishment of delinquents in that kind, or disposed of as the King and Council shall think meet.

And this is the story of this Deliverance, and end of JOHN RAWLINS's voyage.

Now, gentle Reader! I hope you will not call in question the power and goodness of GOD, who, from time to time, extendeth His mercy to the miraculous preservation of His servants; nor make any doubt that He hath still the same arm and vigour as He had in times past, when GIDEON's three hundred men overcame the Midianites: and many ancient stratagems are recorded to have had a passage of success, even within our memories, to execute as great a wonder as this. Nor do I think you will be startled at anything in the discourse touching the cruelty and inhumanity of Turks and Moors themselves: who, from a native barbarousness, do hate all Christians and Christianity; especially if they grow into the violent rages of piracy, or fall into that exorbitant course of selling of slaves, or enforcing of men to be Mahomedans.

Nor can I imagine, you will call in question our natural desire of liberty, and saving of our lives, when you see, from instinct of nature, all the creatures of the world come to the law of preservation: and our Saviour Himself, alloweth the flying out of one city into another, in the time of persecution; and PAUL, by saying "He was a Roman!" procured his delivery.

Well, then, it is only the truth of the story that you are amazed at: making doubt whether your belief of the same may be bestowed to your own credit! I can say no more.

The actors in this comic tragedy are most of them alive. The Turks are in prison! the ship is to be seen! and RAWLINS himself dare justify the matter! For he hath presented it to the Marquis! a man not to be dallied withal in these things; nor any way to be made partaker of deceit.

Nay, I protest I think he durst not, for his ears! publish (concerning the substance) such a discourse to open overlooking, if it were not true! As for illustration, or cementing the broken pieces of well-tempered mortar, blame him not in that! For precious stones are worn enamelled and wrought in gold; which otherwise would still be of value and estimation; but published and receiving the addition of art and cunning, who doth not account [them] the better, and esteemeth himself the ruler for their possession.

So, then, entertain it for a true and certain discourse! Apply it! make use of it! and put it to thy heart for thy comfort! It teacheth the acknowledgment of a powerful, provident, and merciful GOD, who will be known in His wonders, and make weak things the instruments of His glory! It instructeth us in the practice of thanksgiving when a a benefit is bestowed, a mercy shown, and a deliverance perfected. It maketh us strong and courageous in adversity, like cordial restoratives to a sick heart; and our patience shall stand like a rock, against the impetuous assaults of affliction. It is a glorious sun to dissipate the clouds of desperation; and cheer us thus far that GOD can restore us, when we are under the pressure of discomfort and tribulation: for preferment comes neither from the East, nor the West; but from Him that holdeth the winds in His hands, and puts a hook in the nostrils of Leviathan.

So that if He do not give way to our contentment, it is because He will supply us with better graces, or keep us from the adder's hole of Temptation, whereat, if we tarry, we shall be sure to be stung unto death.

In a word, it is a Mirror to look Virtue in the face! and teach men the way to industry and noble performances; that a brave spirit and honest man shall say, with NEHEMIAH, "*Shall such a man as I! fly?* Shall I fear death or some petty trial; when GOD is to be honoured! my country to be terved! my King to be obeyed! Religion to be defended! the Commonwealth supported! honour and renown obtained! and, in the end, the crown of immortality purchased?"

THE names of those [four] English Renegadoes as consented, and joined with the Slaves, in the recovery of the Ship, were these:

RICHARD CLARKE, the Gunner; called in Turkish, JAFAR.

GEORGE COOKE, Gunner's Mate; called in Turkish, RAMEDAM.

WILLIAM WINTER, Carpenter; in Turkish, MUSTAPHA.

JOHN BROWNE, in Turkish, MEMME.

One Dutch Renegado.

Four Dutch Slaves.

One French Slave.

Five Englishmen and a boy, taken but three days before.

Nine English Slaves, which they took with them from Argier.

In all twenty-four men and a boy: which were all safely landed at Plymouth, the 13th of February, 1621 [*i.e.*, 1622].

They saved alive, of the forty-five Turks and Moors, the Captain, one HENRY CHANDLER (born in Southwark), an English Renegado: and five Turks more, who are at this present in Plymouth Gaol, &c.

THREE TO ONE.

Being an English-Spanish combat performed by a Western Gentleman of Tavistock in Devonshire, with an English quarterstaff, against three Spaniards [at once] with rapiers and poniards; at Sherries [*Xeres*] in Spain, the 15th day of November 1625: in the presence of Dukes, Condes, Marquises, and other great Dons of Spain; being the Council of War.

The author of this book, and the actor in this encounter;

R[ICHARD] PEEKE.

Printed at London for I. T. and are to be sold at his shop.

TO THE KING'S MOST EXCELLENT MAJESTY.

GRACIOUS SOVEREIGN,

IF I were again in Spain, I should think no happiness on earth so great as to come into England; and at your royal feet, to lay down the story of my dangers and peregrination: which I tell, as a late sea-wrecked man, tossed and beaten with many misfortunes; yet, setting my weary body at last on a blessed shore: my hands now lay hold on your altar, which is to me a sanctuary. Here I am safe in harbour.

That psalm of kingly DAVID, which I sang in my Spanish captivity,

When as we sate in Babylon &c. [Psal. cxxxvii.]

I have now changed to another tune; saying, with the same prophet,

Great is Thy mercy towards me, O LORD! for Thou hast delivered my soul from the lowest grave! [Psal. xvi. 16.]

And, as your Majesty hath been graciously pleased both to let your poor soldier and subject behold your royal person, and to hear him speak in his rude language: so if your Majesty vouchsafe to cast a princely eye on these his unhandsome papers: new sunbeams shall spread over him, and put a quickening soul into that bosom, which otherwise must want life for want of comfort. Those graces from your excellent clemency already received being such, that I am ashamed and sorry not to have endured and to have done more in foreign countries for the honour of Yours: when from so high a throne, my Sovereign deigns to look down on a creature so unworthy, whose life he prostrates before your Highness.

Ever resting Your Majesty's
Most humble and loyal subject.

RICHARD PEEKE.

Three to One.

BEING

AN ENGLISH-SPANISH COMBAT.

LOVING Countrymen! Not to weary you with long preambles, unnecessary for you to read and troublesome for me to set down; I will come roundly to the matter: entreating you, not to cast a malicious eye upon my actions nor rashly to condemn them, nor to stagger in your opinions of my performance; since I am ready with my life to justify what I set down, the truth of this relation being warranted by noble proofs and testimonies not to be questioned.

I am a Western man; Devonshire my country, and Tavistock my place of habitation.

I know not what the Court of a King means, nor what the fine phrases of silken Courtiers are. A good ship I know, and a poor cabin; and the language of a cannon: and therefore as my breeding has been rough, scorning delicacy; and my present being consisteth altogether upon the soldier (blunt, plain and unpolished) so must my writings be, proceeding from fingers fitter for the pike than the pen. And so, kind Countrymen! I pray you to receive them.

Neither ought you to expect better from me, because I am but the chronicler of my own story.

After I had seen the beginning and end of the Algiers' voyage; I came home somewhat more acquainted with the world, but little amended in estate: my body more wasted and weather-beaten; but my purse, never the fuller, nor my pockets thicker lined.

Then the drum beating up for a new expedition, in which

many noble gentlemen and heroical spirits were to venture their honours, lives and fortunes; cables could not hold me: for away I would, and along I vowed to go; and did so.

The design opening itself at sea for Cadiz, proud I was to be employed there; where so many gallants and English worthies did by their examples encourage the common soldiers to honourable darings.

The ship I went in was called the *Convertine*, one of the Navy Royal. The captain, THOMAS PORTAR.

On the two and twentieth day of October, being a Saturday, 1625; our fleet came into Cadiz, about three o'clock in the afternoon: we, being in all, some 110 sail.

The Saturday night, some sixteen sail of the Hollanders, and about ten White Hall Men (who in England are called Colliers) were commanded to fight against the Castle of Punthal, standing three miles from Cadiz: who did so accordingly; and discharged in that service, at the least, 1,600 shot.

On the Sunday morning following, the Earl of ESSEX going up very early, and an hour at least before us, to the fight; commanded our ship, the *Convertine*, being of his squadron, to follow him: the Castle playing hard and hotly upon his Lordship.

Captain PORTAR and the Master of our ship whose name is Master HILL, having upon sight of so fierce an encounter an equal desire to do something worthy of themselves and their country; came up so close to the Castle as possibly men in such a danger either could or durst adventure, and there fought bravely. The Castle bestowed upon us a hot salutation (and well becoming our approach) with bullets; whose first shot killed three of our men, passing through and through our ship; the second killed four; and the third two more at least; with great spoil and battery [*battering*] to our ship: the last shot flying so close to Captain PORTAR that with the windage of the bullet, his very hands had almost lost the sense of feeling, being struck into a sudden numbness.

Upon this, Captain PORTAR perceiving the danger we and our ship were in, commanded a number of us to get upon the upper deck; and with our small shot [*musketry fire*] to try if we could not force the cannoniers from their ordnance.

We presently advanced ourselves, fell close to our work

and plied them with pellets [*bullets*]. In which hot and dangerous service, one Master WILLIAM JEWELL behaved himself both manly and like a noble soldier, expressing much valour, ability of body, and readiness: with whom and some few more (I, among the rest) stood the brunt which continued about three hours.

Our ship lay all this while with her starboard side to the fort; which beat us continually with at least two hundred muskets, whose bullets flew so thick that our shrouds were torn in pieces, and our tacklings rent to nothing: and when she came off, there were to be seen five hundred bullets, at the least, sticking in her side. I, for my part (without vain-glory be it spoken) discharged at this time, some threescore and ten shot; as they recounted to me, who charged my pieces for me.

In the heat of this fight, Sir WILLIAM SAINT LEGER, whether called up by my Lord of ESSEX or coming of himself I know not, seeing us so hardly beset; and that we had but few shot upon our deck in regard of the enemy's numbers which played upon us: came, with a valiant and noble resolution, out of another ship into ours; bringing some forty soldiers with him. Who there with us, renewed a second fight as hot or hotter than the former: where in this fight, one of our bullets [*cannon-balls*] was shot into the mouth of a Spanish cannon; where it sticketh fast and putteth that roarer to silence.

Upon this bravery, they of the fort began to wax calmer and cooler: and in the end, most part of their gunners being slain, gave over shooting; but yielded not the fort until night.

Whilst this skirmish continued, a company of Spaniards within the castle, by the advantage of a wall whose end jutted out, they still as they discharged retired behind it, saving themselves and extremely annoying us: I removed into the forecastle of our ship, and so plied them with hailshot, that they forsook their stand.

What men on our own part were lost by their small shot I cannot well remember, but sure I am, not very many: yet the Spaniards afterwards before the Governor of Cadiz, confessed they lost about fifty; whose muskets they cast into a well because [*in order that*] our men should not use them, throwing the dead bodies in after.

My hurts and bruises here received, albeit they were neither many nor dangerous, yet were they such that when the fight was done; many gentlemen in our ship, for my encouragement, gave me money.

During this battle the Hollanders and White Hall Men, you must think, were not idle; for their great pieces went off continually from such of their ships as could conveniently discharge their fire, because our ship lay between them and the fort: and they so closely plied their work that at this battery, were discharged from their ordnance, at least four thousand bullets [*cannon balls*].

The castle being thus quieted, though as yet not yielded; the Earl of ESSEX, about twelve at noon, landed his regiment close by the fort, the Spaniards looking over the walls to behold them. Upon the sight of which, many of those within the castle (to the number of six score) ran away; we pursuing them with shouts, halloings and loud noises, and now and then a piece of ordnance overtook some of the Spanish hares, and stayed them from running further.

Part of our men being thus landed, they marched up not above a slight [musket] shot off, and there rested themselves. Then, about six at night, the castle yielded upon composition to depart with their arms and colours flying, and no man to offend them; which was performed accordingly.

The Captain of the fort, his name was Don FRANCISCO BUSTAMENTE; who, presently upon the delivery, was carried aboard the Lord General's ship, where he had a soldierly welcome: and the next day, he and all his company were put over to Puerto Real upon the mainland, because they should not go to Cadiz, which is an island.

On the Monday [October 24th], having begun early in the morning; all our forces, about noon, were landed: and presently marched up to a bridge between Punthal and Cadiz. In going up to which, some of our men were unfortunately and unmanly surprised; and before they knew their own danger, had there their throats cut. Some had their brains beaten out with the stocks of muskets; others, their noses sliced off; whilst some heads were spurned up and down the streets like footballs; and some ears worn in scorn in Spanish hats. For when I was in prison in Cadiz, whither some of these Spanish *picaroes* [robbers] were brought in for flying from the castle, I was an eyewitness of Englishmen's ears being worn in that despiteful manner.

What the forces being on shore did or how far they went up I cannot tell, for I was no land soldier; and therefore all that while kept aboard. Yet about twelve o'clock, when they were marched out of sight, I (knowing that other Englishmen had done the like, the very same day) ventured on shore likewise, to refresh myself: with my sword only by my side; because I thought that the late storms had beaten all the Spaniards in, and therefore I feared no danger.

On therefore I softly walked, viewing the desolation of such a place: for I saw nobody. Yet I had not gone far from the shore, but some Englishmen were come even almost to our ships; and from certain gardens had brought with them many oranges and lemons. The sight of these sharpened my stomach the more to go on; because I had a desire to present some of those fruits to my Captain. Hereupon I demanded of them, "what danger there was in going?" They said, "None, but that all was hushed; and not a Spaniard stirring." We parted; they to the ships, I forward.

And before I had reached a mile, I found (for all their talking of no danger) three Englishmen stark dead; being slain, lying in the way, it being full of sandy pits, so that I could hardly find the passage: and one, some small distance from them, not fully dead. The groans which he uttered led me to him; and finding him lying on his belly; I called to him, and turning him on his back saw his wounds, and said, "Brother! what villain hath done this mischief to thee?" He lamented in sighs and doleful looks; and casting up his eyes to heaven, but could not speak. I then resolved, and was about it, for Christian charity's sake and for country's sake; to have carried him on my back to our ships, far off though they lay; and there, if by any possible means it could have been done, to have recovered him.

But my good intents were prevented. For on a sudden, came rushing in upon me, a Spanish horseman, whose name, as afterwards I was informed, was Don JUAN of Cadiz, a Knight. I seeing him make speedily and fiercely at me with his drawn weapon, suddenly whipped out mine, wrapping my cloak about mine arm. Five or six skirmishes we had; and for a pretty while, fought off and on.

At last, I getting, with much ado, to the top of a sandy hillock, the horseman nimbly followed up after. By good fortune to me (though bad to himself) he had no petronel or pistols about him: and there clapping spurs to his horse's sides; his intent, as it seemed, was with full career to ride over me, and trample me under his horse's feet. But a providence greater than his fury, was my guard.

Time was it for me to look about warily and to lay about lustily; to defend a poor life so hardly distressed. As therefore his horse was violently breaking in upon me, I struck him in the eyes with a flap of my cloak. Upon which, turning sideward, I took my advantage; and, as readily as I could, stepping in, it pleased GOD that I should pluck my enemy down, and leave him at my mercy for life: which notwithstanding I gave him, he falling on his knees, and crying out in French to me. *Pardonnez-moi, je vous prie, je suis un bon Chrêtien.* "Pardon me, Sir! I am a good Christian."

I, seeing him brave, and having a soldier's mind to rifle him, I searched for jewels but found none, only five pieces of eight about him in all, amounting to twenty shillings English. Yet he had gold, but that I could not come by. For I was in haste to have sent his Spanish knighthood home on foot, and to have taught his horse an English pace.

Thus far my voyage for oranges had sped well; but in the end, it proved a sour sauce to me: and it is harder to keep a victory than to obtain one. So here it fell out with mine.

For fourteen Spanish musketeers spying me so busy about one of their countrymen, bent [*aimed*] all the mouths of their pieces to kill me; which they could not well do, without endangering Don JUAN's life. So that I was enforced (and glad I escaped so too) to yield myself their prisoner.

True valour, I see, goes not always in good clothes. For he, whom before I had surprised, seeing me fast in the snare; and as the event proved, disdaining that his countrymen should report him so dishonoured; most basely, when my hands were in a manner bound behind me, drew out his weapon, which the rest had taken from me to give him, and wounded me through the face, from ear to ear: and had there killed me had not the fourteen musketeers rescued me from his rage.

Upon this, I was led in triumph into the town of Cadiz: an owl not more wondered and hooted at; a dog not more cursed.

In my being led thus along the streets, a Fleming spying me, cried out aloud "Whither do you lead this English dog? Kill him! Kill him! he is no Christian." And with that, breaking through the crowd, in upon those who held me; ran me into the body with a halbert, at the reins [*groin*] of my back, at the least four inches.

One Don FERNANDO, an ancient Gentleman, was sent down this summer from the King at Madrid, with soldiers: but before our fleet came, the soldiers were discharged; they of Cadiz never suspecting that we meant to put in there.

Before him, was I brought to be examined: yet few or no questions at all were demanded of me; because he saw that I was all bloody in my clothes, and so wounded in my face and jaws that I could hardly speak. I was therefore committed presently to prison, where I lay eighteen days: the noble gentleman giving express charge that the best surgeons should be sent for: lest being so basely hurt and handled by cowards, I should be demanded at his hands.

I being thus taken on the Monday when I went on shore; the fleet departed the Friday following from Cadiz, at the same time when I was there a prisoner. Yet thus honestly was I used by my worthy friend Captain PORTAR. He, above my deserving, complaining that he feared that he had lost such a man; my Lord General, by the solicitation of Master JOHN GLANVILLE, Secretary to the Fleet, sent three men on shore to enquire in Cadiz for me; and to offer, if I were taken, any reasonable ransom. But the town thinking me to be a better prize than indeed I was; denied me, and would not part from me.

Then came a command to the Terniente or Governor of Cadiz to have me sent to Sherrys, otherwise called Xerez, lying three leagues from Cales.

Wondrously unwilling, could I otherwise have chosen,

was I to go to Xerez, because I feared I should then be put to torture.

Having therefore a young man (an Englishman and a merchant, whose name was GOODROW), my fellow prisoner who lay there for debt, and so I thinking there was no way with me but one (that I must be sent packing to my long home); thus I spake unto him, "Countryman! what my name is, our partnership in misery hath made you know; and with it, know that I am a Devonshire man born, and Tavistock the place of my once abiding. I beseech you! if GOD ever send you liberty, and that you sail into England; take that country [*Tavistock*] in your way. Commend me to my wife and children, made wretched by me; an unfortunate husband and father. Tell them and my friends (I entreat you, for GOD's cause) that if I be, as I suspect I shall be, put to death in Sherris [*Xerez*], I will die a Christian soldier: no way, I hope, dishonouring my King, country, or the justice of my cause, or my religion."

Anon after, away was I conveyed with a strong guard by the Governor of Cadiz and brought to Xerez on a Thursday about twelve at night.

On the Sunday following, two friars were sent to me; both of them being Irishmen, and speaking very good English. One of them was called Padre JUAN (Father JOHN). After a sad and grave salutation, "Brother," quoth he, "I come in love to you and charity to your soul to confess you; and if to us, as your spiritual ghostly fathers, you will lay open your sins, we will forgive them and make your way to heaven: for to-morrow you must die."

I desired them that they would give me a little respite that I might retire into a private chamber; and instantly I would repair to them, and give them satisfaction. Leave I had; away I went; and immediately returned. They asked me "if I had yet resolved, and whether I would come to confession?" I told them, that "I had been at confession already." One of them answered "With whom?" I answered, "With GOD the Father." "And with nobody else," said the other. "Yes," quoth I, "and with JESUS CHRIST my Redeemer; who hath both power and will to forgive all men their sins, that truly repent. Before these Two have I fallen on my knees, and confessed my grievous offences; and trust They will give me a free absolution and pardon."

"What think you of the Pope?" said Father JOHN. I answered "I knew him not." They, hereupon, shaking their heads; told me "they were sorry for me:" and so departed.

Whilst thus I lay at Xerez, the Captain of the fort [at Punthal], Don FRANCISCO BUSTAMENTE, was brought in prisoner for his life, because he delivered up the castle; but whether he died for it or not, I cannot tell.

My day of trial being come; I was brought from prison into the town of Xerez, by two drums [*drummers*] and a hundred shot [*musketeers*], before three Dukes, four Condes or Earls, four Marquises; besides other great persons. The town having in it, at least, five thousand soldiers.

Duke of MEDINA, Duke of MACADA, Duke FERDINANDO GIRON, Marquis DE ALQUENEZES &c.

At my first appearing before the Lords; my sword lying before them on a table, the Duke of MEDINA asked me, "if I knew that weapon." It was reached to me. I took it and embraced it with mine arms; and, with tears in mine eyes, kissed the pummel of it. He then demanded, "how many men I had killed with that weapon?" I told him, "If I had killed one, I had not been there now before that princely assembly: for when I had him at my foot, begging for mercy, I gave him life: yet he, then very poorly, did me a mischief." Then they asked Don JOHN (my prisoner) "what wounds I gave him?" He said "None." Upon this he was rebuked and told "That if upon our first encounter, he had run me through; it had been a fair and noble triumph: but so to wound me, being in the hands of others, they held it base."

Then said the Duke of MEDINA to me, "Come on! Englishman! what ship came you in?" I told him "The *Convertine*." "Who was your Captain?" "Captain PORTAR." "What ordnance carried your ship?" I said "Forty pieces." But the Lords looking all this while on a paper, which they held in their hands; the Duke of MEDINA said, "In their note, there were but thirty-eight."

In that paper—as after I was informed by my two Irish interpreters—there was set down the number of our ships; their burden, men, munition, victuals, captains, &c., as perfect as we ourselves had them in England.

"Of what strength," quoth another Duke," is the fort at Plymouth?" I answered, "Very strong." What ordnance in it? "Fifty," said I. "That is not so," said he, "there are but seventeen." "How many soldiers are in the fort?" I answered, "Two hundred." "That is not so," quoth a Conde, "there are but twenty."

The Marquis ALQUENEZES asked me "Of what strength the little island was before Plymouth?" I told him, "I knew not." "Then," quoth he, "we do."

"Is Plymouth a walled town?" "Yes, my Lords." "And a good wall?" "Yes," said I, "a very good wall." "True," says a Duke, "to leap over with a staff!" "And hath the town," said the Duke of MEDINA, "strong gates?" "Yes." "But," quoth he, "there was neither wood nor iron to those gates; but two days before your fleet came away."

Now before I go any further, let me not forget to tell you, that my two Irish confessors had been here in England the last summer; and when our fleet came from England, they came for Spain: having seen our King at Plymouth when the soldiers there showed their arms, and did then diligently observe what the King did, and how he carried himself.

"How did it chance," said the Duke GIRON, that "you did not in all this bravery of the fleet, take Cadiz as you took Punthal?" I replied, "That the Lord General might easily have taken Cadiz, for he had near a thousand scaling ladders to set up, and a thousand men to lose; but he was loth to rob an almshouse, having a better market to go to." "Cadiz," I told them, "was held poor, unmanned and unmunitioned." "What better market?" said MEDINA. I told him, "Genoa or Lisbon." And as I heard there was instantly, upon this, an army of six thousand soldiers sent to Lisbon.

"Then," quoth one of the Earls, "when thou meetest me in Plymouth, wilt thou bid me welcome?" I modestly told him, "I could wish they would not too hastily come to Plymouth; for they should find it another manner of place, than as now they slighted it."

Many other questions were put to me by these great Dons; which so well as GOD did enable me I answered. They speaking in Spanish, and their words interpreted to me by those two Irishmen before spoken of; who also related my several answers to the Lords.

And by the common people, who encompassed me round, many jeerings, mockeries, scorns and bitter jests were to my face thrown upon our nation: which I durst not so much as bite my lip against, but with an enforced patient ear stood still, and let them run on in their revilings.

At the length, amongst many other reproaches and spiteful names; one of the Spaniards called Englishmen, *Gallinas* (hens). At which the great Lords fell a laughing. Hereupon one of the Dukes, pointing to the Spanish soldiers; bade me note how their King kept them—and indeed they were all wondrously brave in apparel; hats, bands, cuffs, garters, &c.: and some of them in chains of gold—and asked further, "If I thought these would prove such hens as our English; when next year they should come into England?" I said, "No." But being somewhat emboldened by his merry countenance, I told him as merrily, "I thought they would be within one degree of hens." "What meanest thou by that?" said a Conde. I replied, "They would prove pullets or chickens." "Darest thou then," quoth the Duke of Medina, with a brow half angry, "fight with one of these Spanish pullets?"

"O my Lord!" said I, "I am a prisoner and my life at stake; and therefore dare not to be so bold as to adventure upon any such action. There were here of us English, some fourteen thousand; in which number, there were above twelve thousand better and stouter men than ever I shall be: yet with the license of this princely assembly, I dare hazard the breaking of a rapier." And withal told him, "He is unworthy of the name of an Englishman, that should refuse to fight with one man of any nation whatsoever." Hereupon my shackles were knocked off; and my iron ring and chain taken from my neck.

Room was made for the combatants; rapier and dagger were the weapons. A Spanish champion presented himself, named Signior TIAGO: when, after we had played some reasonable good time, I disarmed him, as thus. I caught his rapier betwixt the bars of my poniard and there held it, till I closed with him; and tripping up his heels, I took his weapons out of his hands and delivered them to the Dukes.

I could wish that all you, my dear Countrymen! who read this relation had either been there, without danger, to have beheld us: or that he with whom I fought were here in prison, to justify the issue of that combat.

I was then demanded, "If I durst fight against another?"

I told them, "My heart was good to adventure; but humbly requested them to give me pardon, if I refused."

For to myself I too well knew that the Spaniard is haughty, impatient of the least affront; and when he receives but a touch of any dishonour, disgrace or blemish (especially in his own country, and from an Englishman) his revenge is implacable, mortal and bloody.

Yet being by the nobleman pressed again and again, to try my fortune with another; I (seeing my life in the lion's paw, to struggle with whom for safety there was no way but one, and being afraid to displease them) said "that if their Graces and Greatnesses would give me leave to play at mine own country weapon called the quarterstaff; I was then ready there, an opposite against any comer, whom they would call forth: and would willingly lay down my life before those Princes to do them service; provided my life might by no foul means, be taken from me."

Hereupon, the head of an halbert, which went with a screw, was taken off, and the steel [*handle*] delivered to me; the other butt end of the staff having a short iron pike in it. This was my armour: and in my place I stood, expecting an opponent.

At the last, a handsome and well-spirited Spaniard steps forth, with his rapier and poniard. They asked me "What I said to him?" I told them, "I had a sure friend in my hand that never failed me, and therefore made little account of that one to play with: and should show them no sport."

Then a second, armed as before, presents himself. I demanded, "If there would come no more?" The Dukes asked, "How many I desired?" I told them, "Any number under six." Which resolution of mine, they smiling at in a kind of scorn; held it not manly, it seemed, not fit for their own honours, and the glory of their nation, to worry one man with a multitude: and therefore appointed three only, so weaponed, to enter into the lists.

Now, Gentlemen! if here you condemn me for plucking, with mine own hands, such an assured danger upon mine own head; accept of these reasons for excuse.

To die, I thought it most certain; but to die basely, I would not. For three to kill one had been to me no dishonour; to them, weapons considered, no glory. An honourable subjection, I esteemed better than an ignoble conquest. Upon these thoughts I fell to it.

The rapier men traversed their ground; I, mine. Dangerous thrusts were put in, and with dangerous hazard avoided. Shouts echoed to heaven to encourage the Spaniards: not a shout nor hand to hearten the poor Englishman. Only heaven I had in mine eye, the honour of my country in my heart, my fame at the stake, my life on a narrow bridge, and death both before me and behind me.

It was not now a time to dally. They still made full at me; and I had been a coward to myself, and a villain to my nation, if I had not called up all that weak manhood which was mine to guard my own life, and overthrow my enemies.

Plucking up therefore a good heart, seeing myself faint and wearied; I vowed to my soul to do something, ere she departed from me: and so setting all upon one cast, it was my good fortune (it was my GOD that did it for me), with the butt end, where the iron pike was, to kill one of the three; and within a few bouts after, to disarm the other two; causing the one of them to fly into the army of soldiers then present, and the other for refuge fled behind the bench.

I hope, if the braving Spaniards set upon England as they threaten; we shall every One of us, give repulse to more than Three. Of which good issue for the public, I take this my private success to be a pledge.

Now was I in greater danger, being, as I thought, in peace; than before when I was in battle. For a general murmur filled the air, with threatenings at me: the soldiers especially bit their thumbs, and was it possible for me to escape?

Which the noble Duke of MEDINA SIDONIA seeing, called me to him; and instantly caused proclamation to be made that none, on pain of death, should meddle with me: and by his honourable protection I got off, not only with safety but with money. For by the Dukes and Condes were given me in gold, to the value of four pounds, ten shillings sterling: and by the Marquis ALQUENEZES himself, as much; he, embracing me in his arms, and bestowing upon me that long Spanish russet cloak I now wear; which he took from one of his men's backs, and withal, furnished me with a clean band and cuffs. It being one of the greatest favours a Spanish

Lord can do to a mean man to reward him with some garment, as recompense of merit.

After our fight in Xerez, I was kept in the Marquis ALQUENEZES' house; who, one day, out of his noble affability, was pleasant in speech with me: and, by my interpreter, desired I would sing. I, willing to obey him (whose goodness I had tasted), did so: and sang this psalm,

When as we sate in Babylon, &c.

The meaning of which being told; he said to me "Englishman comfort thyself! for thou art in no captivity."

After this, I was sent to the King of Spain, lying at Madrid. My conduct [*guard*] being four gentlemen of the Marquis ALQUENEZES': he allowing unto me in the journey twenty shillings a day when we travelled, and ten shillings a day when we lay still.

At my being in Madrid, before I saw the King, my entertainment by the Marquis ALQUENEZES' appointment, was at his own house; where I was lodged in the most sumptuous bed that ever I beheld: and had from his noble Lady a welcome far above my poor deserving, but worthy the greatness of so excellent a woman. She bestowed upon me whilst I lay in her house a very fair Spanish shirt, richly laced: and at my parting from Madrid, a chain of gold and two jewels for my wife, and other pretty things for my children.

And now that her noble courtesies, with my own thankfulness, lead me to speak of this honourable Spanish Lady; I might very justly be condemned of ingratitude, if I should not remember with like acknowledgement, another rare pattern of feminine goodness to me a distressed miserable stranger: and that was the Lady of Don JUAN of Cadiz. She, out of a respect she bare me for saving her husband's life, came along with him to Xerez; he being there to give evidence against me: and, as before when I lay prisoner in Cadiz, so in Xerez, she often relieved me with money and other means. My duty and thanks ever wait upon them both!

Upon Christmas Day, I was presented to the King, the Queen, and Don CARLOS the Infante.

Being brought before him: I fell, as it was fit, on my knees. Many questions were demanded of me; which, so well as my plain wit directed me, I resolved.

In the end, His Majesty offered me a yearly pension (to a good value) if I would serve him either at land or at sea. For which his royal favours, I (confessing myself infinitely bound and my life indebted to his mercy) most humbly intreated, that with his Princely leave, I might be suffered to return unto mine own country: being a subject only to the King of England, my Sovereign.

And besides that bond of allegiance, there was another obligation due from me to a wife and children: and therefore I most submissively begged that His Majesty would be so Princely minded as to pity my estate, and let me go. To which he, at last, granted; bestowing upon me one hundred pistolets [=£25=£150 *in present value*] to bear my charges.

Having thus left Spain, I took my way through some part of France. Where by occasion, happening into company of seven Spaniards; their tongues were too lavish in speeches against our nation. Upon which, some high words flying up and down the room; I leaped from the table, and drew. One of the Spaniards did the like, none of the rest being weaponed; which was more than I knew. Upon the noise of this bustling, two Englishmen more came in: who, understanding the abuses offered to our country; the Spaniards, in a short time, recanted on their knees, their rashness.

And so hoisting sail for England, I landed on the three and twentieth day of April 1626, at Foy in Cornwall.

And thus endeth my Spanish pilgrimage. With thanks to my good GOD, that in this extraordinary manner preserved me, amidst these desperate dangers.

Therefore most gracious GOD! Defender of men abroad! and Protector of them at home! how am I bounden to thy Divine Majesty, for thy manifold mercies?

On my knees I thank Thee! with my tongue will I praise Thee! with my hands fight Thy quarrel! and all the days of my life serve Thee!

Out of the Red Sea I have escaped; from the lion's den been delivered, aye rescued from death and snatched out of the jaws of destruction, only by Thee! O my GOD! Glory be to Thy Name for ever and ever! Amen.

Certain Verses written by a friend in commendation of the Author, RICHARD PEEKE.

SELDOM DO clouds so dim the day,
But SOL will once his beams display;
Though NEPTUNE drives the surging seas,
Sometimes he gives them quiet ease:
  And so few projects speed so ill,
  But somewhat chanceth at our will.

I will not instance in the great,
Placed in Honour's higher seat;
Though virtue in a noble line
Commends it, and the more doth shine.
  Yet this is proved by sword and pen,
  Desert oft dwells in private men.

My proof is not far hence to seek;
There is at hand brave RICHARD PEEKE,
Whose worth his foes cannot revoke:
Born in the town of Tavistock
  In Devon; where MINERVA sits
  Shaping stout hearts, and pregnant wits.

This well-resolved and hardy spark
Aiming at fame, as at a mark;
Was not compelled against his will,
In MARS his field to try his skill:
  As voluntary he did go
  To serve his King against his foe.

If he had pleased, he might have spent
His days at home in safe content;
But nursing valour in his breast
He would adventure with the best:
  Willing to shed his dearest blood,
  To do his Prince and Country good.

Thus bent, he, adding wings to feet,
Departed with the English fleet.
There was no rub, no stay at all,
The ships sailed with a pleasant gale:
  In setting forth they by their hap,
  Seemed lulled in AMPHITRITE's lap.

At length they did arrive at Cales;
Where restless PEEKE against the walls
Made fourscore shot towards the shore,
Making the welkin wide to roar:
  He kept his standing in this strife,
  Setting a straw by loss of life.

Into a vineyard afterward
He marched, and stood upon his guard;
There he an horseman did dismount,
By outward port of good account:
  But did on him compassion take,
  And spared his life, for pity's sake.

The next assault uneven he felt,
For with twelve Spaniards he dealt
At once, and held them lusty play;
Until through odds, theirs was the day:
  From ear to ear, they pierced his head,
  And to the town him captive led.

In prison, they him shut by night,
Laden with chains of grievous weight;
All comfortless, in dungeon deep,
Where stench annoys, and vermin creep:
    He grovelled in this loathsome cell,
    Where ghastly frights and horrors dwell.

Yet nothing could his courage quail,
Hunger, nor thirst, nor wound, nor gaol;
For being brought before a Don,
And asked "Why England did set on
    A scraping, no a pecking hen?
    He answered "Stain not Englishmen!

"That England is a nation stout,
And till the last will fight it out;
Myself could prove by chivalry,
If for a captive this were free."
    "Why," quoth the Duke, "durst thou to fight
    With any of my men in sight?"

"Of thousands whom in war you use;
Not one," quoth PEEKE, "do I refuse."
A chosen champion then there came;
Whose heels he tripped, as at a game:
    And from his hand his rapier took,
    Presenting it unto the Duke.

Then Three at once did him oppose;
They rapiers, he a long staff chose:
The use whereof so well he knows,
He conquered them with nimble blows:
    One that beside him played his round
    He threw as dead unto the ground.

The noble Duke who this did see,
Commended PEEKE, and set him free.
He gave him gifts, and did command
That none should wrong him in their land.
So well he did him entertain,
And sent him to the Court of Spain.

There he was fed with no worse meat
Than which the King himself did eat;
His lodging rich, for he did lie
In furniture of tapestry.
The King what of him he had heard,
Did with his treasure well reward.

Our then Ambassador was there,
PEEKE's pike and praise he doth declare:
At Spanish Court while he attends,
He thrives for virtue's sake: as friends,
Foes sent him in triumphant sort,
Home from a foe and foreign port.

If thus his very foes him loved,
And deeds against themselves approved;
How should his friends his love embrace
And yield him countenance and grace?
The praise and worth how can we cloke
Of manly PEEKE of Tavistock.

FINIS.

J. D.

The noble Duke who this did see,
Commended Lenox, and set him free.
He gave him gifts, and did command
That none should wrong him in their land.
[illegible]
And sent him to the [illegible]

[illegible]
Then [illegible]
His lodging [illegible]
In [illegible]
The [illegible] he had heard
Did [illegible] well reward.

[illegible]
[illegible] death decreed
Sent [illegible] friends;
[illegible],
[illegible] sent him in [illegible] sort,
[illegible] from a [illegible] foreign port.

[illegible]
[illegible] approved
[illegible]
[illegible]
[illegible]
Of [illegible]

FINIS.

A
TRUE RELATION
OF A BRAVE ENGLISH STRATAGEM PRACTISED

lately upon a sea town in Galicia, one of the kingdoms in Spain ; and most valiantly and successfully performed by one English ship alone of thirty tons, with no more than 35 men in her.

AS ALSO

With two other remarkable Accidents between the English and Spaniards, to the glory of our Nation.

Printed for *Mercurius Britanicus*.
1626.

A True Relation of a Brave English

Stratagem practised lately upon a sea town in Galicia, one of the kingdoms in Spain; and most valiantly and successfully performed by one English ship alone of thirty tons, with no more than 35 men in her.

With two other remarkable Accidents between the English and Spaniards, to the glory of our Nation.

YOU SHALL here, loving Countrymen! receive a plain, full and perfect relation of a stratagem bravely attempted, resolutely seconded with bold English spirits, and by them as fortunately executed upon our enemies, the Spaniards: who, albeit upon what kingdom soever they once set but footing, they write *Plus ultra*; devouring it up in conceit, and feeding their greedy ambition that it is all their own. Yet this golden faggot of dominion may have many sticks plucked out of it, if cunning fingers go about to undo the band: as by this Galician enterprise may appear.

A pregnant testimony hereby being given, that if the great warriors of the sea would join together, and thunder all along the Spanish coasts; the Castilian kingdoms might easily be shaken: when so poor a handful of our English being spread before one of their sea towns, was the forerunner of so terrible a storm to all the inhabitants.

Such a brave mustering of all the gods of the Ocean into one conjoined army, would quickly make the great Dons to alter their proud and insolent poesy of *Non sufficit orbis*, "the world is too little" to fill their belly (when the East Indies lies upon one of their trenchers, and the West Indies upon another), yea, and compel them to dwell quietly at home in their own hot barren country of Spain; contented with a dinner of a few olives, a handful of raisins, and such poor trash: not intruding into other King's territories (especially these fruitful ones of ours) to eat up our fat beefs [*oxen*], veals [*calves*], muttons [*sheep*] and capons; victuals too good for such insatiable feeders, when whole countries—might they swallow down their fill—are nothing to be devoured at one meal.

Come forth, therefore, you renowned English! and by the example of a few countrymen of yours, plough up the furrows of your enemy's seas! and come home ladened, as we have done, with spoils, honours, victory and richly purchased prizes.

Fear not to fight! albeit five Kings bring their men of war into the field: for you have a JOSHUA [? *CHARLES I.*] to stand up in your defence, and to bid them to battle.

And when you go to draw your swords, or to discharge your cannon against the iron ribs of the Armadas of this potent and bloody Enemy: pray unto the LORD toward the way of the city which he hath chosen! and toward the house which in that place is built for His name! and He in heaven will hear your prayers and supplications, and judge your cause; and deliver these wild boars and bulls of Tarifa into your toils.

To arm you for action for your country, for your fames, for wealth, and the credit of your nation: whensoever it pleaseth GOD that you put to sea, may you be prosperous! and speed no worse than these have done! whose story I am now going to set down.

One Captain QUAILE, born in Portsmouth, desiring to attempt something for the honour of England and the benefit of himself and followers: by the license and authority of those in England, who might give him leave; got a bark of Plymouth, which by him and his friends, was sufficiently furnished with men, victuals and munition. The bark being but of thirty tons, and the men in her to the number of 34 or 35.

This captain and the resolute gang with him, went merrily to sea, and sailed to and fro; without fastening on any purchase answerable to their expectation or defraying such a charge as they and their ship had been at. Their fortunes in England were not great, and if they should return home without some exploits, their estates would be less. Hereupon, the Captain discovering his mind to his Lieutenant, whose name was FROST; they two, after consultation between themselves, persuaded the rest of their company to try their uttermost adventures rather than like cowards to go back: who, hearing the Captain's resolution, were on fire to follow him through all dangers, happen whatsoever could. And so they clapped hands upon this desperate bargain, yet protesting and seriously vowing not to turn pirates; thereby to make booty either of their own countrymen or friends to the State.

Good hope thus, and a prosperous wind filling their sails; they hovered along the coast of Galicia, which lies upon the head of Portugal to the northward. In passing by which, the ship being clear [? of enemies] and the shores quiet; the Captain commanded them to cast anchor before a certain town called Cris, which had a platform or fort with ordnance to defend it. And this was done at noon day.

Then he, being perfect in the French tongue, wrote a letter in that language to the Governor or Captain of the fort, importing thus much. "That they were poor distressed Frenchmen, driven thither by some Turkish Men of War; and flying to them (as to their friends) for succour: pretending their greatest want to be wood for firing, and fresh water to relieve them. Of both which necessaries, they knew that place to be abundantly stored; and for which they would give any reasonable content." Thus riding at anchor in sight of the town, and their cock-boat being lost in a storm; they had no other device to convey the letter to the Spanish Commander, than by sending a sailor upon an empty hogshead, with an oar in his hand to guide him to land; he being very skilful both in French, and in swimming.

The Spaniards seeing a man making to them in that strange manner, thought verily they were men distressed indeed: and thereupon manning out a skiff to meet and receive him, they took him in.

The letter spake his business to the Spanish Captain, who talking further in French to the mariner, and being thereupon certainly assured of their distress; determined to sell to them such commodities as they wanted at as dear a rate as he could: and for that purpose commanded another skiff to be manned out with certain Spaniards; who, suspecting nothing, hastened to go aboard the Pinnace, with their Captain in company.

In the meantime, Captain QUAILE had shut his portholes close and hid his ordnance; discovering not above five men above the hatches, who seemed to carry sickly faces and weak bodies, and were all unarmed. The Spaniards were joyfully embraced and welcomed. Such poor victuals as they had aboard, were with arguments of much love set before them. Holland cheeses were cut in the middle; and such wine and beer offered them, as they were furnished with.

This entertainment carrying away all suspicion with it: Captain QUAILE invited the Spanish Captain and the rest of his company to his cabin. In passing into which, the Spanish commander espied a piece of ordnance: at which, starting back, and, not half well pleased, demanding "why it lay there;" QUAILE excused it and said "that it was all the protection they carried about them to defend them from dangers:" and so, with much cunning as he could, he drew by compliment and disguised fair language all the Spaniards into his cabin. Whither with good words he welcomed them, and saluted them with cans of wine: which, while they were tossing—albeit the Spaniard is the most temperate drinker in the world—Captain QUAILE, with his foot giving a knock for more; that sign of the foot was a watchword to fetch up all mariners. Who, crying "St. George!" appeared in their full number, every man armed with a charged pistol and a short sword drawn in his hand.

The Spaniards, astonished at this unexpected surprisal, seeing no remedy, yielded themselves; and so were all taken prisoners: an assurance being given them by the English Captain—upon the oath of a soldier (his honour) and the faith of an Englishman (which to an enemy he scorns to break)—that not a Spaniard there should be in any danger for his life, so they would be quiet and silent; otherwise death!

Certain fishermen were all this while round about them, at their labour; yet perceived nothing.

With all speed therefore that possibly could be used, Captain QUAILE and his Lieutenant, making their prisoners sure; manned out the two Spanish skiffs with his English musketeers: every one of them lying down in the skiffs flat on his belly; none that might be mistrusted being seen, but such only as rowed the two skiffs.

Then, with great circumspection (attended upon by a resolution to meet death face to face) they landed themselves; and, active as fire, suddenly, with little or no danger at all, surprised the platform, and, with the same dexterity, were masters of the fort. For the act being quick as lightning, so amazed the Spaniards: that it took from them all apprehension not only of fear, but of prevention or acknowledgment of that danger which trod upon their heels. So that Captain QUAILE, what with his own success and the others' astonishment, in a short time, and without resistance, seized upon the ordnance of the platform, which turning and discharging upon the town, and his own bark likewise giving fire to her pieces on the other side: away ran the people, to the number of two hundred persons, besides women and children. At the noise of these sudden terrors, the fishermen likewise, cutting their nets, hastened as fast as they could to the shore; having more care to save themselves than to catch any fish. And so the people flying up into the country, the town was left naked, and let to new landlords.

Who, meeting no Spaniards willing to be their tenants; and the Englishmen themselves being loth to tarry among such bad neighbours: they rifled both the fort and the town, and had the pillaging of both for eight hours together. In which time, they hurried to their ship anything that was of value: and besides the abundance of much riches; they brought away the ordnance of the fort, the bell out of the church, and the chalice. And so, without wrong to their persons, putting their Spanish prisoners into their own skiffs; to shore they sent them: with a warlike triumphing farewell from their own pieces; and are now with much honour arrived in England.

If this example, noble Countrymen! cannot give you sufficient encouragement: do but look back into the former ages, and take a brief survey what honourable attempts, exploits, undertakings and stratagems have in foreign countries been enterprized and achieved by the English. When brave JOHN of GAUNT, Duke of LANCASTER, &c., being but a subject, without borrowing or charging of the King's treasures; out of his own purse and coffers, and assisted by his friends and such voluntary gentlemen as craved dependence upon his fortunes, without press or compelling any man, beating up his drums, levied so sufficient an army that with it he conquered all Spain, removed the usurper and reinstated the expulsed Don PEDRO: and after by interchangeable marriages, made himself and successive issue, competitors and allies to the Crown and Dignity Imperial.

Of what honours our nation have purchased from the French, even their own Chronicles without the flattery of ours, give ample and sufficient testimony. Witness the battles of Poitiers and Cressy, fought by "the Invincible Soldier" (for the great terror, which he brought into France) called the Black Prince; who, with inimitable valour, courage undaunted, and expedition almost beyond human apprehension, against infinite odds, and nothing in his own party to encourage him, save want of numbers and disadvantage of place: yet notwithstanding, not only disrouted their mighty armies, killing many and defeating all, but brought the King, Dauphin, and all the Prince Peers of the land, prisoners, and presented them at the feet of his father.

The Scotch King, taking the advantage of the King of England then being in France, who lay at Calais; made inroads and excursions into this land: whom the Queen PHILIPPA—then destitute of all her nobility and gentry, as being then with the King her husband in France—met with an army of priests, husbandmen, artificers and some few gentlemen; gave him battle, vanquished his army, took him prisoner, and added one thing more to the eternising of her husband's and son's famous and renowned valours.

I omit the great battle fought by HENRY V. at Agincourt, with many others; and lest I be taxed of [*with*] too great a degression, return to the former discourse; by me promised, and I make no question by you expected.

In Lisbon, not long since, a young merchant, who for divers respects desires to have his name concealed, being in the company of certain Dons, and falling into discourse about the valour of several nations, they so far exceeded in the hyperboles of their own praise, that they blushed not to affirm that one Spaniard was able to beat two Englishmen out of the field, which they in their braggadesme [*braggadacio*] enforced so far; that though the rest were silent, this young gentleman, not able to conceal a true English spirit, after some retort of language, there made a protestation, "That if it pleased the Governor to give him leave, he himself would undertake (making choice of his weapon) to fight singly against three of the proudest champions they could produce against him." To cut off circumstance; the challenge was accepted. The Governor prepared the combatants, with the time and place appointed. A great confluence of people assembled: where one young merchant, armed only with his sword and a Spanish pike, in the lists appeared, who by the three adversaries was boldly and resolutely charged. But GOD and his good cause defended him so well, that the combat continued not long till one of them he had laid dead at his foot; and having received from them some few scratches with the loss of a small quantity of blood and without danger, he so actively and resolutely behaved himself against the survivors that they, after divers wounds from him received, began to quail in their former courage and fight more faintly and further off: which the Governor perceiving, commanded the combat to cease, and withal to guard the Englishman from the fury of the displeased multitude who could have found in their hearts to have plucked him in pieces. There calling him up to him, conveyed him safe to his house and, after much commendation of his valour, very nobly secured him to his ship; wishing him for his own safety to be seen no more ashore: whose counsel he followed; and since with much envy from them and great honour to us, he is arrived in his own country.

I desire to be tedious in nothing, but will acquaint you with another exploit; no less remarkable than the former, performed in the beginning of this last month,* April: and thus it was.

A worthy gentleman, one Captain WARNER, with two small Pinnaces, was bound towards some part of the West Indies: neither of them being of above thirty tons burthen. He, being

* It is clear from this, that this tract was written in May, 1626. The foregoing incident is a confused and inaccurate account of R. PEEKE's brave act, which will be found, narrated by himself, on pages 621–643.

thus at sea, was chased by a tall Man of War, a Dunkirker [*coming from Dunkirk*]; who came towards them, as if she meant to overrun them at once and bury their ruins [*fragments*] in the bottom of the ocean. Which WARNER perceiving, pretended to make away with one of his Pinnaces; as if he purposed to save a stake, and leave the other to the enemy's fury and spoils. The Dunkirker, not able to fasten on both at once, took the advantage of the first; intending when he had seized her to make like prize of the other: hails her, boards her; his sailors and soldiers, being all greedy of booty, neglect their own ship; only busying themselves in the rifling of the other, where I leave them all busy at work.

Which WARNER perceiving, and not willing to slack so good an opportunity, takes advantage of the wind, suddenly casteth about [*tacks*] and seizeth upon the Dunkirk's ship, whose men were, most of them, aboard the other pinnace; boards her, takes her, mans her: and now being armed with her strength; commands both his other Pinnace and all the enemies aboard her. By which stratagem, he not only ransomed his own, but subdued his enemies; made prize both of ship and goods, and took all the men prisoners. A noble encouragement to all the brave captains and commanders of our nation to try to imitate him in his resolution and valour.

And thus, worthy Countrymen! you see that notwithstanding the proud braves [*bravados*] of the Public Enemy, their scandals and calumnies with all the aspersions of disgrace that their malice can devise, to cast upon our Kingdom and country; maugre their invasions threatened on land or their naval triumphs boasted at sea: how the great Creator of all things (in whose sight pride, vainglory and ambition are abominable) can when He pleases, by the hand of the young man DAVID stoop the stiff neck of the strongest GOLIATH. And, noble countrymen! may these few encouragements put into you the ancient courage of your ancestors; whose memories through all seas, nations and languages, have been and ever shall be sacred to all posterities. Now is the time of acting, and to show yourselves as you have been ever held and esteemed; brave in attempting, and bold in performing. And so, without question, your expeditions shall be successful, as the fame of your virtues immortal.

FINIS.

The Sequestration of Archbishop ABBOT from all his Ecclesiastical Offices, in 1627.

JOHN RUSHWORTH, Esq., of Lincoln's Inn.

[*Historical Collections*, i. 435. Ed. 1659.]

ARCHBISHOP ABBOT, having been long slighted at Court, now fell under the King's high displeasure; for refusing to license Doctor SIBTHORP's sermon, entituled *Apostolical Obedience*, as he was commanded; and, not long after, he was sequestered from his Office, and a Commission was granted to the Bishops of LONDON, DURHAM, ROCHESTER, OXFORD, and Doctor,

LAUD, Bishop of BATH AND WELLS, to exercise archiepiscopal jurisdiction.

The Commission is followeth—

CHARLES, by the grace of GOD, King of England, Scotland, France, and Ireland; Defender of the Faith, &c. To the Right Reverend Father in GOD, GEORGE [MONTAIGNE], Bishop of LONDON; and to the Right Reverend Father in GOD, our trusty and well beloved Councillor, RICHARD [NEYLE], Lord Bishop of DURHAM; and to the Right Reverend Father in GOD, JOHN [BUCKERIDGE], Lord Bishop of ROCHESTER; and to the Right Reverend Father in GOD, JOHN [HOWSON], Lord Bishop of OXFORD; and to the Right Reverend Father in GOD, our Right Trusty and Well Beloved Councillor, WILLIAM [LAUD], Lord Bishop of BATH AND WELLS.

WHEREAS GEORGE, now Archbishop of CANTERBURY, in the right of the Archbishopric, hath several and distinct Archiepiscopal, Episcopal, and other Spiritual and Ecclesiastical Powers and Jurisdictions, to be exercised in the Government and Discipline of the Church within the Province of Canterbury, and in the Administration of Justice in Causes Ecclesiastical within that Province, which are partly executed by himself in his own person, and partly and more generally by several persons nominated and authorised by him, being learned in the Ecclesiastical Laws of this Realm, in those several places whereunto they are deputed and appointed by the said Archbishop: which several places, as We are informed, they severally hold by several Grants for their several lives, as namely,

Sir HENRY MARTIN Knight hath and holdeth by the grants of the said Archbishop, the Offices and Places of the Dean of the Arches, and Judge or Master of the Prerogative Court, for the natural life of the said Sir HENRY MARTIN.

Sir CHARLES CÆSAR Knight hath and holdeth by grants of the said Archbishop, the Places or Offices of the Judge of the Audience, and Master of the Faculties, for the term of the natural life of the said Sir CHARLES CÆSAR.

Sir THOMAS RIDLEY Knight hath and holdeth by the grant of the said Archbishop, the Place or Office of Vicar General to the said Archbishop.

And NATHANIEL BRENT, Doctor of the Laws, hath and

holdeth by grant of the said Archbishop, the Office or Place of Commissary to the said Archbishop, as of his proper and peculiar diocese of Canterbury.

And likewise the several Registrars of the Arches, Prerogative, Audience, Faculties, and of the Vicar General and Commissary of Canterbury, hold their places by grants by the said Archbishop respectively.

Whereas the said Archbishop, in some or all of these several Places and Jurisdictions, doth and may sometimes assume unto his personal and proper Judicature, Order, or Direction, some particular Causes, Actions, or Cases, at his pleasure. And forasmuch as the said Archbishop cannot, at this present, in his own person, attend these services which are otherwise proper for his Cognisance and Jurisdiction; and which as Archbishop of CANTERBURY, *he might and ought in his own person to have performed and executed in Causes and Matters Ecclesiastical, in the proper function of Archbishop of the Province.*

WE, therefore, of Our regal power, and of Our princely care and providence, that nothing shall be defective in the Order Discipline, Government, or Right of the Church, have thought fit by the service of some other learned and reverend Bishops, to be named by Us, to supply those which the said Archbishop ought or might, in the cases aforesaid, to have done; but, for this present, cannot perform the same.

Know ye, therefore, That We, reposing special trust and confidence in your approved wisdoms, learning, and integrity, have nominated, authorised, and appointed, and do, by these presents, nominate, authorise, and appoint You, the said GEORGE, Lord Bishop of LONDON; RICHARD, Lord Bishop of DURHAM; JOHN, Lord Bishop of ROCHESTER; JOHN, Lord Bishop of OXFORD; and WILLIAM, Lord Bishop of BATH AND WELLS, or any four, three, or two of you, to do, execute, and perform all and every those acts, matters, and things any way touching or concerning the Power, Jurisdiction, or Authority of the Archbishop of CANTERBURY *in Causes or Matters Ecclesiastical, as amply, fully, and effectually, to all intents and purposes, as the said Archbishop himself might have done.*

And We do hereby Command you, and every of you, to attend, perform, and execute this Our Royal Pleasure in and touching the premises, until We shall declare Our Will and Pleasure to the contrary.

And We do further hereby Will and Command the said Archbishop of CANTERBURY, *quietly and without interruption, to permit and suffer you the said* GEORGE, *Bishop of* LONDON; RICHARD, *Bishop of* DURHAM; JOHN, *Bishop of* ROCHESTER: JOHN, *Bishop of* OXFORD; *and* WILLIAM, *Bishop of* BATH AND WELLS; *any four, three, or two of you, to execute and perform this Our Commission, according to Our Royal Pleasure thereby signified.*

And We do further Will and Command all and every other person and persons, whom it may any way concern in their several Places or Offices, to be attendant, observant, and obedient to you and every of you, in the execution and performance of this Our Royal Will and Command; as they and every of them will answer the contrary at their utmost perils.

Nevertheless, We do hereby declare Our Royal Pleasure to be That they the said Sir HENRY MARTIN, *Sir* CHARLES CÆSAR, *Sir* THOMAS RIDLEY, *and* NATHANIEL BRENT, *in their several Offices and Places; and all other Registrars, Officers, and Ministers in the several Courts, Offices, and Jurisdictions appertaining to the said Archbishop, shall, quietly and without interruption, hold, use, occupy, and enjoy their several Offices and Places, which they now hold by the grant of the said Archbishop, or of any other former Archbishop of* CANTERBURY, *in such manner and form, and with those benefits, privileges, powers, and authorities which they now have, hold, and enjoy therein or thereout, severally and respectively: they, and every of them, in their several Places, being attendant and obedient unto you, the said* GEORGE, *Bishop of* LONDON; RICHARD, *Bishop of* DURHAM; JOHN, *Bishop of* ROCHESTER; JOHN, *Bishop of* OXFORD; *and* WILLIAM, *Bishop of* BATH AND WELLS; *or to any four, three, or two of you, in all things according to the tenour of this our Our Commission; as they should or ought to have been to the said Archbishop himself, if this Commission had not been had or made.*

In witness whereof, We have caused these our Letters to be made Patents. Witness Our Self, at Westminster, the ninth day of October [1627] *in the third year of our reign.*

Per ipsum Regem.

EDMONDS.

Archbishop ABBOT's own Narrative.

[RUSHWORTH. *Historical Collections, idem.*]

Pars Prima.

IT IS an example, so without example, that in the sunshine of the Gospel; in the midst of profession of the true religion; under a gracious King, whom all the world must acknowledge to be blemished with no vice; a man of my place and years, who has done some service in the Church and Commonwealth, so deeply laden with some furious infirmities of body, should be removed from his ordinary habitation, and, by a kind of deportation, should be thrust into one end of the Island (although I must confess into his own diocese), that I hold it fit that the reason of it should be truly understood, least it may someways turn to the scandal of my person and calling. Which Declaration, notwithstanding, I intend not to communicate to any, but to let it lie by me privately; that it being set down impartially, whilst all things are fresh in memory, I may have recourse to it hereafter, if questions shall be made of anything contained in this Relation.

And this I hold necessary to be done, by reason of the strangeness of that, which, by way of Censure, was inflicted upon me; being then of the age of sixty-five years, encumbered with the gout, and afflicted with the stone: having lived so many years in a Place of great service, and, for ought I know, untainted in any of my actions; although my Master, King JAMES (who resteth with GOD) had both a searching wit of his own to discover his servants, whom he put in trust, whether they took any sinister courses or not; and wanted not some suggesters about him, to make the worst of all men's actions whom they could misreport.

Yet this innocency and good fame to be overthrown in a month! and a Christian Bishop suddenly to be made *fabula vulgi*, to be tossed upon the tongues of friends and foes, of Protestants and Papists, of Court and Country, of English and Foreigners, must needs, in common opinion, presuppose some crime, open or secret; which, being discovered by the

King, albeit not fully appearing to the world, must draw on indignation in so high a measure.

I cannot deny that the indisposition of my body kept me from Court, and thereby gave occasion to maligners to traduce me, as, "withdrawing myself from public services, and therefore misliking some courses that were taken": which abstaining, perhaps, neither pleased the King, nor the Great Man that set them on foot.

It is true, that in the turbulency of some things, I had not great invitements to draw me abroad; but to possess my soul in patience till GOD sent fairer weather. But the true ground for my abstaining from solemn and public places, was the weakness of my feet, proceeding from the gout: which disease being hereditary unto me, and having possessed me now nine years, had debilitated me more and more; so that I could not stand at all, neither could I go up or down a pair of stairs but, besides my staff, I must have the service of one at least, of my men, who were not fit to be admitted in every place where I was to come.

And although I was oft remembered by the wisest of my friends, that "I might be carried, as the old Lord Treasurer BURLEIGH was!" yet I did not think my service so necessary for the commonwealth, as his Lordship's, by long experience, was found to be. I did not value myself at so high a rate; but remembered that it was not the least cause of overthrow to ROBERT [DEVEREUX], Earl of ESSEX, that he prized himself so, as if Queen ELIZABETH and the Kingdom could not well have stood, if he had not supported both the one and the other.

Now for me, thus enfeebled, not with gout only, but with the stone and gravel, to wait on the King or the Council Table, was, by me, held a matter most inconvenient. In the Courts of Princes, there is little feeling of [*for*] the infirmities belonging to old age. They like them that be young and gallant in their actions, and in their clothes. They love not that men should stick too long in any room of greatness. Change and alteration bringeth somewhat with it; what have they to do with kerchiefs and staves, with lame or sickly men? It is certainly true, there is little compassion upon the bodily defects of any. The Scripture speaketh of "men standing before Kings." It were an uncouth sight to see the subject sit the day before the Coronation: when, on the morrow, I had work enough for the strongest man in England, being weak in my feet, and coming to Whitehall to see things in readiness against the next day. Yet, notwithstanding the stone and gout, I was not altogether an inutile servant in the King's affairs; but did all things in my house that were to be done: as in keeping the High Commission Court, doing all inferior actions conducing thereto; and despatching references from His Majesty that came thick upon me.

These Relations which are made concerning me, be of certain truth; but reach not to the reason I was discarded.

To understand therefore the verity, so it is, that the Duke of BUCKINGHAM (being still great in the favour of the King; could endure no man that would not depend upon him) among other men, had me in his eye, for not stooping unto him, so asto become his vassal.

I (that had learned a lesson, which I constantly hold, *To be no man's servant, but the King's*: for mine old royal Master which is with GOD, and mine own reason did teach me so) went on mine own ways; although I could not but observe, that as many as walked in that path did suffer for it upon all occasions, and so did I: nothing wherein I moved my Master taking place; which, finding so clearly (as if the Duke had set some ill character upon me), I had no way but to rest in patience; leaving all to GOD, and looking to myself as warily as I might. But this did not serve the turn; his undertakings were so extraordinary, that every one that was not with him, was presently [*instantly*] against him: and if a hard opinion were once entertained, there was no place left for satisfaction or reconciliation. What befell the Earl of ARUNDEL, Sir RANDAL CAREW, and divers others, I need not to report; and no man can make doubt but he blew the coals.

For myself, there is a gentleman called Sir H. S., who gave the first light what should befall me.

This Knight, being of more livelihood than wisdom, had married the Lady D., sister of the now Earl of E.; and had so treated her, both for safeguard of her honour, blemished by him scandalously; and for her alimony or maintenance, being glad to get from him; she was forced to endure a suit in the High Commission Court.

So to strengthen his party, he was made known to the Duke; and, by means of a dependent on his Grace, he got a letter from the King, that "The Commissioners should proceed no further in hearing of that cause; by reason that it being a difference between a Gentleman and his Wife, the King's Majesty would hear it himself." The solicitor for the lady, finding that the course of Justice was stopped, did so earnestly, by petition, move the King, that, by another letter, there was a relaxation of the former restraint, and the Commissioners Ecclesiastical went on.

But now, in the new proceeding, finding himself by justice like[ly] enough to be pinched; he did publicly in the Court, refuse to speak by any Counsel, but would plead his cause himself: wherein he did bear the whole business so disorderly and tumultuously, and unrespectively [*disrespectfully*], that, after divers reproofs, I was enforced, for the honour of the Court and the reputation of the High Commission, to tell him openly that "If he did not carry himself in a better fashion, I would commit him to prison!"

This so troubled the young gallant, that, within few days after, being at dinner or supper (where some wished me well), he bolted it out that "As for the Archbishop, the Duke had a purpose to turn him out of his Place, and that he did but wait the occasion to effect it." Which being brought unto me, constantly, by more ways than one; I was now in expectation, what must be the issue of this Great Man's indignation; which fell out to be, as followeth.

There was one SIBTHORP, who, not being so much as a Bachelor of Arts (as it hath been credibly reported unto me), by means of Doctor PEIRCE, Dean of Peterborough (being Vice Chancellor of Oxford), did get to be confirmed upon him, the title of a Doctor.

This man is Vicar of Brackley, in Northamptonshire; and hath another benefice not far from it, in Buckinghamshire: but the lustre of his honour did arise from being the son-in-law of Sir JOHN LAMB, Chancellor of Peterborough, whose daughter he married; and was put into the Commission of Peace.

When the Lent Assizes were, in February last [1627], at Northampton, the man that preached [*on the 22nd of the month*] before the Judges there, was this worthy Doctor: where, magnifying the authority of Kings (which is so strong in the Scripture, that it needs no flattery any ways to extol it), he let fall divers speeches which were distasteful to the auditors, and namely, "That Kings had power to put poll money upon their subjects' heads": when, against those challenges, men did frequently mourn.

He, being a man of low fortune, conceived that the putting his sermon [*entitled* "*Apostolical Obedience*"] in print, might gain favour at Court and raise his fortune higher, on he goeth with the transcribing of his sermon; and got a bishop or two to prefer this great service to the Duke. It being brought unto the Duke, it cometh in his head, or was suggested to him by some malicious body, that, thereby, the Archbishop might be put to some remarkable strait. For if the King should send the sermon unto him, and command him to allow it to the press, one of these two things would follow: that, either he should authorise it, and so, all men that were indifferent should discover him for a base and unworthy beast; or he should refuse it, and so should fall into the King's indignation, who might pursue it at his pleasure as against a man that was contrary to his service.

Out of this fountain flowed all the water that afterwards so wet. In rehearsing whereof, I must set down divers particulars; which some man may wonder how they should be discovered unto me: but let it suffice, once for all, that in the word of an honest man and a Bishop, I recount nothing but whereof I have good warrant; GOD Himself working means.

The matters were revealed unto me, although it be not convenient that, in this Paper, I name the manner how they came unto me; lest such as did, by well doing, farther me, should receive blame for their labour.

Well, resolved it is, that "I be put to it! and that, with speed!" and therefore Master WILLIAM MURRAY (nephew as, I think, unto Master THOMAS MURRAY, sometimes Tutor to Prince CHARLES), now of the King's Bedchamber, is sent to me with the written Sermon: of whom, I must say, that albeit he did the King his Master's service; yet he did use himself temperately and civilly unto me.

For avoiding of *inquit* and *inquam*, as TULLY saith, *I said this* and *he said that*, I will make it by way of dialogue: not setting down every day's conference exactly by itself, but mentioning all things in the whole; yet distinguishing of times where, for the truth of the Relation, it cannot be avoided.

MURRAY. My Lord! I am sent unto you by the King, to let you know that his pleasure is, That whereas there is brought unto him, a Sermon to be printed: you should allow this Sermon to the press.

Archbishop. I was never he that authorised books to be printed: for it is the work of my Chaplains to read over other men's writings, and what is fit, to let it go; what is unfit, to expunge it.

MURRAY. But the King will have you yourself to do this, because he is minded that no books shall be allowed, but by you and the Bishop of LONDON [*then GEORGE MONTAIGNE*]: and my Lord of LONDON authorised one the other day, COSENS's book; and he will have you do this.

Archbishop. This is an occupation that my old Master, King JAMES, did never put me to; and yet I was then young, and had more abilities of body than I now have: so that I see I must now learn a new lesson. But leave it with me! and when I have read it, I shall know what to say unto it. A day or two hence, you shall understand my mind.

When I had once or twice perused it; I found some words which seemed to me to cross that which the King intended, and, in a sort, to destroy it; and therefore upon his return a day or two after, I expressed myself thus:

Master MURRAY! I conceive that the King intended that this Sermon shall promote the service now in hand about the Loan of Money: but in my opinion he much crosseth it. For he layeth it down for a rule (and because it should not be forgotten, he repeateth it again) that *Christians are bound in duty one to another, especially all subjects to their Princes, according to the Laws and Customs of the Kingdom wherein they live*. Out of this, will men except this Loan; because there is neither Law nor Custom for it, in the Kingdom of England.

Secondly. In my judgement, there followeth a dangerous speech, *Habemus necessitatem vindicandae libertatis*. (For this was all that was then quoted out of CALVIN, no mention being made of any the other words which are, now, in the printed copy.) For when, by the former rule he hath set men at liberty whether they will pay or not; he imposeth upon them a necessity to vindicate this liberty; and *vindicare* may be extended to challenge with violence, *cum vi*. But, for my part, I would be most unwilling to give occasion to Sedition and Mutiny in the kingdom!

Again, here is mention made of Poll Money; which, as I have heard, hath already caused much distaste where the Sermon was preached.

Moreover, what a speech is this? *That he observes the forwardness of the Papists to offer double according to an Act of Parliament so providing; yea, to profess that they would part with the half of their goods*: where he quoteth in the margent, *Anno* I. *CAROLI, the Act for the Subsidy of the Laity, whereby Popish Recusants were to pay double*; when indeed there is *no such Act*!

And in the fifth place, it is said in this Sermon, that *the Princes of Bohemia have power to depose their Kings, as not being hereditary*. Which is a great question: such a one as hath cost much blood; and must not in a word be absolutely defined here, as if it were without controversy.

I pray you, make His Majesty acquainted with these things! and take the book with you!

Where it is to be noted, that, all this time, we had but one single copy [*manuscript*]; which was sometimes at the Court, and sometimes left with me.

MURRAY. I will faithfully deliver these things to the King, and then you shall hear further from me!

Some two or three days after, he returneth again unto me, and telleth me, That he had particularly acquainted the King with my objections; and His Majesty made this answer.

First. For the Laws and Customs of the Kingdom, he did not stand upon that. He had a precedent for that which he did, and thereon he would insist.

Archbishop. I think that to be a mistaking; for I fear there will be found no such precedent. King HENRY VIII., as the Chronicle sheweth, desired but a Sixth Part of men's estates,

Ten Groats in the Pound: our King desireth the whole six parts, full out; so much as men are set at in the *Subsidy Book*. And in the time of King HENRY, although he were a powerful King; yet, for that taxation, there began against him little less than a rebellion; so that he held it wisdom to desist; and, laying the blame upon Cardinal WOLSEY, professed that "he knew nothing of the matter."

MURRAY. Secondly. The King saith for the words, *Habemus necessitatem vindicandae libertatis*; he taketh them to be for him, and he will stand upon his liberty.

Thirdly. For Poll Money, he thinketh it lawful.

Fourthly. It is true, there was no such Act passed; and therefore it must be amended. (And yet in the printed book, it is suffered still to stand! Such slight, and, I may say, slovenly care was had, by them that published this Sermon.)

And fifthly. For that of Bohemia: he hath crossed it out of the book.

Some other matters there were, against which I took exception; but Master MURRAY being a young gentleman, although witty and full of good behaviour: I doubted that, being not deeply seen in Divinity, he could not so well conceive me or make report of my words to His Majesty: and therefore I, being lame and so disabled to wait on the King, did move him, that "He would, in my name, humbly beseech His Majesty to send [*WILLIAM LAUD, then*] the Bishop of BATH AND WELLS unto me; and I would, by his means, make known my scruples." And so I dismissed Master MURRAY; observing with myself, that the Answers to my five Objections especially to two or three [of them], were somewhat strange; as if the King were resolved (were it to his good, or to his harm) to have the book go forth.

After one or two days more, the young Gentleman cometh to me again, and telleth me, that "The King did not think it fit to send the Bishop of BATH unto me; but that expecteth I should pass the book."

In the meantime, had gone over one High Commission day; and this Bishop (who used otherwise on very few days, to fail) was not there: which being joined to His Majesty's message, made me, in some measure to smell that this whole business might have that Bishop's hand in it; especially I knowing in general, the disposition of the man.

The minds of those that were Actors for the publishing of the book, were not quiet at the Court, that the thing was not despatched. Therefore, one day, the Duke said to the King, "Do you see how this business is deferred! If more expedition be not used, it will not be printed before the end of the Term: at which time, it is fit that it be sent down into the countreys [*counties*]." So eager was he, that either by my credit, his undertakings might be strengthened; or at least, I might be contemned and derided, as an unworthy fellow.

This so quickened the King, that the next message which was sent by Master MURRAY, was in some degree minatory, "That if I did not despatch it, the King would take some other course with me!"

When I found how far the Duke had prevailed; I thought it my best way, to set down in writing, many objections, wherefore the book was not fit to be published: which I did modestly, and sent them to the King.

1. (Page 2.) These words deserve to be well weighed, *And whereas the Prince pleads not the Power of Prerogative.*

2. (Page 8.) *The King's duty is first to direct and make Laws.* There is no law made till the King assent unto it; but if it be put simply to *make Laws,* it will make much startling at it.

3. (Page 10.) If *nothing may excuse from Active Obedience, but what is against the Law of GOD, or of Nature, or impossible;* how doth this agree with the first fundamental position: (Page 5.) *That all subjects are bound to all their Princes, according to the Laws and Customs of the Kingdom wherein they live.*

4. (Page 11.) This is a fourth Case of Exception. The Poll Money, mentioned by him in *Saint MATTHEW*, was imposed by the Emperor as a Conqueror over the Jews: and the execution of it in England, although it was by a Law, produced a terrible effect in King RICHARD II.'s time; when only it was used, for ought that appeareth.

5. (Page 12.) It is, in the bottom, *View of the reign of HENRY III.*; and whether it be fit to give such allowance to the book; being surreptitiously put out?

6. (In the same page.) Let the largeness of those words be well considered! *Yea, all Antiquity to be absolutely for Absolute Obedience to Princes, in all Civil and Temporal things.* For such cases as NABOTH's Vineyard, may fall within this.

7. (Page 14.) SIXTUS V. was dead before 1580.

8. (In the same page.) Weigh it well, How this Loan may be called a Tribute! and when it is said, *We are promised, it shall not be immoderately imposed,* how agreeth that, with His Majesty's Commission and *Proclamation,* which are quoted in the margent?

It should seem that this paper did prick to the quick; and no satisfaction being thereby accepted, Bishop LAUD is called, and he must go to answer to it in writing.

This man is the *only* inward [*intimate*] counsellor with BUCKINGHAM: sitting with him, sometimes, privately whole hours; and feeding his humour with malice and spite.

His life in Oxford was to pick quarrels in the Lectures of the Public Readers, and to advertise [*denounce*] them to the then Bishop of DURHAM [? *T. MATTHEW, or his successor, W. JAMES*], that he might fill the ears of King JAMES with discontents against the honest men that took pains in their Places, and settled the truth (that he called Puritanism) in their auditors.

He made it his work, to see what books were in the press; and to look over *Epistles Dedicatory*, and *Prefaces to the Reader*, to see what faults might be found.

It was an observation what a sweet man this was like[ly] to be, that the first observable act that he did, was the marrying of the Earl of D[EVONSHIRE] to the Lady R[ICH] [*See Vol. I. p.* 483]: when it was notorious to the world, that she had another husband, and the same a nobleman, who had divers children then living by her.

King JAMES did, for many years, take this so ill, that he would never hear of any great preferment of him: insomuch that Doctor WILLIAMS, the Bishop of LINCOLN (who taketh upon him, to be the first promoter of him) hath many times said "That when he made mention of LAUD to the King, His Majesty was so averse from it, that he was constrained oftentimes to say that 'He would never desire to serve that Master, which could not remit one fault unto his servant.'"

Well, in the end, he did conquer it, to get him [*on the* 10*th October*, 1621] the Bishopric of ST. DAVIDS: which he had not long enjoyed; but he began to undermine his benefactor, as, at this day, it appeareth.

The Countess of BUCKINGHAM told LINCOLN, that "St. DAVIDS was the man that undermined him with her son." And, verily, such is his aspiring nature, that he will underwork any man in the world! so that he may gain by it.

This man, who believeth so well of himself, framed an Answer to my Exceptions.

But to give some countenance to it; he must call in three other Bishops, that is to say, DURHAM, ROCHESTER, and OXFORD, tried men for such a purpose! and the style of the Speech runneth, "We, and We." This seemed so strong a Confutation, that, for reward of their service, as well as for hope that they would do more, Doctor NEYLE, Bishop of DURHAM, and the Bishop of BATH, were sworn of the Privy Council.

The very day, being Sunday, Master MURRAY was sent unto me, with a writing: but finding me all in a sweat, by a fit of the stone which was then upon me, he forbore, for that time, to trouble me, and said, "That on the morrow, he would repair to me again."

I got me to bed, and lying all that night in pain; I held it convenient not to rise the next day.

And on the Monday, Master MURRAY came unto me; which was the eighth time that he had been with me, so incessantly was I plied with this noble work.

I had shewed it [the *Apostolical Obedience*] to a friend or two: whereof the one was a learned Doctor of Divinity; and the other had served many times in Parliament with great commendation. We all agreed that it was an idle work of a man that understood not Logic, that evidently crossed [*contradicted*] himself, that sometimes spake plausibly; and, in the end of his Sermon, [it] fell so poor and flat, that it was not worth the reading.

Master MURRAY coming to my bedside, said, "That he

was sent again by the King, and had a paper to be shewed unto me."

Archbishop. You see in what case I am, having slept little all this last night; but nevertheless since you come from the King, I will take my spectacles, and read it.

MURRAY. No, my Lord! You may not read it, nor handle it; for I have charge not to suffer it to go out of my hands.

Archbishop. How then, shall I know what it is?

MURRAY. Yes, I have order to read it unto you! but I may not part with it.

Archbishop. I must conceive, that if I do not assent to it, His Majesty will give me leave to reply upon it; which I cannot do, but in my study, for there are my books.

MURRAY. I must go with you into your study; and sit by you, till you have done.

Archbishop. It is not so hasty a work. It will require time; and I have not been used to study, one sitting by me. But first read it, I pray you!

The young gentleman read it from the one end to the other; being two or three sheets of paper.

Archbishop. This Answer is very bitter; but giveth me no satisfaction. I pray you leave the writing with me; and I shall batter it to pieces.

MURRAY. No, my Lord! I am forbidden to leave it with you, or to suffer you to touch it.

Archbishop. How cometh this about? Are the authors of it afraid of it, or ashamed of it? I pray you tell His Majesty that I am dealt with neither manly, nor scholar like. Not manly, because I must fight with adversaries that I know not: not scholar like, because I must not see what it is that must confute me. It is now eight and forty years ago [*i.e., in* 1579], that I came to the University; and, since that time, I have ever loved a learned man. I have disputed and written divers books, and know very well what appertaineth to the Schools.

This is a new kind of learning unto me. I have formerly found fault, that the author of this Sermon quoteth not the places, whereupon he grounds his doctrine: and when I have oft called for them, it is replied to me that "I must take them upon the credit of the Writer," which I dare not do.

For I have searched but one place, which he quoted in general, but sets down neither the words, nor the treatise, nor the chapter; and I find nothing to the purpose for which it is quoted: and therefore I have reason to suspect all the rest.

I pray you, therefore, in the humblest manner, to commend my service to the King my Master, and let him know that, unless I may have all the quotations set down, that I may examine them: and may have that Writing, wherein I am so ill used: I cannot allow the book!

Before I go further, it shall not be amiss to touch some particulars of that which I sent in writing to the King.

The First was Page 2. These words deserve to be well weighed. *And whereas the Prince pleads not the power of Prerogative.*

To this, Master MURRAY said, "The King doth not plead it."

But my reply was, "But what then, doth he coerce those refractories? for I have not heard of any Law, whereby they are imprisoned; and therefore I must take it to be by the King's Prerogative."

To the Second (Page 8). *The King's duty is first to direct and make Laws.* There is no Law made till the King assent unto it; but if it be put simply to *make Laws*, it will cause much startling at it.

To this I remember not any material thing was answered; neither to the Third.

(Page 10.) *If nothing may excuse from Active Obedience, but what is against the Law of GOD, or of Nature, or impossible;* how doth this agree with the first fundamental position: (Page 5.) *That all subjects are bound to all their Princes, according to the Laws and Customs of the kingdom wherein they live.*

This is a fourth case of Exception.

And here, before I go to the rest, the Doctor did truly hit upon a good point, in looking *to the Laws and Customs*, if he could have kept him to it.

For in my memory, and in the remembrance of many Lords and others that now live, Doctor HARSENET, the then Bishop of CHICHESTER, and now of NORWICH, in Parliament time, preached at Whitehall, a sermon (which was afterwards burned) upon the text, *Give unto CÆSAR, the things that be CÆSAR's!* wherein he insisted that "Goods and Money were CÆSAR's; and therefore they were not to be denied unto him."

At this time, when the whole Parliament took main offence thereat, King JAMES was constrained to call the Lords and Commons into the Banquetting House at Whitehall: and there His Majesty called all, by saying "The Bishop only failed in this, when he said *The goods were CÆSAR's*, he did not add *They were his, according to the Laws and Customs of the Country wherein they did live.*"

So moderate was our CÆSAR then, as I myself saw and heard, being then an Eye and Ear Witness: for I was then Bishop of LONDON.

> To the Fourth. The Poll Money, in *Saint MATTHEW*, was imposed by the Emperor, as a Conqueror over the Jews: and the execution of it in England, although it was by a Law, produced a terrible effect in RICHARD II.'s time; when only it was used, for ought that appeareth.

Here the Bishop, in the Paper, excepted divers things "That sometimes among us, by Act of Parliament, strangers are appointed to pay by the poll:" which agreeth not with the Case: and that "It was not well to bring examples out of weak times; whereas we live in better: but it was a marvellous fault, the blame was not laid upon the rebels of that Age."

Those are such poor things, that they are not worth the answering.

But my Objection, in truth, prevailed so far, that in the printed book, it was qualified thus: *Poll money, other persons, and upon some occasions.*

Where, *obiter*, I may observe that my refusing to sign the Sermon, is not to be judged by the printed book: for many things are altered in one, which were in the other.

> To the Fifth (Page 12). It is in the bottom, *View of the reign of HENRY III.*, whether it be fit to give such allowance to the book; being surreptitiously put out?

To this, it was said, "That being a good passage out of a blameworthy book, there was no harm in it."

But before the question of SIBTHORP's treatise; the Bishop

of BATH himself, being with me, found much fault with that Treatise, as being put out for a scandalous Parallel of those times.

To the Sixth, in the same page. Let the largeness of those words be well considered! *Yea, all Antiquity to be absolutely for Absolute Obedience to Princes, in all Civil and Temporal Things.* For such cases as NABOTH's Vineyard may fall within this.

Here the Bishop was as a man in a rage, and said, "That it was an odious comparison! for it must suppose, that there must be an AHAB, and there must be a JEZEBEL, and I cannot tell what!"

But I am sure my Exception standeth true; and reviling and railing doth not satisfy my argument. *All Antiquity* taketh the Scripture into it: and if I had allowed that proportion for good, I had been justly beaten with my own rod.

If the King, the next day, had commanded me to send him all the money and goods I had; I must, by mine own rule, have obeyed him! and if he had commanded the like to all the clergymen in England, by Doctor SIBTHORP's proportion and my Lord of CANTERBURY's allowing of the same; they must have sent in all! and left their wives and children in a miserable case.

Yea, the words extend so far, and are so absolutely delivered, that by this Divinity, If the King should send to the city of London, and the inhabitants thereof, commanding them "to give unto him all the wealth which they have," they are bound to do it!

I know our King is so gracious, that he will attempt no such matter: but if he do it not, the defect is not in these flattering Divines! who, if they were called to question for such doctrine, they would scarce be able to abide it.

There is a *Meum* and a *Tuum* in Christian commonwealths, and *according to Laws and Customs*, Princes may dispose of it. That saying being true, *Ad reges, potestas omnium pertinet, ad singulos, proprietas.*

To the Seventh (p. 14.), PIUS V. was dead before the year 1580; they make no reply, but mend it in the printed book: changing it into GREGORY XIII.

To the last (on the same page). Weigh it well!

How this Loan may be called a Tribute; and when it is said, *We are promised it shall not be immoderately imposed.* How that agreeth with His Majesty's Commission and Proclamation, which are quoted in the margent?

They make no answer but in the published Sermon, distinguish a Tribute from a Loan or Aid: whereby they acknowledge it was not well before, and indeed it was improper and absurd: worthy of none but Doctor SIBTHORP.

I have now delivered the grounds, whereupon I refused to authorise this book: being sorry at my heart, that the King, my gracious Master, should rest so great a building upon so weak a foundation; the Treatise being so slender, and without substance, but that it proceeded from a hungry man.

If I had been in Council, when the Project for this Loan was first handled, I would have used my best reasons to have had it well grounded; but I was absent, and knew not whereupon they proceeded: only I saw, it was followed with much vehemency. And since it was put in execution, I did not interpose myself to know the grounds of one, nor of the other.

It seemed therefore strange unto me, that, in the upshot of the business, I was called in, to make that good by Divinity, which others had done; and must have no other inducement to it, but Doctor SIBTHORP's contemptible treatise!

I imagined this, for the manner of the carriage of it, to be somewhat like unto the Earl of SOMERSET's case; who having abused the wife of the Earl of ESSEX, must have her divorced from her husband, and must himself marry her. And this must not be done; but that the Archbishop of CANTERBURY must ratify all, judicially!

I know the cases are different; but I only compare the manner of the carriage.

When the approbation of the Sermon was by me refused, it was carried to the Bishop of LONDON, who gave a great and stately allowance of it [*It was entered at Stationers' Hall, under his authority, on the 3rd May,* 1627] : the good man being not willing that anything should stick which was sent unto him from the Court; as appeareth by the book which is commonly called *The Seven Sacraments,* which was allowed by his Lordship, with all the errors! which since that time have been expunged and taken out of it.

But before this passed the Bishop's file, there is one accident which fitly cometh in to be recounted in this place.

My Lord of LONDON hath a Chaplain, Doctor WORRAL by name; who is scholar good enough, but a kind of free fellow like man, and of no very tender conscience.

Doctor SIBTHORP's Sermon was brought unto him; and "hand over head" as the proverb is, he approved it, and subscribed his name unto it: but afterwards, being better advised, he sendeth it to a learned gentleman of the Inner Temple; and writing some few lines unto him, craveth his opinion of that which he had done.

The Gentleman read it; but although he had promised to return his judgement by letter, yet he refused so to do: but desired Doctor WORRAL would come himself. Which being done, he spake to this purpose, "What have you done? You have allowed a strange book yonder! which, if it be true, there is no *Meum* or *Tuum*! no man in England hath any·thing of his own! If ever the tide turns, and matters be called to a reckoning; you will be hanged for publishing such a book!"

To which, the Doctor answered, "Yea, but my hand is to it! What shall I do?"

For that, the other replied, "You must scrape out your name! and do not suffer so much as the sign of any letter to remain in the paper!"

Which, accordingly he did; and withdrew his finger from the pie.

But what the Chaplain, well advised, would not do; his Lord, without sticking, accomplished: and so, being un-sensibly hatched, it came flying into the world!

But in my opinion, the book hath persuaded very few understanding men; and hath not gained the King, sixpence.

Pars Secunda.

HITHERTO, I have declared, at length, all passages concerning the Sermon; and, to my remembrance, I have not quitted anything that was worthy the knowing. I am now, in the second place, to shew what was the issue of this not allowing the worthy and learned Treatise.

In the height of this question, I privately understood from a friend in the Court, that "for a punishment upon me, it was resolved that I should be sent to Canterbury, and confined there." I kept this silently, and expected GOD's pleasure, yet laying it up still in my mind: esteeming the Duke to be of the number of them, touching whom, TACITUS observeth, *that such as are false in their love, are true in their hate!* But whatsoever the event must be, I made use of the report, that *jacula prœvisa minus feriunt.*

The Duke, at the first, was earnest with the King, that I must be presently sent away before his going to sea [*He left Portsmouth, on the Rochelle Expedition, on the 27th June*]. "For, saith he, "if I were gone, he would be every day at Whitehall, and at the Council table! and there, will cross all things that I have intended."

To meet with this objection, I got me away to Croydon, a month sooner than, in ordinary years, I have used to do; but the Term was ended early, and my main [*strong*] fit of the stone did call upon me to get me to the country, that there on horseback, I might ride on the downs: which I afterwards performed, and, I thank GOD! found great use of it in recovering of my stomach, which was almost utterly gone.

The Duke hastened his preparations for the fleet: but still that cometh in for one memorandum, "That if he were once absent, there should no day pass over but that the Archbishop would be with the King, and infuse things that would be contrary to his proceedings."

What a miserable and restless thing ambition is! When one talented, but as a common person; yet by the favour of his Prince, hath gotten that Interest, that, in a sort, all the

Keys of England hang at his girdle (which the wise Queen ELIZABETH would never endure in any subject); yet standeth in his own heart, in such tickle terms, as that he feareth every shadow, and thinketh that the lending of the King's ear unto any grave and well seasoned report, may blow him out of all! which in his estimation, he thinketh is settled on no good foundation, but the affection of the Prince; which may be mutable, as it is in all men, more or less. If a man would wish harm unto his enemy; could he wish him a greater torment, than to be wrested and wringed with ambitious thoughts!

Well, at first, it went current, that "with all haste, I must be doffed!" but, upon later consideration, "it must be stayed till the Duke be at sea, and then put in execution by the King himself; that, as it seemeth, BUCKINGHAM might be free from blame, if any should be laid upon any person."

Hence it was, that, after his going, there was a new prosecution of the Yorkshire men; and the refusing Londoners were pursued more fervently than before: and it is very likely that the arrow came out of the same quiver, that the Bishop coming to the election at Westminster, was driven back so suddenly to Bugden.

Take heed of these things, noble Duke! You put your King to the worst parts! whereof you may hear, one day! So when your Sovereign, in the Parliament time, had spoken sharply to both Houses, commanding them "To go together again, and to give more money!" and commanding them to "meddle no more with the Duke of BUCKINGHAM!" you came, the next day, and thought to smooth all, taking the glory of qualifying disturbances to yourself! Whereas, if you read books of true State Government (wherewithal you are not acquainted!), sweet things are personally to be acted by Kings and Princes, as giving of honours, and bestowing of noted benefits; and those things that are sour and distasting, are to be performed by their Ministers. You go the contrary way!

But as before the whole house falleth on fire, some sparks do fly out; so, before the message of the King was brought by the Secretary [of State], there were some inklings that such a thing would follow. And upon the naming of me, by occasion [*incidentally*], it was said by a creature of the

Duke, that "It would not be long, before the Archbishop should be sequestered!" that was the word. So well acquainted are the Duke's followers, with great actions that are likely to fall out in State.

Accordingly on Tuesday, the 5th of July, 1627, the Lord CONWAY [Secretary of State] came to me to Croydon, before dinner-time; "having travelled," as he said, "a long journey that morning, even from Oatlands thither."

He would say nothing till he had dined. Then, because he was to return to Oatlands that night, I took him into the gallery: and when we were both sat down, we fell to it, in this manner.

My Lord! I know you, coming from Court, have somewhat to say to me.

Secretary. It is true, My Lord! and I am the most unwilling man in the world, to bring unpleasing news to any Person of Quality, to whom I wish well; and especially to such a one, as of whose meat I have eaten, and been merry at his house: but I come from the King, and must deliver his pleasure (I know who you are! and much more) with very civil language.

Archbishop. I doubt not, my Lord! but you have somewhat to say; and therefore, I pray you, in plain terms, let me have it!

Secretary. It is then His Majesty's pleasure, that you should withdraw yourself unto Canterbury! for which, he will afford you some convenient time.

Archbishop. Is that it! Then I must use the words of the Psalmist, "He shall not be afraid of any evil tidings; for his heart standeth fast, and believeth in the LORD!" But, I pray you, what is my fault that bringeth this upon me?

Secretary. The King saith, you know!

Archbishop. Truly, I know none, unless it be that I am lame; which I cannot help. It is against my will, and I am not proud of it.

Secretary. The King bade me tell you, "That if any expostulation were used"——

Archbishop. No, I will not use any expostulation! If it be his pleasure, I will obey. I know myself to be an honest man, and therefore fear nothing; but, my Lord! do you think it is for the King's service, in this sort, to send me away?

Secretary. No, by GOD! I do not think it: and so, yesterday, I told the King with an oath; but he will have it so.

Archbishop. I must say, as before, "He shall not be afraid of any evil tidings; for his heart standeth fast, and he believeth in the LORD!" But, I pray you, my Lord! is the King precisely set upon my going to Canterbury. There are questions in law between me and that town, about the liberties of my Archbishopric; which I, by my oath, am bound to maintain: and if I should be among them, I have many adversaries of the citizens. I have there some tenants, and the Dean and Chapter are interested in the question. I would be unwilling that my servants and their people should fall together by the ears, while I am in the town.

His Majesty knoweth this difference to be between us, by the token that a suit, which I lately brought against them, by a *Quo Warranto* in the King's Bench, was stopped: justice being denied me, which is not usual to be denied to any subject; and the King well knoweth, by whose means it was stayed.

I have therefore another house called Foord, five miles beyond Canterbury, and more out of the way. His Majesty may be pleased to let me go thither.

Secretary. I can say nothing to that, but I will acquaint the King with it; and I conceive nothing to the contrary, but that His Majesty will yield so much unto you.

I have a second Charge to deliver unto you, and that is that "His Majesty will not have you, from henceforth, to meddle with the High Commission. He will take care that it shall be done otherwise."

Archbishop. I do not doubt but it shall be better managed than it hath been by me: and yet, my Lord! I will tell you, that, for these many years that I have had the direction of that Court, the time is to come, that ever honest man did find fault that he had not there justice done.

Secretary. It is now Vacation time, and so consequently little to do; and by Michaelmas, His Majesty may set all in order.

Archbishop. I am sorry the King proceedeth thus with me, and letteth me not know the cause.

Secretary. Although I have no commission to tell you so. It is for a book which you would not allow, which concerned the King's service.

Archbishop. If that be it; when I am questioned for it, I doubt not but to give an honest answer.

Secretary. You will never be questioned for it!

Archbishop. Then am I the more hardly dealt withal; to be Censured, and not called to my answer.

Secretary. Well, my Lord! I will remember that of Foord: and will your Grace command me any more service?

Archbishop. No, my Lord! but GOD be with you! Only I end where I began, with the words of the Prophet, "He shall not be afraid for any evil tidings; for his heart standeth fast, and believeth in the LORD!"

It comforted me not a little, that the word was now out: "My confining must be, for not allowing of a book!" I had much ado to forbear smiling when I heard it: because now it was clear, it was not for felony or treason that was laid to my charge, nor for intelligence with the Spaniards or French, nor for correspondency [*correspondence*] with Jesuits and Seminary Priests; I thank GOD for that!

I had almost forgotten that, among many other memorable speeches that passed between us, I used this one, that "Peradventure, the King might be offended at me, because I was no more present at the matter of the Loan; but," said I, "my lameness hindered me therein; and I hoped thereby to do my Master better service. Because if ever course were taken to reconcile the King and his people (which if it be not, this Kingdom will rue it in the end!), I would hope, among many others, to be a good instrument therein, since my hand hath not been in those bitternesses, which have, of late, fallen out."

"You say well!" said the Secretary; "would you that I should tell the King so much?"

"Yea," said I, "if you please, I hold it not unfit that His Majesty should know it."

What he reported therein, I know not: but matters proceeded in the former course, as if there were no regard had of any such thing.

The Lord CONWAY being gone from me for two or three days; I expected to hear the resolution [as] to what place in Kent, I should betake myself. And receiving no news, I tossed many things in my mind, as perhaps that the King desired to hear somewhat from the Duke, how he sped on his journey [*expedition*]; or that peradventure he might alter his purpose, upon report of my ready obeying; or that it might so fall out, that some of the Lords at the Court, understanding, upon the Secretary's return from Croydon, that which was formerly concealed from them, might infuse some other counsels into the King.

These thoughts I revolved. At last, not forgetting the courses of the Court, and imprinting that into my heart, that *there was no good intended towards me, but that any advantage would be taken against me*, I sent a man to Whitehall, whither the King was now come for a night or two, and by him, I wrote to the Lord CONWAY, in these words

MY VERY GOOD LORD,

I Do not forget the message, which you brought unto me on Thursday last; and because I have heard nothing from you since that time, I send this messenger on purpose to know what is resolved touching the house or houses where I must remain. There belong to the Archbishopric, three houses in Kent: one at Canterbury; another five miles beyond, called Foord; and a third, on the side of Canterbury, but two miles off, the name whereof is Beeksburn.

I pray your Lordship to let me know His Majesty's pleasure, whether he will leave the choice of any of those houses to reside in, to me?

I have reason to know the resolution thereof: because I must make my provision of wood and coals and hay for some definite place; and when I shall have brewed, it is fit I should know where to put it, or else it will not serve the turn. It is an unseasonable time to brew now, and as untimely to cut wood (it being green in the highest degree), and to make coals; without all which, my House cannot be kept. But when I shall know what must be my habitation, I will send down my servants presently [at once] *to make the best provision they can.*

And so, expecting your Lordship's answer, I leave you to the Almighty, and remain,

Your Lordship's very loving friend,

G. CANT.

Croydon, July 10, 1627.

He made my servant stay: and when he had gone up to know the King's pleasure, he returned me the answer following.

MAY IT PLEASE YOUR GRACE,

I AM ashamed, and do confess my fault, that I wrote not to your Grace before I received your reproof, though a gracious one; but, in truth, I did not neglect, nor forget: but the continual oppression of business would not permit me to advertise to your Grace, the King's Answer.

His Majesty heard seriously your professions and answers, and commanded me to signify unto you that "He knew not the present differences between you and the town [i.e., of Canterbury]*; and if he had, he would not have cast you into that inconvenience." He was well pleased you should go to your house at Foord; and said, "He did not expect when the question was ended between your Grace and the town, that you should go to Canterbury."*

And he further said, "He would not tie you to so short a time, as might be any way inconvenient; but doth expect that your Grace will govern it so, as His Majesty shall not need to warn you a second time."

I will not fail to move His Majesty to give you liberty to choose either of the houses you name, and give you knowledge of his pleasure, and in all things be ready to obey your commandments, or take occasion to serve you in the condition of

Your Grace's

Most humble servant,

CONWAY.

Whitehall, July 10, 1627.

I could not but observe therein that passage, that the King *doth expect your Grace will so govern it, as His Majesty shall not need to warn you a second time.*

I needed no interpreter to expound those words, and therefore did take order that one of my officers was presently despatched unto Foord, to see the house ready.

While necessaries were caring for, and I lay for some days at Croydon, and afterwards at Lambeth; the city of London was filled with the report of "my confining" (for so they did term it), and divers men spake diversely of it.

I will not trouble myself to mention some idle things; but some other of them require a little consideration. A main matter, that the Duke was said "to take in ill part," was the resort which was made to my house, at the times of dinner and supper, and that, oftentimes, of such as did not love him.

My answer unto that is, That, by nature, I have been given to keep a house according to my proportion, since I have had any means, and GOD hath blessed me in it. That it is a property, by Saint PAUL required in a Bishop, that "He should be given to hospitality"; that it is another of his rules, "Let your conversation be without covetousness!" and those things, I had in mine eyes. Besides I have no wife, nor child: and as for my kindred, I do that for them which I hold fit; but I will not rob the Church, nor the poor, for them!

Again, it is so rare a fault in these things, that men not feeding on the King's meat, but of their own charge, should frankly entertain their friends when they come unto them; that I deserve to be pardoned for it!

But this is not all. When King JAMES gave me the Bishopric, he did once between him and me, and another time before the Earl of SALISBURY, charge me that "I should carry my house nobly!" that was His Majesty's word, "and live like an Archbishop!" which I promised him to do. And when men came to my house, who were of all Civil sorts, I gave them friendly entertainment: not sifting what exceptions the Duke made against them; for I knew he might as undeservedly think ill of others, as he did of me. But I meddled with no man's quarrels: and if I should have received none, but such as cordially, and in truth had loved him; I might have gone to dinner many times without company!

There, frequented me Lords Spiritual and Temporal, divers Privy Councillors, as occasion served, and men of the highest rank: where, if the Duke thought that we had busied ourselves about him, he was much deceived. Yet, perhaps the old saying is true, "A man who is guilty of one evil to himself; thinketh that all men that talk together, do say somewhat of him!" I do not envy him that happiness; but let it ever attend him!

As for other men, of good sort, but of lesser quality; I have heard some by name, to whom exception has been taken: and these are three. I know from the Court by a friend, that my house, for a good space of time, hath been watched; and I marvel that they have not rather named sixty, than three.

The First of these, is Sir DUDLEY DIGGES, a very great mote in the Duke's eye, as I am informed: for it is said that this Knight hath paid him in Parliament, with many sharp speeches. If this be so, yet what is that to me? He is of age to answer for himself!

But in the time of the late Parliament, when the Earl of CARLISLE came unto me, and dealt with me thereabouts; I gave him my word, and I did it truly, that I was not acquainted with these things: only, being sick as I was, I had in general given him advice that he should do nothing that might give just offence to the King. And I have credibly heard that when Sir DUDLEY was last in the Fleet, committed from the Council table; he was much dealt with, to know whether he was not instigated by me to accuse the Duke in Parliament: the Knight, with all the protestations and assurances that could come from a Gentleman, acquitted me of the part and whole: wherein he did me but right.

And I do remember, when that man, now so hated! was a great servant of the Duke. So that if he have now left him, it cannot but be presumed that it is for some unworthy carriage, which the Gentleman conceiveth hath, by that Lord, been offered unto him.

Moreover, how can I but imagine the words and actions of Sir DUDLEY DIGGES have been ill interpreted and reported; when I myself saw the Duke stand up nine times in a morning, in a Parliament House, to fasten upon him words little less, if at all less than treason; when by the particular votes of all the Lords and Commons in both Houses, he was quit [*acquitted*] of those things, which the other would have enforced upon him. And a little while before, he was hastily clapped into the Tower; and within a day or two released again, because nothing was proved against him!

And I assure you, I am so little interested in his actions, that, to this day, I could never learn the reason why he was imprisoned in the Fleet; although he was kept there for seven or eight weeks.

I distinguish the King, from the Duke of BUCKINGHAM. The one is our Sovereign, by the laws of GOD and men! the other, a subject! as we are: and if any subject do impeach another, though of different degrees; let the party grieved, remedy himself by Law, and not by Power!

But, to speak further for this Knight, I may not forget that when he was publicly employed (one time to the Hague, a second time to Muscovia, and thirdly into Ireland about Affairs of the State), such opinions as were then held of his good endeavours.

As for my own part, ever since the days of Queen ELIZABETH, I have been nearly acquainted with him. He was my pupil at Oxford, and a very towardly one; and this knowledge, each of the other, hath continued unto this time. He calleth me, Father; and I term his wife, my daughter. His eldest son is my godson; and their children are in love accounted my grandchildren.

The Second that I have heard named, was Sir FRANCIS HARRINGTON: a Gentleman, whom for divers years, I have not seen; and who, for ought I know, was never in my house but once in his life.

The Third was Sir THOMAS WENTWORTH [*who after FELTON murdered BUCKINGHAM on the 23rd August*, 1628, *went over to the Court, and ultimately became Earl of STRAFFORD*]; who had good occasion to send unto me, and sometimes to see me; because we were joint executors to Sir GEORGE SAVILE, who married his sister, and was my pupil at Oxford. To whose son also, Sir THOMAS WENTWORTH and I were Guardians, as may appear in the Court of Wards; and many things passed between us in that behalf: yet, to my remembrance, I saw not this gentleman but once, in these three-quarters of a year last past [*i.e., since October*, 1626]: at which time, he came to seek his brother-in-law, the Lord CLIFFORD, who was then with me at dinner at Lambeth.

For one of the punishments laid upon me, it was told me by the Lord CONWAY, that "I must meddle no more with the High Commission." Accordingly, within a few days after, a Warrant is sent to the Attorney-General, that the Commission must be renewed, and the Archbishop must be left out. This, under hand, being buzzed about the town, with no small mixture of spite; I conceived it to be agreeable to [*correspond with*] the proceedings with [*against*] the Lords and Gentlemen, who refused to contribute to the Loan: they all being laid aside in the Commissions for Lieutenancy, and of the Peace, in their several counties.

For my part, I had no cause to grieve at this, since it was His Majesty's pleasure! but it was, by the actors therein understood otherwise; they supposing that this power gave me the more authority and splendour in the Church and Commonwealth.

To deliver therefore, truly, the state of this question. It cannot be denied but that it was a great point of policy for the establishing of order in the Ecclesiastical, and consequently Civil Estate also, to erect such a Court: whereby Church-men [*clergy*] that exorbitated [*exceeded bounds*] in any grievous manner, might be castigated and rectified; and such sort of crimes in the laity might be censured [*judged*] as were of Ecclesiastical Cognisance. And, verily, this is of great use in the kingdom, as well for cherishing the study of the Civil Law, as otherwise; so that it be kept incorruptible, and with that integrity as so grave a Meeting and Assembly requireth. This was principally my care; who took much pains and spent much money that, in fair and commendable sort, justice was indifferently [*impartially*] administered to all the King's people that had to do with us.

But every one might see that this was to my singular trouble! For besides that to keep things in a straight course, sometimes in fits of the gout I was forced to be carried into the Court by my servants; where I could not speak much, but with difficulty: I was, at no time, free from petitions;

from examinations; from signing of warrants to call some, to release others; from giving way to speeding, and forwarding Acts of Court. Suitors, as their fashion is, being so importunate as that, in summer and winter, in the day and in the night, in sickness and health, they would not be denied!

These things were daily despatched by me out of Duty; and more, out of Charity; no allowance of pay being from the King, or of fee from the subject to us that were the Judges. Nay, I may say more. The holding of that Court, in such sort as I did, was very expenseful to me, out of my private purse, in giving weekly entertainment to the Commissioners. The reason whereof was this. King JAMES being desirous, when he made me Archbishop, that all matters should gravely and honourably be carried, directed me that I should always call some of the Bishops that were about London, and some Divines and Civilians [*Doctors of the Civil Law*], that, by a good presence, causes might be handled for the reputation of the action: and willed me withal, to imitate therein the Lord Archbishop WHITGIFT, who invited weekly some of the Judges to dinner, the rather to allure them thither. This advice proceeded from [JOHN BRIDGMAN] the Bishop of Durham that now is; which was not ill, if it came from a good intention.

I obeyed it, singly; and did that which was enjoined. But whereas in those times, the Commissioners were but few: since that time there hath been such an inundation of all sorts of men into that Company [*i.e., the High Commission*], that, without proportion, both Lords Spiritual and Temporal, Commissioners and not Commissioners, resorted thither; and divers of them brought so many of their men, that it was truly a burthen to me. I think it may, by my Officers, be justified upon oath, that since I was Archbishop, the thing alone hath cost me, out of my private estate [*i.e., official income as Archbishop*], one and a half thousand pounds; and if I did say two thousand pounds, it were not much amiss: besides all the trouble of my servants, who, neither directly nor indirectly, gained sixpence thereby in a whole year, but only travail and pains for their Master's honour; and of that, they had enough! my houses being like a great host[el]ry every Thursday in the Term; and for my expenses, no man giving me so much as thanks!

Now this being the true case, if the Church and Commonwealth be well provided for, in the administration of justice, and regard be had of the public [welfare]; can any discreet man think that the removing of me from this molestation, is any true punishment upon me? I being one that have framed myself to Reality, and not to Opinion: and growing more and more in years, and consequently into weakness; having before surfeited so long of worldly shews, whereof nothing is truly gained temporally but vexation of spirit, I have had enough of these things, and do not dote upon them. The world, I hope, hath found me more stayed and reserved in my courses.

Nevertheless, what was expedient for this, was despatched by me while I lived at Lambeth and Croydon; albeit I went not out of door.

"Yea, but you were otherwise inutile, not coming to the Star Chamber, nor to the Council table?"

My pain or weakness by the gout, must excuse me herein. When I was younger, and had my health, I so diligently attended at the Star Chamber, that, for full seven years, I was not one day wanting.

And for the Council table, the same reason of my indisposition may satisfy. But there are many other things that do speak for me.

The greatest matters there handled, were for money, or more attempts of war.

For the one of these, we of the Clergy had done our parts already: the Clergy having put *themselves* into payments of Subsidy, by an Act of Parliament; not only for these last two years (when the Temporalty lay in a sort dry), but yet there are three years behind, in which our payments run on, with weight enough unto us. And no man can justly doubt but my hand was in those grants, in a principal fashion.

And concerning the Provisions for War, I must confess my ignorance in the facts thereof. I knew not the grounds whereon the controversies were entered, in general. I thought that before wars were begun, there should be store of treasure; that it was not good to fall out with many great Princes at once; that the turning of our forces another way, must needs be some diminution from the King of Denmark;

who was engaged by us into the quarrel for the Palatinate and Germany, and hazarded both his person and dominions in the prosecution of the question. These matters I thought upon, as one that had sometimes been acquainted with Councils; but I kept my thoughts unto myself.

Again, I was never sent for to the Council table but I went; saving one time, when I was so ill that I might not stir abroad.

Moreover, I was sure that there wanted no Councillors at the Board; the number being so much increased as it was.

Besides, I had no great encouragement to thrust my crazy body abroad; since I saw what little esteem was made of me, in those things which belonged to mine own occupation. With Bishoprics and Deaneries, or other Church places I was no more acquainted; than if I had dwelt at Venice, and understood of them but by some *Gazette*.

The Duke of BUCKINGHAM had the managing of these things, as it was generally conceived. For what was he not fit to determine in Church or Commonwealth, in Court or Council, in peace or war, at land or at sea, at home or in foreign parts?

MONTAGUE had put out [*published*] his Arminian book. I, three times, complained of it: but he was held up against me; and by the Duke magnified, as a well deserving man.

COSENS put out his treatise, which they commonly call *The Seven Sacraments*: which, in the first edition had many strange things in it, as it seemeth. I knew nothing of it, but as it pleased [JOHN BRIDGMAN] my Lord of DURHAM, and [WILLIAM LAUD] the Bishop of BATH, so the world did read.

We were wont, in the High Commission, to repress obstinate and busy Papists.

In the end of King JAMES his time, a Letter was brought me, under the hand and signet of the King, that "We must not meddle with any such matter: nor exact the twelve pence for the Sunday, of those which came not to the Church (with which forfeit, we never meddled)." And this was told us to be, in contemplation of a marriage intended with the Lady MARY, the Daughter of France.

After the death of King JAMES, such another Letter was

brought from King CHARLES; and all execution against Papists was suspended.

But when the Term was at Reading, by open divulgation in all Courts under the Great Seal of England, we and all magistrates were set at liberty to do as it was prescribed by law. And our pursuivants must have their warrants again, and take all the priests they can; whereof Master CROSS took fourteen or fifteen in a very short space.

Not long after, all these are set free! and Letters come from the King, under his royal signet, that "All warrants must be taken from our messengers, because they spoiled the Catholics, and carried themselves unorderly unto them, especially the Bishops' pursuivants:" whereas we had in all, but two; CROSS, my messenger, for whom I did ever offer to be answerable; and THOMLINSON, for whom my Lord of LONDON, I think, would do as much. But the caterpillars, indeed, were the pursuivants used by the sectaries [*Puritans*]: men of no value, and shifters in the world; who had been punished and turned away by us, for great misdemeanours.

But truth of religion and GOD's service was wont to overrule human policies, and not to be overruled; and I am certain that things best prosper, where those courses are held. But be it what it may be, I could not tell what to make of this Variation of the Compass, since it was only commanded unto me, to put such and such things in execution: but I never understood anything of the counsel, whereby I might give my judgement how fit or unfit they were, or might speak to alter the tenour; whereunto, in former times, I had been otherwise used. Variety [*diversity*] of reasons breedeth variety of actions.

For the matter of the Loan, I knew not, a long time, what to make of it. I was not present when the advice was taken, I understood not what was the foundation whereupon the building was raised; neither did ever any of the Council acquaint me therewith.

I saw, on the one side, the King's necessity for money; and especially it being resolved that the war should be pursued. And, on the other side, I could not forget that in the Parliament, great sums were offered, if the Petitions of the Commons might be hearkened unto.

It still ran in my mind, that the old and usual way was best; that in kingdoms, the harmony was sweetest where the Prince and the people tuned well together; that, whatsoever pretence of greatness [he might have], he was but an unhappy man! that set the King and the Body of the Realm at division; that the people, though not fit to be too much cockered, yet are they that must pray! that must pay! that must fight for their Princes! that it could not be, but [that] a man so universally hated in the kingdom as the Duke was, must (for the preservation of himself) desperately adventure on anything! if he might be hearkened unto.

These meditations I had with myself, and, GOD knoweth! I frequently, in my prayers, did beg that he whom these things did most concern, would seriously think upon them.

It ran in my mind, that this new device for money could not long hold out! that then, we must return into the Highway, whither it were best, to retire ourselves betimes; the shortest errors being the best.

But these thoughts, I suppressed within my soul: neither did I ever discourage any man from lending, nor encourage any man to hold back; which I confidently avouch.

At the opening of the Commission for the Loan, I was sent for, from Croydon. It seemed to me a strange thing: but I was told there that "howsoever it shewed, the King would have it so; there was no speaking against it."

I had not heard [*i.e., at any time before*] that men, throughout the kingdom, should lend money against their will! I knew not what to make of it! But when I saw in the instructions that refusers should be sent away for soldiers to the King of Denmark; I began to remember URIAH, that was sent in the forefront of the battle: and, to speak truth, I durst not be tender in it.

And when, afterwards, I saw that men were to be put to their oath, "With whom they had had conference, and whether any did dissuade them?" and yet further beheld that divers were to be imprisoned; I thought this was somewhat a New World! yet, all this while, I swallowed my own spittle, and spake nothing of it to any man.

Nay, when after some trial in Middlesex; the first sitting was for Surrey, in my House [*the Palace*] at Lambeth; and the Lords were there assembled, with the Justices of the whole county: I gave them entertainment in no mean fashion.

And I sat with them, albeit I said nothing; for the confusion was such, that I knew not what to make of it. Things went on every day, and speech was of much money to be raised out of some counties, yet afterwards it was not so readily paid as preferred [? *deferred*]: and, at length, some refused, even in London itself, and Southwark; besides many gentlemen of special rank, and some Lords, as it was said. And though it was reported that "they were but a contemptible company!" yet the prisons in London demonstrated that they were not a very few, but persons both of note and number.

The Judges, besides, concurring another way, that "They could not allow the legality of the demand, and the enforcement that is used thereupon," did somewhat puzzle me, for being too busy in promoting of that for which I might, one day, suffer. Yet, hitherto, I remained silent; hoping that time would break that off which was almost come to an absolute period [*full stop*].

But instead of this, by the permission of GOD, I was called up to the King, to look clearly into the question. When the allowance of SIBTHORP's pamphlet was put upon me, I had then some reason, out of the grounds of that sermon to fear (and I pray GOD that my fear was in vain!) that the Duke had a purpose to turn upside down the Laws, and the whole Fundamental Courses, and Liberties of the Subject: and to leave us, not under the Statutes and Customs which our progenitors enjoyed; but to the Pleasure of Princes, of whom, as some are gentle and benign, so some others, to ingreat themselves [*make themselves greater*], might strain more than the string will bear.

Besides, now it came in my heart, that I was present at the King's Coronation: where many things, on the Prince's part, were solemnly promised; which, being observed, would keep all in order, and the King should have a loving and faithful people, and the Commons should have a kind and gracious King.

The contemplations of these things made me stay my judgement, not any unwillingness to do my Prince any dutiful service: whom I must, and do honour above all the creatures in the world, and will adventure as far for his true good, as any one whatsoever.

But I am loath to plunge myself, so over head and ears, in these difficulties, that I can neither live with quietness of conscience, nor depart out of the world with good fame and estimation. And, perhaps, my Sovereign (if, hereafter, he looked well into this paradox) would, of all the world hate me! because one of my profession, age, and calling, would deceive him; and, with base flattery, swerve from the truth. *The hearts of Kings are in the hands of GOD, and He can turn them as rivers of water.*

I DRAW to a conclusion. Only repute it not amiss, because so much falleth in here, to observe a few words of the Duke of BUCKINGHAM—not as now he is, but as he was in his rising.

I say nothing of his being in France, because I was not present; and divers others there be, that remember it well: but I take him at his first repair to Court [*in* 1614].

King JAMES, for many insolencies, grew weary of SOMERSET: and the Kingdom groaning under the Triumvirate of NORTHAMPTON, SUFFOLK, and SOMERSET (though NORTHAMPTON soon after died [*in June*, 1614]) was glad to be rid of him.

We could have no way so good to effectuate that which was the common desire, as to bring in another in his room. "One nail," as the proverb is, "being to be driven out by another."

It was now observed that the King began to cast his eye upon GEORGE VILLIERS, who was then Cup-bearer, and seemed a modest and courteous youth. But King JAMES had a fashion, that he would never admit any to nearness about himself, but such a one as the Queen should commend unto him, and make some suit on his behalf: that if the Queen, afterwards, being ill intreated, should complain of this "Dear One!"; he might make his answer, "It is 'long of yourself! for you were the party that commended him unto me!" Our old Master took delight strangely, in things of this nature.

That noble Queen, who now resteth in heaven, knew her

husband well; and having been bitten with Favourites, both in England and Scotland, was very shy to adventure upon this request.

King JAMES, in the meantime, more and more loathed SOMERSET; and did not much conceal it, that his affection increased towards the other.

But the Queen would not come to it; albeit divers Lords (whereof some are dead; and some, yet living) did earnestly solicit Her Majesty thereunto.

When it would not do; I was very much moved [*i.e.*, *desired by others*] to put to, my helping hand: they knowing that Queen ANNE was graciously pleased to give me more credit than ordinary; which, all her attendants knew, she continued to the time of her death.

I laboured much, but could not prevail. The Queen oft said to me, "My Lord! you and the rest of your friends know not what you do! I know your Master better than you all! For if this young man be once brought in, the first persons that he will plague, must be you that labour for him! Yea, I shall have my part also! The King will teach him to despise and hardly intreat us all; that he [*BUCKINGHAM*] may seem to beholden to none but himself."

Noble Queen! how like a Prophetess or Oracle did you speak!

Notwithstanding this, we were still instant, telling Her Majesty that "the change would be for the better! for GEORGE was of a good nature, which the other was not; and if he should degenerate, yet it would be a long time before he were able to attain to that height of evil, which the other had."

In the end, upon importunity, Queen ANNE condescended [*agreed to it*]; and so pressed it with the King, that he assented thereunto: which was so stricken, while the iron was hot, that, in the Queen's Bedchamber, the King knighted him with a rapier which the Prince [CHARLES] did wear. And when the King gave order to swear him of the Bedchamber, SOMERSET (who was near) importuned the King with a message that he might be only sworn a Groom. But myself and others, that were at the door, sent to Her Majesty that "She would perfect her work, and cause him to be sworn a Gentleman of her Chamber!"

There is a Lord, or two, living that had a hand in this achievement. I diminish nothing of their praise for so happy a work: but I know my own part best; and, in the word of an honest man, I have reported nothing but truth.

GEORGE went in with the King; but no sooner he got loose, but he came forth unto me, in the Privy Gallery, and there embraced me. He professed that "He was so infinitely bound unto me that, all his life long, he must honour me as his father." And now, he did beseech me, that I would give him some Lessons how he should carry himself.

When he had earnestly followed this chase, I told him, I would give him three short lessons, if he would learn them.

> The First was, That, daily, upon his knees, he should pray to GOD to bless the King his Master, and to give him (*GEORGE*) grace studiously to serve and please him.
>
> The Second was, That he should do all good offices between the King and the Queen; and between the King and the Prince.
>
> The Third was, That he should fill his Master's ears with nothing but truth.

I made him repeat these three things unto me: and then I would have him, to acquaint the King with them! and so tell me, when I met him again, what the King said unto him.

He promised he would. And the morrow after, Master THOMAS MURRAY (the Prince's Tutor) and I standing together, in the gallery at Whitehall, Sir GEORGE VILLIERS coming forth, and drawing to us, he told Master MURRAY how much he was beholden unto me, and that I had given him certain instructions: which I prayed him to rehearse; as, indifferently well he did, before us. Yea, and that he had acquainted the King with them; who said, "They were instructions worthy of an Archbishop, to give to a young man."

His countenance of thankfulness continued for a few days, but not long! either to me or any others, his well wishers. The Roman historian, TACITUS, hath somewhere a note that "Benefits, while they may be requited, seem courtesies; but when they are so high, that they cannot be repaid, they prove matters of hatred."

THUS, to lie by me, to quicken my remembrance, I have laid down the Cause and the Proceedings of my sending [*being sent*] into Kent; where I remain at the writing of this Treatise. Praying GOD, to bless and guide our King aright! to continue the prosperity and welfare of this Kingdom, which, at this time, is shrewdly shaken! to send good and worthy men to be Governors [*i.e., Bishops*] of our Church! to prosper my mind and body, that I may do nothing that may give a wound to my conscience! and then, to send me patience quietly to endure whatsoever His Divine Majesty shall be pleased to lay upon me! *Da quod jubes, et jube quod vis!* and, in the end, to give me such a happy deliverance, either in life or death, as may be most for His glory; and for the wholesome example of others! who look much on the actions and passions of Men of my Place.

THOMAS, third Lord FAIRFAX.

Short Memorials of some things to be cleared during my Command in the Army.

[1645 to 1650 A.D.]

THOMAS, third Lord FAIRFAX.

Short Memorials of some things to be cleared during my Command in the Army.

[1645 to 1650 A.D.]

[From the holograph, now *Fairfax MS.* 36, in the Bodleian Library, Oxford.]

NOw when GOD is visiting the nation [? *an allusion to the Plague of London in* 1665] for the transgressions of their ways, as formerly he did to one sort of men so doth he it to another sort; so that all may see their errors and his justice: and as we have cause to implore his mercy, having sinned against him; so must we still vindicate his justice, who is always "clear when he judgeth." [*Ps.* li. 4.]

Now therefore, by his grace and assistance, I shall truly set down the grounds my actions moved upon during that unhappy War; and those actions which seemed to the World the more questionable in my steering through the turbulent and perilous seas of that time.

The first embarking into the sad calamities of War was about the year 1641 when the general distemper of the Three Kingdoms had kindled such a flame even in the hearts (I mean the Difference between the King and Parliament), as every one sought to guard his own house by the authority of both these. But the different judgements and ways were so contrary that, before a remedy could be found out, almost all was consumed to ashes.

I must needs say my judgement was for the Parliament, as the King's, and Kingdom's, great and safest Council; as others were for the King, and averse to Parliament, as if it could not go high enough for the Perogative.

Upon which division, different Powers were set up, viz.: The Commission of Array for the King; and [the Militia for] the Parliament. But those of the Array so exceeded their Commission by oppressing many honest people; whom, by way of reproach, they called Roundheads: they being (for Religion, Estates, and Interest) a very considerable part of the country; that occasioned them to take up arms in their own defence, which was afterwards confirmed by Parliamentary authority.

Now my father being yet at his house at Denton, where I then waited on him, though he had notice from his friends that it was resolved that he should be sent for, as a prisoner, to York: yet he resolved not to stir from his own house; not knowing anything in himself to deserve it. But the country [*Yorkshire*] suffering daily more and more, many were forced to come and intreat him to join with them in defence of themselves and country [*Yorkshire*]; which [were] being sadly oppressed by those of the Array, which afterwards had the name of Cavaliers.

And being much importuned by those that were about him; he was resolved, seeing his country [*Yorkshire*] in this great distress, to run the same hazard with them for the preservation of it.

Then did the Parliament grant a Commission to him, to be General of the Forces in the North: myself also having a Commission under him, to be General of the Horse. But it is not my intention, in this place, to mention the several Services that were done in this Cause of the Parliament: being rather desirous to clear my actions in it than to declare them. Therefore I shall say no more [*See however pp.* 577-610] of this Three Years' War in the North; there being nothing, I thank GOD! in all that time to be alleged against me.

But now I shall come to say something how I came to be engaged in the South.

There being some years spent, in those parts, in a lingering War between the forces of the King and [the] Parliament; and several battles so equally fought, as could scarce be known on which side the business in dispute would be determined; though it must be confessed the Parliament's Army was under the command of a very noble and gallant person, [ROBERT DEVEREUX] the Earl of ESSEX: yet finding Time and Delay gaining more advantage on their affairs than Force had done; the Parliament resolved to make a change in the constitution of their Army; hoping by it to find a change also in businesses, which were then something in a declining condition.

So as, in this distemper of affairs, the Army was New Modelled; and a new General was proposed to command it. For which, by the Votes of the Two Houses of Parliament [in February 1645], myself was nominated; though most unfit: and so far from desiring of it, that had not so great an authority commanded obedience, [I also] being then unseparated from the royal Interest; besides the persuasions of nearest friends, not to decline so free and general a Call; I should have "hid myself [among the stuff," 1 *Samuel* x. 22.] to have avoided so great a charge. But whether it was from a natural facility in me, that betrayed my modesty; or the powerful hand of GOD, which all things must obey: I was induced to receive the Command.

Then was I immediately voted by the Parliament [in February 1645], to come to London to take up my charge [*where he arrived on* 18*th February* 1645]; though not fully recovered of a dangerous wound, which I had received a little before; and which, I verily believe, without the miraculous hand of GOD had proved mortal.

But here, alas! when I bring to mind the sad consequences that designing men have brought to pass since, from these first innocent undertakings, I am ready to let go that confidence I had, with JOB to say: "Till I die, I will not remove my integrity from me; nor shall my heart reproach me so long as I live" [*Job* xxvii. 5]. But now more fit to take up his Complaint with a little alteration and to say, Why did I not die when I had that hurt? Why did I not give up the ghost when my life was on the confines of the grave? [See *Job* x. 18.]

But GOD having been pleased thus to give me my life as a prey; I took my journey southward: hoping I might be someway serviceable to the Public. But when I came thither, had it not been in the simplicity of my heart, I could not have supported myself under the frowns and displeasures showed me by those who were disgusted at this alteration; in which many of them were themselves so much concerned: and these did not only outwardly express it, but sought by all means to obstruct my proceedings in this new charge. Who though they could not prevent what the necessity of affairs pressed most to do, viz.: To march speedily out with the Army; yet were we, by them, made so inconsiderable for want of fit and necessary accommodations, as it rather seemed that we were sent to be destroyed and ruined than to do any service for the Kingdom by it. Insomuch as when I went to take my leave of a Great Person [*Can this have been* DENZIL HOLLES *?*]; he told me, He was very sorry I was going out with the Army, for he did believe we should be beaten.

Surely then had some of our ends been Self Interest merely, this might have discouraged us: but it working no such effects, gave the more hopes of future success; as it did to the Parliament's advantage. But if any ill use hath been made of such mercies, let the mercies be acknowledged from GOD: but let the abuses receive their due reward of shame and punishment.

Thus, being led on by good success, and clear intentions of a Public Good; some of us could not discern the serpent which was hid in these spreading leaves of so Good Fortune: nor could believe the fruits of our hopes would prove as cockatrice's eggs; from whence so viperous a brood should afterwards spring up.

But, how ill deserving so ever we were: yet still it pleased GOD to give the Army such success in the years [16]45 and

[16]46; that there remained in England neither Army nor fortress to oppose the Parliament in settling the peace of the Kingdom.

But this shining mercy soon became clouded with the mists of abominable hypocrisy [and] deceit; even in those men, who had been instrumental in bringing this War to a conclusion. Here was the vertical point on which the Army's honour and reputation turned into reproach and scandal. Here the power of the Army, which I once had, was usurped by the Forerunners of Confusion and Anarchy, viz.: the Agitators. [*The Army appointed a Committee of Adjutators on* 14*th May* 1647.]

My Commission as General bound me to act with [the co-operation of my] Council: but the arbitrary and unlimited power of this new Council would act without a General: and all that I could do, could not prevail against this stream; especially when the Parliament itself became divided, so that the pay was withheld from the Army, which heightened their distempers.

Then followed, Free Quarter [in November 1647]; and that brought a general discontent through the whole nation: which gave these factious Agitators matter enough for the carrying on of their designs; viz., To raise their own fortunes by the ruin of others.

But now, being much troubled to see things in this condition, I did rather desire to be a sufferer than to be a Commander: but, before I laid down my Commission, I thought it fit to consult with some friends rather than gratify my private sense and reason, which much desired it; especially having received it from a Public Authority, which might justly expect to have notice of it before I laid it down. Which was the cause of my continuing in the Army longer than I would have done (seeing I could not have my desire granted): which did indeed preserve the Parliament for some time, from those confusions and breakings, which afterwards Time and Confidence emboldened these men to.

But now I shall descend to some particulars of their Agitation:

At Nottingham was the first time that I took notice of it, by the soldiers' meetings to frame a *Petition* to the Parliament about their arrears [of pay]. The thing seemed just: but, not liking the way, I spake with some Officers that were principally engaged in it; and got it suppressed for that time.

Which was but as the cutting off of Hydra's head, which soon sprang up again (though not so near the Head Quarters; but in more remote corners of the Army, which I could not so timely prevent) so that they presented it to the Parliament; which they were highly displeased with. And now falling into difference[s]; the consequence of which proved fatal not only to the King, but also destructive to one another. The one striving to uphold his authority: the other (who had a spirit of unsettlement) to preserve themselves from the ruin they feared. This (with a natural inclination to change) I believe created the thoughts of a New Government; which, in time, attained the name of a Common Wealth: though it never arrived to the perfection of it; being sometimes Democratical, sometimes Oligarchial, lastly Anarchical—as indeed all the ways attaining to it seemed nothing but a Confusion.

For now the Officers of the Army were placed and displaced by the will of the new Agitators; who, with violence, so carried all things, as it was above my power to restrain it. This made me have recourse to my friends to get me a discharge of my Command; so as there was a consultation with several Members of Parliament, who met about it: but none would undertake to move it to the House, as affairs then stood. And they perceiving that such a Motion would be unpleasing to them: which was the answer I received from them. And further that I should satisfy myself: for it would be the Parliament's care to compose all things in as good order as might be most for the good and settlement of the Kingdom. But these hopes, though they something supported my spirit; yet could not they balance the grief and trouble I had, that I could not get my discharge. So that, if you find me carried on with this stream; I can truly say, It was by the violence of it, and no consent of mine.

But the Army, having gotten this power and strength by correspondence with some in Parliament (who themselves did after find it [to their disadvantage] in the end) they] *the*

Army] march nearer London [26th June 1647]: and, at Windsor [20th November 1647], after two days' debate in a Council of War, it was resolved to remove all out of the House [of Commons] whom they conceived to "obstruct," as they called it, "the Public Settlement."

Upon which expedition in this march, I was vehemently pressed: but here I resolved to use a restrictive power, when I had not a persuasive one. So when the Lieutenant General [OLIVER CROMWELL] and others pressed me to sign orders for marching, I still delayed the doing of it [in November 1647]; as always dreading the consequences of breaking Parliament, and at a time when the Kingdom was falling into a new War: which was so near, that my delaying but three or four days giving out Orders, diverted this humour of the Army from being Statesmen to their more proper duty of soldiers.

For, even then, Colonel POYER declared [for the King] in Wales; great forces were raised with the Lord GORING in Kent; and Duke [of] HAMILTON (almost at the same time) with a powerful Army of the Scots. All which set out work enough for that summer [of 1648].

This I write to shew how, by Providence, a few days' delay did prolong the Parliament more than a year from the violent breaches that afterwards happened to them.

Here again might be mentioned the great and difficult businesses the Army went through that year [1648]: hoping, as well aiming, it would be a good service to the Kingdom. But, seeing the factious Party grew more insolent as success made them more powerful, I shall forbear to relate those Actions; which would, otherwise, have deserved a better remembrance than, in modesty, [it] were fit for me to record: and [I] will rather punish myself here, with the continuance of the Story of the Army's Irregularities.

But one thing, of very great concernment in all after changes, should have been inserted before the mention of this Second War: but [it] will come in well enough in this place, without much interruption of this Discourse, viz.:

THE KING'S REMOVAL FROM HOLMBY,

the sad consequences whereof fill my heart with grief with

the remembrance of it now; as it did then, with thoughts and care how to have prevented it.

Being then at Saffron Walden in Essex, I had notice that Cornet JOYCE (an arch-Agitator that quartered about Oxford) had [on 4th June 1647] seized on the King's person, and removed his Quarters: and [had] given such a check to the Commissioners of Parliament which were ordered to attend His Majesty, that they refused to act any further in their Commission; being so unwarrantably interrupted.

But, as soon as I heard it, I immediately sent away two Regiments of Horse, commanded by Colonel WHALLEY to remove this force; and to set all things again in their due order and course.

But before he reached Holmby [or Holdenby]; the King was advanced two or three miles [from thence] on his way towards Cambridge; attended by JOYCE. Here Colonel WHALLEY acquainted the King, That he was sent by the General to let him know how much he was troubled at those great insolencies that had been committed so near his person: and as he had not the least knowledge of it before it was done, so he had omitted no time in seeking to remove the force; which he had orders from me to see done. And therefore [Colonel WHALLEY] desired that His Majesty would be pleased to return again to Holmby, where all things should again be settled in as much order and quietness as they were before. And also he [*Colonel WHALLEY*] desired the Commissioners to resume their Charge, as the Parliament had directed them: which he had in charge also to desire them to do, from the General.

But the King refused to return; and the Commissioners refused also to act any more as Commissioners. Which Colonel WHALLEY still further urged, saying, He had an express command to see all things well settled again about His Majesty; which could not be but by his returning again to Holmby.

Which the King said positively, He would not do.

So Colonel WHALLEY pressed him no further: having indeed a special direction from me to use all tenderness and respect, as was due, towards His Majesty.

So the King came that night, or the second [6th June

1647] to Sir JOHN CUTT's house [at Childerley] near Cambridge: where, the next day, I waited on His Majesty. It being also my business to persuade his return to Holmby. But he was otherwise resolved.

I pressed the Commissioners also to act again, according to the power that Parliament had given them: which they also refused to do.

So having spent the whole day [7th June 1647] about this business; I returned to my Quarters.

But before I took my leave of the King, he said to me, "Sir, I have as great an Interest in the Army as you." By which I plainly saw the broken reed he leaned upon.

These Agitators [*or Adjutators*], chameleon-like, could change into that colour which best served their ends; and so had brought the King into an opinion that the Army was for him: though [it was] never less for his safety and rights, than when it was theirs.

And that it might appear what real trouble this act was to me; notwithstanding the Army was almost wholly infected with the humour of Agitation, I called for a Court of War, to proceed against JOYCE for this high offence, and the breach of the *Articles of War*. But the Officers (whether for fear of the distempered soldiers; or rather, as I fear, from a secret allowance of what was done) made all my endeavours herein ineffectual: and now (no punishment being able to reach them) all affairs steer after this compass:

The King and all his Party are in hopes. Those of the Parliament, and others who kept to their Covenant Interest, in fears. So as, for many months, Public Councils were turned into private Junto's. Which would have been less criminal, if it had ended in General Consent. But, on the contrary, it begat greater emulations and jealousies one of another. So that the Army would not entrust the King any longer with the liberty he had; nor would the Parliament suffer the King to undertake that which was properly their work to do, viz.: [the] Settling [of] the Kingdom with its just rights and liberties. And the Army were as jealous of the Parliament, that they [*the Parliament*] would not have care enough of their [*the Army's*] security.

All things growing worse and worse made the King endeavour his own escape, as he did [11th-14th November 1647]; but out of a larger confinement at Hampton Court, to a straiter one in the Isle of Wight.

Here the Parliament treated upon *Propositions of Peace* with the King. But, alas, the Envious One sowed tares that could not be rooted out, without plucking up the corn also.

And here was the King, as the golden ball, tossed before the two great Parties; the Parliament, and the Army: [which] grew to a great contest, which must again have involved the kingdom in blood.

But the Army, having the greater power, got the King again into their hands; notwithstanding all the means that could be used. The *Treaty* [*? of Newport, ? October* 1648] was scarcely ended, before the King was seized upon by the hands of the same person, Lieutenant Colonel COBBETT, who took him from Holmby [; *and who now removed him, on* 1*st December* 1648, *from Carisbrooke Castle to Hurst Castle*]. Soon after followed his Trial.

But to prepare a way to this work [*the Trial*] this Agitating Council had thought first how to remove out of the Parliament all those who were likely to oppose them in that work; which they carried on with that secrecy as that I had not the least intimation of it, till it was done: as some Members of the House can witness, with whom I was met, at that very time, upon especial business, when that horrible attempt was made by Colonel PRIDE upon the Parliament [on 6th December 1648]. It was so secretly carried on that I should get no notice of it: because I always prevented those designs when I knew of them. But by this "Purging of the House," as they called it, the Parliament was brought into such a consumptive and languishing condition as that it could never recover again that healthful Constitution which always kept the Kingdom in its strength and vigour.

But now, this Three-fold Cord being cut by the sword, the Trial of the King was the easier for them to accomplish. My afflicted and troubled mind for it, and my earnest endeavours to prevent it, will, I hope, sufficiently testify my abhorrence of the fact. And what might they not now do to the lower shrubs, having thus cut down the cedar? For, after this, [the] Duke [of] HAMILTON, [the] Earl of HOLLAND, and Lord CAPEL, and others, were condemned to death.

But here it is fit to say something for my own vindication about my Lord CAPEL, Sir CHARLES LUCAS, and Sir GEORGE LISLE; who were *prisoners at mercy* upon the rendition of Colchester: seeing some have questioned the just performance of those *Articles* [*of Surrender*].

I (having laid siege to the town, and several assaults being made upon it) finding their forces within [to be] much more numerous than those I had without, forced me to take another course: blocking them up; and so, by cutting off all supplies, to bring them to a surrender. Which, after [a] four months' siege, they were necessitated to; and that *upon mercy*: they being between 3,000 and 4,000 men.

Now by *Delivering upon mercy* is to be understood, that some are to suffer, and the rest to go free.

So those forementioned persons only were to suffer; and all the rest freed.

So immediately after our entrance into the town [on 26th August 1648], a Council of War being called; those persons were sentenced to die, the rest to be quit.

Yet, on they being so resolved, I thought fit to manumit the Lord CAPEL, the Lord NORWICH, &c. over to the Parliament (being the Civil Judicature of the Kingdom, consisting then of Lords and Commons) as the most proper Judges of their cases: being considerable for estates and families.

But Sir CHARLES LUCAS and Sir GEORGE LISLE being mere Soldiers of Fortune; and falling into our hands by the chance of war, execution was done upon them. And in this distribution of Justice I did nothing but according to my Commission, and the trust reposed in me.

But it may be objected that I went into the Court during the Trial.

To this, I answer. It was upon the earnest entreaties of my Lord CAPEL's friends; who desired me to explain there, what I meant by *Surrendering to mercy*: otherwise I had not gone, being always unsatisfied with the Court.

But for this I shall need to say no more: seeing I may as well be questioned for the *Articles* of Bristol, Oxford, Exeter; or [for] any other Action in the War, as for this.

And now I have related the most remarkable things that might be alleged against me during the prosecution of the War.

Yet one thing more requires that I should say something to it, before I conclude, viz.: Concerning Papers and Declarations of the Army that came out in my name and the Council of Officers. I must needs say. From the time they declared their Usurped Authority at Triplow Heath [10th June 1647], I never gave my free consent to anything they did: but (being then undischarged of my place) they set my hand [*signature*], by way of course, to all their Papers; whether I consented or not.

And unto such failings all Authority may fall. As sometimes Kingly Authority may be abused to their, and the Kingdom's, prejudice; sometimes, under a Parliamentary Authority, much injury hath been done: so here, hath a General's Power been broken and crumbled into a Levelling Faction, to the great unsettlement of the Nation.

Yet, even in this, I hope all impartial judges will interpret as a force and ravishment of a good name; rather than a voluntary consent whereby it might make me seem to become equally criminal. Though I must confess, if in a multitude of words, much more in a multitude of actions, there may be some transgressions: yet, I can as truly say, they were never designedly or wilfully committed by me.

But now, when all the power was got into the Army, they cut up the root of Kingly Government. After this, were Engagements to relinquish the Title. Then [was] War declared against Scotland for assisting the King [CHARLES II.]: and several Leagues made with foreign Princes to confederate with their new Government, which was now a Common Wealth, against the Kingly Power.

Seeing which, with grief and sorrow, though I had as much the love of the Army as ever; though I was with much importunity solicited by the remaining Parliament, the Lieutenant General [OLIVER CROMWELL], and other

Officers and soldiers, to continue my Command; and though I might, so long as I acted their designs, attain to the height of power and other advantages I pleased (for so I understood from themselves): yet (by the mercy and goodness of GOD, ever valuing Loyalty and Conscience before this perishing felicity) I did, so long as I continued in the Army, oppose all those ways in their counsels; and, when I could do no more, I also declined their actions, though not their Commission I had from the Parliament, till the remaining part of it, took it from me [25th June 1650].

Thus I have given you, in short, the sum of the most considerable things that the World may censure me for, during this unhappy War. Yet, I hope, among many weaknesses and failings there shall not be found crimes of that magnitude [for me] to be counted amongst those who have done these things through ambition and dissimulation. Hoping also that GOD will, one day, clear this Action we undertook, so far as concerns his honour; and the integrity of such as faithfully served in it. For I cannot believe that such wonderful successes shall be given in vain. Though cunning and deceitful men must take shame to themselves; yet the purposes and determination of GOD shall have happy effects to his glory, and the comfort of his people.

THOMAS, third Lord FAIRFAX.

A Short Memorial of the Northern Actions; during the War there, from the year 1642 till the year 1644.

I DID not think to have taken up my pen any more, to have written on this subject: but that my silence seemed to accuse me of ingratitude to GOD for the many mercies and deliverances I have had; and of injuriousness to myself in losing the comfort of them, by suffering them to be buried in the grave of Oblivion in my lifetime.

Wherefore I shall set down, as they come to my mind, such things wherein I have found the wonderful assistance of GOD to me in the time of the War I was in the North: though not in that methodical and polished manner as might have been done; being but intended only for my own satisfaction, and the help of my memory.

As I said, in the First Part [*p.* 353], my father was called forth by the importunity of the country [*Yorkshire*], to join with them in the defence of themselves: and [was] confirmed by a Commission of the Parliament [*by Vote on the 23rd August* 1642. *He however did not actually receive the Commission till the 3rd December following.*]

The first Action we had was at Bradford, where we had about 300 men. The Enemy, having about 700 or 800 and

2 pieces of ordnance, came thither to assault us [in October 1642]. We drew out close to the town to receive them. They had [the] advantage of [the] ground, the town being compassed with hills; which made us more exposed to their cannon shot, from which we received some hurt. Yet notwithstanding, our men defended the passages, which they [*the Enemy*] were to descend, so well that they got no ground of us. And now, the day being spent, they drew off; and returned back again to Leeds.

A few days after, Captain HOTHAM, with 3 Troops of Horse and some Dragoons, came to me; and then we marched to Leeds. But the Enemy, having notice of it, quitt[ed] the town in haste; and fled to York.

And that we might have more room, and be less burthensome to our friends; we presently advanced [in November 1642] to Tadcaster, 8 miles from York.

Now we being increased to 1,000 men, it was thought fit, for securing of the West Riding, at least the greatest part of it, from whence our greatest supply came, to keep the Pass at Wetherby; whither my father sent me with about 300 Foot and 40 Horse. The Enemy's next design, from York, was to fall on my Quarters there; which was a place very open and easy for them to do: there being so many back ways to enter in; and friends enough to direct and acquaint them with all we did.

About six of the clock in the morning [in November 1642], they set upon us with 800 Horse and Foot. The woods thereabouts favoured them so much as that our Scouts could get no notice of them; so as no alarm was given till they were ready to enter the town, which they might soon do for the Guards were all asleep in houses.

For in the beginning of the War, men were as impatient of Duty as ignorant of it.

Myself only was on horseback; going out, at the other end of the town, to Tadcaster: where my father lay.

One came running to me, and told me, The Enemy was entering the town. I presently galloped to the Court of Guard [*the Piquet*], where I found not above four men at their arms; as I remember, two Foot Sergeants and two

Pike men, [who] withstood with me when Sir THOMAS GLENHAM, with about six or seven Commanders more, charged us: where, after a short but sharp encounter, in which Major CARR was slain, they retired. And in this time more of the Guard were gotten to their arms. But I must confess I know [of] no strength, but the powerful hand of GOD, that gave them this repulse.

Afterward they made another attempt, in which Captain ATKINSON was slain.

And here again, there fell out another remarkable Providence. During this conflict, our Magazine was blown up: which struck such a terror in the Enemy, thinking we had cannon (which they were informed we had not), that they instantly retreated. And though I had but a few Horse; they pursued the Enemy some miles, and took many prisoners.

We lost about eight or ten men, whereof seven were blown up with [the] powder: the Enemy, many more.*

At this time [HENRY CLIFFORD] the Earl of CUMBERLAND commanded the Forces in Yorkshire for the King.

* *Sir HENRY SLINGSBY gives the following Account of this Action:*

My Lord of CUMBERLAND sent out Sir THOMAS GLENHAM once again to beat up Sir THOMAS FAIRFAX's Quarters at Wetherby; commanding out a party both of Horse and Dragoons. He comes close up to the town, undiscovered, a little before sunrise; and PRIDEAUX and some others enter the town through a back yard. This gave an alarm quite through the town.

Sir THOMAS FAIRFAX was, at this juncture, drawing on his boots, to go to his father at Tadcaster. He gets on horseback, draws out some Pikes, and so meets our Gentlemen. Every one had a shot at him: he only making at them with his sword; and then retired again, under the guard of his Pikes.

At another part, Lieutenant Colonel NORTON enters with his Dragoons. Captain ATKINSON encounters him on horseback: the other being on foot. They meet. ATKINSON missed with his pistol. NORTON pulls him off horseback by the sword-belt. Being both on the ground; ATKINSON's soldiers come in, fell NORTON into the ditch with the butt ends of their muskets, to rescue their Captain. NORTON's soldiers come in, and beat down ATKINSON; and with repeated blows break his thigh; of which wound, he died. A sore scuffle between two that had been neighbours and intimate friends. After this they [*NORTON's Dragoons*] retreated out of the town; with the loss of more than one Trooper killed, and one Major CARR, a Scotchman.

Memoirs, p. 40, Ed. 1806, 8vo.

But (being of a peaceable nature; and by his amiable disposition having but few enemies, or rather because he was an enemy to few) he did not suit with their present condition and apprehension of fears. Therefore they sent to [WILLIAM CAVENDISH] the Earl of NEWCASTLE, who had an Army of 6,000 men, to desire his assistance: which he answered by a speedy march to York.

Being now encouraged by this increase of force, they resolved to fall on Tadcaster. My father drew all his men thither. But by a Council of War the town was judged untenable; and that we should draw out to an advantageous piece of ground by the town. But before we could all march out; the Enemy advanced [on 7th December 1642] so fast that we were necessitated to leave some Foot in a slight Work above the bridge to secure our retreat.

But the Enemy pressing still on us, forced us to draw back [*return back*], and maintain that ground.

We had about 900 men. The Enemy above 4,000: who, in Brigades, drew up close to the Works, and stormed us. Our men reserved their shot till they were very near; which then they disposed to so good purpose as forced them to retire, and shelter themselves behind the hedges that were hard by.

And here did the fight continue from 11 a clock at noon till 5 at night, with cannon and musket, without intermission.

They had, once, possessed a house by the bridge; which would have cut us [off] from our reserves that were in the town: but Major General GIFFORD, with a commanded party, beat them out again; where many of the enemies were slain and taken prisoners.

They attempted at another place; but were also repulsed by Captain LISTER, who was there slain: which was a great loss, [he] being a discreet Gentleman.

And now, it growing dark, the Enemy drew off into the fields hard by; with intention to assault us again the next day. They left that night about 200 dead and wounded upon the place.

But our ammunition being all spent in this day's fight; we drew off that night, and marched to Selby: and the Enemy entered, the next day [8th December 1642], into the town [of Tadcaster]. And thus, by the mercy of GOD, were a few delivered from an Army who, in their thoughts, had swallowed us up.

Now, the Earl of NEWCASTLE lay between us and our friends in the West Riding; and so [was] equally destructive to us both. But, to give them encouragement and help, I was sent [on Friday, 9th December 1642], with about 200 Foot and 3 Troops of Horse and some arms, to Bradford. I was to go by Ferrybridge: our intelligence being that the Enemy was advanced yet no further than Sherburn.

But when I was within a mile of the town [*i.e. Ferrybridge*]; we took some prisoners who told us That my Lord NEWCASTLE laid at Pontefract, 800 men in Ferrybridge, and the rest of the Army in all the towns thereabouts.

So as now, our advance, or retreat, seemed [to be] alike difficult. But, there being not much time to demur in, a retreat was resolved on back again to Selby. 300 or 400 of the Enemy's Horse shewed themselves in our rear, without making any attempt upon us; and so, through the goodness of GOD, we got safe thither.

[*Here, chronologically, comes in the Fight at Sherburn in Elmet, on Wednesday, 14th December* 1642, *described at page* 372.]

And, in three days after,* having better intelligence how they lay, with the same number as before, I marched in the night by several towns where they lay, and arrived, the next

* *This is clearly wrong, and a slip of the memory. The Writer did not again go to Bradford until after the Victory of the Club Men there, on Sunday, 18th December 1642; which is thus described by FERDINANDO, Lord FAIRFAX, in a letter from Selby on 29th December* 1642.

I have formerly advertised that the Earl of NEWCASTLE's Army have seized upon Leeds: where they plunder the well-affected party; and raise a very great sum of money out of those that they can draw to compound for their securities.

And from Leeds, they marched on Sunday, the 18th of this month, with 5 Troops of Horse, 6 Companies of Dragoons, 200 Foot, and two drakes [*small cannon, or field pieces*], of the Earl of NEWCASTLE's Army; besides Sir WILLIAM SAVILE and divers other Gentlemen of Yorkshire and their forces, that joined themselves with them: and came to Bradford, about ten a clock in the morning; intending to surprise the town, in [the] time of Prayer.

day, at Bradford: a town very untenable; but, for their good affections, deserving all we could hazard for them.

But the town, having scouts abroad, had notice of their coming; and gave the alarm to the country [*district*]: who came in to their succour from the parts adjoining.

Yet they had not in all above 80 muskets: the rest being armed with clubs and such rustic weapons; with which small force, they put the cause to trial with [*against*] the great strength of the Enemy. - Who planted their drakes, and discharged each of them seventeen times upon the town; until a townsman, with a fowling piece, killed one of the Cannoniers. And then they all, with great courage, issued from the town upon the enemies; and killed many of them, and took about 30 prisoners: and forced the rest to retreat, leaving 40 of their muskets and [a] barrel of powder, with much other provision, behind them. And this, with [the] loss of 3 Bradford men.

The report of the country is that [of] the enemies, amongst those that were killed were Colonel EVERS, and Captain BINNS, and another Commander; and that Colonel GORING, General of the Horse with the Earl of NEWCASTLE, was wounded; and Serjeant Major CARR, taken prisoner. And it is generally spoken, That 150 more are run away, upon the retreat; and are not since returned to Leeds.

In which victory the hand and power of GOD was most evident, the town being open on all sides and not defensible; assaulted on every side by a malicious and bloody Enemy; and defended by a few half-naked [*half-armed*] men: there being in the town not above 80 muskets before they got 40 more by the spoils of their enemies; so that [the] slaughter was, for the most part, with clubs and scythes mounted on poles, and came to hand blows.

With this defeat, the enemies are so enraged as they threaten revenge to Bradford.

Whereupon the Bradford men sent to me for succour of men and arms. And I have sent my son [Sir THOMAS FAIRFAX] and Sir HENRY FOULIS to them, with 3 Troops of Horse and 120 Dragooners; who are safely arrived there: and [have been] received with great joy and acclamation of the country [*district*]; who flock to him and offer themselves most willingly to serve against their Popish enemies, if arms could be furnished to them.

He hath already surprised some victuals [*convoys af provisions*] sent in, upon warrants [*requisitions*], to the Enemy at Leeds, by the overawed country [*district*]. And he hath sent Captain MILDMAY, with his Troop of Horse, into Craven [*i.e. the upper Wharfe-dale*] to stop the raising of forces and money in that country: which is attempted by the Earl of CUMBERLAND; who is lately retired from York to Skipton. And I hope he may leave nothing unattempted that may conduce to the safety of the country, so far as can be expected from the few forces he hath with him.

A Second Letter from the Lord FAIRFAX. Printed 5th Jan. 1642[-3]. British Museum Press Mark, E. 84. (15).

Our first work there was to fortify ourselves; for we could not but expect strong opposition in it: seeing there lay at Leeds 1,500 of the Enemy, and 1,200 at Wakefield; neither above six or seven miles from us. They visited us every day with their Horse; for ours went not far from the town, being so unequal in number: yet they seldom returned without loss. Till, at length, our few men grew so bold; and theirs, so disheartened: as they durst not stir a mile out of their garrison.

But while these daily skirmishes were among the Horse; I thought it necessary to strengthen ourselves with more Foot. So, summoning the country [*i.e. the West Riding of Yorkshire*], which now our Horse had given some liberty to come into us; I presently armed them with the arms we brought along with us: so that, in all, we were now about 800 Foot.

But being too many to lie idle, and yet too few to be in continual duty; we resolved rather, through the assistance of GOD, to attempt them in their garrison than endure longer this trouble. So summoning the country in again; we made a body of about 1,200 or 1,300 men: with which we marched to Leeds, and drew them up [on Monday, 23rd

Another Account of the Bradford Vietory, dated 21st December 1642, *states:*

They appeared in Barker End, about 9 a clock, when we had not in [the] town above 40 Musketeers; planted their ordnance in WILLIAM COOKE's Barn; marched down the Causey [*Causeway*] with their Foot, whilst their Horse coasted about the town to hinder aid from coming in; possessed themselves of those houses under the Church; and from thence played hotly upon our Musketeers in the Church till 11 a clock: about which time [the] Halifax men, and other neighbours, came in to our help.

The fight, before hot, was then hotter. Our men, impatient to be cooped up in the Church, rushed out [and] forced a passage into the foresaid houses; and there our Club Men did good execution upon them. Thereabouts the fight continued till it was dark. Many of theirs were slain. . . . . .

Their cannon, one of which shoots a 9 lb. ball [*if so, it was a Demi-Culverin: see Vol. IV., p.* 251] played all that time upon the town: but hurt no man, praised be GOD! who hath delivered those that were ordained to death, &c.

Brave News of the taking of Chichester, &c. &c. Printed 30th Dec, 1642. British Museum Press Mark, E. 83. (36).

January 1643] within [a] half cannon shot of their Works, in Battalia; and then sent in a Trumpet[er] with a Summons to deliver up the town to me, for the use of [the] King and Parliament.

They presently returned this answer, That it was not civilly done to come so near before I sent the Summons; and that they would defend the town, the best they could, with their lives.

So presently ordering the manner of the Storm, we all fell on at one time. The business was hotly disputed for almost two hours: but, after, the Enemy were beaten from their Works. The Barricadoes were soon forced open into the streets: where Horse and Foot resolutely entering, the soldiers cast down their arms, and rendered themselves prisoners. The Governor and some chief Officers swam the river and escaped. One Major BEAUMONT was drowned, as was thought. In all, there were about 40 or 50 slain; and [a] good store of ammunition [was] taken, which we had much want of.

But the consequence of this Action was yet of more importance. For those that fled from Leeds and Wakefield, (for they also quitted that garrison) gave my Lord NEWCASTLE such an alarm at Pontefract, where he lay; as he drew all his Army back again to York: leaving once more a free intercourse between my father [at Selby] and me, which he had so long time cut off.

But, after a short time, the Earl of NEWCASTLE returned again to the same Quarters [at Pontefract]; and we to our stricter duties.

But, after some time, we found that our men must either have more room, or more action. [*This Fight at Sherburn took place on the* 14*th December* 1642; *and should have been mentioned earlier in this Narrative.**] Therefore Captain

* *Sir HENRY SLINGSBY says of this Fight:*

Two days after, His Excellency [the Earl of NEWCASTLE] came to York [5th December 1642]; he undertook to attempt to beat Lord FAIRFAX out of Tadcaster: in this he succeeded pretty well [on 7th December 1642]; and marched to Pomfret [*Pontefract*], which he made his Head Quarters. His Horse [was] at Sherburn, and towns next adjacent.

Here we were a little too secure. Sir THOMAS FAIRFAX (with a

HOTHAM and I took a resolution, early in the morning to beat up a Quarter [*Encampment*] of the Enemy that lay at [Church] Fenton. But they being gone, we marched towards Sherburn [in Elmet]; intending only to give them an alarm there.

But they might see us, a mile or two, march over a plain common which lay by the Town; and therefore had sent about 20, or 30, Horse to guard a Pass near the town. I having the Van (For, at this time we [*FAIRFAX and HOTHAM*] commanded our Troops distinct one from another; both making 5 Troops of Horse and 2 of Dragoons), I told him, If he would second me, I would charge those Horse; and if they fled, I would pursue them so close[ly] as to get into the town with them. He promised to second me. I went to the head of my Troops, and presently charged them: who fled, and we pursued [them] close to the Barricado. But they got in, and shut it upon us; where my horse was shot at the breast. We so filled the lane; being strait [*narrow*], that we could not retreat without confusion, and danger of their falling in our rear. So we stood to it; and stormed the Work with pistol and sword. At the end of the Barricado, there was a straight passage for one single horse to go in. I entered there, and others followed one by one. Close at one side of the entrance stood a Troop of Horse: but so soon as eight or ten of us got in they fled. And by this time, the rest of our men had beaten them from their Barricado, and entered the town; which soon cleared the streets, and pursued those that fled. And now my horse, which was shot in the lane, fell down dead under me: but I was presently mounted again.

party of 300 Horse; and, it seems, hearing the Officers in Sherburn were to have a feast) comes at noon-day, beats up our Quarters; [and] takes Commissary WINDHAM, Sir WILLIAM RIDDALL, and many others, prisoners. *Memoirs*, p. 42, Ed. 1806, 8vo.

The date of this Fight is fixed by the following passage:

On Tuesday last [13th December 1642], about four of the clock in the morning, Sir THOMAS FAIRFAX marched from Selby; fetching a compass, as if he declined Sherburn: yet, at last, [he] wheeled about, and assaulted that town about one of the clock, the next day [14th December 1642] &c. &c. *A True Relation of the Fight at Sherburn, &c.* Written on [Friday] 16th December 1642. British Museum Press Mark, E. 83. (15).

They in the towns about having taken the alarm, now made us think of securing our retreat with the prisoners we had gotten: and some of them [were] very considerable; among whom was Major General WINDHAM. But we scarce[ly] got into good order before General GORING came, with a good body of Horse, up to us: and as we marched on, he followed close in the rear, without [our] receiving any hurt; only my Trumpet[er] had his horse shot close by me. So we returned again to Selby.

But though this could not free us wholly from a potent Enemy; yet we lay more quietly by them a good while after.

In this recess of action, we had several treaties [*negotiations*] about prisoners. And this I mention the rather, for that Captain HOTHAM here began to discover his intention of leaving the Parliament's Service, by making conditions for himself with the Earl of NEWCASTLE (though [it was] not discovered till a good while after): which had almost ruined my father, and the forces that were with him.

For, being now denied help and succour from Hull and the East Riding; he was forced to forsake Selby, and retire to Leeds and those western parts where [I] myself was.

But to make good this retreat, I was sent to, to bring what men I could to join with him at Sherburn. For NEWCASTLE's forces lay so, as he might easily intercept us in our way to Leeds: which he had determined [to do], and to that end lay with his Army on Clifford Moor; having perfect intelligence of our march.

But while my father, with 1,500 men ordnance and ammunition, continued [on 2nd April 1643] his way from Selby to Leeds; I, with those I brought to Sherburn, marched a little aside, between my Lord NEWCASTLE's Army and ours. And to amuse [*deceive*] them the more, [I] made an attempt upon Tadcaster: whither they had 300 or 400 men; who presently quitted the town, and fled to York. Here we stayed three or four hours sleighting [*destroying*] the Works.

This put NEWCASTLE's Army to a stand, which was on their march to meet us: thinking that he was deceived in his intelligence; and that we had some other design upon York.

He presently sent back the Lord GORING, with 20 Troops of Horse and Dragoons, to relieve Tadcaster. We were newly drawn off when they came. GORING pressed over the river to follow us.

But seeing we were far unequal to him in Horse, for I had not above 3 Troops; and [having] to go over Bramham Moor, a large plain: I gave direction to the Foot to march away, while I stayed with the Horse to interrupt the Enemy's passage in those narrow lanes that lead up to the Moor. Here was much firing at one another. But, in regard of their great number, as they advanced we were forced to give way: yet had gained by it sufficient time for the Foot to be out of danger.

But when we came up to the Moor again, I found them where I left them: which troubled me much, the Enemy being close upon us, and a great plain yet to go over. So [I] marched the foot in two Divisions, and the Horse in the rear. The Enemy followed, about two musket shot from us, in three good bodies: but yet made no attempt upon us. And thus we got well over the open *campania*.

But having again gotten to some little enclosures, beyond which was another Moor, called Seacroft Moor [*now called Whin Moor. It is about five miles from Leeds*], much less than the first. Here our men thinking themselves more secure, were more careless in keeping order; and while their officers were getting them out of houses, where they sought for drink, [it] being an exceedingly hot day; the Enemy got, another way, as soon as we, on to the Moor. But we had almost passed this plain also.

They [*the Royalists*] seeing us in some disorder, charged us both in Flank and Rear. The countrymen presently cast down their arms, and fled. The Foot soon after: which, for want of pikes, were not able to withstand their Horse. Some were slain; and many taken prisoners. Few of our Horse stood the charge. Some Officers, with me, made our retreat with much difficulty; in which Sir HENRY FOULIS had a slight hurt. My Cornet was taken prisoner. Yet [we] got to Leeds about two hours after my father, with those forces with him, was arrived safe thither.

This was one of the greatest losses we ever received. Yet was it a great Providence that it was a part, and not the whole, [of the] Force which received this loss: it being the Enemy's intention to have fought us that day with their whole Army, which was, at least, 10,000 men; had not the Attempt at Tadcaster put a stand to them. And so concluded that day with this storm that fell on us.

But now, being at Leeds, it was thought fit to possess some other place also: wherefore I was sent to Bradford, with 700 or 800 Foot and 3 Troops of Horse. These two towns being all the garrisons we had. At Wakefield, six miles off, lay 3,000 of the Enemy: but yet [we] had not much disturbance from them.

Being most busied about releasing our prisoners that were taken at Seacroft Moor, most of them being countrymen [*Yorkshire peasants*]; whose wives and children were still importunate for their release: which was as earnestly endeavoured by us; but no conditions would be accepted. So their continual cries, and tears, and importunities compelled us to think of some way to redeem these men: so as we thought of attempting Wakefield; our intelligence being that the Enemy had not above 800 or 900 men in the town.

I acquainted my father with our design: who approved of it; and sent [to Bradford] some men from Leeds; which enable us to draw out 1,100 Horse and Foot.

So upon Whit-Sunday [21st May 1643], early in the morning, we came before the town. But they had notice of our coming, and had manned all their Works, and set about 800 Musketeers to line the hedges about the town: which made us now doubt our intelligence; which was too late. Notwithstanding, after a little consultation, we advanced, and soon beat them back into the town; which we stormed in three places.

After two hours' dispute, the Foot forced open a Barricado, where I entered with my own Troop. Colonel ALURED, and Captain BRIGHT, followed with theirs. The street which we entered was full of their Foot: which we charged through, and routed; leaving them to the Foot which followed close behind us. And presently we were charged again with Horse led by General GORING: where, after a hot encounter, some were slain; and [he] himself taken prisoner by [the brother of] Colonel ALURED.

And I cannot but here acknowledge GOD's goodness to me this day: who being advanced a good way single [*alone*] before my men, having a Colonel and a Lieutenant Colonel, who had engaged themselves to be my prisoners, only with me; and many of the enemies between me and my men, I light[ed] on a Regiment of Foot standing in the Market Place.

Thus encompassed, and thinking what to do; I espied a lane which I thought would lead me back to my men again. At the end of this lane, there was a Corps du Guard [*Piquet*] of the Enemy's, with 15 or 16 soldiers; who were then just quitting it, with a Serjeant leading them off: whom we met. Who, seeing their [two] Officers, came up to us; taking no notice of me. They asked them, What they would have them do? for they could keep the Work no longer; because the Roundheads, as they called them, came so fast upon them.

But the Gentlemen, who had passed their words to me to be my true prisoners, said nothing. So, looking upon one another, I thought it not fit now to own them; as so much less to bid the rest to render themselves to me: so, being well mounted, and seeing a place in the Work where men used to go over, I rushed from them, seeing no other remedy, and made my horse leap over the Work. And so, by a good Providence, got to my men again: who, before I came, had, by the direction of Major General GIFFORD, brought up a piece of ordnance, and planted it in the Churchyard, against the body that stood in the Market Place; who presently rendered themselves.

All our men being got into the town, the streets were cleared, [and] many prisoners taken. But the Horse got off almost entire. But this seemed the greater mercy when we saw our mistake: now finding 3,000 men in the town, [and] not expecting half the number. We brought away 1,400 prisoners, 80 Officers, 28 Colours; and [a] great store of ammunition, which we much wanted.*

* Saturday night, the 20th of May [1643]. The Lord General [i.e. FERDINANDO, Lord FAIRFAX] gave Order for a party of 1,000 Foot, 3 Companies of Dragooners, and 8 Troops of Horse, to march from the garrisons of Leeds, Bradford, Halifax, and Howley. Sir THOMAS FAIRFAX commanded in chief. The Foot were commanded by Serjeant

But seeing this was more a Miracle than a Victory; more the effect of GOD's divine power than human force; and more his Providence than the success of our prudence in making so hazardous an attempt: let the honour and praise of it be His only!

After this, we exchanged our men that were prisoners, with these: and were freed, a good while; from any trouble or attempt from [the] Enemy.

But then again it pleased GOD to mix water with our

Major General GIFFORD and Sir WILLIAM FAIRFAX. The Horse were divided into two bodies: 4 Troops commanded by Sir THOMAS FAIRFAX, and the other 4 Troops by Sir HENRY FOULIS.

Howley was the rendezvous, where they all met on Saturday [20th May] last, about twelve a clock at night.

About two, next morning, they marched away: and coming to Stanley, where 2 of the Enemy's Troops lay, with some Dragooners; that Quarter was beaten up, and about one and twenty prisoners taken.

About four a clock in the morning [of 21st May 1643], we came before Wakefield. Where, after some of their Horse were beaten into the town, the Foot, with unspeakable courage, beat the enemies from the hedges, which they had lined with Muskeeters, into the town; and assaulted it in two places, Wrengate and Norgate: and, after an hour and a half's fight, we recovered [*captured*] one of their Pieces [of Ordnance] and turned it upon them; and entered the town, at both places, at one and the same time.

When the Barricadoes were opened, Sir THOMAS FAIRFAX, with the Horse, fell into the town; and cleared the street: where Colonel GORING was taken by Lieutenant ALURED, brother to Captain ALURED, a Member of the House [of Commons].

Yet in the Market Place, there stood 3 Troops of Horse; and Colonel LAMPTON's Regiment: to whom Major General GIFFORD sent a Trumpet[er], with offer of Quarter, if they would lay down their arms.

They answered, They scorned the motion.

Then he fired a Piece of their own Ordnance upon them: and the Horse fell in upon them, [and] beat them out of [the] town. We took 39 Officers, 27 Colours of Foot, 3 Coronets of Horse, and about 1,500 common soldiers.

The Enemy had in the town 3,000 Foot and 7 Troops of Horse: besides Colonel LAMPTON's Regiment; which came into the town, after we had entered the town.

The Enemy left behind them 4 Pieces of Ordnance, with Amunition; which we brought away.

THOMAS FAIRFAX. JOHN GIFFORD. JOHN HOLMAN. TITUS LEIGHTON.
HENRY FOULIS. WILLIAM FAIRFAX. ROBERT FOULIS. FRANCIS TALBOT.

A Miraculous Victory . . . . at Wakefield. Printed 27th May 1643. British Museum Press Mark, E. 104. (13).

wine; and to bring us into a better condition by the brinks of ruin and destruction.

Hitherto, through His mercy, we had held up near[ly] two years against a potent Army: but they finding us now almost tired, with continual Services; treacherously used by our friends; and in want of many things necessary for support and defence—the Earl of NEWCASTLE marched with an Army of 10,000 or 12,000 men to besiege us; and resolved to sit down before Bradford, which was a very untenable place.

My father drew all the forces he could spare out of the garrisons hither.

But seeing it impossible to defend the town but by strength of men; and not [having] above ten or twelve days' provisions for so many as were necessary to keep it: we resolved [on 29th June 1643] the next morning, very early, with a party of 3,000 men, to attempt his whole Army, as they lay in their Quarters, three miles off; hoping thereby, to put him into some distraction; which could not, by reason of the unequal numbers, be done any other way.

For this end, my father appointed four of the clock next morning [30th June 1643] to begin the march. But Major General [JOHN] GIFFORD, who had the ordering of the business, so delayed the execution of it that it was seven or eight before we began to move: and not without much suspicion of treachery in it; for when we came near the place we intended, the Enemy's whole Army was drawn up in Battalia.

We were to go up a hill to them, which our Forlorn Hope [*or Advanced Guard*] gained by beating theirs into their Main Body; which was drawn up half a mile further, upon a plain called Adderton [*the correct spelling is Adwalton*] Moor. [*It is also spelt Atherston and Atherton.*]

We, being all up the hill, drew into Battalia also. I commanded the Right Wing, which was about 1,000 Foot and 5 Troops of Horse; Major General [JOHN] GIFFORD, the Left Wing, which was about the same number. My father commanded all in chief.

We advanced through the enclosed grounds till we came to the Moor; beating the Foot that lay in them to their Main Body.

10 or 12 Troops of Horse charge us in the Right Wing [*which was at the head of Warren's Lane*]. We kept [to] the enclosures, placing our Musketeers in the hedges next the Moor; which was a good advantage to us, that had so few Horse.

There was a gate, or open place, to the Moor: where five or six might enter abreast. Here they strove to enter: we, to defend. But, after some dispute, those that entered the pass found sharp entertainment; and those that were not yet entered, as hot welcome from the Musketeers, that flanked them in the hedges. All, in the end, were forced to retreat; with the loss of Colonel HOWARD, who commanded them.

The Left Wing, at the same time, was engaged with the Enemy's Foot. Ours gained ground of them.

The Horse came down again, and charged us: being about 13 or 14 Troops. We defended ourselves as before; but with much more difficulty, many having got in among us: but [they] were beat[en] off again, with some loss; and Colonel HERNE, who commanded that party, was slain. We pursued them [back] to their cannon.

And here I cannot omit a remarkable passage of Divine Justice. Whilst we were engaged in the fight with those Horse that entered the gate, four soldiers had stripped Colonel HERNE naked; as he lay dead on the ground, [and] men still fighting round about him: and so dextrous were these villains, as they had done it, and mounted themselves again, before we had beaten them off. But after we had beaten them to their ordnance, as I said; and [were] now returning to our ground again; the Enemy discharged a piece of cannon in our rear. The bullet fell into Captain COPLEY's Troop, in which these four men were: two of whom were killed; and some hurt or mark remained on the rest, though dispersed into several Ranks of the Troop, which was [the] more remarkable.

We had not yet Martial Law amongst us: which gave me a good occasion to reprove it; by shewing the soldiers the sinfulness of the act, and how GOD would punish when men wanted power to do it.

This charge, and the resolution our soldiers shewed in the Left Wing, made the Enemy think of retreating. Orders were given for it; and some marched off the Field.

Whilst they were in this wavering condition, one Colonel SKIRTON, a wild and desperate man, desired his General to let him charge [on our Left Wing] once more, with a Stand of Pikes. With which he brake in upon our men; and they not [being] relieved by our Reserves, ([which were] commanded by some ill-affected Officers; chiefly Major General GIFFORD, who did not his part as he ought to do), our men lost ground: which the Enemy seeing, pursued this advantage by bringing on fresh troops. Ours, being herewith discouraged, began to flee; and so [were] soon routed.

The Horse also charged us again. We, not knowing what was done in the Left Wing; our men maintained their ground till a command came for us to retreat: having scarce any way now to do it; the Enemy being almost round about us, and our way to Bradford cut off. But there was a lane [*Warren's Lane*] in the field we were in, which led to Halifax: which, as a happy Providence, brought us off without any great loss; save of Captain TALBOT and twelve more, which were slain in this last encounter.

Of those [on the Left Wing] that fled, there were about 60 killed, and 300 taken prisoners.

This business, having such ill success, our hopes of better could not be much: wanting all things that were necessary for defence, and [no] expectations of helps from any place.

The Earl of NEWCASTLE presently lay siege to the town [of Bradford]: but before he had surrounded it, I got in with those men I brought from Halifax.

I found my father much troubled; having neither a Place of Strength to defend ourselves in, nor a garrison in Yorkshire to retreat to. For [Sir JOHN HOTHAM the Elder,] the Governor of Hull had declared himself, If we were forced to retreat thither, that he would shut the gates on us.

But, while he was musing on these sad thoughts, a messenger was sent from Hull to let him know, The townsmen had secured [*taken prisoner*] the Governor [on the morning of the 29th June 1643]; and if he had any occasion to make use of that place, for they were sensible of the danger he was in, he should be very readily and gladly received [there]. Which news was joyfully received, and acknowledged as a great mercy of GOD to us: yet was it not made use of till a further necessity compelled it.

So my father, having ordered me to stay here [at Bradford] with 800 Foot and 60 Horse: he intruded [*retired*] that night [of 30th June 1643] for Leeds, to secure it.

Now NEWCASTLE, having spent three or four days in laying his Quarters about the town; they brought down their cannon: but needed to raise no batteries, for the hills, within half [a] musket shot, commanded all the town; which [cannon], now being planted in two places, shot furiously upon us. [They] making also Approaches; which made us spend very much [ammunition].

Our little store was not above five and twenty, or thirty, barrels of powder at the beginning of the siege: yet, notwithstanding, the Earl of NEWCASTLE sent a Trumpet[er] to offer us Conditions; which I accepted so they were honourable for us to take, and safe for the inhabitants.

Upon which, two Captains were sent to treat with him, and a Cessation [was agreed upon] during the time; but he continued working still, contrary to [the] agreement: whereupon I sent for the Commissioners again, suspecting a design of attempting something against us; but he returned them not till eleven a clock at night [of 1st July 1643], and then with a slight answer.

Whilst they were delivering it to us, we heard great shooting of cannon and muskets. All ran presently to the Works, which the Enemy was storming. Here, for three-quarters of an hour, was very hot service: but, at length they retreated.

They made a second attempt: but were also beaten off.

After this, we had not above one barrel of powder left; and no Match. So I called the Officers together: where it was advised and resolved [*evidently about* 1 *a.m. on the* 2*nd July* 1643] to draw off presently, before it was day; and by forcing a way, which we must do (they having surrounded the town), [in order] to retreat to Leeds

Orders were despatched, and speedily put in execution.

The Foot, commanded by Colonel ROGERS, was sent out, through some narrow lanes; who were to beat up the Dragoons' Quarters [*Encampment*]; and so to go on to Leeds.

[I] myself, with some other Officers, went with the Horse, which were not above 50, in an opener way.

Here I must not forget to mention my Wife, who ran great hazards with us in this retreat as any others; and with as little expression of fear: not from any zeal or delight, I must needs say, in the War; but through a willing and patient suffering of this undesirable condition.

But now I sent two or three Horsemen to discover what they could of the Enemy: which presently returned, and told us, There was a Guard of Horse close by us.

Before I had gone forty paces, the day beginning to break, I saw them on the hill above us; being about 300 Horse.

I, with some 12 more, charged them. Sir HENRY FOULIS, Major General GIFFORD, and myself, with three more [*i.e.*, 6 *out of* 13] brake through. Captain MUDD was slain: and the rest of our Horse, being close by, the Enemy fell upon them, taking most of them prisoners; amongst whom my Wife was, the Officer behind whom she was [on horseback] being taken.

I saw this disaster; but could give no relief. For after I was got through, I was in the Enemy's Rear alone; for those that had charged also through, went on to Leeds; thinking I had done so too.

But being unwilling to leave my company: I stayed till I saw there was no more in my power to do; but to be made a prisoner with them. Then I retired to Leeds.

The like disorder fell amongst the Foot that went the other way, by a mistake. For after they had marched a little way, the Van fell into the Dragoons' Quarters [*Encampment*], clearing the way. But through a cowardly fear of him that commanded those men who were in the Rear; [he] made them face about, and march again into the town [of Bradford]: where, the next day [2nd July 1643], they were all taken prisoners.

Only 80, or thereabouts, of the Front, which got through, came to Leeds; all mounted on horses which they had taken from the Enemy: where I found them when I came thither;

which was some joy to them, all concluding I was either slain or taken prisoner.

I found all in great distraction here [*i.e., at Leeds*].

The Council of War was newly risen, where it was resolved to quit the town, and make our retreat to Hull; which was 60 miles off, and many garrisons of the Enemy on the way. Which, in two hours time was done: for we could expect no less than that the Enemy should presently send Horse to prevent it. For they had 50, or 60, Troops within three miles.

But we got well to Selby; where there was a ferry: and, hard by, a garrison at Cawood.

My father, being a mile before, with a few men getting over the ferry; word came to us that he was in danger to be taken. I hastened to him with about 40 Horse: the rest [of the Horse] coming on after in some disorder. He was newly got into the boat.

The Enemy, with 3 Cornets of Horse, entering the town; I was drawn up in the Market Place, just before the street they came down. When they were almost half come into the Market Place, they turned on the right hand.

With part of my Troop, I charged them in the Flanks; [and] so divided them. We had the chase of them down the long street that goes to Brayton.

It happened, at the same time, [that] those men [which] I left behind, were coming up that street: [but] being in disorder, and under [the] discouragements of the misfortunes of many days before, [they] turned about, and gave way; not knowing that we were pursuing them in the rear. [*That is, there were tearing along the Brayton road;* (1) *FAIRFAX's disordered Cavalry; then* (2) *the Royalist Cavalry; followed by* (3) *FAIRFAX with a part of his Troop.*]

At the end of this street, was a narrow lane which led to Cawood. The Enemy strove to pass away there; but [it] being strait [*narrow*], caused a sudden stop: where we were mingled one among another.

Here I received a shot in the wrist of my arm, which made the bridle fall out of my hand: which [wound], being among the nerves and veins, suddenly let out such a quantity of blood as that I was ready to fall from my horse. So taking the reins in the other hand, wherein I had my sword; the Enemy minding nothing so much as how to get away: I drew myself out of the crowd, and came to our men that turned about; which were standing hard by. Seeing me ready to fall from my horse, they laid me on the ground: and [I] now, [being] almost senseless. My Chirurgeon came seasonably, and bound up the wound, [and] so stopped the bleeding.

After a quarter of an hour's rest there, I got on horseback again.

The other part of our Horse also beat the Enemy to Cawood back again, that way they first came to us.

So, through the goodness of GOD, our passage here was made clear. Some went over the ferry, after my father.

Myself, with others, went through the Levels [*of the Fen Country, in North Lincolnshire; and south of the Humber*] to Hull. But it proved a very troublesome and dangerous passage: having oft interruptions from the Enemy; sometimes in our front, sometimes in our rear.

And now I had been at least twenty hours on horseback, after I was shot [at Selby], without any rest or refreshment: and as many hours before. [40 *hours from* 1 *a.m. on the night of 2nd July* 1643, *when* FAIRFAX *decided to cut his way out of Bradford, would make it about* 5 *p.m. of the 3rd July* 1643.]

And, as a further addition to my affliction, my daughter [*MARY, who afterwards married GEORGE VILLIERS, second Duke of BUCKINGHAM, see p.* 399], not above five years old, being carried before her maid, endured all this retreat on horseback: but, Nature not [being] able to hold out any longer, [she] fell into frequent swoonings; and [was], in appearance, ready to expire her last [breath]. And having now passed the Trent [*and therefore come into North Lincolnshire*], and seeing a house not far off, I sent her, with her maid only, thither: with little hopes of seeing her any more alive; but intending, the next day, to send a ship from Hull for her.

So I went on to Barton [*upon Humber: nearly opposite*

Hull]; having sent before to have a ship ready against my coming thither.

Here I lay down a little to rest; if it were possible to find any in a body so full of pain; and [in] a mind so full of anxiety and trouble. Though I must acknowledge it, as the infinite goodness of GOD, methought my spirits were nothing at all discouraged from doing still that which I thought to be my work and duty.

But I had not laid [down] a quarter of an hour before the Enemy came close to the town [of Barton]. I had now not above 100 Horse with me. We went to the ship; where, under the covert of her ordnance, we got all our men and horses aboard.

So passing [the] Humber, we arrived at Hull; our men faint and tired: [and I] myself having lost all, even to my shirt; for my clothes were made unfit to wear, with rents and the blood which was upon them. Considering which, in all humility and reverence, I may say, I was in JOB's condition when he said, "Naked came I out of my mother's womb, and naked shall I return thither. The Lord gave, and the Lord hath taken away. Blessed be the Name of the Lord." [*Job* i. 21.]

But GOD, who is a GOD of Mercy and Consolation, doth not always leave us in distress.

I having sent a ship, presently after I came into the town, for my daughter: she was brought, the next day [4th July 1643], to Hull; pretty well recovered of her long and tedious journey.

And, not many days after, the Earl of NEWCASTLE sent my Wife back again, in his coach, with some Horse to guard her: which generosity gained more than any reputation he could have gotten in detaining a Lady prisoner upon such terms.

And many of our men, which were dispersed in this long retreat, came hither again to us.

Our first business now, was to raise new forces: which, in a short time, were about 1,500 Foot and 700 Horse.

The town [of Hull] being little; I was sent to Beverley with the Horse and 600 Foot.

But my Lord [of] NEWCASTLE, who now looked upon us as inconsiderable, was marched with his whole Army into Lincolnshire: only leaving some few garrisons at York and other few places. He took in Gainsborough and Lincoln; and intended [to take] Boston next, which was the Key of the Associated Countries [*Counties*]. For his Orders, which I have seen, were to go into Essex; and block up London on that side.

But we, having laid a great while [*from 4th July to 26th August* 1643] still, were now strong enough in the Field for those forces that remained in the Country [*Yorkshire*]. So we sent out a good party to make an attempt upon Stamford Bridge, near York. But the Enemy, upon the alarm, fled thither [*i.e. to York*]; which put them all there in such a fear as they sent earnestly to desire him to return, or the Country [*Yorkshire*] would again be lost: for the Lord FAIRFAX had considerable forces.

Upon which, he returned again into Yorkshire; and, not long after, came to besiege Hull.

I, lying then at Beverley in the way of his march, finding that we were not able to maintain such an open place against an Army, desired Orders from my father to retire back to Hull.

But the Committee there (having always more mind of raising money, than to take care of the Soldiers; yet these [Committee] Men had the greatest share in command at this time) would not let any Orders be given for our retreat; and [it were] unfit for us to return without [them].

The Enemy marcheth from York, with his whole Army, towards us. Retreat, we must not. Keep the town, we could not. So to make our retreat more honourable, and useful both; I drew out all the Horse and Dragoons toward the Enemy, and stood, drawn up by a wood side, all that night.

The next morning [2nd September 1643], by day[time], our Scouts, and theirs, fired on one another. They march[ed] on with their whole body; which was about 4,000 Horse and 12,000 Foot.

We stood till they were come very near [to] us. I then drew off (having given directions before for the Foot to march away toward Hull), thinking to make good the retreat with the Horse.

The Enemy, with a good party, were upon our rear. The lane being but narrow, we made good shift with them till we got into Beverley, and shut the gates: which we had scarce time to do; they being so close upon us. But, in this business, we lost Major LAYTON, and not above 2 more.

The Enemy, not knowing what forces we had in the town, stayed till the rest of the Army came up; which was about a mile behind. This gave our Foot some advantage in their retreat: it being 5 miles to Hull, on narrow banks [and] so fittest for our Foot. I sent the Horse by Cottingham, an opener road; who got well thither.

But they [*the Royalists*] overtook the Foot: which, notwithstanding, made good their retreat till we got to a little bridge, 2 miles from Hull; where we made a stand.

The Enemy following close, our men here gave them a good volley of shot; which made them draw back, and advance no further. So, leaving a small Guard at the bridge, we got safe to Hull.

Thus not only for want of military skill in the Gentlemen of the Committee; but, to say no more, for want of good nature: we were exposed to this trouble and danger.

My Lord of NEWCASTLE now lay siege to Hull, but at a great distance. The sluices being open, drowned the land two miles about the town: yet upon a bank, which was the highway, he approached so near as to shoot cannon shot at random into the town; which were, for the most part, fiery bullets. But the diligence and care of the Governor (who caused every inhabitant to watch his own house; and wheresoever they saw these bullets fall, to be ready to quench them) prevented the danger.

Our Horse was now useless: and many [horses] died every day; having nothing but salt water about the town.

I was therefore sent with the Horse, over [the Humber] into Lincolnshire, to join with [EDWARD MONTAGU,] the Earl of MANCHESTER's forces; which were then commanded by Major General [OLIVER] CROMWELL: who received us at our landing, with his troops.

Sir JOHN HENDERSON lay within three or four miles of this place with 5,000 men, to prevent our conjunction: but durst not attempt [it].

He marched three or four days near to us: but, for want of good intelligence, we did not know so much. For I altogether trusted to the care of our new friends, being a stranger in those parts: till one morning [9th October 1643] he set upon our Guards at Horncastle; which, being but newly raised in that Country [*Lincolnshire*], fled towards Lincoln, without giving any alarm to our Quarters, who lay dispersed and secure.

But Sir JOHN HENDERSON, marching slowly with his Army, gave the alarm to some of our Quarters; which was soon taken by the rest: but, with some disorder, before we could get into a considerable body. My Lord WILLOUGHBY with his Horse, and my Dragoons commanded by Colonel MORGAN, brought up the Rear. After some skirmishes, we lodged that night all in the Field.

And, next day [10th October 1643], the Earl of MANCHESTER came to us with his Foot.

The day following [11th October 1643], we advanced again towards the Enemy; and choosing a convenient ground to fight on, we drew up the Army there. The Enemy did so on the side of another hill close by, having a little plain betwixt us.

Lieutenant General [OLIVER] CROMWELL had the Van [of Horse]; I, the Reserve [of Horse]: my Lord [of] MANCHESTER all the Foot. After we had faced one another a little while; the Forlorn Hopes [*Advanced Guards*] began the fight. Presently the [Main] Bodies met in the plain: where the fight was hot for half an hour; but then we forced them to a rout. Above 200 killed, and 2000 taken prisoners. This was the issue of Horncastle Fight, or, as some call it, Winceby Fight.

At the same instant, we heard great shooting of ordnance towards Hull: which was a sally my father made [out of the town] upon my Lord of NEWCASTLE's Trenches; who drew out most part of his Army to relieve them. But our men charged so resolutely as they possessed themselves of the cannon; and so pursued their advantage as [they] put the enemy into a total rout. Upon which, he raised the Siege, and returned again to York.

These two defeats together, the one falling heavy on the Horse, the other on the Foot, kept the Enemy all that Winter [of 1643-1644] from attempting anything.

And we, after the taking of Lincoln, settled ourselves in Winter Quarters.

But, in the coldest season of it, I was ordered by the Parliament to go and raise the Siege of Nantwich; which the Lord BYRON, with the Irish Army, had reduced to great extremity.

I was the most unfit of all the forces; being ever the worst paid; my men sickly, and almost naked for want of clothes. I desired the Parliament that they would be pleased to supply these wants: not to excuse myself, as some who had no will to stir, though well enough accommodated with all these; and a business of so much importance. But their answer was a positive direction to march; for it would admit of no delay: which indeed was as grievous to me as that injunction was to the Israelites, to make bricks without straw.

But, foreseeing I should have such a return to my desires, I had, seeing the necessity of the business, upon my own credit got so much cloth as clothed 1,500 men: and [they were] all ready to march when these Orders came to me.

So, the 29th of December [1643], we got forwards from Falkingham in Lincolnshire to Nantwich, with 1,800 Horse and 500 Dragoons; and a Power to call the Regiments [of Foot] of Lancashire and Cheshire to make up the body of the Army. But it was not a little trouble to me, when I came to Manchester, to find some of them 30, some 40 miles distant: besides the disaffection of some of their Colonels, who went as their peculiar [*individual*] safety or Interest swayed them. But, finding more readiness in the inferior Officers and common soldiers, I got up, in a few days, near[ly] 3,000 Foot.

With this Army, we marched [from Manchester, on the

21st January 1644] to Nantwich; which was at the point of surrendering.

When we were within two days' march, I had intelligence that the Lord BYRON had drawn off his Siege; and intended to meet us in the Field. I put my men into the order I intended to fight [in]; and so continued my march till we came within 3 miles of the town.

There, was a Pass kept with about 250 men. I sent Colonel MORGAN, with his Dragoons, to beat them off: in which, his brother, who was his Lieutenant, was slain. The Major who commanded the other party, with some others, were taken prisoners.

We marched on till we came within cannon shot of their Works, where half of their Army was drawn up. The river [Weaver], which runs through the town, being raised with the melting of the snow, hindered, as we were informed, those that lay on the other side of the town from joining with them.

We called a Council [of War, on 25th January 1644] wherein it was debated, Whether we should attempt those in their Works [*Entrenchments*], being divided from the rest of the Army: or march into the town and relieve them; and, by increase of more force be better able, the next day [26th January 1644] to encounter them.

The latter was resolved on. So, making a way with [the] Pioneers through the hedges, we marched to[wards] the town.

But, after we had gone a little way, word came that the Enemy were in the Rear. So, facing about two Regiments [of Foot] and my own Regiment of Horse, commanded by Major ROUSBY, we relieving those that were already engaged. And so the fight began on all sides. These that fell on our Rear were those that lay [on] the other side of the town; which had passed the river [Weaver]. Those that were drawn up under their Works [about Acton Church], fell upon our Van, which was marching to the town. Thus was the battle divided; there being a quarter of a mile betwixt us.

In the division first engaged, our Foot, at the beginning, gave a little ground: but our Horse recovered this, by beating the Enemy's Horse out of the lanes that flanked our

Foot; which did so encourage our men as they gained now of the Enemy, so as they made them retire from hedge to hedge till, at length, they were forced to fly to their Works [*Entrenchments*]. But their Horse retreated in better order towards Chester, without much loss.

Our other Wing [*the Van*], being assisted from the town, who sallied out with 700 or 800 Musketeers, beat the Enemy also back into the same Works [at Acton Church]; which we presently surrounded. [" *Where,*" *as Sir T.* FAIRFAX *said in his despatch,* " *they were caught as in a trap.*"]

But, being in great disorder and confusion, [they] sooner yielded themselves prisoners; with all their Chief Officers, arms, Colours, and ammunition.

Thus, by the mercy of GOD, was this victory obtained: being yet the more signal in that we were not to deal with young soldiers, but with men of great experience; and an Army which had ever been victorious.

After this, we took in several garrisons in Cheshire: Lathom [House] only in Lancashire held out; which was besieged by the forces of that Country [*County*], but afterwards [the siege was] raised by Prince RUPERT.

Having spent three or four months in this Expedition; my father commanded me back into Yorkshire, that by the conjunction of forces he might be the more able to take the Field.

We met about Ferrybridge [in April 1644]: he being come out of Hull thither, with intention to fall upon the Enemy's garrison at Selby.

And here I received another Command from the Parliament, to march immediately with my Horse and Dragoons, into Northumberland, to join with the Scots Army. The Earl of NEWCASTLE, who was then at Durham, being much stronger in Horse than they; for want of which they could not advance no further. But it being resolved, within a day or two to storm Selby; I stayed till that business was over: which proved as effectual for the relief of the Scots Army.

The Governor of York lay in the town with 2,000 men. We drew Horse and Foot close to it. Sir JOHN MELDRUM led on the Foot; which had their General Posts appointed, where they should storm: I, with the Horse, ready to second them.

The Enemy within defended themselves [on the 11th April 1644] stoutly a good while. Our men at length beat them from the Line; but could not advance farther because of the Horse within.

I getting a Barricado open, which let us in betwixt the houses and the river. Here we had an encounter with their Horse. [After one charge, they fled over a Bridge of Boats to York.]

Other Horse came up, and charged us again, where my horse was overthrown; [I] being single [*alone*] a little before my men: who presently relieved me, and forced the Enemy back; who retreated also to York. In this charge, we took Colonel [Lord] BELLASIS, Governor of York.

By this, the Foot had entered the town; and also took many prisoners.

This good success put them into great distraction and fears at York: who speedily sent to the Earl of NEWCASTLE, to haste back thither; believing we would presently attempt them. This news suddenly called him back, leaving the Scots: who, with cold and oft alarms, were reduced to great extremity; but now advanced without delay after him.

The Earl of NEWCASTLE gets into York [on 19th April 1644].

The Scots joined their forces with my father's at Wetherby: altogether making 16,000 Foot and 4,000 Horse. They marched on to York [, from Tadcaster, on 19th April 1644].

But for this work, it was thought fit to have more men; the town [of York] being large in compass, and strongly manned. Therefore the Earl of CRAWFORD, [Lord] LINDSAY and myself were sent to the Earl of MANCHESTER, to desire him to join with us in the Siege: which he willingly consented to, bringing an addition of 6,000 Foot and 3,000 Horse [on 2nd June 1644].

So now the Army had three Generals, [ALEXANDER] LESLIE [, Earl of LEVEN], MANCHESTER, and FAIRFAX; who lay apart in three Quarters before the town. But the north side still remained open to the town.

Some time was spent here without any considerable action till, in my Lord of MANCHESTER's Quarters, approaches were made to St Mary's Tower; and soon came to mine it. Which Colonel [LAURENCE] CRAWFORD, a Scotsman, who commanded that Quarter, (ambitious to have the honour alone of springing the mine [on 16th June 1644] undertook, without acquainting of the other two Generals with it, for their advice and concurrence): which proved very prejudicial. For, having engaged his party against the whole strength of the town, without more force to second him, he was repulsed with the loss of 300 men. For which, he had been surely called to account; but that he escaped the better by reason of this triumviral goverment.

So after, Prince RUPERT came to relieve the town. We raised the siege [*which had lasted from Monday the 3rd June to Monday the 1st July* 1644] and Hessa[y] Moor [*a portion of Marston Moor, 7 miles from York*] being appointed the rendezvous, the whole Army drew thither.

About a mile from whence, Prince RUPERT lay; the river Ouse being only betwixt us: which he, that night, passed over at Poppleton. And, the next day, [he] drew his Army into the same Moor we were on: who, being now joined with the Earl of NEWCASTLE's forces, made about 23,000 or 24,000 men. But we, something more.

We were divided in our opinions what do do. The English were for fighting them; the Scots, for retreating, to gain (as they alleged) both time and place of more advantage. This latter being resolved on; we marched away [on Tuesday 2nd July 1644] to[wards] Tadcaster; which made the Enemy to advance the faster.

Lieutenant General CROMWELL, Major General [DAVID] LESLIE, and myself, being appointed to bring up the Rear; we sent word to the Generals, of the necessity of making a stand. For else, the Enemy, having the advantage, might put us in some disorder; but, by the advantage of the ground we were on, we hoped to make it good till they came back to us.

[Which they did.]

The place was Marston Fields, which afterwards gave the name to this battle.

Here we drew up our Army. The Enemy was drawn up in Battalia on the Moor a little below us.

The day being, for the most part, spent in preparation we now began to descend toward them.

Lieutenant General CROMWELL commanded the Left Wing of Horse; and [was] seconded by Major General [DAVID] LESLIE. I had the Right Wing [of Horse], with some Scotch Horse and Lances for my Reserves. The three Generals were with the Foot.

Our Left Wing charged first the Enemy's Right Wing; which was performed for a while with much resolution on both sides; but the Enemy, at length, was put to the worst.

Our Right Wing had not, all, so good success, by reason of the whins [*furze*] and ditches which we were to pass over before we could get to the Enemy, which put us into great disorder: notwithstanding, I drew up a body of 400 Horse. But because the intervals of [their] Horse, in this Wing only, were lined with Musketeers; which did us much hurt with their shot: I was necessitated to charge them. We were a long time engaged one with another; but at last we routed that part of their Wing. We charged, and pursued them a good way towards York.

[I] myself only [*alone*] returned presently, to get to the men I left behind me. But that part of the Enemy which stood [opposite to them], perceiving the disorder they were in, had charged and routed them, before I could get to them. So that the good success we had at first was eclipsed much by this bad conclusion.

But our other Wing, and most of the Foot, went on prosperously till they had cleared the Field.

But I must not forget to remember with thankfulness GOD's goodness to me this day. For having charged through the Enemy, and my [400] men going after [in] the pursuit; returning back [alone] to go to my other troops, I was gotten in among the Enemy, which stood up and down the Field in several bodies of Horse. So, taking the Signal [*a white handkerchief, or a piece of paper*] out of my hat, I passed through, for one of their own Commanders; and so got to my Lord of MANCHESTER's Horse in the other Wing; only with a cut in my cheek which was given me in the first charge, and a shot [which] my horse received.

In which [first] charge also, many of my Officers and soldiers were hurt and slain. The Captain of my own Troop was shot in the arm. My Cornet had both his hands cut, that rendered him ever after unserviceable. Captain MICKELTHWAITE, an honest stout man, was slain. And [there was] scarce[ly] any Officer which was in this charge, which did not receive a hurt.

But Colonel LAMBERT (who should have seconded me; but could not get up to me) charged in another place. Major FAIRFAX, who was Major to his Regiment, had, at least, thirty wounds: of which he died; after he was abroad [*out of doors*] again, and [had] good hopes of his recovery.

But that which nearest of all concerned me, was the loss of my brother [CHARLES FAIRFAX]: who, being deserted of his men, was sore wounded; of which, in three or four days after, he died.

So as, in this charge, as many were hurt and killed as in the whole [Parliamentary] Army besides.*

* A modest Refutation of an Error published in print by Master [THOMAS] FULLER, in his book of *Worthies* [*of England*]. Title, [*Yorkshire*] *Battles*, pagina 225 [, Ed. 1662], in these words, viz.

GORING, [at the fight of Marston Moor,] *so valiantly charged the Right Wing of the Enemy, that they fairly forsook the Field.*

On this, Lord FAIRFAX made the following marginal Note in his copy:

I envy none the honour they deservedly got in this battle; nor am I ambitiously desirous of a branch of their laurel. But I see no reason to be excluded [from] the Lists: in which I underwent equal hazards with any others that day.

But [it] being my lot to be cast upon many disadvantages, having command of the Right Wing, with much difficulty I could get but

Of the Enemy's part, there were above 4,000 slain, and many taken prisoners.

Prince RUPERT returned into the South. The Earl of NEWCASTLE went beyond the seas [on 5th July 1644], with many of his Officers. York presently surrendered [on the 15th July 1644], and the North now was wholly reduced by the Parliament's forces, except some garrisons.

Soon after this, I went to Helmsley, to take in the Castle there: but received a dangerous shot in my shoulder; and was brought back to York. All, for some time, being doubtful of my recovery.

Yet, at the same time, the Parliament voted me to command in the South.

But my intention being only to keep in mind what I had been present in, during this Northern War; I shall put an end to this Discourse, where it pleased GOD to determine my service there.

Yet thus, with some smart from his rod, to let me see I was not mindful enough of returning my humble thanks and acknowledgments for the deliverances and mercies I received; and for which, alas, I am not yet capable enough

5 Troops in order: with which I charged the Enemy's Left Wing; when the business was hotly disputed a long time, at [the] sword's point. We broke through; and had the chase of many of them.

But, indeed, the rest of the Horse, [that] I could not draw up to charge with me, were soon routed with that part of the Enemy we left behind.

But to shew that some did their parts: having routed some of the Enemy, and taken GORING's Major General prisoner; few of us came off without dangerous wounds; and many [of them] were mortal.

Which shews that the Right Wing did not wholly leave the Field; as the Author of that book relates.

F. GROSE, *Antiquarian Repertory*, 2nd Ed., III., p. 31, 1808, 4.

to praise him as I ought. [I] that may say by experience, "Who is a GOD like unto our GOD?" [*Ps.* lxxi. 19.] Therefore, "Not unto us, O Lord; not unto us, but unto Thy Name; give we the praise!" [*Ps.* cxv.]

But as for myself, and what I have done, I may say with SOLOMON, "I looked on all the works that my hands have wrought; and on the labour that I had laboured to do: and, behold, all was Vanity and Vexation of Spirit. For there is no remembrance of the Wise more than of the Fool for ever; seeing that which now is, in the days to come shall be forgotten." *Eccles.* ii. 16.

FINIS.

GEORGE VILLIERS, second Duke of BUCKINGHAM.

An Epitaph on *THOMAS, third Lord FAIRFAX.*

[*A Third Collection of . . . . Poems, Satires, Songs, &c. against Popery and Tyranny.* London, 1689. 4to.

[Lord FAIRFAX, the great General on the side of the Parliament, died in 1671; and his son-in-law, the Writer of this *Epitaph*, in 1688. VILLIERS never wrote a nobler Poem, irregular though it be.]

Under this stone does lie
One born for Victory,

I.

FAIRFAX the valiant; and the only He
Whoe'er, for that alone a Conqueror would be.
Both sexes' virtues were in him combined:
He had the fierceness of the manliest mind,
And eke the meekness too of womankind.
He never knew what Envy was, or Hate.
His soul was filled with Worth and Honesty;
And with another thing, quite out of date,
Called Modesty.

2.

He ne'er seemed impudent but in the Field: a place
Where Impudence itself dares seldom show her face.
Had any stranger spied him in the room
With some of those whom he had overcome,
And had not heard their talk; but only seen
Their gestures and their mien:
They would have sworn he had, the vanquished been.
For as they bragged, and dreadful would appear;
While they, their own ill lucks in war repeated:
His modesty still made him blush to hear
How often he had them defeated.

3.

Through his whole life, the Part he bore
Was wonderful and great:
And yet it so appeared in nothing more
Than in his private last retreat.
For it 's a stranger thing to find
One man of such a glorious mind,
As can dismiss the Power he has got;
Than millions of the Polls and Braves
(Those despicable fools and knaves),
Who such a pother make,
Through dulness and mistake,
In seeking after Power: but get it not.

4.

When all the nation he had won,
And with expense of blood had bought;
  Store great enough, he thought,
  Of fame and of renown:
  He then his arms laid down
  With full as little pride
As if he had been of his Enemies' side;
Or one of them could do that were undone.
  He neither wealth, nor Places sought.
  For others, not himself, he fought.
    He was content to know
    (For he had found it so)
That when he pleased, to conquer he was able;
And left the spoil and plunder to the rabble.
    He might have been a King:
    But that he understood
  How much it is a meaner thing
To be unjustly Great, than honourably Good.

5.

This from the World, did admiration draw;
And from his friends, both love and awe:
Remembering what in fight he did before.
    And his foes loved him too,
    As they were bound to do,

Because he was resolved to fight no more.
So blessed of all, he died. But far more blessed were we,
If we were sure to live till we could see
A Man as great in War, in Peace as just, as he.

A true and just
RELATION
of
Major-General Sir THOMAS MORGAN'S
PROGRESS
in
FRANCE and FLANDERS
with the
Six Thousand English,
in the years 1657 and 1658,
at the taking of
DUNKIRK,
and
other important places.

As it was delivered by the General himself.

LONDON:
Printed for J. NUTT, near Stationers' Hall,
1699.

ADVERTISEMENT.

SIR THOMAS MORGAN drew up the following Relation, at a friend's desire, who was unwilling that posterity should want an authentic account of the actions of the Six Thousand English, whom CROMWELL sent to assist the French against the Spaniards; and thought the Right they did their country, by their behaviour, might make some amends for the Occasion of their being in that service.

It had been printed in the last reign [*i.e.*, of JAMES II.], *if the Authority of it had not interposed, because there was not so much said of some who were* then *in the Spanish army, as they expected: and is published now, to let the world see that more was owing to our country than either Monsieur BUSSY RABUTIN* [ROGER DE RABUTIN, Count DE BUSSY] (Part II. *p.* 135), *or* [*EDMUND*] *LUDLOW* (Part II. *p.* 561), *in their* Memoirs *do allow. The former by his manner of expression seems contented with an opportunity to lessen their merit; and being in the right wing of the French, while this passed in the left, comes under the just reflection he himself makes* (Part II. *p.* 139) *a little after, upon the Describers of Fights, who are particular in what they did not see: and whether the latter was misinformed, or swayed by his prejudice* (Part II. *p.* 496) *to those that were engaged to support the new erected Tyranny, is left to the reader to judge.*

It may not be improper to add, that these papers came to the Publisher's hands, from the gentlemen at whose request they were written: and to whom Sir THOMAS MORGAN confirmed every paragraph of them, as they were read over, at the time he delivered them, to him; which, besides the unaffected plainness of the style, may be urged for the credit of the narrative, since Sir THOMAS was entitled to so much true reputation, that he had no need to grasp at any that was false.

January 24, 1698 [*i.e.*, 1699].

A true and just

RELATION

of

Major-General Sir THOMAS MORGAN'S

PROGRESS

in

FRANCE and FLANDERS

with the

Six Thousand English,

in the years 1657 and 1658.

THE French King, and his Eminence the Cardinal MAZARIN came to view the Six Thousand English, near Charleroi; and ordered Major-General MORGAN with the said Six Thousand English, to march and make conjunction with Marshal TURENNE's army: who, soon after the conjunction, beleaguered a town called St. Venant, on the borders of Flanders.

Marshal TURENNE having invested the town on the east side, and Major-General MORGAN with his Six Thousand English and a Brigade of French Horse on the west; the army encamped betwixt Marshal TURENNE's approaches [*lines or parallels*] and Major-General MORGAN's. And being to relieve Count SCHOMBERG out of the approaches of the west side of the town, Major-General MORGAN marched into the approaches, with 800 English. The English, at that time, being strangers in approaches, Major-General MORGAN instructed the Officers and soldiers to take their place, by fifties; that thereby they might relieve the Point, to carry on the approaches, every hour.

In the meantime, whilst we besieged the town; the enemy had beleaguered a town called Ardres [*p.* 183], within five miles of Calais.

In the evening, Count SCHOMBERG, with six Noblemen, came to the Point, to see how Major-General MORGAN carried on his approaches; but there happened a little confusion, by the soldiers intermingling themselves in the approaches, so as there was never an entire fifty, to be called to the Point.

Count SCHOMBERG and his Noblemen taking notice thereof; Major-General MORGAN was much troubled, leaped upon the Point, and called out fifty to "take up the spades, pickaxes, and fascines, and follow him." But so it happened, that all [*i.e., the* 800] in the approaches leapt out after him; the enemy, in the meantime, firing as fast as they could.

Major-General MORGAN, conceiving his loss in bringing them to their approaches would be greater than in carrying them forward, passed over a channel of water on which there was a bridge and a turnpike, and the soldiers crying out, "Fall on! Fall on!" he fell upon the Counterscarp, beat the enemy from it and three Redoubts: which caused them to capitulate; and, the next morning, to surrender the town, and receive a French garrison. So as the sudden reduction, thereof, gave Marshal TURENNE an opportunity, afterwards, to march and relieve Ardres.

The next place, Marshal TURENNE besieged, was Mardyke; taken, in twice eight and forty hours, by the English and French. After the taking thereof, Major-General MORGAN was settled there; by the order of the French King and OLIVER, with 2,000 English and 1,000 French, in order to the beleaguering Dunkirk, the next Spring. The rest of the English were quartered at Borborch [*Bourbough*].

For the space of four months, there was hardly a week wherein Major-General MORGAN had not two or three alarms by the Spanish army. He answered to them all; and never went out of his clothes all the winter, except to change his shirt.

The next Spring [1658], Marshal TURENNE beleaguered Dunkirk on the Newport side; and Major-General MORGAN on the Mardyke side, with his Six Thousand English, and a Brigade of French Horse. He made a bridge over the canal betwixt that and Bergen, that there might be communication betwixt Marshal TURENNE's camp and his.

When Dunkirk was close invested, Marshal TURENNE sent a summons to the Governor, the Marquis DE LEIDA, a great Captain, and brave defender of a siege: but the summons being answered with defiance, Marshal TURENNE immediately broke ground; and carried on the approaches on his side, whilst the English did the same, on theirs. And it is observable, the English had two miles to march every day, upon relieving their approaches.

In this manner the approaches were carried on, both by the French and English, for the space of twelve nights: when the Marshal TURENNE had intelligence that the Prince DE CONDÉ, the Duke of YORK [*afterwards, JAMES II.*], Don JOHN of AUSTRIA, and the Prince DE LIGNY were at the head of 30,000 horse and foot, with resolution to relieve Dunkirk.

Immediately upon this intelligence, Marshal TURENNE and several Noblemen of France went to the King and Cardinal, at Mardyke; acquainted his Eminence therewith, and desired His Majesty and his Eminence the Cardinal to withdraw their persons into safety, and leave their orders.

His Majesty answered that "He knew no better place of safety than at the head of his army;" but said, "It was convenient the Cardinal should withdraw to Calais."

Then Marshal TURENNE and the Noblemen made answer, "They could not be satisfied, except His Majesty withdrew himself into safety." Which was assented to; and the King and Cardinal marching to Calais, left open orders with Marshal TURENNE that "If the enemy came on; to give battle or raise the siege, as he should be advised by a Council of War."

The enemy came on to Bruges, and then Marshal TURENNE thought it high time to call a Council of War; which consisted of eight Noblemen, eight Lieutenant-Generals, and six *Mareschaux de Camp*: but never sent to [the English] Ambassador LOCKHART, or Major-General MORGAN.

The whole sense of the Council of War was that "It was great danger to the Crown of France to hazard a battle in that strait [*broken*] country, full of canals and ditches of water." And several reasons being shown to that purpose, it ran through the Council of War, "to raise the siege, if the enemy came on."

Within half an hour after the Council of War was risen, Major-General MORGAN had the result of it in his camp; and went immediately to Ambassador LOCKHART to know if he had heard anything of it?

He said, "He had heard nothing of it"; and complained that "he was much afflicted with the stone, gravel, and some other impediments."

Major-General MORGAN asked him "to go with him, the next morning, to the headquarters."

He said, "He would, if he were able."

Next morning, Marshal TURENNE sent a Nobleman to Ambassador LOCKHART, and Major-General MORGAN; to desire them to come to a second Council of War.

Immediately, therefore, Ambassador LOCKHART and Major-General MORGAN went with the Nobleman to Marshal TURENNE's camp: and, by that time they came there, the Council of War was ready to sit down in Marshal TURENNE's tent.

Marshal TURENNE satisfied the Council of War that "He had forgot to send for Ambassador LOCKHART and Major-General MORGAN to the first Council of War; and therefore thought fit to call this, that they might be satisfied!" and then put the question, "Whether if the enemy came on, he should make good the siege on the Newport side, and give them battle: or raise the siege?" and required they should give their reasons for either.

The *Mareschaux de Camp* ran away with it [*i.e., the idea*], clearly to raise the siege; alleging what danger it was to the Crown of France to hazard a battle, within so strait a country, full of canals and ditches of water: further alleging that if the enemy came upon the Bank, they would cut between Marshal TURENNE's and Major-General MORGAN's camps, and prevent their conjunction.

Two of the Lieutenant-Generals ran along with the *Mareschaux de Camp*; and shewed the same reasons.

But Major-General MORGAN (finding that it was high time to speak, and that otherwise it would go round the board [*table*]) rose up, and desired, though out of course, that he might declare his mind in opposition to what the *Mareschaux de Camp* and the two Lieutenant-Generals had declared.

Marshal TURENNE told him, "He should have freedom to speak his thoughts."

Then Major-General MORGAN spoke, and said that "The reasons the *Mareschaux de Camp* and the two Lieutenant-Generals had given for raising the siege, were no reasons: for the straitness of the country was as good for the French and English as for the enemy." And whereas they had alleged that "If the enemy came on the Bank between Furnes and Dunkirk, they would cut between Marshal TURENNE's and Major-General MORGAN's camps." Major-General MORGAN replied, "It was impossible, for they could not march upon the Bank above eight a breast; and that Marshal TURENNE's artillery and small shot would cut them off at pleasure." He added, "That was not the way, the enemy could relieve Dunkirk! but that they would make a bridge of boats over the channel in an hour and a half; and cross their army on to the sands of Dunkirk, to offer Marshal TURENNE battle." Further, Major-General MORGAN did allege, "What a dishonour it would be to the Crown of France! to have summoned the city of Dunkirk, and broke ground before it, and run away! And he desired the Council of War would consider that, if they raised the siege, the alliance with England would be broken the same hour."

Marshal TURENNE answered that, "If he thought the enemy would offer that fair game; he would maintain the siege on the Newport side; and Major-General MORGAN should march, and make conjunction with the French army, and leave the Mardyke side open."

Upon Marshal TURENNE's reply, Major-General MORGAN did rise from the board, and, upon his knees, begged a battle; and said that "he would venture the Six Thousand English, every soul!"

Upon which, Marshal TURENNE consulted the Noblemen that sat next to him; and it was desired that Major-General MORGAN might walk a turn or two without the tent; and he should be called immediately.

After he had walked two turns, he was called in. As soon as he came in, Marshal TURENNE said that "He had considered his reasons; and that himself and the Council of

War resolved to give battle to the enemy, if they came on; and to maintain the siege on the Newport side: and that Major-General MORGAN was to make conjunction with the French army."

Major-General MORGAN then said, "That, with GOD's assistance, we should be able to deal with them!"

The very next day, at four in the afternoon, the Spanish army had made a bridge of boats, crossed their army on the sands of Dunkirk, and drew up into *battalia* [line of battle], within two miles of Marshal TURENNE's lines; before he knew anything of them.

Immediately, all the French horse drew out to face the enemy at a mile's distance; and Marshal TURENNE sent immediate orders to Major-General MORGAN to march into his camp, with the Six Thousand English and the French Brigade of Horse. Which was done accordingly.

The next day, about eight o'clock, Marshal TURENNE gave orders to break avenues on both the lines, that the army might march out in *battalia*.

Major-General MORGAN set his soldiers to break avenues, for their marching out in *battalia* likewise. Several Officers being with him, as he was looking on his soldiers at work; Ambassador LOCKHART comes up, with a white cap on his head, and said to Major-General MORGAN, "You see what condition I am in! I am not able to give you any assistance this day! You are the older soldier, and the greatest part of the work of this day must lie upon your soldiers!" Upon which, the Officers smiled. So he bade "GOD be with us!" and went away with the Lieutenant-General of the Horse, that was upon our left wing. From which time, we never saw him till we were in pursuit of the enemy.

When the avenues were cleared, both the French and English armies marched out of the lines towards the enemy.

We were forced to march up in four lines [? *columns*] (for we had not room enough to wing [? *spread out into line*] for the canal between Furnes and Dunkirk, and the sea) till we had marched above half a mile.

Then we came to a halt on rising hills of sand; and having more room took in [? *spread out*] two of our lines.

Major-General MORGAN seeing the enemy plain, in *battalia*,

said, before the head of the army, "See, yonder are the gentlemen you have to trade withal!"

Upon which, the whole Brigade of English gave a shout of rejoicing, that made a roaring echo betwixt the sea and the canal.

Thereupon, the Marshal TURENNE came up, with above a hundred Noblemen, to know what was the matter, and the reason of that great shout?

Major-General MORGAN told him, "It was a usual custom of the redcoats, when they saw the enemy, to rejoice."

Marshal TURENNE answered, "They were men of brave resolution and courage."

After which, Marshal TURENNE returning to the head of his army; we put on to our march again.

At the second halt, the whole Brigade of English gave a shout, and cast up their caps into the air; saying, "They would have better hats before night!"

Marshal TURENNE, upon that shout, came up again, with several Noblemen and Officers of the army, admiring the resolution of the English, at which time, we were within three-quarters of a mile of the enemy in *battalia*.

Marshal TURENNE desired Major-General MORGAN that, at the next halt, he would keep even front with the French; for says he, "I do intend to halt at some distance, that we may see how the enemy is drawn up; and take our advantage accordingly."

Major-General MORGAN demanded of his Excellency, "Whether he would shock the whole army at one dash; or try one wing first?"

Marshal TURENNE's reply was, "That as to that question, he could not resolve him yet, till he came nearer the enemy."

Major-General MORGAN desired the Marshal, "not to let him languish for orders!" saying that "oftentimes opportunities are often lost, for want of orders in due time."

Marshal TURENNE said, "He would either come himself, and give orders; or send a Lieutenant-General."

And so Marshal TURENNE parted, and went to the head of his army.

In the meantime, Major-General MORGAN gave orders to the Colonels and Leading Officers [*i.e., Captains and Lieu-*

tenants], to have a special care that, when the French came to a halt, they kept even front with them: and further told them, that, "if they could not observe the French, they should take notice when he lifted up his hat," for he marched still above three score [yards] before the centre of the Bodies.

But when the French came to halt, it so happened that the English pressed upon their Leading Officers, so that they came up under the shot of the enemy; but when they saw that Major-General MORGAN was in a passion, they put themselves to a stand. Major-General MORGAN could soon have remedied their forwardness, but he was resolved that he would not lose one foot of ground he had advanced; but would hold it as long as he could.

We were so near the enemy, the soldiers fell into great friendship. One asking, "Is such an Officer in your army?" Another, "Is such a soldier in yours?" And this passed on both sides.

Major-General MORGAN endured this friendship for a little while; and then came up to the centre of the Bodies, and demanded, "How long that friendship would continue?" and told them further that "for anything they knew, they would be cutting one another's throats within a minute of an hour!"

The whole Brigade answered, "Their friendship should continue no longer than he pleased!"

Then Major-General MORGAN bade them tell the enemy, "No more friendship! Prepare your buff coats and scarfs! for we will be with you, sooner than you expect us!"

Immediately after the friendship was broke, the enemy poured a volley of shot into one of our battalions, wounded three or four and one dropped.

The Major-General immediately sent the Adjutant-General to Marshal TURENNE, for orders; "Whether he should charge the enemy's right wing, or whether Marshal TURENNE would engage the enemy's left wing?" and advised the Adjutant-General not to stay, but to acquaint Marshal TURENNE that we were under the enemy's shot, and had received some prejudice already.

But there was no return of the Adjutant-General, nor orders.

By-and-by, the enemy poured in another volley of shot into another of our battalions; and wounded two or three.

Major-General MORGAN (observing the enemy mending faults, and opening the intervals of the Foot to bring the Horse in, which would have made our work more difficult) called all the Colonels and Officers of the Field [*Field Officers, as distinguished from Leading Officers*], together before the centre of the Bodies, and told them, "He had sent the Adjutant-General for orders; but when he saw there was no hope of orders, he told them, if they would concur with him, he would immediately charge the enemy's right wing."

Their answer was, "They were ready, whenever he gave orders."

He told them, "He would try the right wing with the Blue Regiment, and the 400 Firelocks which were in the intervals of the French Horse;" and wished all the Field Officers to be ready at their several posts.

Major-General MORGAN gave orders that "The other five Regiments should not move from their ground; except they saw the Blue Regiment, the White, and the 400 Firelocks shock the enemy's right wing right off the ground:" and further shewed the several Colonels, what Colours they were to charge; and told them moreover that, "If he were not knocked on the head, he would come to them."

In like manner, as fast as he could, he admonished the whole Brigade; and told them, "They were to look in the face of an enemy who had violated and endeavoured to take away their reputation; and that they had no other way but to fight it out to the last man! or to be killed, taken prisoner, or drowned!" And further, that "The honour of England did depend much upon their gallantry and resolution that day!"

The enemy's wing was posted on a sandy hill, and had cast the sand breast-high before them.

Then Major-General MORGAN did order the Blue Regiment and the 400 Firelocks to advance to the Charge. In the meantime, knowing the enemy would all bend upon them that did advance; he removed the White Regiment more to the right, that it might be in the flank of them by that time, the Blue Regiment was got within push of pike.

His Royal Highness, the Duke of YORK, with a select party of Horse, had got into the Blue Regiment, by that time the White came in, and exposed his person to great danger. But we knew nobody at that time.

Immediately, the enemy were clear shocked off their ground; and the English Colours flying over their heads, the strongest Officers and soldiers clubbing them down.

Major-General MORGAN, when he saw his opportunity, stepped to the other five Regiments, which were within six score [yards] of him; and ordered them to advance and charge immediately.

But when they came within ten pikes' length, the enemy perceiving they were not able to endure our charge, shaked their hats, held up their handkerchiefs, and called for "Quarter!"

But the Redcoats cried aloud, "They had not leisure for Quarter!"

Whereupon the enemy faced about, and would not endure our charge; but fell to run: having the English Colours over their heads, and our strongest soldiers and Officers clubbing them down. So that the Six Thousand English carried ten or twelve thousand Horse and Foot before them.

The French army was about musket shot in the rear of us, where they came [*had come*] to a halt; and never moved off their ground.

The rest of the Spanish army, seeing the right wing carried away, and the English Colours flying over their heads, wheeled about in as good order as they could. So that we had the whole Spanish army before us! and Major-General MORGAN called out to the Colonels, "To the right! as much as you can!" that so, we might have all the enemy's army under the English Colours.

The Six Thousand English carried all the Spanish army [before it] as far as from Westminster Abbey to [St.] Paul's Churchyard, before ever a Frenchman came in, on either wing of us. But then, at last, we could perceive the French Horse come powdering [*scattered*] on each wing with much gallantry: but they never struck one stroke; and only carried prisoners back to the camp.

Neither, did we ever see the Ambassador LOCKHART till we were in pursuit of the enemy; and then, we could see him amongst us, very brisk; without his white cap on his head, and neither troubled with gravel or stone.

When we were at the end of the pursuit, Marshal TURENNE and above a hundred Officers of the army came up to us, quitted their horses, embraced the Officers, and said, "They never saw a more glorious action in their lives! and that they were so transported with the sight of it, that they had no power to move, or to do anything." And this high compliment, we had for our pains! In a word, the French army did not strike one stroke in the battle of Dunkirk; only the Six Thousand English!

After we had done pursuing the enemy, Major-General MORGAN rallied his forces, and marched over the sands to where he had shocked them at first, to see what slaughter there was made. But Ambassador LOCKHART went into the camp as fast as he could, to write his letters for England, of what great service he had done! which was just nothing!

Marshal TURENNE and Major-General MORGAN brought the armies close to invest Dunkirk again, and to carry on the approaches.

The Marquis DE LEIDA happened to be in the Counterscarp, and received an accidental shot, whereof he died: and the whole garrison, being discouraged at his death, came to capitulate in a few days.

So the town was surrendered, and Ambassador LOCKHART marched into it, with two Regiments of English for a garrison: but Major-General MORGAN kept the field with Marshal TURENNE, with his other four Regiments of English.

The next siege was Bergen St. Winock, six miles from Dunkirk; which Marshal TURENNE beleaguered with the French army, and the four Regiments of English: and, in four or five days' siege, it was taken upon capitulation.

Marshal TURENNE did rest the army for two days after; and then resolved to march through the heart of Flanders, and take what towns he could, that campaign.

The next town he took was Furnes, the next Menin; after that, Oudenarde: and, in a word, eight towns besides Dunkirk and Ypres. For so soon as the Redcoats came near the counterscarps, there was nothing but a capitulation, and a surrender presently. All the towns we took were towns of strength [*i.e.*, *fortified*].

The last siege we made, was before the city of Ypres, where the Prince DE LIGNY had cast himself in before, for the defence of that city, with 2,500 Horse and Dragoons. Besides, there were in the city, 4,000 burghers, all proper young men, under their arms. So that the garrison did consist of 6,500 men.

Marshal TURENNE sent in a summons; which was answered by a defiance.

Then Marshal TURENNE broke ground, and carried on two approaches towards the Counterscarp. Major-General MORGAN went into the approaches every night, for fear of any miscarriage by the English; and came out of the approaches every morning at sunrising, to take his rest: for then the soldiers had done working.

The fourth morning, Major-General MORGAN went to take his rest in his tent; but, within half an hour afterwards, Marshal TURENNE sent a Nobleman to him, to desire him to come to speak with him. When the Major-General came, there were above a hundred Noblemen and Officers of the army walking about his tent. And his Gentlemen had decked a room for his Excellency with his sumpter cloths; in which homely place, there were about twenty Officers of the army with him: but as soon as Major-General MORGAN came, Marshal TURENNE desired all of them to retire, for he had something to communicate to the Major-General.

The room was immediately cleared, and Marshal TURENNE turned the Gentlemen of his Chamber out, and shut the door himself. When this was done, he desired the Major-General to sit down by him; and the first news that he spake of was that "he had certain intelligence that the Prince of CONDÉ and Don JUAN of AUSTRIA were at the head of 11,000 Horse and 4,000 Foot, within three leagues of this camp: and resolved to break through one of our quarters, to relieve the city of Ypres," and therefore he desired Major-General MORGAN to have all the English, under their arms, every night, at sunset; and the French army should be so likewise.

Major-General MORGAN replied, and said, "The Prince of CONDÉ and Don JUAN of Austria were great Captains; and that they might dodge with Marshal TURENNE, to fatigue his army:" and, further, that "If he did keep the army three nights to that hard shift, they would not care who did knock them on the head!"

Marshal TURENNE replied, "We must do it, and surmount all difficulty!"

The Major-General desired to know of his Excellency, "Whether he was certain, the enemy was so near him?"

He answered, "He had two spies just come from them."

Then Major-General MORGAN told him, "His condition was somewhat desperate!" and said that "A desperate disease must have a desperate cure!"

His Excellency asked, "What he meant?"

Major-General MORGAN did offer him, to attempt the Counterscarp upon [*by*] an assault; and so put all things out of doubt, with expedition.

The Major-General had no sooner said this; but Marshal TURENNE joined his hands, and looked up, through the boards, towards the heavens, and said, "Did ever my Master, the King of France, or the King of Spain attempt a Counterscarp upon an assault; where there were three Half Moons covered with cannon, and the ramparts of the town playing point blank into the Counterscarp?"

Further, he said, "What will the King, my Master, say of me, if I expose his army to these hazards?" And he rose up, and fell into a passion, stamping with his feet, and shaking his locks, and grinning with his teeth, he said, "Major-General MORGAN had made him mad!"

But, by degrees, he cooled, and asked the Major-General, "Whether he would stay to dinner with him?"

But the Major-General begged his pardon, for he had appointed some of the Officers to eat a piece of beef at his tent that day.

His Excellency asked him, "If he would meet him at two o'clock, at the opening of the approaches?"

The Major-General said, "He would be punctual, but desired he would bring none of his train with him (for it was usually a hundred Noblemen with their feathers and ribands); because if he did, he would have no opportunity to take a view of the Counterscarp: for the enemy would discover them, and fire incessantly."

His Excellency said, "He would bring none but two or three of the Lieutenant-Generals."

Major-General MORGAN was at the place appointed, a quarter of an hour before his Excellency: who then came with eight Noblemen, and three Lieutenant-Generals, and took a place to view the Counterscarp.

After he had looked a considerable time upon it; he turned about, and looked upon the Noblemen and Lieutenant-Generals and said, "I don't know what to say to you! Here is Major-General MORGAN has put me out of my wits! for he would have me attempt yonder Counterscarp upon an assault."

None of the Noblemen or Lieutenant-Generals made any reply to him; but Count SCHOMBERG, who said, "My Lord! I think Major-General MORGAN would offer nothing to your Lordship, but what he thinks feasible: and he knows he has good fighting men."

Upon this, Marshal TURENNE asked, "How many English he would venture?"

The Major-General said, "He would venture 600 common men, besides Officers; and fifty pioneers."

Marshal TURENNE said, "600 of Monsieur LA FERTÉ's army and 50 Pioneers; and 600 of his own army and 50 Pioneers more, would make better [*more*] than 2,000 men."

Major-General MORGAN replied, "They were abundance to carry it, with GOD's assistance."

Then his Excellency said, "He would acquaint the King and his Eminence that Major-General MORGAN had put him upon that desperate design."

Major-General MORGAN desired his pardon, "For it was in his [*the Marshal's*] power to attempt it, or not to attempt it."

But in the close, Marshal TURENNE said to the Major-General that "He must fall into Monsieur LA FERTÉ's approaches, and that he should take the one half of Monsieur LA FERTÉ's men; and that he would take the other half into his own approaches."

Major-General MORGAN begged his pardon, and said "He

desired to fall on with the English entire by themselves, without intermingling them."

Marshal TURENNE replied, "He must fall on out of one of the approaches!"

The Major-General replied that "He would fall on in the plain between both approaches."

His Excellency said that "He would never be able to endure their firing; but that they would kill half his men before he could come to the Counterscarp."

The Major-General said that "He had an invention, that the enemy should not perceive him, till he had his hands upon the stockadoes."

Next, his Excellency said, "For the signal, there shall be a captain of Monsieur LA FERTÉ's, with 20 Firelocks; who shall leap upon the Point, and cry, *Sa! Sa! Vive le Roi de France!*" and upon that noise all were to fall on together.

But Major-General MORGAN opposed that signal, saying, "The enemy would thereby be alarmed, and then he should hardly endure their firing."

His Excellency replied then, that "He would give no signal at all! but the Major-General should give it!" and he would not be persuaded otherwise.

Then the Major-General desired his Excellency that he would give order to them in the approaches, to keep themselves in readiness against sunset; for at the shutting of the night he would fall on. He likewise desired his Excellency that he would order a Major out of his own approaches, and another out of Monsieur LA FERTÉ's approaches to stand by him, and when he should be ready to fall on, he would despatch the two Majors into each of the approaches, that they might be ready to leap out when the Major-General passed between the two approaches with the commanded English.

Just at sunset, Marshal TURENNE came himself, and told the Major-General "He might fall on, when he saw his own time."

The Major-General replied, "He would fall on just at the setting of the night, and when the dusk of the evening came on."

The Major-General made the English stand to their arms,

and divided them into Bodies; a Captain at the head of the Pioneers, and the Major-General and a Colonel at the head of the two Battalions.

He ordered the two battalions and the pioneers, each man, to take up a long fascine upon their muskets and pikes; and then, they were three small groves of wood!

Immediately the Major-General commanded the two Majors to go to their approaches; and that they should leap out so soon as they should see the Major-General march between their approaches, and did order the two battalions that when they came within three score [yards] of the stockadoes to slip [off] their fascines, and fall on.

But it so happened that the French never moved out of their approaches, till such time as Major-General MORGAN had overpowered the enemy.

When the Pioneers came within sight of the stockadoes, they slipped the fascines down, and fell on: the Major-General and the two battalions were close to them. When the soldiers began to lay their hands on the stockadoes they tore them down, for the length of six score [yards]; and leaped pell mell into the Counterscarp amongst the enemy. Abundance of the enemy were drowned in the moat; and many taken prisoners, with two German Princes; and the Counterscarp cleared.

The French were in their approaches all this time. Then, the English fell on upon the Half Moons; and immediately the Redcoats were on the top of them; throwing the enemy into the moat, and turning the cannon upon the town. Thus the two Half Moons were speedily taken.

After the manning of the Half Moons, he did rally all the English, with intention to lodge them upon the Counterscarp, that he might be free of the enemy's shot the next morning. And they left the other Half Moon for Marshal TURENNE's party, which was even before their approaches.

Then the French fell on upon the other Half Moon; but were beaten off.

The Major-General considered that that Half Moon would gall him in the day time, and, therefore, did speak to the Officers and soldiers, that "it were best to give them a little help."

The Redcoats cried, "Shall we fall on in order, or happy-go-lucky."

The Major-General said, "In the name of GOD! at it, happy-go-lucky!" And immediately the Redcoats fell on, and were on the top of it, knocking the enemy down, and casting them into the moat.

When this work was done the Major-General lodged the English on the Counterscarp.

They were no sooner lodged, but Marshal TURENNE scrambled over the ditches to find out the Major-General; and when he met with him, he was much troubled the French did no better; for, indeed, they did just nothing!

Then his Excellency asked the Major-General to "go to his approaches to refresh himself."

But the Major-General begged his pardon, and said, "He would not stir from his post, till he heard a drum beat a parley, and saw a white flag over the walls."

Upon that, Marshal TURENNE laughed and smiled, and said, "They would not be at that pass, in six days! and then went to his approaches, and sent the Major-General three or four dozen of rare wine, with several dishes of cold meat and sweetmeats."

Within two hours after sun-rising, a drum beat a parley, and a white flag was seen over the walls.

The Major-General ordered a Lieutenant, with a file of musketeers, to go and receive the drummer, and to blindfold him, and to carry him straight to Marshal TURENNE in his approaches.

Marshal TURENNE came immediately, with the drummer's message, to the Major-General; and was much troubled he would not receive the message, before it came to him.

The Major-General replied that "that was very improper, his Excellency being upon the place."

The message was to this effect, "That whereas his Excellency had offered them honourable terms in his summons, they were now willing to accept of them, provided they might have their Charter and the privileges of the city preserved. That they had appointed four of their Commissioners to treat further with four Commissioners from his Excellency."

Marshal TURENNE was pleased to asked the Major-General "whether he would be one of the Commissioners?" but the Major-General begged his pardon, and desired that he might abide at his post till such time as the city was surrendered up.

Immediately then, his Excellency sent for Count SCHOMBERG and three other Commissioners, and gave them instructions how to treat with the four Commissioners from the enemy. Just as Marshal TURENNE was giving the Commissioners instructions, Major-General MORGAN said "that the enemy were hungry! so that they would eat any meat they could have": whereupon his Excellency smiled, and shortened their instructions, and sent them away.

Within half an hour, the Commissioners had concluded.

> That they should have their City Charter preserved. That they were to receive a French garrison in. And that the Prince DE LIGNY was to march out with all his forces, next morning, at nine o'clock, with one piece of cannon, colours flying, bullet in mouth, and match lighted at both ends; and to have a convoy to conduct him into his own territories.

Marshal TURENNE was in the morning betimes, with several Noblemen and Officers of the army, and Major-General MORGAN attending near the gate, for the Prince DE LIGNY's coming out.

The Prince having noticed that Marshal TURENNE was there, came out of his coach; Marshal TURENNE being alighted from his horse, and Major-General MORGAN: at their meeting there was a great acclamation, and embracing one another.

After a little time, Marshal TURENNE told the Prince "He very much admired [*wondered*] that he should expose his person to a garrison before a conquering army."

The Prince DE LIGNY replied that "If Marshal TURENNE had left his English in England, he durst have exposed his person in the weakest garrison the King of Spain had in Flanders."

So they parted, and his Excellency marched into the town with a French garrison, and the Major-General with him.

So soon as the garrison was settled, Marshal TURENNE

wrote his letters to the French King, and his Eminence the Cardinal, how that "the city of Ypres was reduced to the obedience of His Majesty, and that he was possessed of it; and that Major-General MORGAN was instrumental in that service, and that the English did wonders!" and sent the Intendant of the Army with his letters to the King and Cardinal.

Monsieur TALLON, the Intendant, returned back from the King and Cardinal to the army within eight days, and brought a compliment to Major-General MORGAN that "the King and his Eminence the Cardinal did expect to see him at Paris, when he came to his winter quarters! where there would be a Cupboard of Plate [*i.e., of gold and silver plate*] to attend him."

Major-General MORGAN, instead of going for his Cupboard of Plate, went for England; and His Majesty of France had never the kindness to send him his Cupboard of Plate. So that this is the reward that Major-General MORGAN had had from the French King, for all his service in France and Flanders.

Killed at the Battle of Dunkirk.

Lieutenant-Colonel FENWICK, two Captains, one Lieutenant, two Ensigns, two Sergeants, thirty-two soldiers.

And about twenty wounded.

Killed at the Storming of Ypres.

One Captain, one Sergeant, eight private soldiers. [Wounded], about twenty-five officers, out of thirty-five; and about six soldiers slightly wounded after they were lodged upon the Counterscarp.

Sir THOMAS MORGAN himself slightly hurt by a shot in the calf of his leg.

THE END.

England's Joy

OR A

RELATION

OF THE

Most Remarkable passages, from his MA-
JESTY'S Arrival at *DOVER*, to His
entrance at *WHITEHALL*.

London, Printed by Thomas Creak, 1660.

ENGLAND'S JOY.

BEING come aboard one of the fairest of those ships which attended at Sluce [? *Helvoetsluys*] for wafting him over from the Hague in Holland; and therein having taken leave of his sisters, the Princess Royal; he set sail for England on Wednesday evening, May 23rd, 1660. And having, during his abode at sea, given new names to that whole navy (consisting of twenty-six goodly vessels), he arrived at Dover on the Friday following [May 25th] about two o'clock in the afternoon.

Ready on the shore to receive him, stood the Lord General MONK, as also the Earl of WINCHELSEA Constable of Dover Castle, with divers persons of quality on the one hand; and the Mayor of Dover, accompanied by his brethren of that Corporation of the other, with a rich canopy. As soon as he had set foot on the shore, the Lord General presenting himself before him on his knee, and kissing his royal hand; was embraced by his Majesty: and received divers gracious expressions of the great sense he had of his loyalty, and in being so instrumental in his Restoration.

There also did the Corporation of Dover, and the Earl of WINCHELSEA do their duties to him, in like sort; all the people making joyful shouts: the great guns from the ships and castle telling aloud the happy news of this his entrance upon English ground.

From thence, taking coach immediately, with his royal brothers, the Dukes of YORK and GLOUCESTER, he passed to Barham Down—a great plain lying betwixt Dover and Canterbury—where were drawn up divers gallant troops of horse, consisting of the nobility, knights and gentlemen of note, clad in very rich apparel; commanded by the Duke of BUCKINGHAM, Earls of OXFORD, DERBY, NORTHAMPTON, WINCHELSEA, LICHFIELD, and the Lord, Viscount MORDAUNT:

As also the several foot regiments of the Kentish men. Being entered the Down on horseback, where multitudes of the country people stood making loud shouts, he rode to the head of each troop—they being placed on his left hand, three deep—who bowing to him, kissed the hilts of their swords, and then flourished them above their heads, with no less acclamations; the trumpets in the meantime also echoing the like to them.

In the suburb at Canterbury stood the Mayor and Aldermen of that ancient city, who received him with loud music, and presented him with a cup of gold of two hundred and fifty pounds value. Whence, after a speech made to him by the Recorder, he passed to the Lord CAMPDEN's house, the Mayor carrying the sword before him.

During his stay at Canterbury (which was till Monday morning) he knighted the Lord General MONK, and gave him the ensigns of the most honourable Order of the Garter: And by Garter Principal King of Arms sent the like unto Lord Admiral MONTAGUE, then aboard the navy, riding in the Downs. There likewise did he knight Sir WILLIAM MAURICE, a member of the House of Commons; whom he constituted one of his principal Secretaries of State.

From Canterbury he came on Monday to Rochester, where the people had hung up, over the midst of the streets, as he rode, many beautiful garlands, curiously made up with costly scarves and ribbons, decked with spoons and bodkins of silver, and small plate of several sorts; and some with gold chains, in like sort as at Canterbury: each striving to outdo the other in all expressions of joy.

On Tuesday, May the 29th (which happily fell out to be the anniversary of his Majesty's birthday) he set forth from Rochester in his coach; but afterwards took horse on the farther side of Blackheath: on which spacious plain he found divers great and eminent troops of horse, in a most splendid and glorious equipage; and a kind of rural triumph, expressed by the country swains, in a morrice dance with the old music of taber and pipe; which was performed with all agility and cheerfulness imaginable.

And from this Heath these troops marched off before him; viz. Major General BROWN, the Merchant Adventurers, Alderman ROBINSON, the Lord MAYNARD, the Earls of

Norwich, Peterborough, Cleveland, Derby, Duke of Richmond, and His Majesty's own Life Guards.

In this order proceeding towards London, there were placed in Deptford, on his right hand—as he passed through the town—above an hundred proper maids, clad all alike in white garments, with scarves about them: who having prepared many flaskets covered with fine linen, and adorned with rich scarves and ribbons; which flaskets were full of flowers and sweet herbs, strewed the way before him as he rode.

From thence passing on he came into Saint George's Fields in Southwark, where the Lord Mayor and Aldermen of London in their scarlet, with the Recorder and other City Council, waited for him in a large tent, hung with tapestry; in which they had placed a chair of state, with a rich canopy over it. When he came thither the Lord Mayor presented him with the City sword, and the Recorder made a speech to him; which being done, he alighted and went into the tent, where a noble banquet was prepared for him.

From this tent the proceeding was thus ordered, viz. First the City Marshal, to follow in the rear of His Majesty's Life Guards. Next the Sheriff's trumpets. Then the Sheriff's men in scarlet cloaks, laced with silver on the capes, carrying javelins in their hands. Then divers eminent citizens well mounted, all in black velvet coats, and chains of gold about their necks, and every one his footman, with suit, cassock and ribbons of the colour of his Company: all which were made choice of out of the several Companies in this famous City and so distinguished: and at the head of each distinction the ensign of that Company.

After these followed the City Council, by two and two, near the Aldermen; then certain Noblemen and Noblemen's sons, Then the King's trumpets. Then the Heralds at Arms.

After them the Duke of Buckingham. Then the Earl of Lindsey, Lord High Chamberlain of England; and the Lord General Monk. Next to them Garter Principal King of Arms; the Lord Mayor on his right hand bearing the City sword, and a Gentleman Usher on his left: and on each side of them the Sergeants at Arms with their maces.

Then the King's Majesty with his equerries and footmen on each side of him; and at a little distance on each hand his royal brothers, the Dukes of York and Gloucester: and after them divers of the King's servants who came with him from beyond sea. And in the rear of all, those gallant troops, viz. The Duke of BUCKINGHAM, Earls of OXFORD, NORTHAMPTON, WINCHELSEA, LICHFIELD, and Lord MORDAUNT: as also five regiments of horse belonging to the army.

In this magnificent fashion, His Majesty entered the Borough of Southwark, about half-past three o'clock in the afternoon; and within an hour after, the City of London, at the Bridge: where he found the windows and streets exceedingly thronged with people to behold him, and the wall adorned with hangings and carpets of tapestry and other costly stuff: and in many places sets of loud music; all the conduits as he passed running claret wine; and the several Companies in their liveries, with the ensigns belonging to them; as also the trained bands of the city standing along the streets as he passed, welcoming him with loyal acclamations.

And within the rails where Charing Cross formerly was, a stand of six hundred pikes, consisting of knights and gentlemen, as had been officers in the armies of his late Majesty, of blessed memory: the truly noble and valiant Sir JOHN STOWELL, Knight of the Honourable Order of the Bath (a person famous for his eminent actings and sufferings) being in the head of them.

From which place, the citizens in velvet coats and gold chains being drawn up on each hand, and divers companies of foot soldiers; his Majesty passed betwixt them, and entered White Hall at seven o'clock: the people making loud shouts, and the horse and foot several volleys of shots, at this his happy arrival. Where the House of Lords and Commons of Parliament received him, and kissed his royal hand.

At the same time likewise, the Reverend Bishops of ELY, SALISBURY, ROCHESTER and CHICHESTER in their episcopal habits, with divers of the long oppressed orthodox clergy; met in that royal Chapel of King HENRY the SEVENTH of Westminster, and there also sung *Te DEUM &c.*, in praise and thanks to Almighty GOD, for this His unspeakable mercy, in the deliverance of his Majesty from many dangers, and so happily restoring him to rule these kingdoms, according to his just and undoubted right.

FINIS.

A

RELATION

OF THE

great sufferings

AND

strange adventures

of HENRY PITMAN,

Chirurgeon to the late Duke of MONMOUTH, containing an account

1. Of the Occasion of his being engaged in the Duke's service. 2. Of his trial, condemnation, and transportation to Barbadoes; with the most severe and unchristian *Act* made against him and his fellow sufferers, by the Governor and General Assembly of that island. 3. How he made his escape in a small open boat with some of his fellow-captives, namely, JOHN WHICKER, PETER BAGWELL, WILLIAM WOODCOCK, JOHN COOKE, JEREMIAH ATKINS, &c. And how miraculously they were preserved on the sea. 4. How they went ashore on an uninhabitable island, where they met with some Privateers, that burnt their boat, and left them on that desolate place to shift for themselves. 5. After what manner they lived there for about three months; until the said HENRY PITMAN was taken aboard a Privateer and at length arrived safe in England. 6. How his companions were received on board another Privateer, that was afterwards taken by the Spaniards, and they all made slaves: and how, after six months' captivity, they were delivered; and returned to England also.

Licensed, June 13th, 1689.

London. Printed by ANDREW SOWLE: and are to be sold by JOHN TAYLOR, at the sign of the *Ship* in Paul's Churchyard, 1689.

A RELATION &c.

AS A necessary introduction to the following *Relation*, it will be convenient that I give account of the Occasion of my being engaged with the rest that went in to the Duke of MONMOUTH; and how far I was concerned in that action.

Being, at that time, but newly returned from a voyage to Italy, I went to see my relations at Sandford in Somersetshire: where I had not been long, before the Duke landed at Lyme; and making forwards, was advanced as far as Ilminster. Upon which, I was induced (partly out of my own curiosity, and partly by the importunity of some of my acquaintance) to go and see whether his strength and number were answerable to what the common rumour had spread abroad: and to that purpose, rode, accompanied by my brother and some other friends, to Taunton; whither the Duke by this time was marching, with such forces as he had got together.

After some stay there, having fully satisfied my curiosity, by a full view both of his person and his army; I resolved to return home: and in order thereunto, I took the direct road back again, with a friend, who had the same intention as myself: but understanding, upon the road, that if we went forward, we should be certainly intercepted by the Lord of OXFORD's Troop, then in our way; we found ourselves, of necessity, obliged to retire back again to the Duke's forces, till we could meet with a more safe and convenient opportunity.

But, after some time, losing my horse, and no opportunity presenting itself; I was prevailed with, by the importunate desires of my friends and aquaintance then in the army, to stay and take care of the sick and wounded men. To which I was the rather induced, in regard I thought myself liable to the same punishment, should the Duke be defeated, as those who still remained in the army: but more especially, for that I saw many sick and wounded men miserably lamenting the want of chirurgeons to dress their wounds. So that pity and compassion on my fellow creatures, more especially being my brethren in Christianity, obliged me to stay and perform the duty of my calling among them, and to assist my brother chirurgeons towards the relief of those that, otherwise, must have languished in misery; though, indeed, there were many who did, notwithstanding our utmost care and diligence. Whose lives, perhaps, might have been preserved to this day, had we had a garrison wherein to have given them rest; and not have been constrained, through the cruelty and inhumanity of the King's soldiers, to expose their wounded and fractured limbs to the violent agitation and shogging of the carts, in our daily marches.

But as I was never in arms myself, so neither was I wanting in my care to dress the wounds of many of the King's soldiers, who were prisoners in the Duke's army: using the utmost of my care and skill for both. And thus I continued in full employment, dressing the wounded in the night-time and marching by day: till the fatal rout and overthrow of the whole army [*at Sedgmoor on July* 6, 1685].

In my flight homewards, I was taken prisoner, and commited to Ilchester Gaol by Colonel HELLIER; in whose porch, I had my pockets rifled and my coat taken off my back, by my guard: and, in that manner, was hurried away to prison; where I remained, with many more under the same circumstances, until the Assizes at Wells; though, perhaps, there could not anything have been proved against most of us, to have done us much harm, had they not extorted confessions from us, by sending certain persons to the prisons where we were.

Who called us forth, one after another, and told us, that "the King was very gracious and merciful, and would cause none to be executed but such as had been Officers or capital offenders: and therefore if we would render ourselves fit objects of the King's grace and favour, our only way was to give them an account where we went into the Duke's army, and in what capacity we served him, &c. Otherwise we must expect no mercy or favour from the King, who would certainly punish all such wilful and obstinate offenders."

By which means, they drew us into the acknowledgement of our guilt, and our Examinations and Confessions were written and sent to the King, before the Lord Chief Justice JEFFRIES came to try us: so that he knew beforehand our particular crimes; and likewise received orders from the King, as it is supposed, who, and what number to execute.

But seeing our former Confessions were sufficient only to find the [True] Bill against us, by the Grand Jury; and not to prove us "Guilty"; the Petty Jury being obliged to give their verdict according to the evidence in Court: the Lord Chief Justice (fearing lest we should deny what we formerly confessed, and by that means, put them to the trouble of proving it against us) caused about twenty-eight persons at the Assizes at Dorchester, to be chosen from among the rest, against whom he knew he could procure evidence, and brought them first to their trial. Who pleaded "Not Guilty"; but evidence being produced, they were immediately condemned, and a warrant signed for their execution the same afternoon.

The sudden execution of these men so affrightened the rest, that we all, except three or four, pleaded "Guilty" in hopes to save our lives: but not without large promises of the King's grace and favour. For the Lord Chief Justice told us that "if we would acknowledge our crimes, by pleading Guilty to our Indictment, the King, who was almost all mercy [!], would be as ready to forgive us as we were to rebel against him; yea, as ready to pardon us, as we would be to ask it of him."

And now was that common saying verified, "Confess, and be hanged!" For, notwithstanding his large promises of grace and favour, we were all condemned "to be hanged, drawn, and quartered." And by his order, there were two hundred and thirty executed; besides a great number hanged immediately after the Fight.

The rest of us were ordered to be transported to the

Caribbee Islands. And in order thereunto, my brother and I, with nearly a hundred more, were given to JEREMIAH NEPHO; and by him, sold to GEORGE PENNE, a needy Papist, that wanted money to pay for our transportation, and therefore was very importunate with my relations, to purchase mine and my brother's freedom.

Which my relations, at first, were unwilling to do, having no assurance of his performing *Articles* at such a distance; and therefore thought it best to defer it until we came to Barbadoes, or otherwise to agree to pay him as soon as they should receive an account of our being set free. But this not satisfying him, having present occasion of money, he threatened that if they would not pay him now, he would give orders to his brother-in-law at Barbadoes, that our freedom should not be sold us after we came there: but that he should treat us with more rigour and severity than others.

With these threats, on the one hand; and promises of particular favour on the other: he, at length, prevailed with our relations to give him £60, upon condition that we should be free when we came to Barbadoes; only owning some person, whom we should think fit to nominate, as a titular Master. And in case that these, with other conditions, were not performed; the said GEORGE PENNE was bound with his brother JOHN PENNE, in a bond of £120, to pay the £60 back again.

And thus we may see the buying and selling of free men into slavery, was beginning again to be renewed among Christians, as if that heathenish custom had been a necessary dependence on Arbitrary Power.

And in order to our transportation, we were removed to Weymouth, and shipped on board a vessel that belonged to London: which, in a few days, sailed for Barbadoes, where we arrived in about five weeks' time; but had a very sickly passage, insomuch that nine of my companions were buried in the sea.

We had not been many days in Barbadoes, before the Governor [EDWARD STEED] of the said island summoned the General Assembly, who welcomed us with the following inchristian and inhuman *Act*.

An Act for the governing and retaining within this island, all such rebels convict, as by His most sacred Majesty's Order or Permit, have been, or shall be transported from his European dominion to this place.

WHEREAS a most horrid, wicked, and execrable Rebellion was lately raised and prosecuted within His Majesty's Dominions, by JAMES SCOT, late Duke of MONMOUTH, and ARCHIBALD CAMPBELL, late Earl of ARGYLE, and their traitorous complices, with intent to destroy His Majesty's most sacred Person and Royal Family, to overthrow his Crown and Government, and to render his Dominions the theatres of blood and misery. In prevention whereof, it hath pleased the Divine Providence (which is ever peculiarly watchful to guard the thrones of Princes) to accompany His Majesty's counsel and arms with such success and victory that the said rebels and traitors were utterly defeated: for which impious fact, many of them have since deservedly suffered the pains of death, according to law; which the rest were liable unto, being equally guilty of those barbarous crimes, and must have undergone, but that His Majesty, in his Princely and unparalleled grace and clemency, hath been pleased to extend his mercy in sparing the lives of several thousands of them, by commuting the execution of their sentence into a Temporary Service in his American Colonies.

And forasmuch as His sacred Majesty hath signified it, as his royal pleasure, that the said rebels or so many of them as should be transported to his said American colonies, should be there held and obliged to serve the Buyers of them, for and during the space of Ten Years at least; and that they be not permitted in any manner whatsoever, to redeem themselves by money or otherwise, until that time be fully expired.

Therefore, We, His Majesty's most dutiful and loyal subjects, his Lieutenant Governor, Council, and General Assembly of this His Majesty's said island, taking the premises into our serious consideration; and being zealous, to render all due and ready obedience to His Majesty's command, as also to make apparent with how great abhorrence and detestation, we resent the said late wicked inhuman and damnable Rebellion, and all those that were promoters and actors therein, have thought it becoming our duty to Enact: and it is hereby Enacted by the Right Honourable EDWARD STEED Esquire, Lieutenant Governor and Commander in Chief of this and other the Caribbee Islands, the Honourable the Council, and General Assembly of this island, and authority of the same :

That what person or persons soever were guilty of the aforesaid Rebellion, and have been therefore convict[*ed*], *which either already have been, or hereafter shall be brought to this island; either by His Majesty's order or permit for the purpose aforesaid, shall be held compelled and obliged to serve and obey the Owner or Purchaser of him or them, in their plantations within this island, in all such labour or service as they shall be commanded to perform and do by their Owners, Masters, or Mistresses, or their Overseers, for the full time and term of Ten Years from the day of their landing, and disposed of fully to be completed and ended; any bargain, law, usage or custom in this island to the contrary, in any wise, notwithstanding.*

And to the intent that no disobedience may be suffered or done upon His Majesty's said Orders and Expectations concerning the said rebels convict[*ed*], *but that they may become fully liable unto and bear the aforesaid mark of their monstrous villainy. It is further Enacted :*

That if any Master of a ship, Importer, Owner, Master or Purchaser of any of the said rebels aforesaid, shall acquit, release, or discharge them or any of them, or permit them or any of them to redeem themselves by money or other reward or recompense or consideration whatsoever, respecting either themselves or the said rebels convict[*ed*], *before the term of Ten Years' Service in this island as aforesaid, be fully completed and ended; or shall connive at or assist unto their, or any of their removes, withdrawings, or escapings from off this island: the Party or Parties so offending herein shall therefore forfeit and pay unto His Majesty his heirs and successors, the sum of Two Hundred Pounds* [= £500 now] *sterling for each, or every one of the said rebels, which by him or them shall be either acquitted, released, discharged, or permitted to be redeemed; or connived at or assisted unto a remove, withdrawing, or escaping off this island before the full end of the Term aforesaid : over and above the value or recompense for which it was permitted or done; and further shall suffer imprisonment in the common gaol of this island for the space and term of One whole Year without bail or mainprize: and be for ever thereafter uncapable of bearing any Public Office within this island.*

And it is hereby further Enacted and ordained by the Authority aforesaid:

That if one or more of the aforesaid Servants [i.e., Slaves] *or rebels convict*[*ed*], *shall attempt, endeavour, or contrive to make his or their escape from off this island before the said Term of Ten Years be fully complete*[*d*] *and ended; such Servant or Servants, for his or their so attempting or endeavouring to make escape, shall, upon proof thereof made to the Governor, receive, by his warrant, Thirty-nine lashes on his bare body, on some public day, in the next market town to his Master's place of abode: and, on another market day in the same town, be set in the pillory, by the space of one hour; and be burnt in the forehead with the letters* **F. T.** *signifying* Fugitive Traitor, *so as the letters may plainly appear in his forehead. But for all other misdemeanours and miscarriages, they shall be prosecuted and punished according to the laws of this island, provided for the governing of other Servants.*

And to the end the said convict rebels may be the better known and distinguished; it is hereby further Enacted and Ordained:

That, within eight days after the arrival of any ship or vessel to this island, in which any of the said convict rebels are brought, the Master of the said ship shall deliver to the Governor, and into the Secretary's Office of this island, a true list or catalogue of those names, upon oath; and the Merchant or Merchants to whom they come consigned, or who have the disposal of them, shall also, within eight days after finishing the Sale, give unto the said Office a just account of the persons' names to whom they were sold and disposed of: and in case of failure herein, the same shall forfeit to the King his heirs and successors, the sum of Two Hundred Pounds sterling; and the Merchant or Merchants shall forfeit in like manner, the sum of Two Hundred Pounds sterling.

And for such of the said convict rebels as have been already imported, before the making and publishing of this Act, *the Master and Merchant of such vessels are hereby required forthwith to deliver to the Secretary, such list or catalogue as aforesaid, upon penalty of the like forfeiture: which said list or catalogue, the said Secretary is required to receive, and write out fairly, and cause to be hung up in his Office, that all persons concerned may have free recourse thereto.*

And in case the first Buyer shall sell or assign over any such rebel or rebels convict, to any other inhabitant or inhabitants of this island, the Vendor is hereby required to give notice thereof to the Secretary, to the end the name or names of such Servant or Servants may be changed in the Secretary's Office, from the first, to the second or other purchaser or assigns, [*that they*] *may stand charged as the first.*

And in case of the death of any of the Servants aforesaid, it is hereby further Enacted:

That the present Owner, shall, within fourteen days, make, or cause oath to be made, before the next or some Justice of the Peace, of the name and death of such Servant, and that he really was in the Record, and not another of the same name; that by means of the certificate sent to the Secretary's Office, the Secretary may charge him, Dead.

And if any Owners or Vendors shall fail, in either of the cases aforesaid, he or they shall forfeit to His Majesty his heirs and successors, the sum of Twenty-five Pounds sterling: and for the Secretary's pains therein, and also in case of changing Masters and Mistresses, the Secretary may receive for such person dead or assigned over, Six Pence, and no more.

And to the end, none of the Servants or convict rebels may remove or escape from this island, by obtaining Tickets under wrong names, or other fraudulent or illegal methods of this kind; it is hereby further Enacted and Ordained by the Authority aforesaid:

That all Justices of the Peace that shall hereafter take Affidavits *(to be sent to the Secretary's Office) for persons that design to go off this island, shall always express and insert in those* Affidavits, *that the person so going off, and desiring a Ticket, is not one of these Servants and convict rebels: without which, the Secretary is hereby forbidden to grant or produce a Ticket.*

And the Secretary is also required to use the same method in such Affidavits *as shall be taken before himself, under the penalty of forfeiting to His Majesty his heirs and successors, the sum of Two Hundred Pounds sterling, for his neglect in either of these cases.*

And whosoever obtaining a Ticket lawfully out of the Secretary's Office, being of the name of any of those rebels, or otherwise, and shall permit any of the said rebels of that name, or others, to have such Tickets, by which he may be in a probable way of making his escape off this island, shall forfeit to the use of our Sovereign Lord the King his heirs and successors, the sum of One Hundred Pounds sterling, if he be able to pay the same; and also suffer imprisonment in the common gaol, by the space of six months, without bail or mainprize. The said commitment to be made, and execution to be levied, by Warrant *from the Governor, upon proof made before him, by two witnesses, or one witness with pregnant circumstances. But in case such persons be uncapable to make payment of such forfeiture, he is hereby ordered to lie in prison during the space of six months, and be set once in the pillory, by the space of two hours at a time, in each of the four market towns of this island, on four several days.*

And for the encouragement of all such as shall inform or discover any false, fraudulent, or wicked practice of this kind; it is hereby Enacted:

That One Fifth part of all forfeits in the Act *mentioned, shall be to the use and benefit of such Informers.*

And to the end the restraint continuing and holding the said rebels convict within this island, during the Term aforesaid, may be the [more] effectually and fully secured and provided for; and also for preventing the Servants, Slaves, and Debtors of this island from running off, by which some have perished in the sea; it is hereby further Enacted and Ordained, by the Authority aforesaid:

That every Owner or Keeper of any small vessel, sloop, shallop, wherry, fishing-boat, or any other sort of boat belonging to this island, shall, within twenty days after publication hereof, give into the Secretary's Office of this island, [security] in the sum of Two Hundred Pounds sterling (excepting the small boats and wherries, who are to enter in the sum of Ten Pounds sterling), that he will not convey or carry off from this island any of the aforesaid rebels convict, or any other person that hath not a lawful Ticket; or will permit, suffer, or consent to the same: but will use his utmost skill, care, and diligence in securing and guarding his small vessel, sloop, shallop, or boat, in such manner as may most probably prevent the escapes of such fugitives.

And if any Owner or Keeper of such small vessel, sloop, shallop, or boat shall hereafter make sale, change, or any other alienation thereof, without first giving notice in the Secretary's Office, that new security may be taken then: such vessel, shallop, or boat, shall be forfeited to His Majesty his heirs and successors; and the Vendor to be further obliged to put in security to answer all damages that may happen, by reason of such sale, before security so given.

And the like method and forfeitures is hereby required and appointed unto Masters of ships, in case they shall sell or dispose of any boat to any of the inhabitants of this island.

And whosoever shall hereafter build or set up in this island, any small vessel, sloop, shallop, or boat, shall, when he or they build the same, enter into the security aforesaid, under the penalty of forfeiting the materials thereof to His Majesty his heirs and successors.

And be it further ordained and Enacted:

That the Secretary shall have and receive for the Bond and Certificate for wherries, fishing-boats, and other small boats, only Fifteen Pence; and for all other vessels of greater bulk, Five Shillings each, as has been customary.

And it is further Enacted by the Authority aforesaid:

That it shall be Felony in every Master of every shallop, sloop, wherry, or other boat belonging to this island, that runneth away with any shallop, sloop, wherry, or other boat which they command [although such boats should be their own property!].

And it is further Enacted by the Authority aforesaid:

That if any woman in this island, Owner or Mistress of any such convict rebels, by any means whatsoever, shall intermarry with any of the said convict rebels, whereby the said rebels may become free from their servitude; or suffer or consent to the marriage of their daughters or other near relations, by which such Servant is freed, connived at, or eased from his servitude aforesaid: that upon notice thereof given to the Governor and Council, of such marriage or marriages, such rebel or rebels shall, notwithstanding, be, by the Governor and Council ordered to serve the remainder of his time to some other person, whom the Governor and Council shall think fit; and the woman so marrying as aforesaid, is to forfeit to our Sovereign Lord the King his heirs or assigns, the sum of Two Hundred Pounds sterling, and suffer Six Months' imprisonment for such her intermarrying with any of the said rebels convict.

And, lastly, it is Enacted by the Authority aforesaid:

That the Act *be published by the Ministers of the several parishes in this island, in their several parish churches, once in every six months from the date hereof, upon such penalty as the Governor and Council for the time being, shall think fit to impose on the person so neglecting to publish the same.*

Given under my hand, the Fourth day of January, 1685[-6],

EDWARD STEED.

But to return to my discourse

We were consigned to CHARLES THOMAS and his Company, with particular orders and instructions from GEORGE PENNE not to sell me or my brother, but permit us to make choice of some person to own as a titular Master. However, they were so unkind, they would not allow us that liberty; but compelled us, contrary to our desires and inclinations, to live with one ROBERT BISHOP: pretending that they had not absolutely sold us to him; but could remove us again, in case we disliked our place.

And that the before-mentioned GEORGE PENNE might not be obliged to repay the money we gave him; they told us, we should have the yearly salary of £20, which they were to receive for our service.

But these pretences were only to amuse us, for afterwards when we were constrained, by the great unkindness of our Master, to address ourselves unto them, not only in person, but also by many importunate and affectionate letters, intreating them to use their utmost endeavour and Interest with our Master, in order to remove us; we found it in vain: for they had positively sold us, and also given it in, on their oaths, at the Secretary's Office.

When our Master perceived that we were uneasy, and unwilling to serve him; he grew more and more unkind unto us, and would not give us any clothes, nor me any benefit of my practice, whereby to enable me to provide for myself: for I was obliged to give him an account of what physic I administered out of his plantation, and he received the money for the same.

Our diet was very mean. 5 lbs. of salt Irish beef, or salt fish, a week, for each man; and Indian or Guinea Corn [*maize*] ground on a stone, and made into dumplings instead of bread.

Which coarse and mean fare brought me to a violent flux [*diarrhœa*], insomuch that I was forced to complain to my Master, desiring him to allow me some flour, instead of Indian corn, to make dumplings withal; and humbly recommended to his consideration my Profession and practice, which I hoped would render me deserving of better accommodation than was usually allowed to other Servants.

But he, not moved with pity, angrily replied, "I should not have so good!"

Whose unkind answer moved me so, that I had the confidence to tell him that "I would no longer serve him, nor any other, as a Surgeon, unless I were entertained according to the just merits of my Profession and practice; and that I would choose rather to work in the field with the Negroes than to dishonour my Profession by serving him as Physician and Surgeon, and to accept the same entertainment as common Servants."

My angry Master, at this, was greatly enraged, and the fiery zeal of his immoderate passion was so heightened by some lying stories of a fellow Servant, that he could not content himself with the bare execution of his cane upon my head, arms, and back, although he played so long thereon, like a furious fencer, until he had split it in pieces; but he also confined me close prisoner in the Stocks (which stood in an open place), exposed to the scorching heat of the sun; where I remained about twelve hours, until my Mistress, moved either with pity or shame, gave order for my release.

It would be too tedious to give a particular account of the many other abuses and unkindnesses we received at his hands; and therefore it shall suffice to say, that in this condition we lived with him about fifteen months [*to about April*, 1687], until by his debauched and extravagant course of life, he had run himself so extremely in debt, and particularly to those merchants that sold us to him, that he could not well pay for us. For which reason, we were removed from him; but the merchants were forced to remit the money due for our service, before he would return us.

And now, being returned again, we remained in the merchants' hands, as goods unsold; and because I would not consent to be disposed of, at their pleasure; they threatened to horsewhip me and put me to servile employment.

But we had not been long here, before my brother died, and I being wearied with long and fruitless expectation of my Pardon; and no less perplexed and tired with the great abuses I had received at their hands, resolved to attempt the making of my escape from off the island: to which purpose, after several contrivances and ways that came into my head, and those well weighed with the consequent circumstances that possibly I could foresee; I concluded at length to proceed after this manner.

Being introduced by a friend into the acquaintance of one JOHN NUTHALL [*Not a White Slave, but a Debtor, see p.* 355], a carver; whose condition was somewhat mean, and therefore one that wanted money to carry him off the island: I imparted my design unto him, and employed him to buy a boat of a Guiney Man [*a ship trading to Guinea*] that lay in the road; promising him for his reward, not only his passage free, and money for his present expenses, but to give him the boat also, when we arrived at our port.

By the way, it is to be understood, that the means which enabled me to defray these extraordinary expenses, was a private consignation [*consignment*] of goods from my relations, to a particular friend in the island; who took care to dispose of them for me.

JOHN NUTHALL therefore readily consented to what I proposed; and after I had enjoined him to secresy, I delivered him £12 to buy the boat; which accordingly he did, and gave in security for the same at the Secretary's Office, conformable to the custom and laws of the island. Nevertheless all that would not prevent the jealousy of the magistrates, that sprang from the consideration of his poverty, and the little service they knew the boat would do him.

Whereupon, they sent for JOHN NUTHALL, and strictly commanded him to discover who it was that had employed him to buy the boat; and threatened to put him to his oath. Nevertheless, they could get nothing out of him, for the man had so much courage that he confidently denied that any person had employed him; but that he bought the boat merely for his own use. Yet was not all this sufficient. They still threatened to seize the boat, unless he gave in better security. Upon which, he came to me, to advise what it were best to be done. I ordered him forthwith to sink the boat: which as it very much abated the suspicion of the Magistrates, so it secured the boat from seizure.

While these things were in agitation, one of JOHN NUTHALL's creditors, to whom he owed £7 for tools, threatened to arrest him, unless he paid him down the money; which was no small surprise to a man that had no money to make his payment: however, having a day's respite to procure satisfaction, he came and told me, that "Unless I would supply him with money to pay his debt, necessity would constrain him to discover my design." So that, well knowing the danger I was in, I was forced to supply him.

And here, I must not omit to relate, that, by this time, I had discovered my design to two of my acquaintance under the same circumstances [*i.e.*, *White Slaves*], THOMAS AUSTIN and JOHN WHICKER; who readily agreed to be my companions, and gave me what money they could well spare, to help to carry on the design: but I myself was the chief contriver and manager of the whole, having more time and liberty than they. For I usually met JOHN NUTHALL every night, at some convenient place remote from the town by the sea side; where, after we had consulted together, he took his instructions how to proceed.

In this interval of time, the boat being sunk, and by that means, the suspicion of the Magistrates quite over; JOHN NUTHALL's debt being paid, and he again secured to secresy: we began to think of providing necessaries for our intended voyage; which, as they occurred to my thoughts, I set them down, that so nothing might be forgotten. Which take as followeth. A hundredweight of bread, a convenient quantity of cheese, a cask of water, some few bottles of Canary and Madeira wine and beer; these being for the support of Nature: and then for use, a compass, quadrant, chart, half-hour glass, half-minute glass, log and line, large tarpaulin, a hatchet, hammer, saw and nails, some spare boards, a lantern and candles. All which were privately conveyed to a friend's house, not far from the water side, to be in a readiness against the time.

Which after I had bethought myself; who besides, to make choice of for my companions was the next thing to be considered of; but that a lucky chance, after a short expectation, presented itself to us.

For within few days the Governor of Mevis putting in at the Barbadoes; the Governor, for his more noble entertainment, caused the Militia of the town to be in arms: which was attended with revelling, drinking, and feasting to excess; the consequence of which, I easily conjectured would be drowsy security and carelessness.

This time, I therefore thought most proper for our intended enterprise; and gave notice thereof to my intended companions (most of whom I kept ignorant of my design until now, fearing it should by any means be discovered): and ordered them not to carry home their arms, but to bring them, after it was night, to a certain storehouse by the wharf; where I designed to put to sea. The storehouse was then under the care of JOHN WHICKER, one of my confederates; and therefore a most happy convenience to conceal both them and their arms, till it was time to sail.

In the meantime, JOHN NUTHALL employed two lusty blacks to empty the water out of our skiff, and set her afloat; and then brought her to the wharf before the storehouse: whither by this time, we had conveyed our necessaries; keeping the blacks within the storehouse, that they might have no opportunity to discover our design.

About 11 o'clock at night [9*th May*, 1687], thinking it time to embark in our small vessel, we assigned one of our company to stand sentry at the head of the wharf, to give us notice if the Watch should happen to come that way; and then, with all speed, we put our provisions and necessaries aboard: which we had no sooner done, but we had an alarm that the Watch was approaching to the head of the wharf. A misfortune which so surprised us, that we all, of an instant, betook ourselves to our heels. And I, for my own part, soon recovered a friend's house, giving all for lost; supposing my companions were fallen into the enemy's hands.

But whilst I was condoling my misfortune to my friend, and giving him a lamentable account of our attempt and discovery; and also consulting whether to retire in the country, to lie dormant if possible till some better opportunity offered itself, I heard a person at the window inquiring for me.

At first, I was in a dreadful fear, lest it was one of the Watch in quick pursuit after me: but knowing him, by his voice to be one of my companions, I gladly received the account he gave me. Which was, that the Watch came only to call up one of their number, that was to watch with them that night; and then went away, without taking the least notice of the boat.

However, I was so disheartened by this unlucky accident, that I was altogether unwilling to make a second attempt, till at length overruled by the importunity of my friend; more especially when he told me that they all waited for me, and could not go without me, for none of them had any skill in navigation. So, considering the baseness of disappointing so many persons, whom I had engaged in so much danger; I resolved, once more, to hazard a burnt forehead and sore back: and going with him to the water side, I found my companions by the boat, waiting for me, and not a little glad to see me come again.

Then we put the Negroes into the storehouse, charging them not to stir forth or make any noise till the morning: and to encourage them to be faithful to us, I gave them three Half-Pieces of Eight [=6*s*.=18*s*. *now*] for their good service.

This done, and thus delivered from our fears, we embarked in our small vessel; being in number eight, viz., JOHN WHICKER, PETER BAGWELL, WILLIAM WOODCOCK, JOHN COOKE, JEREMIAH ATKINS, and myself, which were Sufferers on the account of the Duke of MONMOUTH: the other two were JOHN NUTHALL, who bought the boat for me, and THOMAS WAKER. THOMAS AUSTIN, of whom I formerly spake, was so possessed with fear of being cast away, that he would not go with us.

About midnight, we put off to sea, designing for Curaçoa, a Dutch island that lies about 200 leagues thence: for we durst not go to any English island, for fear we should be taken and sent back.

We rowed softly forward, within a pistol's shot of the Fort; and there lay at that time, a man-of-war in the road: which made us not a little afraid of being discovered by those watchful enemies; but Providence so ordered it, that we passed both without discovery.

However, by the time that we were got clear of the Fort and the shipping, our boat being so extremely leaky, had taken in so much water, that we were almost ready to sink; not daring to heave it out before, for fear of making a noise to alarm our enemies.

But having the conveniency of a tub and a large wooden bowl; we now fell to work, and in a little time, we pretty well emptied our boat: and then we set our mast, and hoisted our sail, and steered our course south-west as near as I could judge, intending to make the Great Grenada. Our candles being bruised into one mass of tallow, and our tinder and matches being wet, we could not strike a light to steer by our compass; neither indeed had we any candles lighted for the same reason, during our whole voyage: so that, in the night, we were forced to steer by the stars; and when it was cloudy, by the wind.

That which troubled us most was the leakiness of our little vessel. For although we endeavoured all we could to stop her gaping seams with our linen and all the rags we had, which we tallowed with our bruised candles: yet she was so thin, so feeble, so heavily ladened, and wrought [*laboured*] so exceedingly by reason of the great motion of the sea, that we could not possibly make her tight, but were forced to keep one person almost continually, day and night, to throw out the water, during our whole voyage.

The same night, most of my companions were so sea-sick, that notwithstanding we were all ready to sink, I could hard persuade them to throw out the water; and my place being at the helm, to guide and govern the boat, I could not safely go thence. However, at length, through great importunity and earnest persuasions, I prevailed with them to take a little pains to preserve us from drowning. My companions now began to wish themselves at Barbadoes again; and would willingly have returned: but I told them there was no possibility of it, being so far to the leeward of the island.

One of them, through carelessness in heaving out the water, threw over our wooden bowl; and we running away with a large [*full*] wind, could not go back to take it up; so that we had nothing left to throw out the water with, but our tub; which obliged them to be more careful of it, for our lives were concerned therein.

May the 10th [1687], in the morning, we were got almost out of sight of the island; at least far enough from being descried from thence. And perceiving no sort of vessel in pursuit of us, we began to be cheered up with the thoughts of our liberty, and the hopes of our safe arrival at our desired port.

But then, alas, the night no sooner approached, but we were assailed with a brisk gale of wind; under which misfortune, another worse befel us, that we split our rudder so that we were forced to lower our sail, and with an oar to keep our boat before the sea, whilst one of my company, a joiner, mended our helm by nailing to it two pieces of boards. That done, we went cheerily on again.

May the 11th, we had indifferent good weather. My companions being pretty well recovered of their sea-sickness, we now had time to put things in a better posture in our boat; and to raise her, which we did by nailing on tarpolings [*tarpaulings*] from her sides to our oars that were lashed fast about nine inches above, which did us good service in keeping out the sea. We likewise made a tilt [*awning*] with a hammock over the hinder part of our boat, to defend us from the scorching heat of the sun.

May the 12th. This morning, notwithstanding we steered south-west, to weather the Great Grenada, the current had set us so much to the northward, that we made the Grenadilloes to bear west of us: which obliged us to steer more southerly to weather the Great Grenada.

May the 13th. The last night, we weathered the Great Grenada, and steered down the south side of the same; and then shaped our course for the Testigos. For I could not take any true observation by my quadrant, because of the uneven motion of the sea, and the nearness of the sun to the zenith, and therefore was constrained to steer a course from island to island, though the further way about.

May the 14th. We had fair weather, and a fresh gale of wind; and about noon, as I remember, we made the Testigos, bearing south-south-west; and before night, made the north-east end of the Margarita.

But, by this time, being so extremely spent for want of sleep, having been obliged for the most part, night and day, to steer the boat; I was desirous to take a little rest: but first I directed one of my companions how to steer down by the said island; and then composed myself to sleep.

In which interval of time, my companions eagerly longing

for fresh water, in regard ours stank so extremely as it did, stood in for the land; and lowered the sail, designing to go ashore. At which time, I happily [*by chance*] awoke; and apprehending the great danger of falling into the hands of the Indians, who had already kindled a fire on the shore not far from us, I caused the sail again to be hoisted up, and hasted away with all expedition: and being favoured with a brisk gale of wind, we soon got out of fear or danger of those savage cannibals.

May the 15th. We had fair weather, and very pleasant sailing down the north side of this island [*Margarita*]. But when we had got about the middle of the island, my companions were no less importunate than before, to go ashore for fresh water. To which I, at length, consented, partly because I saw that part of the island free from inhabitants, and partly enticed by the fair appearance of a sandy bay and that the water seemed so smooth that I thought we could not injure our boat by running her ashore, in regard we had neither anchor nor grapling to ride her off.

But, contrary to our expectations, and to our great surprisal, we found the ground near the shore extremely foul; and the sea heaved us so fast in, that we could not possibly have avoided being split on the rocks, had not I leaped into the sea to fend her off, which whilst I laboured to do with my feet against the rock till I was almost spent, my companions with their two oars rowed her off. At which, our hearts were filled with joy, and our mouths with praises to the LORD, who had so wonderfully preserved us from being cast away on this island: where probably we must either have been starved ourselves, or have become food for those inhuman man-eaters.

From the west end of this island, we directed our course for Saltatudos; but that afternoon, the wind increased, and a white ring encircled the moon, which I thought presaged ill weather, and to our great sorrow, proved too true. For about nine at night, a dreadful storm arose, which made us despair of ever seeing the morning sun. And now the sea began to foam, and to turn its smooth surface into mountains and vales. Our boat was tossed and tumbled from one side to the other; and so violently driven and hurried away by the fury of the wind and sea, that I was afraid we should be driven by the island in the night-time: and therefore we brought our boat to, with her head against the sea: but the wind and sea still increasing, we were forced to bear up before it, with only sail sufficient to give her steerage way.

And now, in vain we began to wish ourselves at the Barbadoes again, or (which was worse) on that island on which we were so lately like to have been wrecked, believing that a misery then which now we should have thought a happiness, and that which confirmed us the more in the certainty of our approaching ruin, was an unexpected voice, which (to our thinking) seemed to hallow [*holloa*] to us at a great distance. But the Omnipotent (who is never unmindful of the cries of his people in distress) heard our prayers; so that when all our hopes were given over, and we had resigned ourselves into his hands, expecting every moment when the wide gaping sea would devour and swallow us up: GOD, of his infinite mercy and unspeakable goodness, commanded the violence of the winds to cease, and allayed the fury of the raging waves. Eternal praises to his Name for evermore!

May the 16th. This morning, at break of day, we saw the island of Saltatudos just before us, and when it was sufficiently light, that we could discern how the land lay, we steered down the north side of it, intending to go ashore at some convenient place to refresh ourselves after that dreadful storm, and to take on board some fresh water, and if possible to stop the leaks of our boat, in order to proceed in our voyage for Curaçoa: and accordingly, when we came to the leeward of a small island hard by the other, we stood in directly for the shore, thinking it a convenient place to land. Which we had no sooner done, but we saw a canoe coming thence, directing her course towards us. At which sight, being a little surprised, my companions provided their arms, and charged their muskets and blunderbusses with glass bottles: for we coming from Barbadoes in so great a hurry and fear; through forgetfulness they left their bag of bullets on the wharf.

When they were come somewhat nearer, that we could perceive them to paddle like Indians, we bore up and were running from them.

Which as soon as they perceived, they waved their hats and hailed us; by which we knew they were not Indians as we supposed: and therefore we permitted them to come nearer, and perceiving them to be white men, we enquired "What they were?"

They told us, "They were Englishmen in distress, &c., and waited for an opportunity to go off the island."

The account we gave them of ourselves was very short That we came from one of the Windward islands: by which, they supposed we had fled for debt; and should have continued in that belief, had not THOMAS WAKER, one of my companions, privately informed them, That there were only he and JOHN NUTHALL that were debtors: the rest of us being rebels: for he thought thereby to ingratiate himself and friend in their friendship.

But these privateers, for so they were, as we afterwards understood, hated them the more for their treachery; and loved us the better, confessing that they were rebels too, adding that "if the Duke of MONMOUTH had had 1,000 of them, they would soon have put to flight the King's army."

But to proceed. When we came to the shore, the privateers assisted us to haul up our boat that she might not be injured by the sea; having no conveniency to ride her off [*i.e., at anchor*].

Which done, they shewed us the well of fresh water which was hard by their huts; where we refreshed ourselves a little; and with our sail we made a shade to keep the sun from us: and when we had so done, we lay down under it, to refresh ourselves with rest and sleep; having had but little of either, all our voyage, being so extremely thronged together in our little boat.

These privateers at first were very kind to us, and gave us some of their provisions: and related to us the story of their adventures; which, to the best of my memory, was thus:

That they formerly belonged to one Captain YANCHE, Commander of a Privateer of 48 guns, that designed to plunder a Spanish town by the Gulf of Florida, called St. Augustine. And in order thereunto, he sent 30 of them out into the Gulf of Florida, to take canoes from the Indians; for the more convenient and speedy landing of their men. But they going ashore on the Main to turn turtle [*i.e., on their backs*], were set upon by the Indians, and two of them killed on the place. However, at length, they put the Indians to flight; and some time afterwards, took two or three canoes, and one Indian prisoner: who conducted them to his own and his father's plantations, on condition they would afterwards set him free; where they stored themselves with provisions and other necessaries. But it cost them dear. For their Quartermaster and one more of the company were poisoned, by their unwary eating of casader [*cassava*] roots.

The rest of them went, with those canoes and the Indian they had taken, to the place appointed, expecting to meet their man-of-war: but could not find her, and therefore being necessitated to shift for themselves as well as they could, they came to this island, hoping to meet here with some vessel loading of salt in which they might get a passage for some English port: but were disappointed here also, for the ships were all gone before they came.

After we had sufficiently refreshed ourselves with rest and sleep, and returned to the LORD the praises due to his Name, for his wonderful and miraculous deliverance; we thought it time to consider how to stop the leaks of our boat, and to raise a deck over her with rinds [*barks*] of trees, &c., that we might proceed in our intended voyage for Curaçoa.

Our intentions were no sooner perceived by the privateers, but they endeavoured to persuade us from it: alleging the insufficiency of our boat, and the dangers we were so lately exposed unto; and advising us rather to go with them in their pereagoes [*piraguas*] a privateering than to hazard our lives by a second attempt. With the like argument, they would have easily prevailed with my companions to consent to go with them; had I not persuaded them to the contrary.

But when the privateers saw it was in vain to persuade, they thought to compel us, by burning our boat: supposing then that we would choose rather to go with them, than to stay upon the island till shipping came for salt, which would be eight or nine months; and in the meantime, to be in danger of being taken by the Spaniards for privateers, or otherwise to be starved with hunger, for we had no more than 4lbs. or 5lbs. of bread for each man left.

But this contrivance answered not their expectations. For notwithstanding they burnt our boat and took our sails and other utensils from us, I continued my resolution, and chose rather to trust Divine Providence on that desolate and uninhabitable island than to partake or be any ways concerned with them in their piracy: having confidence in myself, that GOD, who had so wonderfully and miraculously preserved us on the sea and brought us to this island, would, in like manner, deliver us hence, if we continued faithful to Him.

And in order to our better accommodation and preservation on this island, I gave the privateers 30 Pieces of Eight [=£6=£18 *now*] for the Indian they took on the Main, but were not so true to their promise as to set him at liberty; who I expected would be serviceable unto us in catching fish, &c.

About the 25th of May [1687], 22 of the privateers, having first raised the sides of their pereagoes [*piraguas*] with boards, fastened with the nails they saved in the burning of our boat, and fitted them for sea; they set sail: leaving four of their company behind, that refused to go with them; as also a Spanish boat that was of no service to them, neither could be of any use to us, unless we had sails to sail her, and a rudder to guide her, both of which we wanted.

In this situation, they left us, deprived of all ways and means of getting off until the season aforesaid: unless GOD, by a particular Providence, should direct some vessel or other to touch here.

But before I proceed to give account of our manner of life in this place, I think it necessary to give a short description of the island itself; which is situated in the latitude of 11° 11′ N. Lat. Its extent is about twelve miles in length, and two or three in breadth; and is about 120 leagues from Barbadoes.

It is called by the Spaniards, *Tortuga*, from the plenty of turtle that resort thither: but our English give it the name of *Saltatudos*, because there is such a great quantity of salt yearly brought from thence. The Spaniards claim the propriety of this island, lying so near the Main [*South America*], where they inhabit; and therefore will sometimes take our English vessels as they are loading salt: of which they took two, the season before we came there.

The east and west ends of this island are for the most part

sand. The middle consists of hard and craggy rocks, that are very porous, and resemble honeycombs: and therefore we called them Honeycomb Rocks. There are plenty of small bushes growing out of the sand, and of shrubs from between the rocks: but there are no timber trees on the whole island.

On the south side, near the east end, are the *salinas* or salt ponds; from whence the salt is brought; which is thus made. The sea or salt water penetrates through the beachy banks of the sea, and overflows a large plain of two or three miles circumference, nearly a foot deep; where, by the scorching heat of the sun, the thin aqueous part is exhaled, and the saline part is coagulated into pure white crystaline salt. And because there is a continual supply of salt water from the sea, the sun continues exhaling and coagulating, until the whole *salinas* is deeply covered over with salt; so that all they have to do, is only to rake it together, and carry it aboard.

There is great plenty of birds and fowl, as pelicans, flammans [? *flamingoes*], paraquets, mocking birds, and an innumerable company of sea fowl: and also some vegetable productions, of which I shall have occasion to treat hereafter.

But to return from this digression. The privateers had no sooner left us, but we found ourselves, of necessity, obliged to seek out for provisions. Being led by the example of those four privateers that stayed behind; we walked along the sea shore to watch for tortoises or turtle: which when they came up out of the sea to lay their eggs in the sand, we turned on their backs. And they being incapable of turning themselves again, we let them remain so till the day following, or until we had conveniency of killing them: for if they were sufficiently defended from the heat of the sun by a shade, which we usually built over them, they would live several days out of the water.

And thus we walked to and fro in the night-time, to turn turtle; and in the day-time, we were employed in killing them: whose flesh was the chiefest of our diet, being roasted by the fire on wooden spits. And sometimes when we designed a festival, we left some part of the flesh on the calapatch and calapee, that is, the back and breast shells;

which we roasted, by setting them upright in two forked sticks thrust into the sand, before a large fire.

What we did not eat, we cut into long and slender pieces; and after we had salted it very well, we dried it carefully in the sun, on ranges of sticks set up for that purpose: for we had no other way of preserving it, having nothing to wet salt in. But we found it so difficult to divide their shells, that we broke our knives; and were forced to make new ones out of the swords my companions brought with them: which we did after this manner. First, we broke them into suitable lengths, and softened them in the fire; and then rubbed them on a stone to a fit shape and thinness: and after we had hardened them again, we fixed them in hafts, and made them more serviceable than our former.

And here for the better information of some persons, I think fit to describe these sea beasts, if I may so call them. They are somewhat of an oval form, strongly defended on the back and on the breast with a thick shell; and have four fins covered with thick scales, that serve them instead of legs when they come ashore. They feed on Woose or Sea Grass that grows out of the rocks; which I judge is the true reason they do not eat fishy. They breathe, and therefore are obliged to come frequently up to the surface of the water; on which they sometimes float so soundly asleep, that they give seamen an opportunity with a boat to take them up. Their flesh is very delightsome and pleasant to the taste, much resembling veal; but their fat is more yellow. The she or female turtle come up on the shore to lay their eggs in the sand, three times in the year, in the months of April, May, and June; where they are brought to maturity by the sweet influence of the sun. When the young ones are hatched, they muster out of their cells and march into the sea: but not without danger of being devoured by the sea fowl that wait to destroy them. Each of these tortoises lays about 140 eggs at one time, in about an hour's space; which are fully as large as hens' eggs, but with this difference, that these are round, and covered only with a thick strong membrane or skin, nor will their whites harden by heat as the whites of hens' eggs. Their yolks we beat in calabashes with some salt; and fried them with the fat of the tortoise, like to pancakes, in a piece of an earthen jar found by the sea-side: which we did eat instead of bread.

I never saw any creature so long a-dying as these: for after we had cut their throats, divided their bodies, and cut their flesh into small and minute parts; every part and portion would continue twitching and moving itself a long time. They have a threefold heart, said to be the heart of a fowl, of a beast, and of a fish; which will stir and pant several hours after it is taken out of their body.

Our continual feeding on these tortoises brought us to a violent looseness [*diarrhœa*] which I speedily stopped with an opiatic tincture, which I had provided on another occasion. For before we came from Barbadoes, I thought of a way to deliver ourselves out of our enemies' hands, in case we should be taken, without shedding of blood. And it was thus. I dissolved a sufficient quantity of opium in a bottle of rich cordial water, which we carried with us in the boat: intending to give it to those persons that should take us, which I supposed they would readily drink, and by that means would be overtaken with so profound a sleep that we should have opportunity sufficient to make our escape from them.

We were obliged to go many miles from the well of fresh water, to turn turtle, and to fetch salt from the *salinas*. This necessitated us to carry our water with us in a cask, over those uneven rocks, which soon wore out our shoes, and compelled us to make use of our soft and tender feet, unwilling to salute those hard and craggy rocks: which was very irksome to us at first, but time and necessity made it more familiar and easy, that, at length, the bottoms of our feet were hardened into such a callous substance that there were scarcely any rocks so hard but we could boldly trample them under our feet.

When the season of the tortoises' coming ashore was expired, and we had gotten a considerable quantity of their flesh salted and dried for our winter store; we set about building houses to defend us from the stormy weather, which we were shortly to expect, which we did so artificially, and covered them so well with coarse grass that grew by the sea-side, that neither the violence of winds, nor fierceness of storms could easily injure or offend us. Our household goods consisted chiefly in two or three earthen jars left us by the privateers, some few calabashes, and shells of fish that we found by the sea-side. In our houses, we formed a kind of little cabins to repose ourselves in, with as much ease as possibly we could.

In these little huts or houses, we spent most of our time; sometimes reading or writing. And at other times, I went abroad with my Indian a-fishing, at which he was so dexterous that with his bow and arrow, he would shoot a small fish at a great distance. Sometimes we caught some craw-fish, which we broiled over the coals; and for change of diet, we sometimes ate a sort of shell fish that live on the rocks, and are like snails, but much larger, called W[h]ilks.

And as there is no mountain so barren, on which there may not be found some medicinal plant; so neither was this island so unfruitful, but it afforded us two vegetable productions of great service unto us. The one we called Turks' Heads, being of an oval form, beset on every side with sharp prickles like a hedgehog; out of which there grew in the upper part, a longish red and pleasant fruit, about the bigness of a small nut, in taste resembling a strawberry. The other was much more serviceable to us, called *Curatoe* [*? the Agave*], of an oval body or stump, like the former: but out of this grew long thick leaves, whose edges were prickly, and its juice so exceeding sharp and pungent that it was not easily suffered on the bare skin; with which we washed our linen as with soap, for it would scour excellently well. Through the leaves are dispersed long and thready fibres, with which, when we had separated and dried them in the sun, we made very good thread, and mended our clothes therewith, in needles which we made of bones. With the leaves, I made a most excellent balsom [*poultice*] for wounds, by boiling them in the fat of the tortoises, which I brought to a sufficient consistency by adding bees' wax thereunto. Thus much of its external use.

Its internal use follows. After we had cut off the leaves about three or four inches from the body, we digged a great hole or pit in the sand, and heated it exceedingly hot; and put the said body therein, covering it up in the hot sand: where we permitted it to remain five or six days, in which time, the juice that was before extraordinarily sharp and corrosive, by this digestion became so strangely changed that it was extremely sweet and pleasant, like the syrup of baked pears. And after we had pressed it forth, and fermented it with a proportionable quantity of water; it became a most pleasant and spirituous liquor to drink. The innermost part of the body or stump, we cut into slices, and ate it like bread.

At this island, there is an innumerable company of sea fowl that lay their eggs in the sand, overspreading at some places, nearly twenty yards as near together as the birds can well sit to lay them. And when the young ones are hatched, they run about in great companies, like chickens, a considerable time before they are able to fly; which often afforded us pleasant diversion, to pursue and take them: which, when we had skinned, salted, and dried in the sun, we could preserve a long time. But they did eat extremely fishy; much like red herrings.

We endeavoured to make a pot to boil our turtle in, by tempering the finest sand with the yolks of turtles' eggs and goats' hair: for we could find no clay or earth in the whole island: but we could not possibly make them endure the drying; so that we were forced to eat our turtle roasted by the fire on wooden spits.

There is a pleasant fragrant herb grows out of the sand among the rocks, which we call Wild Sage; whose leaves we smoked instead of Tobacco: and for want of a pipe, I smoked it in a crab's claw; of which crabs there were plenty, but they were so poor that we did not eat them.

There is also an insect called a Soldier [? *the hermit crab*]; having a shell like a snail: but some say this shell is not proper to themselves. For having weak and tender bodies, they get possession of these shells to defend themselves against the injury of the air, and attempts of other creatures. As they grow bigger, they shift their shells, and get into large; being commonly those of Peridwinkles. They have, instead of a foot, an instrument like a crab's claw, wherewith they close the entrance of their shells, and thereby secure their whole body. When they are set near the fire, they presently forsake their quarters; and if it be presented to them again, they go backwards. They commonly keep in great companies about the rocks near the well of fresh water. When they intend to change their lodgings, there sometimes happens a serious engagement, managed with that clasping instrument; still the strongest, by conquest, gets possession, which he carries about with him, on his back, during his pleasure.

Another little insect is worthy to be mentioned, called Lizards. They were so familiar and friendly, that they would come boldly among us, and do us no harm. They have four legs and their bodies are adorned with divers delightsome colours. They feed on flies, and for that reason were serviceable unto us in killing them: which they performed with great nimbleness and cunning. For they lay down where they supposed the fly would come, putting their heads into as many different postures as the fly shifts places; and when they find their advantage, they start so directly on their prey with open mouth, that they seldom miss it. They are so very tame that, when we were eating, they would come on our meat and hands to catch flies.

After we had spent about three months [*May–August*, 1687] in this desolate and disconsolate island; we saw a ship, attended by a small sloop, steering towards the shore. At which, we were at once possessed with hopes and fears: with hopes, that it was some English vessel, in which we might probably get a passage thence; and with fear, lest it should be a Spaniard, who doubtless would make us prisoners, if they could take us, supposing that we were privateers.

The four privateers that remained with us all this time, drew near the sea-side, where the ship was at an anchor, and after they had discovered them to be privateers, made signs to them to send their boat ashore: which accordingly they did.

And after they had carried them on board, the Captain of the man-of-war sent up the sloop to that part of the island where I and my companions were: and when they came ashore unto us, they inquired, "Which was the Doctor?"

My companions informed them it was I. One of them therefore addressed himself particularly to me, desiring me, in the name and on the behalf of their Captain, to go with them on board the man-of-war; where I should be kindly entertained, and have liberty to come [*go*] ashore when I pleased.

I readily embraced this kind invitation; but could not procure liberty for any of ny companions to go with me.

When we came to the man-of-war, I was very honourably handed up the side, the trumpets in the meantime sounding; and very kindly received and welcomed aboard by the Captain and Doctor: who invited me aft into the Great Cabin, where I was not only feasted with wine and choice provisions; but had given me by the Doctor a pair of silk stockings, a pair of shoes, and a great deal of linen cloth to make me shirts, &c.

After a long discourse concerning the affairs of England, more particularly of the progress and defeat of the Duke of MONMOUTH, which they seemed to deplore; I addressed myself to the Captain in the behalf of myself and companions, humbly entreating him to permit us to go with them either to that port to which they were bound, or otherwise to put us on board some English ship that they should accidentally meet withal. For I understood by their discourse, that they had taken a rich prize; and were bound directly for a port, to spend their money, as they usually do: so that I apprehended no danger in going with them.

But the Captain not being able to take us aboard without the consent of the Company, having but two votes and as many shares in the ship and cargo; the Company were called together, and, after some debates, they voted that they would take me with them, but none of my companions. However they were so kind that they sent them a cask of wine, some bread and cheese, a gammon of bacon, some linen cloth, thread and needles to make them shirts, &c. And the next day, they permitted them to come on board, and entertained them very courteously.

In about two days' time, we set sail; leaving my companions on the island, not a little grieved at my departure. We stood away to the northward, with a design to go to Illa Terra.

From which, at present I shall digress to give an account of what became of those privateers that left us; who were the occasion of my being delivered from this place.

The next day [26th *May*, 1687], after they went from us, they arrived at the main continent, where they hauled up their piraguas, and stayed there about a fortnight, waiting to seize some Spanish vessel that might come that way, which they designed, if possible, speedily to board before the Spaniards could get themselves in a posture of defence. But not meeting here with any prize, they went to the windward; where they took a canoe ladened with pork: and meeting with some English vessel at one of the Windward Islands, they parted company. Some went for Carolina. The others went in a small sloop to Blanco: where they met with a man-of-war, a Privateer, that had taken a Portuguese, a great ship called the *Grand Gustaphus*, laden with wine and linen cloth, &c. When these had shared her cargo, they parted company: the French with their shares went it for Petty Guavas, in the *Grand Gustaphus*; and the English being informed by those other privateers of our being on Saltatudos, came thither with their man-of-war, as is before expressed.

In about five or six days after we left Saltatudos, we made Porto Rico. Our vessel being so extremely leaky, some of the Company were for putting into Mena. But the rest not consenting, we steered betwixt Porto Rico and Hispaniola, and so to the eastward of the *Abroletas* or "Handkerchers": where there were divers vessels on the Wrack, diving for plate. But we stopped not here, but continued our course to the northward until we came into the latitude of Illa Terra, and then steered away west for the island.

As we were running down, we saw a ketch, to which we gave chase, and in a few hours came up with her; who told us that they came from New York, and were bound for Providence.

As soon as the privateers understood that Providence [*one of the Bahamas*] was inhabited again; they altered their resolutions, and designed to go with them to that place: and accordingly kept them company.

The night following, we met with bad weather, and were like to run ashore on Illa Terra, through the carelessness of our pilot; had not a person from the quarter-deck, that was more watchful than the rest, espied the land just before us.

But this was not all. For after we had tacked about, and

were lying by, with the heads of both vessels off ashore, the men on board the ketch were so drunk with the wine the privateers had given them, that they suffered their ketch to drive aboard us, and, with the violence of the blow she gave us, broke down our cat-head: and had we not by a particular Providence, got free from her: we had both unavoidably sunk down in the sea. For our vessel was so extremely leaky before, that at the same time she had three feet of water in her hold; and our pumps being both out of order, we were forced to convey it out with tubs.

The next day, we steered into Providence, and came to anchor under the command of a small *stochadoe* fort [*stockade*], built by the new inhabitants; who had not been there above eight months. But they had so well improved their time, that they had built a town by the seaside; and elected a Governor from among themselves: who, with the consent of twelve more of the chief men of the island, made and enacted divers laws for the good of their little commonwealth; being as yet under the protection of no Prince.

The privateers found here a kind reception by the inhabitants. After they had gotten their goods ashore, they ran their ship aground, and burnt her; giving their guns to the inhabitants to fortify the island: designing to divide themselves into small numbers, and to go thence, to some other place where they might sell their goods, and betake themselves to an honest course of life.

The Governor of this island was a very sober man, an Independent; and usually preached to the inhabitants every First Day of the week: at which time, he caused a gun to be fired for a signal, to give notice to the people, when he was going to begin.

Whilst I remained here, the privateers had two false alarms; supposing the Spaniards were come again to dispossess them of the island. For this being formerly a harbour for privateers, and a nest of robbers; the Spaniards, on a time when most of the men were on the Old Wrack, pillaged and burnt their towns; carried away, as it was reported, £30,000 [=£90,000 *now*] in plate and money; and took some of the inhabitants prisoners. The others fled to Illa Terra, where they remained till this island was resettled by those few inhabitants that came from Jamaica and other parts.

The island itself is very fruitful, and if the report of the inhabitants be true, the quickest in production of any I ever heard or read of. There is plenty of wild hogs in the woods, which the inhabitants often kill; and good store of wild grapes, with which they make good wine; and divers sorts of fruits, as oranges, lemons, limes, guavas: also medicinal herbs as *tea radix*, *Contra yerva*, *Jesuit's bark*, &c. Of eatable roots, there are partatoes, yams, edders, &c.

The ketch, with whom we came in company to this island, sold part of their bread and flour to the privateers, for linen cloth; and some they sold to the inhabitants.

In about a fortnight's time, they set sail for Carolina, and I with them. As we were sailing down among the Bohemia islands [*Bahamas*], towards the Gulf of Florida; we were like to be cast away on the rocks and shoals that lay in our way: but, through mercy, we got clear.

When we came on the coast of Carolina, we met with blowing weather; and by the mistake of our Captain fell in [with the coast] to the Southward, where we came to an anchor: but the wind was so high, that in weighing of it, our cable broke.

The next day we came to an anchor again just before the bar of Carolina [? *Charleston*]: for our Captain was afraid to go in with his vessel, for fear they would seize him, because he had been dealing with the privateers: and for that reason, he only sent in his boat, to get some fresh provisions, and to put on shore a passenger that came with us.

And because I found no vessel here, bound directly for England, I resolved to go with them to New York. And here also, we had the misfortune to lose our other anchor: insomuch that when we came to Sandy Hook, we were forced to ride our vessel by two of her guns, which we had slung for that purpose, until our boat had got us a small anchor from on board some other vessel. The next day, we went up to New York.

Where, as I was walking one morning on the bridge, I accidentally met with a person I knew, that came lately from Barbadoes. At first I was surprised; but having confidence that he would not discover me, I went to him, and desired him to come to some house, where we might privately discourse together.

He was glad to see me safe there: and according to my desire, he went with me to a house hard by: where I gave him an account of my adventures, and what had happened to me since I left Barbadoes.

He, in requital, gave me an account of the different resentments people had at our departure, and how after we were gone, our Masters had hired a sloop to send after us; but thinking it in vain, they did not pursue us. However, they sent our names and the description of our persons to the Leeward Islands, that so, if any of us came thither, we might be taken prisoners and sent up again.

At one time, it was reported that we had gotten aboard a Dutch vessel, and were bound for Holland: at another time, that we were taken prisoners at St. Christophers, and to be sent back in chains; which made our Masters rejoice, and insultingly to boast of the severe punishments they would inflict upon us. They were resolved, as they said, that I should be hanged! for an example to others; because I was the chief contriver and manager of our escape. But these hopes and insultings of theirs were soon over: for when, at length, they could hear no true account of us, they concluded that we had perished in the sea.

I had not been long at New York, before I got passage in a vessel bound for Amsterdam; and in order thereunto took out a Ticket from the Secretary's Office by another name.

In about five weeks' time, we arrived at Cowes, on the Isle of Wight; where this vessel stopped to clear.

As soon as I had got my chest, &c., ashore, I embarked for Southampton; where I left my chest at a friend's house.

I returned in a disguise to my relations: who, before this time, unknown to me, had procured my *Pardon*; and joyfully received me, as one risen from the dead. For having received no account from me, since I left Barbadoes; they did almost despair of ever seeing me any more.

NOw unto the Eternal and True GOD, the sacred Fountain of all mercies, that has been with me in all dangers and times of trial, Who miraculously preserved me on the deep waters, and according to the multitude of His mercies delivered me when appointed to die: unto Him, do I, with sincere gratitude, dedicate the remainder of my days! humbly imploring that the Angel of His Presence may always attend me! and the remembrance of His repeated favours more and more engage my heart to serve Him! that in testimony of my abundant thankfulness, I may return to Him, a perpetual sacrifice of praise and thanksgiving, henceforth and for ever!

From my lodging, at the sign of the *Ship*, in Paul's Churchyard, London. June the 10th, 1689.

HENRY PITMAN.

An Account of the adventures of my Companions, since I left them on Saltatudos.

Communicated to me, by JOHN WHICKER, since his arrival in England.

DEAR DOCTOR,

IN ANSWER to your request, I have given you the following account.

About a fortnight after you left us on Saltatudos [*in August*, 1687], two of our companions, JOHN NUTHALL and THOMAS WAKER [*the two that had not been out with MONMOUTH*], having made sails of the cloth the privateers left us, and fitted the Spanish boat for the sea, went from us, designing for Curaçoa. But the boat was so large and unruly, and they, so unskilful in navigation; that I fear they either perished in the sea, or were driven ashore on the Main among the cruel Spaniards: for we never heard of them since.

The next day after they departed from us, there arrived here a small Privateer boat, of about 4 tons; in which were eight Englishmen and one Negro, that formerly belonged to the ship in which you embarked, but had left her, and went ashore upon an island called Fernando [Po], which lies to the southward, on the coast of Brazil.

Their reason for leaving their ship was this. Having

been out of Carolina, about a year and a half, and had made nothing considerable of a voyage, they had resolved for the South Seas, but coming to the Straits of Magellan, they met with very bad weather, which forced them to put back again; and then they resolved to turn pirates.

But these eight men being averse to the rest of their companions' design, went ashore upon the island aforesaid, carrying with them what they had on board, and intending to go from thence in a small boat, which was given them by the ship's crew, with some rigging and other necessaries; which they designed to build upon and raise higher in case of bad weather, having in their company two carpenters and a joiner.

Taking their leave of each other, the ship put to sea. Next morning, she saw a sail at a considerable distance; but making the best of their way, they soon came up with her; and finding her to be a Portuguese, they laid her aboard, and took her with very little resistance; though she was a bigger ship, and had more men than the Privateer.

Having made her a prize, they brought her away to the same island [? *Fernando Po*], on which were their companions; and turned the prisoners ashore among them, giving them a boat and oars. But this caused no small trouble among the English who were then inhabiters with them. Being well armed, they kept them at a distance from their apartment all that day: but the next night, the Portuguese ran away, carrying with them their own boat and the Englishmen's too.

Then were they in a bad condition, not having a ship nor boat with which they could convey themselves from that desolate island.

Then were they constrained to cut and fell a sort of trees called mangroves; and in the best manner they could, sawed out boats, planks, and other timbers fit for their use; and began to build a new boat from the keel.

In six weeks, or thereabouts, they finished her, being in burden as they judged 4 tons. No one was idle, but employed himself; some about their new vessel, while others, by turns, travelled the island to shoot for provision: which was a sort of birds, called Boobies, something resembling our English seagulls or pies, but bigger.

This island affords a sort of very large and pleasant figs; which they also fed on sometimes. There are a great many wild dogs, very large and fat, which eat very little or nothing but figs. Likewise, in the day-time, there came ashore sea lions [? *walruses*], which will sit by the water-side, and make hideous roaring. They are hairy about their head and neck, much like our land lions; their paws are very large, with a skin like the foot of a swan, which serves them to swim withal. They are very fearful and timorous, not suffering a man to come nigh them but presently they make to the sea. They live under water as well as above.

Having launched and rigged their boat, they put on board their provisions; which was only a small cask of pease that was given them by the ship, which they kept by them for their sea store.

Having water and all things aboard, they took their departure from Fernando aforesaid, committing themselves to the protection of Almighty GOD and the mercies of the seas, and directing their course for Tobago. But missing it, the pilot ordered to bear up the helm for Saltatudos: at which place they arrived, but almost famished; for they had had neither peas nor water for the space of five or six days before.

Having lain some days at the east end of the island unknown to us, and being in great want of provisions, they resolved to travel over the island to see if they could find out any food. By chance, they found some salt turtle, which we had laid upon a tree, and covered it over with a calapatch to secure it from the weather.

Three of these men being very unprincipled and loose kind of fellows, waiting their opportunity when three of their companions were abroad, went aboard and fetched their arms: then came to the hut, where the other two were, and presented a pistol to each of their breasts, and swore "If they would not carry everything aboard, they were dead men!"

The two men being surprised, and not able to make any resistance (the three having all the arms in their custody) were forced to comply, and carry all aboard.

Which done, they charged them that "if they did not acquaint them when the others came home, they would make them examples!"

They promised very fair.

Having done this, they went aboard, waiting for their coming home.

In the evening, the other three men came to their hut, not mistrusting what had happened; but finding the hut rifled and everything gone, inquired the meaning of it. Which having understood, they bethought what to do.

To tarry, they were afraid: to go, they could not tell where. For they had travelled all day, and could not find a drop of fresh water; neither was there any at the hut, for the others had carried all aboard.

Being very faint, one was resolved to hail the boat, and beg a little. The others kept close [*hid*] to see how he would fare.

Who having hailed them, they made answer "He should have some." So coming ashore, they laid hold on him, and tied his hands behind him; and left him in custody with one of them, while they went to look for the rest. The reason why they endeavoured to take them, was because they had hid their money in the sand, and did not keep it in their chests.

But in the meantime, while they were looking for the others, the prisoner, by means of a knife he had in his pocket, cut loose the line with which his hands were tied, and made his escape.

Being thus exiled from his companions, he bethought himself of ranging the island to look for men: for the turtle which they had found came afresh in his memory. All this time he had no victuals, nor a drop of water; being excessively hot.

At length, having travelled about the island till almost ready to faint; he came near our huts; and seeing us dressing of turtle with nothing on but a pair of drawers; the man made a stand, thinking we had been Indians, for we were tanned with the sun almost as yellow as them.

At length, he advanced, and inquired if we were Englishmen?

We told him, "We were."

Then he begged for a little water, which we gave him, and some of our turtle.

And after some conference, he told us of his condition, and desired us to help him to regain what was so ungratefully taken from him and his fellow sufferers, by their own countrymen and boat's crew. Which we readily agreed to.

And when we had fixed our arms, we travelled all night till we came where the boat lay; which was about six or seven miles from that place.

When we came near the place, we hid ourselves in the bushes by the sea-side, waiting their coming ashore next morning, which they usually did, as we were informed.

Morning being come; two of them came ashore, and the Negro slave bearing a vessel to fetch water: they with their arms, and leaving one aboard, with twelve pieces by him ready loaded.

When they were come ashore, we appeared, with our arms ready cocked, enclosed them and took them prisoners.

Then we brought them to the water-side, and shewed the other aboard what we had done, commanding him not to fire, but to jump overboard, and swim ashore to us: which he immediately did.

So taking them all three prisoners, we put them ashore, leaving them some of our provisions.

[? *Did* DEFOE *get his idea of* WILL. ATKINS *&c. from this.*]

The rest we put aboard, in order to prosecute our voyage for New England. So victualling and watering our small frigate in the best manner we could, we left them upon the island; and the 24th of August [1687] we took our departure from Saltatudos.

In about six days' time, we made the island of Porto Rico; but our pilot not being very well acquainted with that country, supposed it to be the high land of Santo Domingo upon Hispaniola; and therefore ordered to bear up the helm and stand away to the westward before the wind.

The next day, we could see no land; which caused no small trouble amongst us, being dubious where we were.

Towards the evening, we made the east end of Hispaniola. Then our pilot saw his error, and that we had lost our passage between the islands Hispaniola and Porto Rico.

We were sailing down the south side of Hispaniola about nine days, having sometimes very little wind, and at other times tornadoes that we could carry no sail. Our water was all spent.

Running along close aboard the shore, we espied three men running with all the haste that possibly they could, till they came to a canoe which lay at the mouth of a creek; which immediately they rowed up into the country among the woods. We imagined they were afraid of us, supposing us to be Spaniards.

Then we came to an anchor, and I myself with one more, a carpenter, swam ashore: but with a great deal of difficulty, for the rocks lying so far off the shore, had like to have dashed out our brains.

Coming ashore, we swam up the creek; but the tide being so strong against us, we were forced to return back again, neither finding the men nor hope of getting fresh water. Therefore we swam aboard again.

Weighing our anchor, we steered within the isle of Ash, which lies almost to the west end of Hispaniola. Our pilot looking over his Waggoner, found that within this island was a fresh-water creek, into which we designed to run; but through mistake ran about two leagues up into a wrong creek where we could find no fresh water: so that with drinking salt water, our mouths were almost grown together and hardly able to speak. But GOD Almighty was pleased to send us a very great shower of rain, which lasted so long that, by means of a sheet held up by the four corners, with a weight in it, we caught about two gallons of water.

So lowering our sails we hauled up the creek into the woods, and went ashore, and concluded to dig a well. When we had digged about four or six feet deep, we found fresh water to our great comfort and satisfaction.

Lying ashore all night to take up the water as it sprang, we were almost stung to death with a sort of flies, called *Musquitoes* and *Merrywings*, which drew blisters and bladders in our skin, that we looked as if we had the smallpox; which were very tedious for our bodies too.

By next morning, we had got about forty gallons of water aboard; with which we put to sea again.

But we had not been at sea above three hours, before we saw a sail within the west end of the isle of Ash before mentioned. We bore up our helm, and stood away for her. In a short time, we saw her come to an anchor.

Supposing her to be a Jamaica sloop, for she had our King's Jack [*arms*] and ancient [*colours*]; we hailed them.

Whose answer was "From Jamaica."

So coming to anchor by their side, they laid us aboard with two canoes, full of Spaniards, all armed as pirates, and carried us aboard their sloop, stripped us naked, and put us down in their hold: having nothing to lay our naked bodies upon but their ballast stones, or atop of their water cask.

The provisions they allowed us were coarse and short: about half a pint of Indian corn a day for a man, for nine days together.

The place where they carried us is called St. Jago, a Spanish town upon Cuba.

We remained in this condition above six months. When they went to sea, we were carried as their slaves; to pump ship, wash their clothes, and beat corn in great wooden mortars; with Negroes, with naked swords, always standing by as overseers: so that our hands have been bladdered, and so sore that we could hardly hold anything. When at home, our business was to row the canoe up two leagues into the country; full of jars, to fetch water, which we were forced to carry upon our naked backs a great way, to fill them; sometimes, into the woods to cut wood, barefooted and barelegged, with neither a shirt to our back, nor a hat to our head, but only a rag sufficient to cover our nakedness. Our provisions, as I told you before, were Indian corn boiled in water; but a larger share than the first.

About the latter end of October [1687], we were divided: myself with three more were put on board a small bark, the rest of my companions remained aboard the sloop; both vessels being bound down to leeward of Cape [de] Cruz; having information of a Dutch trader that lay there, before a small town, called Byan.

In which voyage, we were all taken very sick in the ague, as well Spaniards as English; which reduced us to a deplorable condition, having nothing to yield us any comfort.

In this distemper, died one of our companions, JEREMIAH ATKINS, of Taunton. During his sickness, they were very cruel to him; not suffering us to carry him down into the hold, but made him lie day and night upon the deck. All we could do for him, was to cover him with the bark of a cabbage tree, to keep the sun from him by day, and the dew by night. In this languishing condition, he lay about a week; and then died. When dead, they threw him overboard, letting him float astern; without using any means to sink him, as is usual.

Returning back again for St. Jago, without their expected prize; myself and one more of our companions were taken again from on board the bark, and put aboard the sloop; and two others of our English were put aboard the bark, which took its departure from us at Cape [de] Cruz aforesaid, bound for Cartagena, a Spanish town upon the main continent.

In five days, we arrived at our port of St Jago, where we lay about a month.

Having careened our sloop, we put to sea again, bound for the north side of Hispaniola, to take Frenchmen.

Turning up to windward of Cuba, we met with a Jamaica sloop bound for the Wrack. The Spaniard commanded him to hoist out his canoe, and come aboard: which he refusing, went his way.

Having weathered Cape Myceze [*Maysi*], which is the eastward point of Cuba, we stood along shore, bound for a small town, called Barracco [*Baracoa*], where in two days we arrived.

We lay there till the latter end of October, [1687], at which place our sloop drave ashore, and struck off about fourteen feet of her false keel: but after a great deal of trouble, we got her off again. At this place, they got two hogs; and a quantity of plantains, a sort of food that grow upon trees, and are made use of instead of bread, among the inhabitants in the West Indies.

We then proceeded in our voyage for Hispaniola, and fell in with a place called the Mould. Off which place, we saw two sail: an English vessel that came from Jamaica, bound for New York; and a French sloop bound for Petty Guavas, a French town to leeward, on the north side of the said Hispaniola.

Having a fresh gale, we came up with the Englishman, brought him by the lee, commanded the Captain with four of his men aboard, and put twelve Spaniards aboard his ship.

Then chasing the Frenchman, we came up with him, about an hour after night. The Frenchman stood it out and fought us, making a stout resistance; although they had not above seven or eight men, and of the Spaniards, there were thirty-five men, eight guns, six patteroes, and every man his small arms. The French making such a bold resistance kept them off till such time as they had an opportunity to run their sloop aground in the Mould, in the dark; by which means they saved their lives: otherwise they had been all dead men, as the Spaniards swore if they took them.

In the next morning, we ran into the Mould, and brought out their sloop; and put about ten men aboard: bringing both prizes away for St. Jago.

From the English Captain, they took £900 in money, and plundered him of all he had, save a suit of clothes that he wore: and but waited the Governor's [of St. Jago] motion, to make a prize of the ship. Which would have been done, had not the Spanish Governor received advice of the Duke of ALBEMARLE's arrival at Jamaica.

Upon which news, the Governor paid the English Captain £600 of his money back again, and sent him away to Jamaica; and all the English prisoners, that would go with him, were freed by his consent.

By this time, arrived the bark in which were the other three of our companions; who were very glad to hear of our and their redemption.

We embarked once again free men together, by GOD's grace, bound for Jamaica: where we safely arrived about the latter end of March [1688].

So separating ourselves, we endeavoured in the best manner we could, to get passage for England, our native country, desiring GOD Almighty to deliver us, and all our dear countrymen Protestants, from the barbarous cruelty of the Spaniards and Papists.

FINIS.

A true and exact Account of The Retaking of a Ship, called The *Friends' Adventure*, of Topsham, from the FRENCH;

After she had been taken six days, and they were upon the coasts of France with it four days.

Where One Englishman and a boy set upon Seven Frenchmen, killed two of them, took the other Five prisoners, and brought the ship and them safe to England.

---

*Their Majesties' Customs of the said ship amounted to £*1,000 *and upwards.*

Performed and written by
ROBERT LYDE, Mate of the same ship.

LONDON,
Printed for R. BALDWIN, near the *Oxford Arms*, in Warwick lane.
1693.

Courteous Reader,

I Here present you with a token of GOD's almighty goodness in relieving me, by His special Providence, from the barbarity, inhumanity, and most cruel slavery of the Most Christian Turk of France: whose delight it is, to make his own subjects, slaves; and his chief study to put prisoners of war to the most tedious and cruel lingering deaths of hunger and cold, as I have experimentally, to my own damage, both felt and seen, by a four months' confinement in his country. Whereas, by their cruel usage, I was reduced to the last gasp of life: but, through the merciful goodness of GOD, I did recover; notwithstanding that of 600 *prisoners, upwards of* 400 *were starved to death, as by the sequel more fully will appear.*

What I have written is really matter of fact: and it had never appeared in print, were it not to vindicate myself, and to free myself from the many calumnies and aspersions of unreasonable men: who have not so much civility as to commend the action; but, on the con-

trary, tell the World, that I attacked the Frenchmen in cold blood, and murdered the two men I fairly killed; and that the spirits of them have haunted me ever since, and will till I am hanged.

Others say, that I retook the ship without a Commission, and I might have as well taken any other ship, and so been hanged for a pirate.

And others, more unreasonably, say, that the boy solicited me, for many days together, to stand by him in the attempt, before I consented to it.

And others say, that I had the help of the Devil to bring home the ship.

And therefore to convince these, and to satisfy others; I have here represented you with an exact Relation of the whole matter of fact, with an account of my bringing the ship and prisoners home together, also with the ingratitude and unkindness of the owners of the ship and cargo to me.

It is not so methodical as I could wish it was; but I hope your candour will excuse it: for it was not ambition, but respect to my native country, together with the reasons before hinted, that prompted me to make it public.

I shall detain you no longer: but wishing prosperity to Their Majesties, and the settlement and happiness of these nations, I subscribe myself,

Courteous Reader,

Your cordial and real friend,

ROBERT LYDE.

A true and exact Account of the retaking of the Friends' Adventure, *of Topsham, from the French; after she had been taken six days, and upon the coast of France four days: by one Englishman and a boy.*

IT IS natural for all men living to have a certain kind of a natural affection for the country from whence they first have their being: and every man ought as much to vindicate his native country as he would his own posterity! for the fall or ruin of the one is the *Prodromus* of the other; besides the duty and allegiance which we owe, by GOD's command, to our most gracious Sovereigns, the King [*WILLIAM III.*] and Queen [*MARY*].

And how much we ought, at this time particularly, to fight in vindication of all, I presume none can be ignorant of. For if the enemy fall upon and assault us, with all the strength they have, we ought in like manner to resist as powerfully: and if unhappily they prove victors at any time, this book will inform you how cruelly they use their prisoners of war, contrary to the ancient custom of nations. The very report of which, before I experimentally knew their tyranny, did so exasperate me against them, that if I could possibly have had any assistance, next to Providence, to have stood by me, I would never have gone into France, a captive at all! for I had resolved to myself rather to die upon the deck fighting, than ever to be subject to those that, NERO like, rejoice over them that lie languishing under their torments. And so I will first give you an account of my being taken the first time.

In the month of February, 1689, I [*ROBERT LYDE, a native of Topsham, "a lusty young man, aged about twenty-three," see p.* 453] shipped myself on board a Pink [*a fishing boat*] in Topsham, of 80 tons burden, Mr. ISAAC STONEHAM, Master, bound for Virginia, and from thence to Topsham again: and on the 18th of May following, we arrived there.

After we had taken in our lading, we set sail homeward bound, with 100 Sail of merchantmen, under the convoy of two Men-of-war.

About a fortnight after, the winds separated us from our convoy: so that our ship with several others, made the best of our way for England; but, soon after, left each other's company.

The 19th of October following, we came up with two Plymouth vessels that were of our said fleet: being then about 40 leagues to the westward of Scilly, having the wind easterly.

On the 21st of the same month, we saw four other ships to leeward of us; which we took to be some of our said fleet. But one of them proved to be a French Privateer; which came up under our lee quarter, and went ahead of us, and took a Virginia-man of our former fleet, belonging to London: which gave us three an opportunity to make our escape from the said Privateer. But the two Plymouth men being in great want of provisions, and an easterly wind being likely to continue; they bore away for Galicia in Spain. But our ship kept on her way for England.

The Mate of our ship and I made an agreement, in case we should be taken by the French, and left on board our own ship; although they should put ten men on board with us, to carry the ship and us to France: yet, if we lost sight of the Privateer, to stand by each other and attack them; and if it did please GOD that we should overcome them, to carry home the ship.

On the 24th of this month [*October*, 1689], we were, as I feared, taken by a Privateer of St. Malo, of 22 guns, 8 patteroes [*carronades*], and 100 and odd men. But the Mate's design and mine was spoiled: for we were put on board the Privateer with three more of our men; and the Master with four men and a boy left on board, with eight Frenchmen, to navigate the prize to St. Malo.

On the 26th, we had as much wind as could well blow at south-south-west, so that the Privateer could not take care of the prize, and so left her: and in some time after, she arrived at Havre de Grace.

Then I made it my endeavour to persuade our Mate and the [*three*] other prisoners, to attack the Frenchmen [*about a hundred*] on board the Privateer; being very positive, with the assistance of GOD and theirs, to overcome them, and carry home the ship (with less trouble to my share than I found in this which is done). But they concluded it impossible; and so we continued attempting no resistance at all.

On the 28th of October [1689], we arrived at St Malo; and were carried on shore and imprisoned, and in all respect, during the space of seventeen days, were used with such inhumanity and cruelty, that if we had been taken by the Turks we could not have been used worse. For bread, we had 6lbs., and one cheek of a bullock, for every 25 men for a day: and it fell out, that he that had half of a bullock's eye for his lot, had the greatest share.

This makes me wish that I could be the prison keeper, and have my liberty to do the Frenchmen that are brought in, their justice.

They daily adding to our number until the prison was so full, that swarms of vermin increased amongst us, not only here at St. Malo, but also at Dinan whereunto we were removed; insomuch, that many of our fellow prisoners died, three of whom were our Mate and two more out of the five of our company: and all that did survive, were become mere skeletons. I was so weak that I could not put my hand to my head. There died out of 600 men, upwards of 400 through their cruelty, in three months' time.

They plundered us of our clothes, when we were taken. Some of us that had money purchased rugs to cover our rags by day, and keep us warm by night: but, upon our return home from France, the Deputy Governor of Dinan (in hopes either to kill us with cold, or to disable us for Their Majesties' service at our return) was so cruel as to order our said rugs to be taken from us; and himself stayed, and saw it performed. And when some of our fellow prisoners lay a-dying; they inhumanly stripped off some of their clothes three or four days before they were quite dead.

These and other their barbarities made so great an impression upon me, as that I did then resolve never to go a prisoner there again; and this resolution I did ever since continue in, and, by GOD's assistance, always will!

And so I was released [? *by exchange*], and, through the goodness of GOD, got to England.

And after I had been at home so long as to recover my health and strength fit to go to sea again; I shipped myself as Mate of a vessel of Topsham [the *Friends' Adventure*] of 80 tons burthen, ROGER BRIANT Master, bound from thence to Oporto in Portugal, and from thence to London.

Accordingly, on the 30th day of September, 1691, we began our voyage; and on the 27th of December following, we arrived at Oporto.

On the 24th of February following [1692], we set sail from thence to London.

On the 29th day, being then about 25 leagues north-west from Cape Finisterre, about six in the morning, we saw a ship, which came up with us at a great pace. At ten in the morning, he was within half a league of us; and then put out French colours and fired a gun, whereby we knew him to be a Frenchman.

Then I took a rope yarn, and seized two parts of the topsail hilliers [*halliards or ropes*] together, that our men might not lower the topsail; for I was desirous to have as much time as possibly I could, to hide some necessaries, to attack the Frenchman [*i.e., the prize crew*].

At which, the Master perceiving and knowing my intention, said, "Mate! are you in the same mind now, as you have been in all the voyage?" for I had often been saying what I would do towards the retaking of our ship.

I answered, "Yes;" and said, "I did not question but, with GOD's assistance, to perform what I had said."

The Master said he believed I could not do it; but if I should, he thought it was impossible for me to carry home the ship.

Notwithstanding all this, I was not discouraged, but desired him to pray for a strong gale of wind after we were taken, that we might be separated from the Privateer, and be out of sight of her.

Then I went down in the forecastle, and hid a blunderbuss and ammunition betwixt decks, amongst the pipes of wine. Before I went aft again the topsails were lowered; and I perceiving that it would not be long before the enemy would be on board us, I took a five gallon vessel of my own wine [*probably Port*], and with a hammer beat in one head, and put several pounds of sugar in it, and then drank to the Master: and said that "I designed that I would drink my fill of it, while I had the command of it: and if it would please GOD that I should be continued on board, I hoped that I should not be long dispossessed of the rest.

Betwixt ten and eleven o'clock, by the Privateer's command, we hauled up the coasts and braced to.

Then the Privateer's boat, full of men, came on board us: and I stept over the side, with my hat under my arm, handing the French gentlemen in, till one of them took hold of my coat, and I (not daring to resist him) helped it off: and ran aft into the cabin, and saved myself from further damage.

After they had taken away almost all our clothes, and what else they pleased; the Lieutenant ordered me and a boy [*JOHN WRIGHT, about sixteen years old*] to stay on board: which I was very glad of; but could heartily have wished they had left a man in the boy's room.

Before the Master and I parted, for he and four of our men and a boy were carried on board the Privateer; I asked him privately, "What he had done with the money he had in a bag?"

He told me he had given it to the Lieutenant, and withal would know of me, why I made that inquiry.

I answered, "Because I did not question but I should have secured that on board, by retaking our ship."

But the Master said, "It was an impossible thing to be done."

I replied, "Although it seemed to him to be so; yet nothing was impossible to be effected by GOD, in whom I put my trust."

Soon after, the Lieutenant and our men returned aboard the Privateer; having left seven of his men on board our ship to navigate her to St. Malo.

In three hours' time, the Privateer was out of our sight, which I was very glad of.

I asked the Master, "If I should fetch a barrel of wine up," in hopes to make them drunk; and then I should command them with the less trouble.

He said I might, if I could find one. Then I fetched a barrel of five gallons of sweet strong wine, and kept it tapped in the steerage. I drank freely of it, hoping that they thereby would be induced to do the like, and so drink to excess; but that stratagem failed me, for they were never the worse for drinking, all the time I was their prisoner.

Then I acquainted the boy with my intent, and persuaded him to assist me in overcoming them; and I would, with the assistance of GOD, carry the ship to Galicia in Spain. I continued soliciting him for his compliance in that, and the third for England [?]; but could not prevail with him.

On the 3rd of March [1692], we saw Ushant in the night. Being within two ships' length of the Fern Rock and in great danger of being lost, they called up me and the boy to save our lives. When I came up and saw that the Frenchmen had got the tackle in the boat and were going to hoist her out, I told the boy "to stay aft; for when the boat is overboard, they may all go in her, if they will! but they shall not come aboard again: for I will not leave the ship, because I shall get the ship off presently." For the wind was west-north-west; and the Frenchmen never minded [*thought*] to trim the sails close by the wind, and I would not tell them of it because I would get them out of the ship, till I saw they did not get out the boat, but gazed at the Rock, some crying, and others calling to saints for deliverance. Then I desired, and helped them to trim the sails, and soon got the ship off again.

On Friday [*4th March*, 1692], at noon, we being about 10 leagues to the eastward of Brest, with the wind easterly: they bore away for Port bean, or some such name they called it; which was about 4 or 5 leagues to the eastward of Brest.

Then I called the boy down betwixt decks, and read two or three chapters in the *Bible*; and then used all my endeavour to persuade him to assist me: but by all the arguments I could use, I could not prevail at this time.

Then I took a brick, and whetted my knife upon it; and told the boy, "I would not use my knife, upon any account, till I was carried into France; except it were to cut the throats of the Frenchmen."

At which words, the boy startled as if his own throat had been cutting; and then left me, and went up on deck.

At four in the afternoon, we were within half a mile of the aforesaid harbour. Then the French fired a patteroe for a pilot to come off: whereupon I went upon deck, with a sorrowful heart, to see how near we were to the shore; but the Frenchmen were as joyful as I was melancholy.

Then considering the inhuman usage I formerly had in France, and how near I was to it again; it struck me with such terror that I could stay no longer upon deck: but went down betwixt decks, and prayed to GOD for a southerly wind, to prevent her going into that harbour; which GOD was graciously pleased immediately to grant me, for which I returned my unfeigned thanks.

Friday night, the wind was westerly; and Saturday, southerly: so that in the evening, I heard the Frenchmen say that they saw Cape Farril [*Frehel*].

At eight on the Saturday night, I prayed again for a south-west wind, that we might not be near the shore in the morning; and immediately I heard them put the helm a lee, and put her about, and got the larboard tacks aboard.

The boy was then lying by my side. I bade him go up and see if the wind was not south-west; which he accordingly did: and at his return, told me it was, and that the ship lay off north-north-west. Then I rejoiced, and gave GOD thanks for this second signal deliverance.

The nearer we came to St. Malo, the surlier the Frenchmen were to me.

At twelve a clock, on Saturday night, they called me to the pumps; as they had done several times before, although I never went but when I pleased: nor would I do anything else for them, thinking it much inferior for an Englishman to do anything for a Frenchman.

But they calling on me several times, at last I turned out, and stood in the Gun Room scuttle; and told the Master that "I had served two years for the French already, and if I went to France again, I should serve three years."

"That is *bien*," said the Master.

Then I told them that "I had nothing in the ship to lose: and that if they would not pump themselves, the ship should sink for me."

Then I went and laid myself down again, fully resolved that if they came to haul me out by force, that I would make resistance, and kill or wound as many of them as I could, before I died myself: but they let me alone.

All that night, when the boy was awake, I endeavoured to persuade him to assist me; but still could not prevail: though I used, as I had done ever since we were taken, many arguments. So that that night, I slept but very little; and when I did slumber at all, I dreamt that I was attacking the Frenchmen.

For sleeping or waking, my mind ran still upon the attacking of them.

Sunday, at seven in the morning, we being then about five leagues off from Cape Farril; I then prayed heartily for a south-south-east wind: and immediately I heard them take in their topsails and haul up the foresail, and brace them aback and lash the helm a lee, and let the ship drive off, with her head to the westward. Then I sent the boy up again, to see if the wind was not come at south-south-east: and he brought me word it was.

Then I gave GOD thanks, and rejoiced at His signal providential mercy on me, and for so immediately strengthening my faith, and confirming my hopes of redeeming myself from slavery: and then I renewed my solicitation to the boy to yield to me, but still he would not consent; which made me think of attempting it myself, and then I went and took a pint of wine, and half a pint of oil, and drank it to make me more fit for action.

At eight in the morning, all the Frenchmen sat round the cabin table at breakfast, and they called me to eat with them. Accordingly I accepted their invitation, but the sight of the

Frenchmen did immediately take away my stomach and made me sweat as if I had been in a stove, and was ready to faint with eagerness to encounter them. Which the Master perceiving, and seeing me in that condition, asked me in French, "If I were sick?" and because he should not mistrust anything, I answered "Yes." But could stay no longer in sight of them, and so immediately went down betwixt decks, to the boy; and did earnestly intreat him to go up presently with me into the cabin and to stand behind me, and knock down but one man in case two laid hold on me; and I would kill and command all the rest presently [*at once*]; "for now," I told him, "was the best time for me to attack them, while they were all around the table; for now I shall have them all before me purely, and it may never be the like opportunity again."

After many importunities, the boy asked me, "After what manner I intended to encounter with them?"

I told him, "I would take the crow of iron, and hold it on the middle with both hands! and I would go into the cabin, and knock down him that stood at the end of the table on my right hand, and stick the point of the crow into him that sat at the end of the table on my left hand: and then for the other five that sat behind the table——" But still he not consenting, I had second thoughts of undertaking it without him: but the cabin was so low that I could not stand upright in it by a foot; which made me desist at that time.

By this time they had eat their breakfast, and went out upon the deck. Then I told the boy, with much trouble [*vexation*] we had lost a brave opportunity, for, by this time, I had had the ship under my command!

"Nay," says the boy, "I rather believe that, by this time, you and I should have both been killed."

In a little time after they had been on deck, they separated from each other, viz., the Master lay down in his cabin; two of the men lay down in the Great Cabin, and one in a cabin between decks, and another sat down upon a low stool by the helm, to look after the Glass [*sand-glass to measure each half-hour of time*], to call to pump, which they were forced to do every half-hour by reason of the leakiness of the ship; and the other two men walked upon the decks.

Then hoping I should prevail with the boy to stand by me;

if not, I was resolved to attack them myself: I immediately applied myself to prayer, and desiring GOD to pardon my sins which I had committed, and to receive my soul and the boy's to mercy. For I thought, if they overcame me, they would give the boy no quarter; although he did nothing against them. I prayed also for my enemies who should happen to die by my hands, because they might not have time to call for mercy themselves. I prayed also that GOD would strengthen me in my design, that my heart fail not in the action.

And then I endeavoured again to persuade the boy, telling him that we should bring a great deal of honour to our native country, besides the particular honour which would accrue to ourselves: but all this, and much more to that purpose, too long to be here insisted on, would not prevail with him to consent.

Then the Glass was out, it being half an hour after eight, and the two men that were upon deck went to pump out the water.

Then I also went upon deck again, to see whether the wind and weather were like to favour my enterprise, and casting my eyes to windward, I liked the weather, and hoped the wind would stand. Then immediately I went down to the boy, and begged of him again to stand by me, while two of the men were at the pump. For they pumped on the starboard side, and the steerage door opened on the larboard side; so that they could not see me go aft to them in the cabin. But I could by no persuasions prevail with the boy; so that by this time the men had done pumping.

Whereupon losing this opportunity caused me again to be a little angry with the boy for not yielding to me. Telling him that "I had prayed three times for the change of the wind, and GOD was pleased to hear my prayers, and to grant my request; and thereupon I had a firm belief wrought in me, that I should not be carried a prisoner into France, where I had suffered such great hardship and misery. Our allowance of food at St. Malo, where we were kept prisoners for seventeen days, was only one cheek of a bullock and 8lbs. weight of bread for 25 men a day; and only water to drink. And at Dinan, where we were kept close prisoners for three months and ten days, our allowance was 3lbs. weight of an old cow beef, without any salt to savour it, for 7 men a day.

But I think we had 2lbs. of bread for each man, but it was so bad that dogs would not eat it; neither could we eat but very little, and that we did eat did us more hurt than good, for it was more orts [*refuse food*] than bread; so we gave some of it to the hogs, and made pillows of the rest to lay our heads on. For they allowed us fresh straw but once every five weeks; so that we bred such swarms of lice in our rags that one man had a great hole eaten through his throat by them; which was not perceived till after his death: and I myself was so weak that it was fourteen weeks after my releasement before I recovered any tolerable strength again. And all this was through their cruel tyranny in not allowing us, as their men are allowed in England."

Said the boy, "If I do find it so bad as you do say, when I am in France, I will go along with them in a Privateer!"

These words of his struck me to the heart, which made me say, "You dog! what! will you go with them against your King and country, and father and mother? Sirrah! I was in France, a prisoner four months, and my tongue cannot express what I endured there; yet I would not turn Papist and go with them! Yet they came daily persuading me and others to go out; and, the time I was there, I think 17 turned Papists, and were kept in a room by themselves; but GOD was pleased to make an example of them; for I think 12 of them died while I was there. And if thou dost turn Papist, thou mayest fare as they did! and if thou, or any of them that be turned, be ever taken again, you will certainly be hanged in England by the law! But I had the command of a Privateer, and should take my brother in a French Privateer, after he had willingly sailed with them, I would hang him immediately!"

I, seeing the boy seemed to be reconciled, told him that "he should not go into France, if he would do as I would have him do!"

The boy asked, "What I would have him do?"

I told him, "to knock down the man at the helm sickore [*for certain*]; and I would kill and command all the rest presently [*at once*].

Saith the boy, "If you be sure to overcome them, how many do you count to kill?"

I answered that "I intended to kill three of them."

Then the boy replied, "Why three, and no more?"

I answered that, "I would kill three, for three of our men that died in prison when I was there. And if it should please GOD that I should get home safe to England, I would, if I could, go in a Man-of-war or fireship, and endeavour a revenge on the enemy, for the death of those 400 men that died in the same prison of Dinan!"

But the boy said "Four alive would be too many for me."

I then replied, "I would kill but three, but I would break the legs and arms of the rest, if they won't take quarter, and be quiet without it."

Then the boy asked me, "Which three I designed to kill?"

I told him, "I designed to kill those three that I judged to be the strongest; which were those that carried themselves most surly towards me: but if any of the rest did take hold on me, and that my life were in danger, I would then endeavour to kill a fourth, and not otherwise."

Then said the boy, "What do you intend to do with the other Frenchmen that shall remain alive?"

I answered, "I will command three of them down into the Forepike [*fore hold*] and nail the scuttle upon them: and I would keep the fourth above deck, to help to carry the ship for England."

Then the boy asked me, "How I thought to carry the ship to England, with only the assistance of him and one Frenchman?"

I answered, "I did not at all question that, but I did verily believe that I should carry the ship safe to an anchor, either in Plymouth or Dartmouth, before twelve o'clock the next day: for this is a fair wind for that purpose."

"But," said the boy, "how do you think to pump out the water, seeing the ship is so very leaky, and to have time to refresh ourselves with sleep; for it may be a longer time than you suppose before we shall come to an anchor?"

I answered that "the assistance of GOD would be sufficient to enable us to do all this and more; for the joy of overcoming them will banish sleep from my eyes! and work will weary me but little!"

The boy's asking me these several questions did encourage me to hope that he would at last be prevailed with to stand by me: and still he proceeded in his inquiries, and asked me, "How I did intend to attack them?"

I told him, "I would take the crow [*crowbar*] of iron, and hold it with both hands in the middle of it; and go into the [Great] Cabin, and knock down one with the claws, and strike the point into the other that lay by his side in the cabin! and I would wound the Master in his cabin! and do thou take the drive-bolt [*a long iron pin for driving out bolts*], and be sure to knock down the man at the helm! so soon as you hear me strike the first blow; for otherwise if he should hear the blow, he may come into the cabin, and lay hold on me, before I shall overcome them three."

And I resolved to myself, of which I said nothing to the boy, that if they should all rise against me before I could get into the cabin, I would strike at them, and either kill them or do them as much hurt as I could before I died myself: concluding that after I had once begun, if I should yield, then I should certainly die by them; and therefore did resolve to sell my life as dear as I could.

Then the boy asked me, "What he should do when he had knocked down the man at the helm?"

I told him, "He should stand without the [Great] Cabin door, and not stir from thence, but to have his eye upon the two Frenchmen that were upon deck: and not to come into the cabin to me, unless he observed them coming towards the cabin; and then he should tell me of it, and come into the cabin.

At nine in the morning, the two men upon deck went to pumping. Then I turned out from the sail, where the boy and I then lay, and pulled off my coat that I might be the more nimble in the action: and having [but] little hair, I hauled off my cap, that if they had the fortune to knock me in the head, they might kill me with it.

Having fitted myself for the action, I went up the Gun Room scuttle into the Steerage, to see what posture they were in; and being satisfied therein, I leapt down the scuttle and went to the boy: who seeing me resolved upon the action, with an earnest entreaty to him to join with me; he, at last, did consent.

Then the boy coming to me, I leapt up the Gun Room scuttle, and said, "LORD! be with us, and strengthen us in the action!": and then I told the boy that the drive-bolt was by the scuttle in the Steerage.

Then I went softly aft into the Cabin, and put my back against the bulk head, and took the iron crow (it was laying without the Cabin door), and held it with both my hands in the middle of it, and put my legs abroad to shorten myself, because the Cabin was very low.

But he that lay nighest to me, hearing me, opened his eyes; and perceiving my intent, and upon what account I was coming, endeavoured to rise, to make resistance against me: but I prevented him, by a blow upon his forehead, which mortally wounded him. And the other man, which lay with his back to the dying man's side, hearing the blow, turned about and faced me; very fiercely endeavouring to come against me. I struck at him, but he let himself fall from his left arm, and held his arm for a guard; whereby he did keep off a great part of the blow: but still his head received a great part of the blow.

The Master laying in his Cabin on my right hand, hearing the two blows, rose, and sat in his cabin; and seeing what I had done, he called me *Boogra!* and *Footra!* But I having my eyes every way, I pushed at his ear betwixt the turnpins with the claws of the crow: but he falling back for fear thereof. It seemed, afterwards, that I struck the claws of the crow into his cheek, which blow made him lie still as if he had been dead.

While I struck at the Master, the fellow that fended off the blow with his arm, rose upon his legs, and ran towards me, with his head low (I suppose he intended to run his head against my breast to overset me): but I pushed the point at his head, and stuck it an inch and a half into his forehead (as it appeared since by the chirurgeon that searched the wound); and as he was falling down, I took hold of him by the back, and turned him into the steerage.

I heard the boy strike the man at the helm, two blows; after I knocked down the first man: which two blows made him lie very still.

As soon as I turned the man out of the Cabin, I struck one blow more at him that I struck first, thinking to leave no man alive aft of myself.

The Master all this while did not stir: which made me

conclude that I had struck him under the ear, and had killed him with the blow.

Then I went out to attack the two men that were at the pump; where they continued pumping, without hearing or knowing what I had done.

As I was going to them, I saw that man that I had turned out of the Cabin into the Steerage, crawling out upon his hands and knees upon the deck; beating his hands upon the deck to make a noise, that the men at the pump might hear: for he could not cry out or speak.

And when they heard him, seeing the blood running out of the hole in his forehead, they came running aft to me, grinding their teeth as they would have eaten me.

But I met them as they came with the Steerage door, and struck at them: but the Steerage being not about four foot high, I could not have a full blow at them. Whereupon they fended off the blow, and took hold of the crow with both their hands close to mine, striving to haul it from me.

Then the boy might have knocked them down with much ease, while they were contending with me; but that his heart failed him, so that he stood like a stake at a distance on their left side.

Two feets' length of the crow being behind their hands, on their left side, I called to the boy to "take hold of it, and haul as they did, and I would let it go all at once!" Which the boy accordingly did. I pushed the crow towards them, and let it go: and was taking out my knife to traverse [*rush in*] amongst them: but they seeing me put my right hand into my pocket, fearing what would follow, both let go the crow to the boy, and took hold of my right arm with both their hands, grinding their teeth at me.

The Master, that I thought I had killed in his Cabin, coming to himself; and hearing that they had hold of me, came out his Cabin and also took hold of me, with both his hands round my middle.

Then one of the men that had hold of my right arm, let go; and put his back to my breast, and took hold of my left hand and arm, and held it close to his breast, and strove to cant me upon his back.

And the Master let go from my middle, and took hold of my right arm, and he, with the other that had hold of my right arm, did strive to turn me over from the other back: thinking to get me off my legs. But I knowing that I should not be long in one piece if they got me down, I put my left foot against the ship's side on the deck for a supporter, and, with the assistance of GOD! I kept upon my feet; when they three, and one more (for the man that the boy knocked down at the helm, rose up and put his hands about my middle, and strove to haul me down) did strive to throw me down.

The boy seeing that man rise, and take hold of me, cried out! fearing then that I should be overcome by them; but did not come to help me, nor did strike one blow at any of them: neither did they touch him all the time.

When I heard the boy cry out, I said, "Do you cry! you villain! now I am in such a condition! Come quickly, and knock this man on the head that hath hold on my left arm!"

The boy perceiving that my heart did not fail me; he took some courage from thence, and endeavoured to give that man a blow on his head with the drive-bolt: but struck so faintly, that he missed his blow; which greatly enraged me against him.

And I feeling the Frenchman which hung about my middle hang very heavy, said to the boy, "Do you miss your blow! and I in such a condition! Go round the binnacle, and knock down that man that hangeth upon my back;" which was the same man the boy knocked down at the helm.

So the boy did strike him one blow upon the head, which made him fall, but he rose up immediately; but being incapable of making any further resistance, he went out upon deck staggering to and fro, without any further molestance from the boy.

Then I looked about the beams for a marlin-speck [*spike*], or anything else to strike them withal: but seeing nothing, I said, "LORD! what shall I do?"

Then casting up my eye upon my left side, and seeing a marlin-speck hanging with a strap to a nail on the larboard side, I jerked my right arm forth and back, which cleared the two men's hands from my right arm, and took hold of the marlin-speck, and struck the point four times, about a quarter of an inch deep, into the skull of that man that had hold of my left arm, before they took hold of my right arm again. I also struck the marlin-speck into his head three times after they had hold of me, which caused him to screech out: but they having hold of me, took off much of the force of the three last blows; and he being a strong-hearted man, he would not let go his hold of me.

The two men finding that my right arm was stronger than their four arms were, and observing the strap of the marlin-speck to fall up and down upon the back of my hand so that it struck him that had his hands nearest to my right one: he let go his right hand and took hold of the strap, and hauled the marlin-speck out of my hand. And I, fearing what in all likelihood would follow, put my right hand before my head for a guard, although three hands had hold of that arm: for I concluded he would knock me on the head with it, or else throw it at my head.

But, through GOD's wonderful providence! it either fell out of his hand, or else he threw it down! for it did fall so close to the ship's side that he could not reach it again, without letting go his other hand from mine. So he did not attempt the reaching of it; but took hold of my arm with his other hand again.

At this time, the Almighty GOD gave me strength enough to take one man in one hand, and throw at the other's head: and looking about again to see for anything to strike them withal, but seeing nothing I said, "LORD! what shall I do now?"

And then it pleased GOD to put me in mind of my knife in my pocket. And although two of the men had hold of my right arm, yet GOD Almighty strengthened me so, that I put my right hand into my right pocket, and took out my knife and sheath, holding it behind my hand that they should not see it. But I could not draw it out of the sheath with my left hand, because the man that I struck in the head with the marlin-speck had still hold of it, with his back to my breast.

So I put it between my legs, and drew it out; and then cut that man's throat with it, that had his back to my breast: and he immediately dropped down, and scarce ever stirred after.

Then with my left arm, I gave both the men a push from me; and hauled my right arm, with a jerk, to me; and so cleared it of them: and fetching a stroke with an intent to cut both their throats at once, they immediately apprehending the danger they were in, both put their hands together, and held them up crying, "*Corte! Corte! Monsieur! moy allay pur Angleterre si vou plea* [Quarter! Quarter! Sir! I will go for England, if you please!]."

With that, I stopped my hand, and said, "Good Quarter you shall have; *Alle a Pro* [Go to the prow]." And then I put my knife into the sheath again.

But they not obeying my command, but standing still; I concluded they had a mind to have the other bout with me; and I drew out my knife again, resolving to cut their throats. But then their countenances immediately changed; and they put off their hats and said, "*Moy alle pro Monsieur. Moy travallay pur Angleterre si vou plea* [I will go for Monsieur. I will work for England, if you please]."

Then I stopped my hand again; and they went out upon deck, and went forwards.

Then I made fast the Steerage door, and ordered the boy to stand by it and to keep it fast; and to look out through the blunderbuss holes; and if he did see any man coming towards the door, with anything in his hand to open the door, he should tell me of it, and come into the Cabin for the blunderbuss and ammunition, which I had hid away before we were taken, but which the Frenchmen had found and kept in the Cabin.

After I had loaded it, I came out with it in the Steerage, and looked forward out of the Companion to see if any man did lie over the Steerage door with a bit [*bight*] of a rope to throw over me, or any other thing that might prejudice me as I should go out. But seeing no man there, I went out upon deck; and looked up to the maintop, for fear the two wounded men were there, and should throw down anything upon my head to do me an injury.

But seeing no man there, I asked the boy, "If he could tell me what was become of the two wounded men that came to themselves, and went out upon the deck, while I was engaged with the three men in the Steerage."

The boy told me, "They had scrambled overboard!" For he said, "he looked through the blunderbuss holes in the bulkhead, and saw them staggering to and fro like men that were drunk."

I thought it very strange they should be accessory to their own deaths.

Then I ordered the boy to stand by the Steerage door, to see if that man betwixt decks did come up; and if he did, to tell me of it, and come forward to me: which he promised to do.

Then I went forward to the two men that cried for Quarter; who stood by the boat side: but they being afraid, ran forwards and were going up in the foreshrouds; but I held up the blunderbuss, and said "*Veni abau e monte a Cuttelia et ally abau* [Come below, and raise the scuttle, and go below!]."

And then they put off their hats, and said, "*Monsieur, moy travalli pur Angleterre si vous plea!* [Sir, I will work for England, if you please]."

But I answered, "*Alle abau* [Go below]; for I don't want your help."

Then they said "*Ouy, Monsieur;*" and unlid[ed] the scuttle, and went down.

Then I went forward, and as I came before the foot of the mainsail, I looked to the foretop, and seeing no man there, I went and looked down into the Forecastle; and shewed the two men a scuttle on the larboard side that went down into the Fore-peak, and said, "*Le monte Cuttelia et ally abau!* [Raise the scuttle and go below!]."

They answered, "*Ouy, Monsieur!*" and then unlid[ed] the scuttle, and put off their hats and went down; giving GOD thanks for His mercy towards them, in giving them a longer life.

Then I called down to them, and asked them, "If they saw any man betwixt decks before they went down?"

And they answered "No!"

Then I called forward the boy, and gave him the blunderbuss; and bid him present it down the Forecastle, and "if he saw any man take hold of me, so that I could not get clear of them, or if I called on him for his help: then, he should be sure to discharge the blunderbuss at us, and kill us all together, if he could not kill them without shooting me."

The boy promised he would, but he would not shoot me.

Then I took the boy's bolt-[driver] and put my head down the scuttle, and looked all round: and seeing no man there, I leaped down in the Forecastle, and looked round that also; but seeing no man betwixt decks, I laid the scuttle and nailed it fast.

Then thought I myself safe; seeing two were killed, and two secured.

Then I went upon deck, and took the blunderbuss from the boy, and gave him the bolt-[driver], and went aft, and ordered the boy as before to stand by the Steerage door, and give me an account if he saw any man coming towards him, with a handspike.

Then I went aft into the Cabin, and cut two candles in four pieces, and lighted them. One I left burning upon the table. The other three I carried in my left hand, and the blunderbuss in my right hand.

I put my head down the Gun Room scuttle, and looked round; and seeing no man there, I leapt down and went to the man that lay all this time asleep in a Cabin betwixt decks, and took him by the shoulder with my left hand, and wakened him.

Presenting the blunderbuss at him with my right hand, I commanded him out of his Cabin; and made him stand still, till I got up into the Steerage.

Then I called the man; and he standing in the scuttle, and seeing the man that had his throat cut, cried out, "O JESU! MARIA!" and called upon some other saints.

I told him "I had nothing to do with MARIA now! *Monte, monte et ally a Pro!* [Go up, go up! and go to the prow]."

Then he came up, and went forward, looking round to see for his companions; but I followed him, and made him go down into the Forecastle, and stand on the starboard side.

Then I gave the boy the blunderbuss, and ordered him to present it at the man; and if he perceived him either to come towards me, or to take anything to throw at me, while I was opening the scuttle, then to shoot him.

Then I took the crow of iron, and leapt down with it, into the Forecastle; and drew the spikes and opened the scuttle, and bade the man go down: which he readily did, and rejoiced when he had found two of his companions there.

After I had nailed down the scuttle again, I went aft, and ordered the boy to stand by the Steerage door again. I then took the candles and the blunderbuss, and went down betwixt decks; and went forward and aft, and looked in all the holes and corners, for the two wounded men: but found them not.

Finding the Gun Room scuttle that went down into the hold, open, I called down: but hearing none make answer, I laid the scuttle. And there being about twenty bags of shumack [? *bark*] in the Gun Room, I rolled two of them, of 6 cwt. [*together*] upon the scuttle; and rolled more close to them, that if the men were there, and did lift up one side of the scuttle, the bags might not roll off.

Then I went upon deck, and told the boy, "I could not find the two men, betwixt decks."

He said, "They were certainly run overboard."

I told him, "I would know what was become of them, before I made sail."

Then I told the boy, "I would go up into the Maintop, and see if they were there; and then I should be sure to see them if they were in the Foretop."

So I gave him the blunderbuss, and bade him present it at the Maintop; and if he saw any man look out over the Top with anything in his hand to throw at me, he should then shoot them.

Then I took the boy's bolt-[driver], and went up; and when I was got to the puddick shrouds, I looked forwards to the Foretop, and there I saw the two men, covered with the Foretopsail, and their sashes bound about their heads to keep in the blood and to keep their heads warm.

Then I called to them. They turned out, and went down upon their knees, and wrang their hands, and cried, "*O Corte! Corte! Monsieur! Moy allay pur Angleterre si vou plea.*"

Then I said, "Good Quarter you shall have!" and I went down, and called to them to come down; and he that the boy wounded [*and that was at the helm*] came down and kissed my hand over and over, and went down into the Forecastle very willingly.

But the other man was one of the three that I designed to kill, and the same that I had struck the crow into his forehead. He knew that he had said ill things of the Prince of ORANGE, meaning our gracious King; and that "an English Man-of-war was no better than a louse!" and did always call me up to pump: these things, I suppose, he thought I'd not forgot, and therefore that I would not give Quarter.

Notwithstanding, I intended to do so. But I suspected him to be an English or Irish man; and I was resolved if it proved so, that I would hang him myself, when it did please GOD that I had help coming aboard from England.

So I called him down. But he being unwilling, delayed his coming.

I took the blunderbuss, and said that "I would shoot him down!" And then he came a little way, and stood still; and begged me to give him Quarter: and if I would, he would then "*trevally pur Angleterre*," and also pump the water.

I told him, "If he would come down, he should have Quarter!" and I presented the blunderbuss at him again. And then he came a little lower, and said, "*O Monsieur, vou battera moy* [O Sir, you will beat me!]."

I told him that "I would not beat him, and withal I would discourse with him no longer. If he would come down, he might! if not, I would shoot him down!"

Then he came down, and I gave the boy the blunderbuss.

The Frenchman took my hand, and wrung it, and kissed it over and over; and called me his *boon Monsieur!* and told me he would help to carry the ship for England.

I told him, "I did not want his help!" and commanded him down in the Forecastle.

Then I made them both stand on the starboard side; and ordered the boy to shoot them, if they offered to throw anything at me, or came near to me, while I went down into the Forecastle to unnail the scuttle.

Then I took the crow of iron, leapt down into the Forecastle, and unnailed the scuttle; and commanded the two Frenchmen down into the hold.

And I called one of the men up that cried first for Quarter, to help me to sail the ship for England. This man was not wounded at all, and was not above twenty-four years of age: and I had least fear of him, because he was indifferent [*somewhat*] kind to me while I was their prisoner. But he was very unwilling to come up: but with much importunity, I prevailed with him to come up.

I sent him aft: and then laid the scuttle, and nailed a piece of oaken plank to each beam, with spikes over it. And I bade them get from under the scuttle. Then I split the scuttle with the crow, and drave it down into the hold to give them air.

Then I went aft, and commanded the man to help to haul out the two men that were dead; which he did accordingly: and so we threw them overboard. But before I threw them both, I took a sash from one of them, because it was red: on purpose to make fast about the white ancient [*the white French flag, and so to make it an English one*] which the Frenchmen put on board; and put it out for a whiff [*signal*]. And I searched his pocket for a steel and flint, but found none: for want whereof, I was forced to keep two candles always burning in the Cabin, till I got the Pilot's [*flint and steel*] on board from Topsham.

Now being about leagues of Cape Farril [*Frehel*], which made half an hour after nine of the clock, and the Glass being almost out; and having secured all the men: I ordered the boy to put the blunderbuss in the boat, for him to command the Frenchman withal, when I was doing anything.

Then I sent the Frenchman to loose the helm, and put him a weather, and weared the ship: and, with the assistance of GOD, I had to cost three topsails, the spritsail, and mizzen trimmed in less than an hour's time, to make the most of a fair wind.

Then I gave down to them in the hold, a basket of bread and butter, and a gimlet and spikes: and ordered them to draw and drink of one of my own casks of wine which I had there; because if they should have drawn out of a Pipe, they might not find the hole in the dark, and so spill a great deal of wine.

And I gave them down their clothes, and some old sails to lie upon. I gave them likewise a bottle of brandy to wash their wounds, and salve which they had brought on board, and candles to see to dress their wounds.

And having no more necessaries for them, I was sorry to see him that the boy wounded, because he was very bad of his wounds.

After we had been some time steering our course for England; the boy asked me, "What I would do, if we should meet with a French Privateer?"

I said, "I did not question but, with the help of GOD, we should be either in Dartmouth or Plymouth, before twelve a clock the next day. If I should see any ship that *will* speak with me, and I cannot get from him, I will either shoot all the Frenchmen that were on board, or knock them all on the head, and heave them overboard! For I do not look for any mercy from the French, if these live or die. And if fall out to be an English ship, they will help to carry our ship to England."

The wind held south-south-east till three in the afternoon, and then veered to the westward. Then I gave GOD thanks, as I had before, for His goodness and mercy to me, in giving me victory over mine enemies.

At four, the wind was at south-west, and at six in the evening, at west. At eight, the wind was north-west-and-by-north, and north-north-east. Then I got two luff tackles, and got the starboard tacks aboard, and stood to the westward: and I prayed to GOD for His protection, to keep me clear from my bloodthirsty enemies.

Then I ordered the boy to walk upon deck, and to look after the Frenchman at the helm: and I went down into the Forecastle, and hove all the moveable things that I could get upon the scuttle over the Frenchmen. And I went up and laid and barred or nailed all the scuttles in the upper deck. Then I knew myself safe from them that were in the hold: for I considered that if they should break through the lower deck, which I thought they could not: yet they could not possibly get through the upper deck, with the assistance of GOD Almighty.

At ten at night, the wind veered to the westward. At eleven, the wind was at west. Then I took the larboard tacks aboard; and having "a topgallant gale," I had the sails trimmed in a quarter of an hour's time.

At one, the wind was west-south-west, "a topsail gale."

At two in the morning, I had as much wind as I could carry the topsails with a reef in of each. The Frenchmen had taken in a reef of each topsail before I retook the ship; and I kept them in, for the more ease in the handling of the ship.

The wind held fresh, and the dawning broke very high, and the clouds looked very dark and showery, and they cleared up in the northward board [*horizon*]: which made me afraid that the wind would be north-west, and blow so hard that I should not be able to handle the ship with the Frenchman; but I put my trust in the LORD for His assistance.

At six, the wind was at west, and blew hard in showers [*squalls*]; and I let three or four showers pass, without lowering either of the topsails.

At eight, the wind was at north-west, and blew very hard: but still I carried more sail than I would have done, if I had had eight Englishmen on board. For I kept up the topsail, till at last the wind in the showers did put the gunhil [*gunwale*] of the ship in the water. Then I hauled down the topsail, and clewed up the sheets, and braced them aback till each shower [*squall*] was over; and then hauled home the sheet, and up with the topsail again. And this I did for four or five hours: which made the ship leak so very much, that I and the boy were forced to pump always between the showers; and yet could not keep her free.

The boy cried many times, that I "would carry the topmast by the board, or the ship to pieces!"

I told him, "I did not fear the topmast, but if they went by the board, I could not help that! For now was the time to carry the topsails, and carry them I would as long as the gunhil was above water! for I had rather carry the ship in pieces than be driven ashore in France!

At nine, the wind was north-north-west and at north, and blew harder. Then I took in the two topsails. The wind increasing, I hauled down the mizzen [sail]; and after we had pumped out the water, we sat down and eat some bread, and drank a glass of wine to refresh ourselves.

And I took brandy and butter and rubbed it into my hands, and especially into my left thumb; which was strained by the man that had his throat cut, and bruised by the boy when he missed his blow at the man's head: so that it was much swelled and enraged; and my hand was sore with pumping and doing other work, for the wind now blew dry.

At two in the afternoon, the wind was at north-north-west, and lynned [? *veered*] a little. I called the boy to hold on the mizzen jacks, and as I was hoisting the mizzen [sail], I looked out upon the luff, and saw land: and after I had set the mizzen, I went up into the maintop, and there made it to be the Start; which I thought was the joyfullest sight that ever I saw.

Then I hove out the maintopsail, and went down, and sent up the boy, and hove out the topsail; and I and the boy set them to get in with the shore. Yet the wind blew very hard, and if all our own crew of men had been on board, I am sure we should have but carried two coasts and a mizzen at the most.

At four, I and the boy bent the cables; and we were sufficiently washed in doing of it.

At six, the Berry Head bore north-north-west, distance four leagues.

In the night, the wind veered north, and north-north-east, and north-east, and north-west; and after twelve at night it proved a little [*slight*] wind.

In the dawning of the day, the wind very hard at north-west; which compelled me to furl both topsails.

This being Tuesday, at eight in the morning, I being then about three leagues south-east from Lyme, the wind grew calm.

At noon, we had a little breeze of wind at north-east and north-north-east.

At two I saw a great ring about the sun, and [it] broke in the east-south-east, and looked but indifferent: but however I did hope to be up with Topsham bar before night. And thereupon I sent up the boy, and let out the reef of the main-topsail, and made all the sail that I could, except the reef in the foretopsail.

At three, I had "a topgallant gale" at east-south-east.

At four, I saw the ring round the sun again, and [it] broke in the south-south-east; and the southward board looked very grim. And having a whole night in hand made me wish that I had six Englishmen on board. For now I was hardly able to lift up my hands to my head, by reason of my frequent pumping, and for want of sleep; but the hopes of getting in over the bar that night, and of bringing such unheard-of news to my native country, did revive my spirits, and my joy increased very much.

At six, I bade the boy fire a patteroe three times, which spent all the powder I had on board; and the French ancient tied in a red sash, I put out for a whiff for the Pilot to come off. But by all the sail that I could make, I got no nearer than a mile from the bar, in the dimps [*dusk*] of the night.

Then I went up to the topmast head, to see if I could perceive the Pilot's boat coming off. But because I could not shew an English ancient [*flag*], they were afraid to come out;

but lay upon their oars near the bar (as afterwards was known), so that I could not see them: and night came on, or else I would, through the assistance of GOD, have ventured to have carried the ship in over the bar myself.

Then I got the larboard tacks aboard, thinking to go into Torbay. And I ordered the boy to furl the spritsail and mizzentopsail, and kept her close by the wind, for to have a good offing, that I might have time to furl all to the mainsail, and that hauled down, before I did come to an anchor.

At eight, I took in the maintopsail.

At night, having a good offing, I took in the foretopsail.

But I considered that it was not best to go into Torbay, because the sheet Cable was carried away by the French Privateer, and the small Bower was not fit for ocam; and having only the best Bower to trust to: and it was to be doubted [*feared*] whether that would bring her up or not, and many casualties might fall out besides; and if that did bring her up, I thought I might sink to an anchor, if the storm did increase (as now it blew a "reef topsail gale") for want of help. For I had no powder to fire the patteroe to invite men on board.

So I kept along, with two coasts and a mizzen, in hopes that the wind would not blow so hard; but that I should be able to carry that sail, and keep her between Dartmouth and Topsham.

The wind veering to the southward, at eleven in the night, I was about half a mile off Dartmouth Range.

The wind blew hard, and I strived to put her about three times; but could not make the ship to stay: which cause made me send the boy up to loose the foretopsail: and after it was sate with one reef in, she stayed; and in half an hour's time, with the assistance of GOD, I had two coasts and the mizzen trimmed: but I clewed up the foretopsail sheets, and braced it aback, for the ease of the vessel, because she leaked very much. And I had not much haste in my way, because the wind was south-south-east, and blew very hard.

At one in the morning, I put the Frenchman to the helm, and hid the blunderbuss, and carried the boy up with me into the maintop to help to reef the maintopsail; and in less than an hour's time, I had taken two reefs of it in. For if the storm did increase, or held as it was, so that the Pilot could not come on board; I would have hauled up the two coasts and the mizzen, and carry the ship in over the bar, with two reef topsails.

After three, I bore away for the bar of Topsham, thinking to go in over the bar in the morning tide; but by five, the wind lined [*veered*].

At six, I sent up the boy to loose the maintopsail.

At seven, I let out the reefs of both topsails, and made all the sail I could: but the wind dying away so, I did not fetch the bar before ten of the clock; which was too late for that tide.

At which time, the Pilot was coming; but seeing no colours, nor no men on deck but myself and the boy, they were afraid: and were rowing away from me.

But I being in hail of them, I asked them, "What they were afraid of? and why they should not come on board?"

They hearing me call to them in English, they lay still upon their oars till I came up with them: and seeing me and the boy, whom they knew; they inquired for the Master.

I told them, "He might be carried into France by this time."

And after they came on board, I gave them an account of all the proceedings, which made them all in a maze; and they would hardly believe it: but to put them out of doubt, I shewed them the five prisoners. Whom the Pilots would have had me let them out to work: but I refused to do that till the ship was over the bar. Because they should not see how the bar did lie; for fear they might become pilots, and go in with their boats hereafter, and so burn or carry away our ships.

This discourse being ended, the Pilots would have me sleep, for they perceived by my countenance, that I stood in need of it: but the joy of having six Englishmen on board banished all sleepiness from me.

Half an hour after ten, I sent two of Pilots' [men] ashore. One to bring me some help on board. And the other, to ride to Exeter, with a letter which I wrote to the owners of the ship, who I thought would have been very well pleased with the news. But they gave him but a French half-crown [2*s.* 3*d.*] and a shilling [=3*s.* 3*d.* *in all* = 10*s.* *now*] for carrying the news to them, eleven miles. For they did not much regard the news, having insured £560 [=£1,700 *now*] upon the ship: and two men since appraised her but at £170 [=£500 *now*].

The Postmaster of Exeter, hearing of my retaking of the ship, sent for the Pilot, to be informed by him of the particulars relating thereunto: who, through forgetfulness, gave an imperfect account of the action: but in the letter I sent to the owners, I gave an account of all, except the action. Both these were sent by an express to London, and printed in the *Gazette*: * which Pilot's account differed from this my Relation.

* *The following account in the* London Gazette, 2,749, *of Monday, March* 14, 1691[-2], *though inaccurate in some respects, gives us the name and age of the boy, and some other particulars about* LYDE *himself.*

Exon, March 12. There has lately happened a remarkable action, by a vessel belonging to this port, called the *Friends' Adventure*, ROGER BRYANT Master.

He came from Oporto on the 24th of last month; and on the 29th, was taken by a French Privateer of 36 guns, and about 250 men, one GERALDINE Commander, twenty-five leagues south-east-and-by-east of Cape Finisterre.

They took away the Master and five of his men, leaving in the said vessel, only the Mate and a boy; and put seven Frenchmen on board to navigate her to St. Malo.

Being come in sight of Cape de Hage [*Hogue*] there arose a south-south-east wind; by which they were driven off the French coast.

On the 6th instant, in the morning, the Mate, whose name is ROBERT LYDE of Topsham, a lusty young man, aged about twenty-three years, who was a prisoner in France last year; and the boy, named JOHN WRIGHT, of about sixteen years, having before agreed on their design, and promised to stand by one another, took their opportunity, while two of the Frenchmen were at the pump, one at the helm, one on the Forecastle, and three sleeping in their cabins. The Mate fell upon the two men at the pump; and with a crow of iron, killed one and wounded the other, at one blow. At the same time, the boy knocked down the Frenchman on the Forecastle: and they afterwards secured the man at the helm.

One of the three that were asleep got up in the meantime, and meeting the Mate, was wounded by him in the head, and driven out upon the deck.

The two others, hearing a noise, came likewise from their cabins, to the rescue of their companions, and laid hold of the Mate: but with the help of the boy, he got the mastery of them, killed one of them, and the other thereupon cried for Quarter.

Of the five Frenchmen that remained alive, two were disabled by the wounds they had received; two, they secured between decks; and the other they took to help to sail the vessel: which they brought into Topsham, on the 9th instant; and the French prisoners are now ashore.

I stayed without the bar till four in the afternoon; and then we went for the bar.

After I was got over in safety and landlocked, and there were many people on board, who were desirous to see the Frenchmen: I ript off the plank which was nailed over the hold; and the prisoners came up, to the confirmation of the truth of this Relation.

By five, I was at anchor at Staircross; and there were as many people on board as could well stand. Immediately, I sent the prisoners to Topsham, in the Custom House wherry, that the doctors might take care of their wounds.

At six, I put all the people ashore, except the boy and Their Majesties' Officers; whom I left on board.

I went to Topsham, where I found my prisoners, with a doctor dressing their wounds. On searching, he concluded that two of them could not live a week. But as soon as I came in, those that were clear of the doctor, put off their hats and kissed my hands, and shewed a great deal of love to me outwardly.

After I had seen them dressed, and good lodging provided for them; I went home to refresh myself with sleep.

And the next day I marched my prisoners to Exeter, and carried them to one of the Owner's house: and afterwards delivered them to the Mayor.

I was creditably informed that, while I was at Exeter, the Owners sent a man on board the ship; who persuaded the boy to go on shore with him, under pretence to drink with him: but his intent was to take possession of the ship on behalf of the Owners, who sent him thither for that very purpose. But the Surveyor of Their Majesties' Custom House chancing to be there; he caused five Tidesmen to be put on board, and so prevented that design.

Then they gave out the report, that they would arrest me, because I would not let them put a Master over me in the ship, to bring her to London; concluding that I could not find bail: but they hearing that I had got bail, in case they did proceed, desisted their design again.

So soon as the owners of the cargo, who lived in London, heard of the arrival of the ship; they got a *Protection* and sent it to a friend of theirs in Exeter, to deliver to me, to get men to bring the ship to London. But the man to whom the *Protection* was sent, being influenced by the Owners, gave the *Protection* to them: which they sent back to London, and endeavoured to get another in the room of it, in the name of one whom they intended to make Master of the ship; who had insured £200 [=£600 *now*] for his brother ROGER BRIANT, the Master of the said ship, that was carried into France.

But they finding that they could not get another *Protection* granted them, than that procured in my name which was sent down! After it was detained a considerable time from me; it was delivered to me with an order to ship men: whom I got, and the ship being ready to sail with the first fair wind, and a strong gale if a convoy did not present.

But they would not let me stay to see the wind settle; but forced me out on the 5th of April [1692], with the first spurt of a fair wind.

On the 6th day of the same, in the morning, being off Portland with a contrary wind; I bore up again: and on the 7th, I went in over the bar of Topsham again.

I had not been three hours at an anchor, before there came two French Privateers from the Eastward, with English colours; supposed to be King JAMES's Privateers, because they were for the most part manned with Irishmen. They went along, about a league from the bar; and went into Torbay, and took and carried away with them, two English ships which came from Oporto. My Owners hearing thereof, and that I was in safety, were very angry with me; and huffed [*blustered*] at me, because I did not stay to be a prey to the enemy.

On the 19th of April, I went out over the bar again, with the wind west-south-west, "a topsail gale."

On the 20th, I went into the Isle of Wight, in hopes to have found some ships bound to the Eastward: but found none.

On the 21st, with a strong south-west wind, I went out again; and got into the Downs on the 22nd, and arrived at London on the 26th.

When I came ashore to the Freighters, that had 115 Pipes of wine on board; they did not so much as bid me welcome!

but bade me go to the Custom House, and enter the cargo: for they said they would unlade the ship forthwith.

Then I asked them for money to pay the men, that helped to bring the ship to London: but they denied to give me any.

There were, besides the Merchants' wine, two Pipes of the Master's; that was in all, 117 Pipes; and 8 Tons of sumach and cork: which paid the King in duties, £1,000 [=£3,000 *now*].

Then I asked the merchants again for money to pay the men, who belonged to Men-of-war: which they again refused to pay.

On the 27th, betimes in the morning, came one of the Freighters on board, with his cooper: who tasted all the wine that he could come at. And the cooper said, "He never knew wine come home in a better condition in his life-time, than that did."

The Freighter having one lighter by the ship's side, and another coming aboard; he bade me to get men to put the wine and other goods into the lighters: for he said he intended to have it all out in twenty-four hours' time.

I perceiving his intention was to get the cargo into his possession, before I should get any friends, said, "Sir, I have ventured my life to save the ship and cargo! For that which was mine on board, was most of it carried away, and what was left I have drunk out of to save the cargo: for I have not drawn one glass of the wine belonging to the cargo; and you see that the wine is good, and the pipes are full! And the Privateer carried but one Pipe of yours, out of the 116. And therefore it is reason that I should have my loss made good out of the cargo: for I have more Adventure money [*i.e., what* LYDE *invested in his own wine*] to pay, than my wages will come to."

"Tush!" he answered, "all the reason is, yours is carried away, and mine is left; and if mine had been carried away, and yours left, I could not have helped it!"

I knowing his mind, I said no more: but told him, "I would go on shore, to get men to load the lighter": but my intent was to deliver a letter that I had, to an Honourable Person, for his favour and assistance in this troublesome affair of mine.

But meeting with a Gentleman, to whom I shewed the

direction of the letter, and gave an account of my proceedings; he went with me, and entered an action in the High Court of Admiralty, for £1,000 upon ship and cargo. And by the assistance of an Honourable Person, I brought it to a trial: and overthrew the Owners and the Freighters, for half the ship and of the cargo.

But they appealed to the High Court of Chancery, and having nothing of truth, disgraced me. Withal they informed the Lords Commissioners [of the Admiralty], that I took a bag of money out of the ship belonging to the Owners: which the Master told me he delivered to the Lieutenant of the Privateer. But I having no proof against the same, this did me a great unkindness.

Yet I overthrew them there [*in Chancery*], for the moiety of the Ship and Cargo; and had a decree for the same: which decree is enrolled, and so is become a precedent in that Court; which will be an advantage to any one that shall hereafter retake their ship from the enemy. If they sue them in Chancery or the High Court of Admiralty for salvage, they will be allowed as much as if it were taken by a Privateer.

Two days after I cast them in the High Court of Admiralty, they gave out a false report concerning me. How that I had no Conduct, for I ran my ship with full sail aboard another ship that was moored in the Thames, ladened with the King's provisions and had sunk her.

Whereupon the owners of the sunk ship, by the wicked instigation of my adversaries, arrested me on the 19th of June [1692], in an action for £400 [=£1,200 *now*], through my adversaries' persuasions; supposing I could not find bail, but must have gone to prison; and then they were in hopes of having their designs upon me. But I being bailed, contrary to their expectation, I was obliged to stay till Michaelmas Term, following [*October*, 1692], before I could bring it to a trial; to my great expense and loss of time.

And I cast them by the evidence of five witnesses, who made it appear that the said ship was not sunk by me.

And so I ended my Law, and the greatest part of my money together.

By the favour of an Honourable Person, I was introduced

to the Right Noble the Marquis of CARMARTHEN; who recommended my case to Her Majesty [*Queen MARY*]: who was pleased, as a token of her extraordinary favour, to order me a gold medal and chain; and recommended me to the Right Honourable the Lords of the Admiralty for preferment in the Fleet; which I am now [1693] attending the Honourable Board for.

Thus I have endeavoured to give an impartial Account of the whole Matter of Fact, from first to last; ascribing all my success to the omnipotent power of the great GOD, who was with me, and protected me throughout the whole action; and made me capable of performing this piece of service for my King and country: in whose defence I am still willing to serve, and shall as long as I remain to be

R. L.

FINIS.

ADVERTISEMENT.

W*HEREAS there has been a report industriously spread abroad, that it was the boy that persuaded me to retrieve ourselves; this is to satisfy the Reader, that that report was maliciously reported of me, and was not true. For it was the boy of another ship, called the* Trial, *of* 50 *tons, that did desire his Master to fall on upon five Frenchmen: and accordingly they did, and overcame them, and brought their ship into Falmouth. For which, the Master was immediately made Commander of the* Mary *Galley: and I, that had used the sea thirteen years* [i.e., from ten to twenty-three years of age], *did but desire the command of a Fire-ship.*

I did design to have given the Reader, a more large account of our sufferings in France; but that it [i.e., such sufferings] *was already published by RICHARD STRUTTON, who has given* A true Relation of the cruelties and barbarities of the French, upon the English prisoners of war. *Printed for RICHARD BALDWIN.*